BRITISH ECONOMIC AND SOCIAL HISTORY
A BIBLIOGRAPHICAL GUIDE

British economic and social history

A bibliographical guide

compiled by

W. H. CHALONER, M.A., Ph.D.
*Reader in modern economic history
in the University of Manchester*

and

R. C. RICHARDSON, B.A., Ph.D., F.R.Hist.S.
*Senior lecturer in history
Thames Polytechnic*

Manchester University Press
Rowman and Littlefield

LIBRARY
WAYNE STATE COLLEGE
WAYNE, NEBRASKA

© 1976 Manchester University Press

All rights reserved

No part of this publication may be reproduced,
stored in a retrieval system, or transmitted
in any form or by any means, electronic,
mechanical or otherwise, including photocopying,
without the permission in writing of the authors
and publisher.

Published by
Manchester University Press
Oxford Road, Manchester M13 9PL

UK ISBN 0 7190 0610 4

USA
Rowman and Littlefield
81 Adams Drive, Totowa, N.J. 07512

US ISBN 0 87471 777 9

 PRINTED BY Unwin Brothers Limited
THE GRESHAM PRESS OLD WOKING SURREY ENGLAND

Produced by 'Uneoprint'
A member of the Staples Printing Group

CONTENTS

Preface xiii

Abbreviations xiv

   HISTORIOGRAPHY AND METHODOLOGY 1

   GENERAL WORKS 3

   (a) Bibliographies 3

   (b) Source material 4

   (c) General surveys 4

   (d) Collections of essays 4

ENGLAND 1066-1300

   GENERAL WORKS 5

   (a) Bibliographies 5

   (b) Sources 5

   (c) General works on the medieval English economy and on post-Conquest society 5

   (d) Monographs and regional studies 6

   DOMESDAY STUDIES 6

   POPULATION 7

   (a) General works 7

   (b) The family 8

   AGRICULTURE AND RURAL SOCIETY 8

   (a) General 8

   (b) Regional studies 8

   (c) The manor 9

   (d) Land tenure and the land market 9

   (e) Estates 10

   (f) Rent 10

   (g) Field systems 10

   (h) Place-name studies 10

   INDUSTRY 10

   (a) General 10

   (b) Textiles 10

   (c) Metals 11

   (d) Building 11

   (e) Miscellaneous 11

   MONEY, PRICES AND PUBLIC FINANCE 11

   (a) Money and prices 11

   (b) Public finance 11

   LABOUR 12

   TOWNS 12

   (a) Sources 12

   (b) Surveys and monographs 13

   COMMERCE 13

   GOVERNMENT 13

   THE JEWS IN ENGLAND 14

   STANDARDS OF LIVING 14

   COMMUNICATIONS AND INTERNAL TRADE 14

   THE MONASTERIES 14

ENGLAND 1300-1500

   GENERAL WORKS 16

   (a) Sources 16

   (b) General surveys 16

   POPULATION 17

   (a) Sources 17

   (b) Secondary works 17

   AGRICULTURE AND RURAL SOCIETY 17

   (a) General 17

   (b) Regional studies 18

   (c) The manor 18

   (d) Estate management 19

   (e) Land tenure 19

   (f) Field systems 19

   (g) Deserted villages 20

   (h) The forests 20

   INDUSTRY 20

   (a) General 20

   (b) Industrial organisation 20

   (c) Textiles 21

- (d) Mining and metallurgy 21
- (e) Salt 21
- (f) Miscellaneous 21
- (g) Sources of power for industry 21

COMMERCE 21
- (a) Sources 21
- (b) General and miscellaneous 22
- (c) The mercantile community 23

PRICES, PUBLIC FINANCE, USURY AND THE ORIGINS OF BANKING 23
- (a) Prices 23
- (b) Public finance 23
- (c) Usury and the origins of banking 24

WAR: ITS IMPACT ON MEDIEVAL SOCIETY AND ECONOMY 24

LABOUR 24
- (a) General and miscellaneous 24
- (b) The Peasants' Revolt 24

STANDARDS OF LIVING 24

GOVERNMENT AND ADMINISTRATION 25

TOWNS 25

COMMUNICATIONS AND INTERNAL TRADE 25
- (a) Inland transport and communications 25
- (b) Markets and fairs 25

ALIEN IMMIGRANTS IN ENGLAND 26

RELIGION 26

THE MONASTERIES 26

EDUCATION AND LEARNING 26

ENGLAND 1500-1700

GENERAL WORKS 28
- (a) Bibliographies 28
- (b) Source material 28
- (c) General surveys 28

- (d) Regional studies 30
- (e) Foreigners' views of England 30

POPULATION 30
- (a) Sources 30
- (b) General 31
- (c) Internal population mobility and emigration 31
  - (1) Internal mobility 31
  - (2) Emigration 31
- (d) Disease 32
- (e) The family 32
- (f) Local and regional studies 32

AGRICULTURE AND RURAL SOCIETY 33
- (a) Sources 33
- (b) General 33
- (c) Miscellaneous 34
- (d) Regional studies 34
- (e) Marketing 34
- (f) The manor 34
- (g) Landholding (including Crown lands) 34
  - (1) Landholding 34
  - (2) The Crown lands 35
- (h) The land market 35
- (i) Rent 35
- (j) Field systems and enclosures 35
- (k) Agricultural improvements 36
- (l) The dissolution of the monasteries 36
  - (1) Sources 36
  - (2) Studies 36
- (m) Risings and riots 37

INDUSTRY 37
- (a) General 37
- (b) Industrial growth 37
- (c) Industrial organisation 37
- (d) Investment 38
- (e) Textiles 38
- (f) Coal 39
- (g) Metals 39

Contents   vii

(h) Salt, leather, paper and glass   40
   (1) Salt   40
   (2) Leather   40
   (3) Paper   40
   (4) Glass   40
(i) Shipping   40
(j) Miscellaneous   40

TOWNS   40
(a) General   40
(b) Specialised studies   41

ALIEN IMMIGRANTS   41
(a) Dutch, Huguenots and Germans   41
(b) Jews   42

COMMERCE AND COLONISATION   42
(a) General   42
(b) England and the age of discovery   43
(c) Trading companies and their organisation   43
   (1) The Merchant Adventurers   43
   (2) The Russia Company   43
   (3) The Eastland Company and trade with the Baltic   44
   (4) The Levant   44
   (5) The East India Company   44
   (6) Miscellaneous   44
(d) The mercantile community   44
(e) Anglo-Dutch commercial relations   44
(f) Coastal trade   45
(g) Smuggling   45
(h) Colonies   45
(i) Miscellaneous   45

THE CONCEPT OF MERCANTILISM   46

COMMUNICATIONS AND INTERNAL TRADE   47
(a) River navigation   47
(b) Roads and their traffic   47
(c) Internal trade   47

PRICES, PUBLIC FINANCE, BANKING AND FINANCIAL DEALINGS   47
(a) Prices   47
(b) Public finance: income and management   48
(c) Banking and financial dealings   49

GOVERNMENT POLICY AND ADMINISTRATION   49
(a) The central government   49
(b) Local government   50

CLASSES AND SOCIAL GROUPS   50
(a) General and miscellaneous   50
(b) The gentry and their estates   51

POOR RELIEF: CHARITY AND THE POOR LAW   52

LABOUR   53

STANDARDS OF LIVING   54

CIVIL WAR, INTERREGNUM, RESTORATION AND REVOLUTION, 1640-89   54
(a) Sources   54
(b) General   55
(c) Regional studies   56
(d) Miscellaneous   57

RELIGION   57
(a) General and miscellaneous   57
(b) Religion and economic development   58

EDUCATION AND LEARNING   59
(a) Schools and schooling   59
(b) The book trade and the newspaper press   60

ENGLAND 1700-1970

BIBLIOGRAPHICAL AND STATISTICAL GUIDES, DOCUMENTARY COMPILATIONS, AND GENERAL WORKS   61
(a) Bibliographical and statistical guides   61
(b) Documentary compilations and readings   61
(c) General works   61
(d) Regional and county studies   62

ECONOMIC AND SOCIAL CHANGES FROM THE 1880s INTO THE TWENTIETH CENTURY 63

(a) The changing structure of the economy 63
(b) Social conditions and social policy 63
(c) The World Wars and their effects 64

POPULATION 64

(a) General works 64
(b) Regional studies 65
(c) Internal migration 65
(d) Immigration 65

AGRICULTURE AND RURAL SOCIETY 65

(a) Bibliographies 65
(b) General works dealing with the process of agricultural change 66
(c) Enclosures 66
(d) Landed society 67
(e) The drovers 67
(f) Farm labourers 67
(g) William Cobbett 67
(h) Regional and local studies 67

ECONOMIC FLUCTUATIONS 68

(a) 1700-1800 68
(b) 1800-1913 68
(c) 1918-1939 68

FOOD AND DRINK 68

(a) General 68
(b) Fish 69
(c) Drink and the temperance movement 69

HOME MARKET, INCLUDING SHOPPING AND THE CO-OPERATIVE MOVEMENT 69

(a) Developments to 1850 69
(b) Co-operation 69
(c) Developments since 1850 69
(d) Advertising 70

SCIENCE AND INVENTION 70

TRUSTS, CARTELS AND COMPETITION 70

BUSINESS HISTORY 70

POWER AND LIGHT 70

(a) Wind and water mills 70
(b) The steam engine 70
(c) Light 71
    (1) General 71
    (2) Gas 71
    (3) Electricity 71

ENGINEERING 71

COAL 72

COPPER AND BRASS 73

LEAD MINING 73

IRON AND STEEL 73

TEXTILES 74

(a) General 74
(b) Cotton 74
(c) Woollens and worsteds 75
(d) Clothing industry 76
(e) Silk 76
(f) Linen and flax 76
(g) Hatting 76
(h) Hosiery 76

CHEMICALS AND SOAP 76

POTTERY 76

GLASS 77

RUBBER 77

MISCELLANEOUS 77

PRINTING AND NEWSPAPERS 77

PAPERMAKING 77

BANKING, CURRENCY AND PUBLIC FINANCE 78

(a) Currency 78
(b) Public finance 78
    (1) The National Debt 78

(2) South Sea Bubble 78
(3) Taxes 78
  (i) *Income Tax* 78
  (ii) *Land Tax* 78
  (iii) *Salt Tax* 78
(4) Administration and budgetary control 78
(c) **Banking and the London money market** 78
(d) **The exchange equalisation account** 79
(e) **Country banking** 79
  (1) General 79
  (2) Regional and local studies 79

ACCOUNTANCY 80

INSURANCE 80

THE PROFESSIONS 80

MANAGEMENT AND MASTERS' ORGANISATIONS 80

CAPITAL FORMATION 81

JOINT STOCK COMPANIES 81

THE WORKING CLASSES 81
(a) **Bibliographical studies and statistics** 81
(b) **Documentary collections** 81
(c) **Socialist theories and theorists** 81
(d) **General studies** 82
(e) **Trade unionism and labour** 82
  (1) Documentary and general studies 82
  (2) Working-class autobiographies 82
  (3) The labour aristocracy controversy 83
  (4) Miscellaneous, including the Labour Party and the Trades Union Congress 83
  (5) Histories of unionism in particular industries 84
    (i) *Agriculture* 84
    (ii) *Engineering and metalworkers* 84
    (iii) *Builders and woodworkers* 84
    (iv) *Railway labour* 84
    (v) *Coal mining* 84
    (vi) *Printing and publishing* 85
    (vii) *White-collar and service workers* 85
    (viii) *Cotton unions* 85
    (ix) *Dockers* 85
    (x) *Footwear and clothing* 85
    (xi) *Miscellaneous* 85
  (6) Local studies 85
  (7) Wages 85
  (8) The General Strike of 1926 86
  (9) The Communist Party, the I.L.P. and the Fabian Society 86
(f) **Friendly societies, etc.** 86
(g) **The standard of living controversy** 86
(h) **Police, popular disturbances and Luddism** 87
(i) **Chartism** 87
  (1) General studies 87
  (2) Regional studies 88
  (3) Biographies 88
(j) **Owenism and Utopianism** 88

INTERNAL TRANSPORT, PORTS AND COASTING TRADE 88
(a) **General** 88
(b) **Roads** 88
(c) **Coasting trade** 89
(d) **Ports and their trade** 89
(e) **Canals** 89
(f) **Postal history and telecommunications** 89
(g) **Motor transport** 89
(h) **The Channel Tunnel** 90
(i) **Railways** 90
  (1) Bibliographies 90
  (2) General 90
  (3) Railway biographies 90

Contents

(4) Locomotives 90

(5) Individual lines and regional studies 91

OVERSEAS TRADE 91

(a) General and statistical 91

(b) Trade with specific areas mainly up to c.1800-15 91

(c) The repeal of the Corn Laws, the free trade era and after 91

    (1) The repeal of the Corn Laws and the coming of free trade 91

    (2) The free trade era and after, 1860-1939 92

(d) Trade relations affecting specific areas from c.1800-15 onwards 92

(e) The slave trade 92

(f) Imperialism 93

OVERSEAS INVESTMENTS 93

OVERSEAS EMIGRATION 93

TOURISM 93

SHIPPING AND SHIPBUILDING 93

(a) General 93

(b) Personnel 94

(c) Steam 94

(d) Shipbuilding 94

AIR TRAVEL 94

ARCHITECTURE AND HOUSING 94

THE BUILDING INDUSTRY 95

BUILDING SOCIETIES 95

URBAN HISTORY 95

(a) General 95

(b) Individual cities and towns 96

(c) The seaside holiday 97

ECONOMIC THOUGHT AND STATE POLICY 97

THE FACTORY SYSTEM AND LEGISLATION 98

POOR LAW, CHARITY AND SOCIAL PROTECTION 99

(a) Poor Law 99

(b) Charity and social protection 99

PUBLIC HEALTH AND MORALITY 100

FOREIGNERS' IMPRESSIONS 100

RELIGION, SOCIETY AND ECONOMIC LIFE 101

(a) General works 101

(b) Nonconformity and economic development 101

(c) Religion and the working class 101

(d) Christian Socialism 101

THE WOMAN QUESTION 101

EDUCATION 102

(a) Schools 102

(b) The public schools 102

(c) Adult education, including public libraries 102

(d) The universities 102

WALES 1700-1966 103

SCOTLAND 1066-1700

GENERAL WORKS 104

(a) Bibliographies 104

(b) Sources 104

(c) Surveys 104

    (1) Medieval 104

    (2) Early modern 104

POPULATION 105

(a) Medieval 105

(b) Early modern 105

AGRICULTURE AND RURAL SOCIETY 105

(a) Medieval 105

(b) Early modern 105

INDUSTRY 105

(a) Medieval 105

(b) Early modern 105

TOWNS 105
(a) **Medieval** 105
(b) **Early modern** 106

COMMERCE 106
(a) **Medieval** 106
(b) **Early modern** 106

PRICES, PUBLIC FINANCE AND BANKING 106
(a) **Medieval** 106
(b) **Early modern** 106

COMMUNICATIONS 106

POOR RELIEF 106

EDUCATION 107

RELIGION 107
(a) **Medieval** 107
(b) **Early modern** 107

SCOTLAND SINCE 1700

GENERAL WORKS 108

POPULATION AND EMIGRATION 108

TRADE AND BUSINESS HISTORY 108

INDUSTRIAL GROWTH 108

AGRICULTURE 108

LABOUR 108

SOCIAL LIFE AND INTELLECTUAL DEVELOPMENT 108

IRELAND 1066-1700

GENERAL WORKS 110
(a) Bibliographies 110
(b) Sources 110
(c) Surveys 110
   (1) Medieval 110
   (2) Early modern 110

POPULATION 111
(a) **Medieval** 111
(b) **Early modern** 111

AGRICULTURE AND RURAL SOCIETY 111

INDUSTRY 111

ANGLO-IRISH RELATIONS IN THE SIXTEENTH AND SEVENTEENTH CENTURIES 111

PRICES AND PUBLIC FINANCE 112
(a) **Medieval** 112
(b) **Early modern** 112

COMMERCE 112
   Early modern 112

TOWNS 112

RELIGION 112

MISCELLANEOUS 112
(a) **Medieval** 112
(b) **Early modern** 112

IRELAND SINCE 1700

GENERAL 113

SOCIAL 113

TRADE 113

TRANSPORT AND INDUSTRY 113

FINANCE, BANKING AND ACCOUNTANCY 114

LAND AND AGRICULTURE 114

POPULATION 114

URBAN STUDIES 114

INDEX OF AUTHORS AND EDITORS 115

Addenda 130

PREFACE

The literature of British economic and social history has been busily proliferating in the course of the last few decades with the appearance of textbook surveys, monographs and innumerable articles in a growing range of specialised periodicals.[1] But surprisingly the consequent need for large-scale bibliographies of the subject has been to a great extent neglected. It is true, of course, that since its inception in 1927 the Economic History Review has provided a valuable annual list of recent publications in the field, and that newer journals such as the Agricultural History Review have followed suit. And it is also true that many very good bibliographies of particular subjects can be found in monograph studies and that there has been published an increasing number of bibliographical introductions to reprint editions of established works. But for all this, no separate large-scale bibliography as such of British economic and social history exists in print.

It is to meet this need among students and their teachers that this present bibliography has been compiled. Its title is deliberately chosen. It is in every sense a guide to—and not a definitively comprehensive list of—the dauntingly enormous literature of British economic and social history from 1066 to 1970. No single-volume bibliography could hope to include everything, and to do so would in any case have been self-defeating in that it would have placed this book outside the price range of those whose needs it is intended to serve. (It is principally for this reason that we have largely restricted ourselves in compiling this bibliographical guide to material written in English.) What follows, then, is a select bibliography, and inevitably—as selection is a very personal business—some may quibble at what has been included or excluded. We can only hope that little of the first importance has been left out and that nothing which can be considered useless has been put in.

The bibliographical guide is chronologically divided at 1300, 1500 and at 1700, and arranged by subject within the different periods. The items in each subject area are then listed under their authors in alphabetical order. All items are numbered, and it is these numbers—not page numbers—which are given in cross-references and in the index. A particular work, of course, is separately numbered only once. Any further reference to that item will be abbreviated and will direct the reader to the entry in the book where fuller bibliographical details can be found. Places of publication are given only when these were outside the British Isles.

The responsibility for the different parts of the bibliographical guide is as follows: Dr Richardson compiled the pre-1700 sections, the opening section on historiography and methodology, and the index. Dr Chaloner is responsible for selecting the entries on the modern period, and both editors joined in preparing the sections on Scotland and Ireland. (We are indebted to Professors S.G.E. Lythe and E.R.R. Green for helpful comments on the two last sections.) Every effort has been made in compiling this bibliographical guide to reach the highest standard of accuracy but doubtless undetected errors still remain in a work of this length. The editors would be grateful, therefore, to receive correspondence pointing out such mistakes and would welcome suggestions for additions to any subsequent edition.

March 1975

W.H.C.
R.C.R.

---

[1] The introduction to N.B. Harte, ed., The Study of Economic History: Collected Inaugural Lectures 1893-1970, 1971, offers a short and very useful survey of the development of the subject.

ABBREVIATIONS

Ag.H.R.	Agricultural History Review
A.H.R.	American Historical Review
B.I.H.R.	Bulletin of the Institute of Historical Research
Birm.Hist.Jnl.	University of Birmingham Historical Journal
Chet.Soc.	Chetham Society
Ec.H.R.	Economic History Review
Ec.J.	Economic Journal
Econ.Hist.	Economic History
E.H.R.	English Historical Review
Hist.Jnl.	Historical Journal
Hist.Rev.	Historical Review
J.E.H.	Journal of Economic History
Jnl.	Journal
Jnl.Mod.Hist.	Journal of Modern History
Jnl.Royal Stat.Soc.	Journal of the Royal Statistical Society
P.P.	Past and Present
Proc.Hug.Soc.	Proceedings of the Huguenot Society of London
Scand.Ec.H.R.	Scandinavian Economic History Review
Scot.H.R.	Scottish Historical Review
T.H.S.L.C.	Transactions of the Historic Society of Lancashire and Cheshire
T.L.C.A.S.	Transactions of the Lancashire and Cheshire Antiquarian Society
T.L.S.	Times Literary Supplement
Trans.	Transactions
T.R.H.S.	Transactions of the Royal Historical Society
V.C.H.	Victoria County History
Yorks.Bull.	Yorkshire Bulletin

HISTORIOGRAPHY AND METHODOLOGY

1. Aitken, H. G. J., 'On the present state of economic history', Canadian Jnl. of Economics and Political Science, XXVI, 1960, 87-95.
2. Andreano, R., ed., The New Economic History. Recent Papers on Methodology, N. Y., 1970.
3. Ashley, W. J., Surveys, Historic and Economic, 1900. Includes two chapters on the study of economic history (1-30).
4. —— 'The place of economic history in university studies', Ec.H.R., I, 1927-8, 1-11. On Ashley see:
5. Scott, W. R., 'Memoir: Sir William Ashley', Ec. H. R., I, 1927-8, 319-21.
6. Ashton, T. S., 'The relation of economic history to economic theory', 1946. In Harte, ed. (55), listed below.
7. —— 'Business history', Business History, I, 1958, 1-2. On Ashton see:
8. John, A. H., 'Thomas Southcliffe Ashton, 1889-1968', Ec.H.R., 2nd ser., XXI, 1968, iii-v.
9. Ashworth, W., 'The study of modern economic history', 1958. In Harte, ed (55), listed below.
10. Ballard, M., ed., New Movements in the Study and Teaching of History, 1970. See Heater (58) and Mathias (78), listed below.
11. Basmann, R.L., 'The role of the economic historian in the productive testing of preferred "economic laws"', Explorations in Entrepreneurial History, 2nd ser., II, 1965, 159-86.
12. Beresford, M. W., 'Time and place', 1960. In Harte, ed. (55), listed below.
13. —— History on the Ground, 2nd ed., 1971.
14. Bloch, M., The Historian's Craft, 1954
15. Bridbury, A., Historians and the Open Society, 1972.
16. Cantor, N. F., Perspectives on the European Past: Conversations with Historians, N. Y., 2 vols., 1971. Amongst the historians included in this collection of interviews are R. S. Lopez on 'Medieval and Renaissance economy and society', G. R. Elton on 'Government and society in Renaissance Europe', R. M. Hartwell on 'The Industrial Revolution', D. S. Landes on 'Labour and the Labour Movement', A. P. Thornton on 'Imperialism' and A. Briggs on 'Modern Britain'.
17. Chambers, J. D., 'The place of economic history in historical studies', 1960. In Harte, ed. (55), listed below. On Chambers see:
17a. Mingay, G. E., 'The contribution of a regional historian: J. D. Chambers 1898-1970', Studies in Burke and his Time, XIII, 1972, 2002-2010.
18. Chandler, J. D. and Galambos, L., eds., Economic History: Retrospect and Prospect. Papers Presented at the Thirtieth Annual Meeting of the Economic History Association, 1971 (A special issue of the J.E.H.

(XXXI, 1, 1971). Contains papers by W. N. Parker, A. Fishlow and R. W. Fogel, J. Swanson and J. Williamson, P. Temin and D. C. North.
19. Clapham, J. H., 'The study of economic history', 1929. In Harte, ed. (55), listed below. On Clapham see:
20. Heaton, H., 'Clapham's contribution to economic history', Political Science Quarterly, LIII, 1938, 599-602.
21. Clark, G. N., 'The study of economic history', 1932. In Harte, ed. (55), listed below.
22. Coats, A. W., 'Economic growth. The economic and social historian's dilemma', 1966. In Harte, ed. (55), listed below.
23. Cole, W. A., Economic History as a Social Science, 1967.
24. Conrad, A. H. and Meyer, J. R., Studies in Econometric History, 1965.
25. —— 'Economic theory, statistical inference and economic history', J.E.H., XVII., 1957, 524-44.
26. Court, W. H. B., 'What is economic history?', in Court (27), listed below, 151-79, and also in Finberg (41), listed below, 17-50.
27. —— Scarcity and Choice in History, 1970. A collection of essays, including a valuable study of 'Two economic historians: R. H. Tawney and Sir John Clapham', 127-50.
28. Cunningham, Audrey, William Cunningham, Teacher and Priest, 1950.
29. David, P., 'Economic history through the looking glass', Econometrica, 32, 1964, 694-6.
30. Davis, L. E., 'Professor Fogel and the new economic history', Ec.H.R., 2nd ser., XIX, 1966, 657-63.
31. —— et al., 'Aspects of quantitative research in economic history', J.E.H., XX, 1960, 539-47.
32. —— '"And it will never be literature": the new economic history: a critique', Explorations in Entrepreneurial History, 2nd ser., VI, 1969, 75-92.
33. Davis, R., 'History and the social sciences', 1965. In Harte ed. (55), listed below.
34. Desai, M., 'Some issues in econometric history', Ec.H.R., 2nd ser., XXI, 1968, 1-16.
35. Dobb, M., 'Historical materialism and the role of the economic factor', History, XXXVI, 1951, 1-11.
36. Douring, F., History as a Social Science, The Hague, 1960.
36a. Drake, M., ed., Applied Historical Studies: An Introductory Reader, 1973. Contains a general introductory chapter on 'Sociology and the historical perspective'.
37. Elton, G. R., The Practice of History, 1967.
38. Federn, K., The Materialist Conception of History: A Critical Analysis, 1939.
39. Finberg, H. P. R., The Local Historian and his Theme, 1952.
40. —— Local History in the University, 1964.
41. —— ed., Approaches to History: A Symposium, 1962.

42 Fisher, F. M., 'On the analysis of history and the interdependence of the social sciences', Philosophy of Science, 27, 1960, 147-58.

43 Fishlow, A., and Fogel, R. W., 'Quantitative economic history. An interim evaluation; past trends and present tendencies', J. E. H., XXXI, 1971, 15-42.

43a Floud, R., An Introduction to Quantitative Method for Historians, 1973.

44 Fogel, R. W., 'The specification problem in economic history', J.E.H., XXVII, 1967, 283-308.

45 —— 'The new economic history: its findings and methods', Ec.H.R., XIX, 1966, 642-56.

46 Glynn, S., 'Approaches to urban history: the case for caution', Australian Ec.H.R., X, 1970, 218-25.

47 Goodrich, C., 'Economic history: one field or two?', J.E.H., XX, 1960, 531-8.

48 Gottschalk, L., ed., Generalization in the Writing of History, Chicago, 1963. Contains a very good bibliography on historiography, 213-48.

49 Gras, N.S.B., Introduction to Economic History, 1922.

50 —— 'The rise and development of economic history', Ec.H.R., I, 1927-8, 12-34.

51 Gunderson, G., 'The nature of social saving', Ec.H.R., 2nd ser., XXIII, 1970, 207-20. A consideration of the 'new economic history'.

52 Habakkuk, H. J., 'Economic history and economic theory', Daedalus, spring 1971, 305-22.

52a Hale, J.R., The Evolution of British Historiography, 1967.

53 Hammond, J. L. See the obituary notice by R. H. Tawney, 'J. L. Hammond, 1872-1949', Proceedings of the British Academy, XLVI, 1960, 267-94.

54 Hancock, W. K.,'Economic history at Oxford', 1946. In Harte, ed. (55), listed below.

55 Harte, N.B., ed., The Study of Economic History, 1971. An extemely useful collection of reprinted inaugural lectures with an introduction by the editor.

56 Hawke, G. R., 'Mr Hunt's study of the Fogel Thesis. A comment', History, LIII, 1968, 18-23. See Hunt (70), listed below.

57 Hayek, F. A., ed., Capitalism and the Historians, 1954.

58 Heater, D., 'History and the social sciences'. In Ballard (10), listed above, 134-46.

59 Heckscher, E. F., 'A plea for theory in economic history', Ec.J. Economic History Supplement, I, 1929, 525-34.

60 Hexter, J. H., Doing History, 1972.

61 —— 'A new framework for social history', in the same author's Reappraisals in History, 1961, 14-25.

62 Hicks, J., A Theory of Economic History, 1969.

63 Holloway, S.J.F., 'Sociology and history', History, XLVIII, 1963, 154-80.

64 Hobsbawm, E. J., 'Karl Marx's contribution to historiography', in R. Blackburn, ed., Ideology in Social Science, 1972, 265-83.

65 —— 'The social function of the past', P.P., 55, 1972, 3-17.

66 Hoskins, W. G., Local History in England, 1959, 2nd ed., 1973.

67 Hughes, J. R. T., 'Fact and theory in economic history', Explorations in Entrepreneurial History, III, 1966, 75-100.

68 —— 'Measuring British economic growth', J. E. H., XXIV, 1964, 60-82.

69 Hughes, H. S., 'The historian and the social scientist', in A. V. Riasanovsky and B. Riznik, eds., Generalizations in Historical Writing, Philadelphia, 1963, 18-59.

70 Hunt, E. H., 'The new economic history', History, LIII, 1968, 3-18. See also Hawke (56), listed above.

71 John, E., 'Some questions on the materialist interpretation of history', History, XXXVIII, 1953, 1-10.

72 Jones, G. Stedman, 'History: the poverty of empiricism', in R. Blackburn, ed., Ideology in Social Science, 1972, 96-118.

73 Kuznets, S., 'Statistics and economic history', J.E.H., I, 1941, 26-41.

74 Lennard, R., 'Agrarian history: some vistas and pitfalls', Ag.H.R., XII, 1964, 83-98.

75 Lythe, S. G. E., 'The historian's profession', 1963. In Harte, ed. (55), listed above.

76 Marczewski, J., 'Quantitative history', Jnl. of Contemporary History, III, 1968, 179-92.

77 Marwick, A., The Nature of History, 1970.

78 Mathias, P., 'Economic history—direct and oblique'. In Ballard (10), listed above, 76-92.

79 Meyer, J. R. and Conrad, A. H., 'Economic theory, statistical inference and economic history', J.E.H., XVII, 1957, 524-53.

80 Morazé, C., 'The application of the social sciences to history', Jnl. of Contemporary History, III, 1968, 207-16.

81 Murphy, G. G. S., 'The "new" history', Explorations in Entrepreneurial History, 2nd ser., II, 1965, 132-46.

82 North, D. C., 'The state of economic history', American Economic Review, LV, 1965, Supplement, 86-91.

83 —— 'Economic history', International Encyclopaedia of Social Sciences, VI, 1968, 468-74.

84 —— 'Institutional change and economic growth', J.E.H., XXXI, 1971, 118-25.

85 Parker, W.N., 'From old to new to old in economic history', J.E.H., XXXI, 1971, 3-14.

86 Payne, P.L., 'The uses of business history', Business History, V, 1962, 11-21.

87 —— ed., Studies in Scottish Business History, 1967 xi-xviii, and the works there cited.

88 Perkin, H.J., 'What is social history?', Bulletin of the John Rylands Library, XXXVI, 1953, 56-74.

89 —— 'Social history'. In Finberg (41), listed above, 51-82.

90 Plumb, J. H., The Death of the Past, 1969.

91 Pollard, S., 'Economic history. A science of Society?', P.P., 30, 1965, 3-22. In Harte, ed. (55), listed above.

92   Postan, M. M., 'The historical method in social science', 1939. In Harte, ed. (55), listed above.
93   —— Fact and Relevance: Essays on Historical Method, 1971.
94   —— 'Function and dialectic in economic history', Ec.H.R., 2nd ser., XIV, 1961-2, 397-407.
95   Power, Eileen, 'On medieval history as a social study', 1933. In Harte, ed. (55), listed above.
96   Powicke, F. M., 'The economic motive in politics', Ec.H.R., XVI, 1946, 85-92.
97   —— Modern Historians and the Study of History, 1955. Includes a study of the Manchester School of historians.
98   Price, L. L., 'The position and prospects of the study of economic history', 1908. In Harte, ed. (55), listed above.
99   Redlich, F., 'New and traditional approaches to economic history and their interdependence', J.E.H., XXV, 1965, 480-95.
100 —— 'Potentialities and pitfalls in economic history', Explorations in Entrepreneurial History, 2nd ser., VI, 1969, 93-108.
101 Rogers, J. E. T., The Economic Interpretation of History, 1888.
102 Rostow, W. W., 'The interrelation of theory and economic history', J.E.H., XVII, 1957, 509-23.
103 Rowney, D. K. and Graham, J. Q., Jnr., eds., Quantitative History: Selected readings in the Quantitative Analysis of Historical Data, Homewood Ill., 1969. Includes sections on 'Social history and social change', 'Historical demography', 'Cliometrics: the new economic history'. Bibliography.
104 Schofield, R. S., 'Historical demography: some possibilities and some limitations', T.R.H.S., 5th ser., 21, 1971, 119-32.
105 Sée, H., The Economic Interpretation of History, trans. and intro. by M. M. Knight, N. Y., 1929.
106 Seligman, E.R.A., The Economic Interpretation of History, N. Y., 1902, 2nd ed. 1922.
107 Shafer, R. J., A Guide to Historical Method, Homewood, Ill., 1969.
108 Sombart, W., 'Economic theory and economic history', Ec.H.R., II, 1929-30, 1-19.
109 Spiegel, H.W., 'Theories of economic development: history and classification', Jnl. of the History of Ideas, XVI, 1955, 518-39.
110 Stephens, W.B., Sources for English Local History, 1973.
111 Stern, F., ed., The Varieties of History from Voltaire to the Present, Cleveland, Ohio, 1956; London, 1971. A collection of extracts from writings on the nature of history with critical notes and introduction. On economic history Unwin, Clapham and Cochran are represented.
112 Supple, B. E., 'Economic history and economic growth', J.E.H., XX, 1960, 548-56.
113 Swanson, J. and Williamson, J., 'Explanations and issues; a prospectus for quantitative economic history', J.E.H., XXXI, 1971, 43-57.
114 Tawney, R. H., 'The study of economic History', 1932. In Harte (55), listed above. On Tawney see Court (27), listed above, and:
115 Stone, L., in P.P., 21, 1962, 73-7.
116 Ashton, T.S., in Proceedings of the British Academy, XLVIII, 1963, 461-82.
117 Chambers, J. D., 'The Tawney Tradition', Ec.H.R., 2nd ser., XXIV, 1971, 355-69.
118 Temin, P., ed., New Economic History, 1973.
119 —— 'General equilibrium models in economic history', J.E.H., XXI, 1971, 58-75.
120 Thomas, K., 'The tools and the job', T.L.S., 7 April 1966, 275-6.
121 —— 'History and anthropology', P.P., 24, 1963, 3-24
122 Thompson, F.M.L., 'Agricultural history', History, XLVIII, 1963, 28-33.
123 Trevor-Roper, H. R., 'The past and the present; history and sociology', P.P., 42, 1969, 3-17.
124 Tuma, E.H., Economic History and the Social Sciences, 1971.
125 Tunzelmann, G. N. von, 'The new economic history: an econometric appraisal', Explorations in Entrepreneurial History, 2nd ser., V, 1968, 175-200.
126 Unwin, G., Studies in Economic History: The Collected Papers of George Unwin, with an introductory memoir by R. H. Tawney, 1927. Part One of the book is taken up with papers on 'The Study and teaching of economic history'. On Unwin see also:
127 Daniels, G. W., George Unwin. A Memorial Lecture, 1926.
128 Webb, S. and Beatrice, Methods of Social Study, 1932.
129 Wilson, B. R., 'Sociological methods in the study of history', T.R.H.S., 5th ser., 21, 1971, 101-18.
130 Wilson, C., 'History in special and in general'. In Wilson (1045), listed below, 201-16.
131 Youngson, A. J., 'Progress and the individual in economic history', 1959. In Harte, ed. (55), listed above.

GENERAL WORKS

(a) Bibliographies

132 Bellot, H. H. and Milne, A. T., eds., Writings on British History, 1901-1933, Royal Historical Society, 5 vols., 1968.
133 Denman, D. R., Switzer, J. F. Q. and Sawyer, O. H. M., eds., Bibliography of Rural Land Economy and Landownership 1900-57: A full List of the Works Relating to the British Isles and Selected Works from the U.S. and Western Europe, 1958.
134 Elton, G. R., Modern Historians on British History, 1485-1945: A Critical Bibliography, 1945-1969, 1970. Economic history is covered, but only sketchily.

135 Frewer, L. B., ed., Bibliography of Historical Writings Published in Great Britain and the Empire 1940-45. 1947
136 Furber, E. C., ed., Changing Views on British History: Essays on Historical Writing Since 1939, Cambridge, Mass., 1966. A useful collection of critical bibliographical essays.
137 Jenkins, R. T. and Rees, W., eds., Bibliography of the History of Wales, 2nd ed., 1962.
138 Kellaway, W., Bibliography of Historical Works Issued in the U.K., 1957-60, 1962. Reprinted 1969.
139 Lancaster, Joan C., ed., Bibliography of Works Issued in the U.K., 1946-56, 1957.
140 Milne, A. T., ed., Writings on British History, 1934-45, Royal Historical Society, 8 vols., 1937-60.

(b) **Source material**

141 Bland, A. E., Brown, P. A. and Tawney, R. H., eds., English Economic History. Select Documents, 1914. Several times reprinted. Covers the period 1000 to 1846.
142 Flinn, M. W., ed., Readings in Economic History, 1964.

(c) **General surveys**

143 Buckatzch, E. J., 'The geographical distribution of wealth in England, 1086-1843', Ec.H.R., 2nd ser., III, 1951, 180-202.
144 Clapham, J.H., Concise Economic History of Britain from the Earliest Times to 1750, 1949.
145 Cunningham, W., The Growth of English Industry and Commerce, 1882, 6th ed., 3 vols., 1915-17.
146 Darby, H.C., ed., Historical Geography of England Before A.D. 1800, 1936, new ed., 1973.
147 Davies, D. J., The Economic History of South Wales Prior to 1800, 1933.
148 Dobb, M., Studies in the Development of Capitalism, 1946.
149 Dodd, A. H., Life in Wales, 1971. A general survey from the Stone Age to the twentieth century.

150 Flinn, M. W., An Economic and Social History of Britain, 1066-1939, 1961.
151 Green, J. R., Short History of the English People, ed. Mrs. J. R. Green and Kate Norgate, 4 vols., 1902. Valuable illustrations.
152 Harding, A., A Social History of English Law, 1966.
153 Hoskins, W. G., The Making of the English Landscape, 1955.
154 King, P., The Development of the English Economy to 1750, 1971. A useful textbook with extended bibliography.
155 Laslett, P., ed., Household and Family in Past Time, 1972.
156 Lipson, E., Economic History of England. I: The Middle Ages, 1915, 12th ed., 1962. II and III: The Age of Mercantilism, 1931, 6th ed., 1961.
157 Murphy, B., A History of the British Economy, 1066-1970, 1973.
158 Pollard, S., and Crossley, D. W., The Wealth of Britain 1085-1966, 1968. A valuable, one-volume survey of English economic history. Good bibliography.
159 Rostow, W. W., The Stages of Economic Growth, 1960.
160 Slicher van Bath, B. H., The Agrarian History of Western Europe, 500-1850, 1964.
161 Stenton, Doris M., The Englishwoman in History, 1957.
162 Trevelyan, G. M., Illustrated English Social History, 4 vols., 1949-52.
163 Zupco, R. E., A Dictionary of English Weights and Measures from Anglo-Saxon Times to the Nineteenth Century, Madison, Milwaukee, 1968.

(d) **Collections of essays**

164 Carus-Wilson, Eleanora M., ed., Essays in Economic History, 3 vols., 1954-62. A reprint collection of important articles. Indispensable.
164a Floud, R., ed., Essays in Quantitative Economic History, 1974. An extensive collection of articles which range from the fourteenth to the twentieth century.
165 Minchinton, W. E., ed., Essays in Agrarian History, 2 vols., 1968. Covers both the medieval and modern periods.

ENGLAND 1066-1300

GENERAL WORKS

(a) Bibliographies

166 Altschul, M., ed., Bibliographical Handbooks: Anglo-Norman England, 1066-1154, 1969. A useful compilation covering all aspects of the period.

167 Bonser, W., ed., An Anglo-Saxon and Celtic Bibliography, 450-1087, 1957.

167a Graves, E.B., ed., A Bibliography of English History to 1485, 1975. A revised and expanded version of Gross (168).

168 Gross, C., ed., The Sources and Literature of English History, 1900, 2nd ed., 1915. In its day extremely comprehensive, but today its usefulness is obviously much more restricted.

169 Hall, H., ed., Select Bibliography for the Study, Sources and Literature of English Medieval Economic History, 1914.

(b) Sources

170 Bagley, J.J., Historical Interpretation: Sources of English Medieval History, 1066-1540, 1965.

171 Douglas, D.C. and Greenaway, G.W., eds., English Historical Documents, 1042-1189, 1955. A valuable collection.

172 Hennings, Margaret A., ed., England under Henry III, 1216-72, (University of London Intermediate Source Books of History), 1924. Section Four, 249-69, is on social and economic aspects of the period.

173 Stenton, F.M., ed., Documents Illustrative of the Social and Economic History of the Danelaw, 1920.

(c) General works on the medieval English economy and on post-Conquest society

174 Baker, T., The Normans, 1966.

175 Barlow, F., The Feudal Kingdom of England, 1042-1216, 1955, 2nd ed., 1962. A very good survey.

176 —— William I and the Norman Conquest, 1965.

177 Barraclough, G., ed., Social Life in Early England, 1960. A varied collection of essays originally issued as Historical Association pamphlets.

178 Barrow, G.W.S., Feudal Britain: The Completion of the Medieval Kingdoms, 1066-1314, 1956. More attention than usual is given to Wales, Scotland and Ireland.

179 Bloch, M., Feudal Society, 2 vols., Paris, 1939-40, English trans., 1960. For background. A brilliant work.

180 Brooke, C.N.L., From Alfred to Henry III, 871-1272, 1961.

181 Brown, R.A., The Norman Conquest, 1969.

182 —— The Origins of English Feudalism, 1973.

183 Chevalier, C.T., ed., The Norman Conquest, 1966. Includes essays by Whitelock and Barlow.

184 Coulton, G.G., Social Life in Britain from the Conquest to the Reformation, 1918, 2nd ed., 1938.

185 —— Medieval Panorama, 1938.

186 —— Medieval Village, Manor and Monastery, 1925. Reprinted 1960.

187 Cronne, H.A., The Reign of Stephen, 1135-54, 1970.

188 Darlington, R.R., The Norman Conquest, 1963 (Creighton Lecture in History for 1962). A very useful summary.

189 Denholm-Young, N., 'Feudal society in the thirteenth century', History, XXIX, 1944, 107-19.

190 Dickinson, J.C., The Great Charter, Historical Association pamphlet, 1955. A readily accessible text of Magna Carta with notes on its background and significance.

191 Douglas, D.C., William the Conqueror: The Norman Impact upon England, 1964.

192 —— 'The Norman Conquest and English Feudalism', Ec.H.R., IX, 1938-9, 128-43.

193 Ganshof, F., Feudalism, English trans., 1952, 3rd ed., N.Y. and London, 1964. For background.

194 Hollings, M., 'The survival of the Five Hide unit in the west Midlands', E.H.R., LXIII, 1948, 435-87.

195 Hollister, C.W., The Making of England, 55 B.C. to 1399, Boston, Mass., 1966.

196 —— The Military Organisation of Norman England, 1965.

197 —— 'The irony of English Feudalism', Jnl. of British Studies, II, 1963, 1-26.

198 —— 'The Norman Conquest and the genesis of English Feudalism', A.H.R., LXVI, 1961, 641-63.

199 —— 'The significance of scutage rates in eleventh and twelfth-century England', E.H.R., LXXV, 1960, 577-88.

200 —— '1066: the "Feudal Revolution"', A.H.R., LXX, 1968, 708-23.

201 —— 'The Five Hide unit and military obligation', Speculum, XXXVI, 1961, 61-74.

202 —— 'The knights of Peterborough and the Anglo-Norman fyrd', E.H.R., LXXVII, 1962, 417-36.

203 —— and Holt, J.C., 'Two comments on the problem of continuity in Anglo-Norman feudalism', Ec.H.R., 2nd ser., XVI, 1963, 104-18.

204 Holt, J.C., Magna Carta, 1965. A major work on the subject.

205 —— 'The barons and the Great Charter', E.H.R., LXIX, 1955, 1-24.

206 —— 'Feudalism re-visited', Ec.H.R., 2nd ser., XIV, 1961, 333-40.

207 —— 'Politics and property in early medieval England', P.P., 57, 1972, 3-52.

208 John, E., 'English feudalism and the structure of Anglo-Saxon society', Bulletin of

the John Rylands Library, XLVI, 1963, 14-41. For background.
209 Jones, R.J., 'Economic organisation and policies in the Middle Ages', Ec.H.R., 2nd ser., XVII, 1965, 570-78. A review article on Postan, Rich and Miller (227), listed below.
210 Lloyd, J.E., History of Wales from the Earliest Times to the Edwardian Conquest, 1911, 3rd ed., 2 vols., 1939.
211 Lopez, R.S., 'Agenda for medieval studies', J.E.H., XXXI, 1971, 165-71.
212 Loyn, H.R., Anglo-Saxon England and the Norman Conquest, 1962. A valuable economic and social history. Good bibliography.
213 —— The Norman Conquest, 1965.
214 Maitland, F.W., Domesday Book and Beyond, 1897. A classic, but one which is preferably read in the light of a modern introduction. Two recent paperback editions of Maitland's book are available: (1) with an introduction by E. Miller, 1960; (2) with an introduction by B.D. Lyon, N.Y., 1966.
215 Matthew, D.J.A., The Norman Conquest, 1966.
216 McKechnie, W.S., Magna Carta: A commentary, 1905, 2nd ed., 1914. Still a standard authority.
217 Miller, E., 'The English economy in the thirteenth century', P.P., 28, 1964, 21-40.
218 —— 'The twelfth and thirteenth centuries: an economic contrast?', Ec.H.R., 2nd ser., XXIV, 1971, 1-14.
219 Painter, S., Studies in the History of the English Feudal Barony, Baltimore, 1943.
220 Poole, A.L., From Domesday Book to Magna Carta, 1087-1216, 1951, 2nd ed., 1955. Good bibliography.
221 —— Obligations of Society in the Twelfth and Thirteenth Centuries, 1946.
222 —— ed., Medieval England, 2 vols., 1958.
223 Postan, M.M., ed., Cambridge Economic History of Europe (1) The Agrarian Life of the Middle Ages, 2nd ed., 1966. An invaluable work.
224 —— The Medieval Economy and Society. An Economic History of Britain 1100-1500, 1972.
225 Postan, M.M., 'The rise of a money economy', Ec.H.R., XIV, 1944, 123-34. Reprinted in Carus-Wilson, ed. (64), listed above, II, 1-12. An important article.
226 —— and Rich, E.E., eds., Cambridge Economic History of Europe II: Trade and Industry in the Middle Ages, 1952.
227 ——, Rich, E.E., and Miller, E., eds., Cambridge Economic History of Europe III: Economic Organization and Policies in the Middle Ages, 1963.
228 Powicke, F.M., The Thirteenth Century, 1216-1307, 1953. A useful survey, though hardly a readable one. Good bibliography.
229 Powicke, M., Military Obligation in England: A Study in Liberty and Duty, 1962.
230 Roehl, R., Patterns and Structure of Demand, 1000-1500, 1970 (Fontana Economic History of Europe, vol. I, section 3). For background.

231 Saunders, I.J., Feudal Military Service in England: A study of the Constitutional and Military Powers of the Barones in Medieval England, 1956.
232 Sawyer, P.H., 'The wealth of England in the eleventh century', T.R.H.S., 5th ser., 15, 1965, 145-64. Argues that England was wealthier than often supposed and that the chief source of this wealth was wool.
233 Sayles, G.O., The Medieval Foundations of England, 1948, 2nd, ed., 1950. A well-known textbook.
234 Southern, R.W., The Making of the Middle Ages, London and New Haven, Conn., 1953.
235 Stenton, Doris M., English Society in the Early Middle Ages, 1066-1307, 1951, 4th ed., 1965.
236 —— ed., Preparatory to Anglo-Saxon England: The Collected Papers of F.M. Stenton, 1970. A useful collection which includes Stenton's essays on 'Norman London', on 'The development of the castle in England and Wales' and on 'The road system of medieval England'.
237 Stenton, F.M., Anglo-Saxon England, c.550-1087, 1943, 3rd ed., 1971. Good bibliography.
238 —— The First Century of English Feudalism, 1066-1166, 1932, 2nd ed., 1961.
239 Tomkieff, O.G., Life in Norman England, 1966.
240 Vinogradoff, P., English Society in the Eleventh Century, 1908. Reprinted 1968. See also Bean (567) listed below, and Clapham (144), Cunningham (145), Lipson (156) and Pollard and Crossley (58), listed above.

(d) Monographs and regional studies

241 Altschul, M., A Baronial Family in Medieval England: The Clares, 1217-1314, Baltimore Md., 1965.
242 Darby, H.C., The Medieval Fenland, 1940.
243 Hoskins, W.G., 'The wealth of medieval Devon'. In Hoskins and Finberg (1055), listed below, 212-49.
244 Jones, G.R.J., 'The tribal system in Wales: a re-assessment in the light of settlement studies', Welsh Hist. Rev., I, 1961, 111-32.
245 Wightman, W.E., The Lacy Family in England and Normandy, 1066-1194, 1966.

DOMESDAY STUDIES

Although many of the entries in this section could quite logically have been placed in other parts of the bibliography—under Agriculture, for example—it has been thought most useful to collect most of them under this heading.

The text of the Domesday Book was printed by the Record Commission as follows:

246 Farley, A., ed., Liber Censualis vocatus Domesday Book, 2 vols., 1783.
247 Ellis, H., ed., Libri Censualis vocati Domesday Book Additamenta, 1816. This contains the texts of the Exon Domesday, the Inquisi-

248 tio Eliensis and the Winchester and Boldon Book surveys.
—— Libri Censualis vocatus Domesday Book Indices, 3 vols., 1816-33.

249 Ballard, A., The Domesday Boroughs, 1904.
250 Bishop, T.A.M., 'The Norman settlement of Yorkshire', in R.W.Hunt, W.A.Pantin, and R.W.Southern, eds., Studies in Medieval History Presented to F.M.Powicke, 1948, 1-14. Reprinted in Carus-Wilson, ed. (164), listed above, II, 1-11.
251 Brooks, F.W., Domesday Book and the East Riding, East Yorkshire Local History Society, 1966.
252 Darby, H.C., ed., The Domesday Geography of Eastern England, 1952, 2nd ed., 1957. The first instalment of a massive historical enterprise.
253 —— and Terrett, I.B., eds., The Domesday Geography of Midland England, 1954, 2nd ed., 1971.
254 —— and Campbell, E.M., eds., The Domesday Geography of South-east England, 1962.
255 —— and Maxwell, I.S., eds., The Domesday Geography of Northern England, 1962.
256 —— and Finn, R.W., eds., The Domesday Geography of South-west England, 1967.
257 —— 'Domesday woodland', Ec.H.R., 2nd ser., III, 1950-1, 21-43.
258 Dodwell, Barbara, 'The making of the Domesday Survey in Norfolk: the Hundred and a Half of Clackclose', E.H.R., LXXXIV, 1969, 79-84.
259 Ellis, H., A General Introduction to Domesday Book, 1833. Reprinted 1972.
260 Finn, R.W., The Domesday Inquest and the Making of Domesday Book, 1961. See also Galbraith (273), listed below.
261 —— Domesday Studies: The Liber Exoniensis, 1964.
262 —— Domesday Studies: The Eastern Counties, 1967.
263 —— Domesday Studies: The Norman Conquest and its Effect on the Economy, 1066-86, 1971.
264 —— 'The immediate sources of the Exchequer Domesday', Bulletin of the John Rylands Library, XL, 1958, 47-78.
265 —— 'The making of the Dorset Domesday', Proceedings of the Dorset Natural History and Archaeological Society, LXXXI, 1960, 50-7.
266 —— 'The Exeter Domesday and its construction', Bulletin of the John Rylands Library, XLI, 1959, 360-87.
267 —— 'The making of the Wiltshire Domesday', Wiltshire Archaeological and Natural History Magazine, LII, 1948, 318-27.
268 —— 'Some reflections on the Cambridgeshire Domesday', Proceedings of the Cambridge Antiquarian Society, LIII, for 1959, 29-38.
269 —— 'The teamland of the Domesday Inquest', E.H.R., LXXXIII, 1968, 95-101. A reply to Moore (278), listed below.
270 Foster, C.W. and Longley, T., eds., The Lincolnshire Domesday and the Lindsey Survey (Lincolnshire Record Society, XIX), 1924.
271 Fowler, G.H., Bedfordshire in 1086, 1922.
272 Fraser, H.M., eds., The Staffordshire Domesday, 1936.
273 Galbraith, V.H., The Making of Domesday Book, 1961. An important and scholarly work.
274 Harvey, S., 'Royal revenue and Domesday terminology', Ec.H.R., 2nd ser., XX, 1967, 221-8.
275 Hoskins, W.G., 'The highland zone in Domesday Book'. In Hoskins (1053), listed below, 15-52.
276 Hoyt, R.S., 'Farm of the manor and community of the vill in Domesday Book', Speculum, XXX, 1955, 147-69.
277 Lennard, R.V., Rural England, 1086-1135, 1959. An extremely useful social and agrarian history.
278 Moore, J.S., 'The Domesday teamland: a reconsideration', T.R.H.S., 5th ser., 14, 1964, 109-30. See Finn (269), listed above.
279 Postan, M.M., 'The Maps of Domesday', Ec.H.R., 2nd ser., VII, 1954, 98-100.
280 Sawyer, P.H., 'The "original returns" and Domesday Book', E.H.R., LXX, 1955, 177-97.
281 Tait, J., ed., Domesday Survey of Cheshire, Chet.Soc., n.s., LXXV, 1916.

POPULATION

(a) General works

282 Hallam, H.E., 'Population density in medieval Fenland', Ec.H.R., 2nd ser., XIV, 1961, 71-81.
283 —— 'Some thirteenth-century censuses', Ec.H.R., 2nd ser., X, 1958, 340-61.
284 —— 'Further observations on the Spalding serf lists', Ec.H.R., 2nd ser., XVI, 1963, 338-50.
285 Harvey, J.B., 'Population trends and agricultural developments from the Warwickshire hundred rolls of 1279', Ec.H.R., 2nd ser., XI, 1958-9, 8-18.
286 Hoskins, W.G., 'The population of an English village, 1086-1801. A study of Wigston Magna', Trans. Leicestershire Archaeological Society, XXXIII, 1957, 15-35. Reprinted in Hoskins (1053), 181-208.
287 Roberts, B.K., 'A study of medieval colonisation in the Forest of Arden, Warwickshire', Ag.H.R., XVI, 1968, 101-13.
288 Russell, J.C., British Medieval Population, Albuquerque, New Mexico, 1949. The main work on the subject, though its conclusions do not command general assent.
289 —— 'The clerical population of medieval England', Traditio, 2, 1944, 177-212.
290 —— 'Recent advances in medieval demography', Speculum, XL, 1965, 84-101.
291 —— 'The pre-Plague population of England', Jnl. of British Studies, V, 1966, 1-21.
292 —— 'A quantitative approach to medieval population change', J.E.H., XXIV, 1964, 1-21.

293 —— Population in Europe, 500-1500 (Fontana Economic History of Europe, vol. I, section I), 1969. Useful for the general background.
294 —— 'Demographic limitations of the Spalding serf lists', Ec.H.R., 2nd ser., XV, 1962, 138-44. A comment on Hallam (282), listed above.
295 Titow, J.Z., 'Some evidence of the thirteenth-century population increase', Ec.H.R., 2nd ser., XIV, 1961, 218-23. See also Hollingsworth (1086) and Wrigley (1096), listed below.

(b) The family

296 Krause, J., 'The medieval household, large or small?', Ec.H.R., 2nd ser., IX, 1957, 420-32.
297 Painter, S., 'The family and the feudal system in twelfth-century England', Speculum, XXXV, 1960, 1-16. An important study of family solidarity in this period.

AGRICULTURE AND RURAL SOCIETY

298 Lamond, Elizabeth, ed., Walter of Henley's Husbandry, 1890. Written in the thirteenth century.
299 Oschinsky, Dorothea, ed., Walter of Henley: and Other Treatises on Estate Management and Accounting, 1971.
On Walter of Henley, see:
300 Denholm-Young, N., 'Walter of Henley', Medievalia et Humanistica, XV, 1962, 61-8.
301 McDonald, D., Agricultural Writers from Walter of Henley to Arthur Young 1200-1800, 1908. For other source material in this field, see Bland, Brown and Tawney (141), listed above, and Titow (329), listed below.

(a) General

302 Ashley, W.J., The Bread of our Forefathers: An Inquiry in Economic History, 1928.
303 Bennett, M.K., 'British wheat yield per acre for seven centuries', Ec.J. Economic History Supplement, III, 1935, 12-29. Reprinted in Minchinton (165), listed above, I, 53-72.
304 Beresford, M.W., and Joseph, J.K.St., Medieval England. An Aerial Survey, 1958. A useful book.
305 Beveridge, W.H., 'The yield and price of corn in the Middle Ages', Ec.J. Economic History Supplement, I, 1927, 155-67. Reprinted in Carus-Wilson, (164), I, 13-25.
306 Butlin, R.A., 'Some terms used in agrarian history: a glossary', Ag.H.R., IX, 1961, 98-104.
307 Cronne, H.A., 'The Royal Forest in the reign of Henry I', in Cronne, Moody and Quinn (1564), listed below, 1-23.
308 Duby, G., Rural Economy and Country Life in the Medieval West, English trans., 1968. A very important comparative history.
309 —— Medieval Agriculture, 900-1500 (Fontana Economic History of Europe, Vol. I, section 5), 1969. For background.
310 Ernle, Lord (R.E. Prothero), English Farming Past and Present, 1912, 6th ed., 1961, with valuable new introductions by G.E. Fussell and O.R. McGregor. A pioneer work of considerable historiographical interest.
311 Fussell, G.E., Farming Technique from Prehistoric to Modern Times, 1966.
312 Higgs, J., The Land, 1964 (part of J. Simmons, ed., A Visual History of Modern Britain). Well illustrated and with a guide to further reading.
313 Homans, G.C., English Villagers of the Thirteenth Century, Harvard, Mass., 1942. Reprinted 1960. An important book.
314 —— 'The rural sociology of medieval England', P.P., 4, 1953, 32-43.
315 —— 'Men and the land in the Middle Ages', Speculum, XI, 1936, 338-51.
316 Hoskins, W.G, 'Sheep farming in Saxon and medieval England'. In Hoskins (1053), listed below, 1-14.
317 Kershaw, I., 'The Great Famine and agrarian crisis in England 1315-1322', P.P., 59, 1973, 3-50.
318 Kosminsky, E.A., Studies in the Agrarian History of England in the Thirteenth Century, 1956. The work of a Marxist historian in which the peasantry receive most attention.
319 Lennard, R.V., 'Statistics of sheep in medieval England. A question of interpretation', Ag.H.R., VII, 1959, 75-81.
320 Neilson, Nellie, 'Early English woodland and waste', J.E.H., II, 1942, 54-62.
321 Parain, C., 'The evolution of agricultural technique'. In Postan (223), listed above, 126-79.
322 Poole, A.L., 'Livestock prices in the twelfth century', E.H.R., LV, 1940, 284-95.
323 Postan, M.M., Essays on Medieval Agriculture and General Problems of the Medieval Economy, 1973.
324 —— 'Medieval agrarian society in its prime: England'. In Postan (232), listed above, 549-632.
325 —— 'Investment in medieval agriculture', J.E.H., XXVII, 1967, 576-87. A pioneer article.
326 —— 'Village livestock in the thirteenth century', Ec.H.R., 2nd ser., XV, 1962, 219-49.
327 Seebohm, M.E.. The Evolution of the English Farm, 1927, 2nd ed., 1952.
328 Slicher van Bath, B.M., Yield Ratios 810-1820, Wageningen, 1963.
329 Titow, J.Z., English Rural Society, 1200-1350, 1969. A valuable general survey. Half the book consists of documents.
330 —— Winchester Yields. A Study in Medieval Agricultural Productivity, 1972. Covers the period 1208-1350.

(b) Regional studies

331 Slade, C.F., ed., The Leicestershire Survey,

Agriculture and Rural Society

332 Chibnall, A.C., Sherington: Fiefs and Fields of a Buckinghamshire Village, 1965. A survey from the twelfth to the eighteenth century.

333 Finberg, H.P.R., West Country Historical Studies, 1969.

334 Hallam, H.E., Settlement and Society: A Study of the Early Agrarian History of South Lincolnshire, 1965. An interesting study which examines land and people in the period between the eleventh century and 1307.

335 Gras, N.S.B. and E.C., The Economic and Social History of an English Village (Crawley, Hants), 909-1928, Cambridge, Mass., 1930. Very well documented.

336 Harvey, P.D.A., A Medieval Oxfordshire Village: Cuxham, 1240-1400, 1965.

337 Hilton, R.H., The Social Structure of Rural Warwickshire in the Middle Ages, Dugdale Society Occasional Paper 9, 1956.

338 —— A Medieval Society: the West Midlands at the End of the Thirteenth Century, 1967. An important study.

339 —— 'Medieval agrarian history', V.C.H. Leicestershire, ed. W.G. Hoskins and R.A. McKinley, II, 145-98.

340 Hoskins, W.G., 'The making of the agrarian landscape'. In Hoskins and Finberg (1055), 289-333. A general survey from medieval times to the nineteenth century.

341 Lennard, R.V., 'The destruction of woodland in the eastern counties under William the Conqueror', Ec.H.R., XV, 1945, 36-43.

342 Moore, J.S., Laughton: A Study in the Evolution of the Wealden Landscape, University of Leicester Department of English Local History, 1966. Occasional Papers, 19, 1966.

343 Scott, Richenda, 'Medieval Agriculture', In V.C.H. Wiltshire, ed. R.B. Pugh, IV, 1959, 7-42.

344 Siddle, D.J., 'The rural economy of medieval Holderness', Ag.H.R., XV, 1967, 40-5.

345 Sylvester, Dorothy, The Rural Landscape of the Welsh Borderland: A Study in Historical Geography, 1969.

346 Thomas, C., 'Thirteenth-century farm economies in North Wales', Ag.H.R., XVI, 1968, 1-14.

347 Vollans, E.C., 'The evolution of farm lands in the central Chilterns in the twelfth and thirteenth centuries', Trans. Institute of British Geographers, XXVI, 1959, 197-241. See also Hoskins (1052), listed below.

(c) The manor

348 Page, F.M., ed., Wellingborough Manorial Accounts, A.D. 1258-1323, Northamptonshire Record Society, 1936.

349 Redwood, B.C. and Wilson, A.E., eds., Custumals of the Sussex Manors of the Archbishops of Canterbury, Sussex Record Society, LVII, 1957.

350 Wilson, A.E., ed., Custumals of the Manors of Laughton, Willingdon and Goring, Sussex Record Society, LX, 1961.

351 Aston, T.H., 'The origins of the manor in England', T.R.H.S., 5th ser., 1958, 59-83. Reprinted in Minchinton (165), listed above, I, 9-35. An important article which considers the development of the manor in the Anglo-Saxon period and in the years following the Norman Conquest.

352 Bennett, H.S., Life on the English Manor, 1937.

353 Bishop, T.A.M., 'The distribution of manorial demesne in the Vale of Yorkshire', E.H.R., XLIX, 1934, 386-406.

354 Davenport, F.G., The Economic Development of a Norfolk Manor, 1086-1565, 1906.

355 Drew, J.S., 'Manorial accounts of St. Swithun's Priory, Winchester', E.H.R., LXII, 1947, 20-41. Reprinted in Carus-Wilson, ed. (164), listed above, II, 12-30. Covers the period from 1248 to 1400.

356 Hilton, R.H., 'Winchcombe Abbey and the Manor of Sherborne'. In Finberg (1051), listed below, 89-113.

357 —— 'Kibworth Harcourt, a Merton College manor in the thirteenth and fourteenth centuries', In Hoskins (1190), listed below, 17-40,

358 —— 'Life on the medieval manor', Amateur Historian, I, 1953, 82-9.

359 Latham, L.C., 'The manor and the village'. In Barraclough (117), listed above, 29-50. Originally published as an Historical Association pamphlet.

360 Levett, Ada E., Studies in Manorial History, 1938. Reprinted 1962.

361 Stenton, F.M., Types of Manorial Structure in the Northern Danelaw, 1910.

362 Sylvester, Dorothy, 'The manor and the Cheshire landscape', T.L.C.A.S., LXX, for 1960, 1961, 1-15.

363 Ugawa, K., 'The economic development of some Devon manors in the thirteenth century', Trans. Devonshire Association, XCIV, 1962, 630-83.

364 Vinogradoff, P., The Growth of the Manor, 1905, 2nd ed., 1911. Book 3, 291-379, covers the feudal period. Needs to be read in the light of Aston (351), listed above. See also Titow (464), listed under the section on Labour.

(d) Land tenure and the land market

Many titles relevant in this connection are listed in the section General Works.

365 Denman, D.R., Origins of Ownership: A Brief History of Land Ownership and Tenure in England from Earliest Times to the Modern Era, 1958.

366 Homans, G.C., 'Partible inheritance of villagers' holdings', Ec.H.R., VIII, 1937-8, 48-56.

367 Hoyt, R.S., The Royal Demesne in English Constitutional History, 1066-1272, Ithaca, N.Y., 1950.

368 Hyams, P.R., 'The origins of a peasant

land market in England', Ec.H.R., 2nd ser., XXIII, 1970, 18-31.
369 King, E., Peterborough Abbey 1086-1310. A Study in the Land Market, 1973.
370 Roden, D., 'Inheritance customs and succession to land in the Chiltern hills in the thirteenth and fourteenth centuries', Jnl. of British Studies, VII, 1967, 1-11.

(e) Estates

371 Stitt, F.B., ed., Lenton Priory Estate Accounts, 1296-1298, Thoroton Society Record series, XIX, 1959.

372 Chibnall, Marjorie, The English Lands of the Abbey of Bec, 1946.
373 Hilton, R.H., 'Gloucester Abbey leases of the late thirteenth century', Birm. Hist. Jnl., IV, 1953-4, 1-17.
374 Lennard, R.V., 'The demesnes of Glastonbury Abbey in the eleventh and twelfth centuries', Ec.H.R., 2nd ser., VIII, 1956, 355-63. A critique of Postan (378), listed below.
375 May, Teresa, 'The estates of the Cobham Family in the later thirteenth century', Archaeologia Cantiana, LXXXIV, 1970, 211-29. Presents a profit and loss account of a large lay manor.
376 Miller, E., The Abbey and Bishopric of Ely: The Social History of an Ecclesiastical Estate from the Tenth to the Early Fourteenth Century, 1951. Reprinted 1969. An important and scholarly work.
377 Oschinsky, Dorothea, 'Medieval treatises on estate management', Ec.H.R., 2nd ser., VIII, 1955-6, 296-309. See also Oschinsky (299), listed above.
378 Postan, M.M., 'Glastonbury estates in the twelfth century', Ec.H.R., 2nd ser., V, 1953, 358-67. See also Lennard (374), listed above.
379 —— 'Glastonbury estates in the twelfth century: a reply'. Ec.H.R., 2nd ser., IX, 1957, 106-18. A reply to Lennard (374), listed below.
380 Ward, J.C., 'The estates of the Clare family, 1066-1317', B.I.H.R., XXXVII, 1964, 114-17.

(f) Rent

381 Hilton, R.H., 'Rent and capital formation in feudal society', International Conference of Economic History, Aix, 1962, 33-68. A valuable general approach.
382 Kosminsky, E.A., 'The evolution of feudal rent in England from the eleventh to the fifteenth centuries', P.P., 7, 1955, 12-36.

(g) Field systems

383 Baker, A.R.H. and Butlin, R.A., (eds.), Studies of Field Systems in the British Isles, 1973. A standard work of reference on the development of British field systems from Anglo-Saxon times to the breakup of the medieval pattern.

384 Bishop, T.A.M., 'Assarting and the growth of the open fields', Ec.H.R., VI, 1935, 13-29. Reprinted in Carus-Wilson, ed. (164), listed above, I, 26-40.
385 Homans, G.C., 'The explanation of English regional differences', P.P., 42, 1969, 18-34. A critique of Thirsk (387), listed below in this section.
386 Pocock, E.A., 'The first fields in an Oxfordshire village', Ag.H.R., XVI, 1968, 85-100.
387 Thirsk, Joan, 'The common fields', P.P., 29, 1964, 3-25. An important article arguing that the growth of the three-field system was slower and less widespread than often assumed.
388 —— 'The origins of the common fields', P.P., 33, 1966, 142-7. A reply to Titow (389), listed below.
389 Titow, J.Z., 'Medieval England and the open-field system', P.P., 32, 1965, 86-102. Takes issue with Thirsk (387), listed above.

(h) Place-name studies

No attempt is made here to provide a comprehensive list of works on this subject. The reader is referred to Altschul's bibliography (166), listed above, 27-9, for details of the publications of the English Place Name Society. Only three items of a general nature are listed below.

390 Cameron, K., English Place Names, 1961.
391 Ekwall, E., Studies on English Place Names, Stockholm, 1936. A work by the leading authority on the subject.
392 Sawyer, P.H., 'The place names of Domesday Book', Bulletin of the John Rylands Library, XXXVIII, 1956, 483-506.

INDUSTRY

(a) General

393 Chaloner, W.H. and Musson, A.E., Industry and Technology (part of J. Simmons, ed., A Visual History of Modern Britain), 1963. A very good brief survey, profusely illustrated. With a bibliographical note.
394 Carus-Wilson, Eleanora M., 'An industrial revolution of the thirteenth century', Ec.H.R., XI, 1941, 39-60. Reprinted in Carus-Wilson, ed. (164), listed above, I, 41-60. An important article. The claims for this industrial revolution rest on evidence relating to water-powered fulling mills.
395 Salzman, L.F., English Industries of the Middle Ages, 1913, 2nd ed., 1923.
396 White, L., Jnr., Medieval Technology and Social Change, 1962. Chapters 2 and 3 on 'The agrarian revolution of the early Middle Ages' and 'The medieval expansion of mechanical power' are useful.

(b) Textiles

397 Carus-Wilson, Eleanora M., 'The English cloth industry in the late twelfth and early thirteenth centuries', Ec.H.R., XIV, 1944, 32-50.

398 —— 'The woollen industry', in Postan and Rich, eds. (226), listed above, 355-429.
399 Miller, E., 'The fortunes of the English textile industry during the thirteenth century', Ec.H.R., 2nd ser., XVIII, 1965, 64-82.

(c) Metals

400 Schubert, H.R., History of the British Iron and Steel Industry from c. 450 B.C. to A.D. 1775, 1957. Particularly useful on the technical aspects.
401 Waites, B., 'Medieval iron-working in N.E. Yorkshire', Geography, XLIX, 1964, 33-43. See also Fell (1362), Gough (1366), Lewis (1376), Raistrick and Jennings (1380) and Straker (1383), listed below.

(d) Building

402 Colvin, H.M., ed., Building Accounts of King Henry III, 1971.
403 —— ed., History of the King's Works, I and II, The Middle Ages (by R.A. Brown, H.M. Colvin and A.J. Taylor), 1963.
404 Edwards, J.G., 'Edward I's castle-building in Wales', Proceedings of the British Academy, XXXII, 1946, 15-81.
405 Johnson, H.T., 'Cathedral building and the medieval economy', Explorations in Entrepreneurial History, 2nd ser., IV, 1967, 191-210.
406 Knoop, D., and Jones, G.P., 'The English medieval quarry', Ec.H.R., IX, 1939, 17-37. See the section on Labour for other titles by Knoop and Jones (448-449).
407 Taylor, A.J., 'Castle building in Wales in the late thirteenth century: the prelude to construction', in E.M. Jope, ed., Studies in Building History, 1961, 104-33. See also Salzman (747), listed below.

(e) Miscellaneous

408 Murray, Kathleen M.E., 'Shipping'. In Poole (222), listed above, I, 168-95.

MONEY, PRICES AND PUBLIC FINANCE

(a) Money and prices

409 Brooke, G.C., English Coins from the Seventh Century to the Present Day, 1932. Reprinted 1966.
410 Craig, J., The Mint. A History of the London Mint from A.D. 287 to 1948, 1953.
411 Dolley, R.H.M., The Norman Conquest and the English Coinage, 1966.
412 —— 'Coinage'. In Poole (222), listed above, I, 264-99.
413 Farmer, D.L., 'Some price fluctuations in Angevin England', Ec.H.R., 2nd ser., IX, 1956-7, 34-43.
414 —— 'Some grain price movements in thirteenth-century England', Ec.H.R., 2nd ser., X, 1957-8, 207-20.
415 Feavearyear, A.E., The Pound Sterling, 1931, 2nd ed., revised by E.V. Morgan, 1963. A valuable work.

415a Harvey, P.D.A., 'The English Inflation 1180-1220', P.P., 61, 1973, 3-30.
416 Homer, S., A History of Interest Rates, New Brunswick, 1963.
417 Lloyd, T.H., The Movement of Wool Prices in Medieval England, 1973. Covers the period from the thirteenth to the fifteenth century.
418 Oman, C., The Coinage of England, 1931.
419 Rogers, J.E.T., A History of Agriculture and Prices in England, 6 vols., 1886-1900.
420 —— Six Centuries of Work and Wages, 1894. Several times reprinted.
421 Shaw, W.A., The History of Currency, 1252-1894, 2nd ed., 1896.
422 Spufford, P., 'Coinage and currency'. In Postan, Rich and Miller, eds. (227), listed above, 576-602.
See also the articles by E.H. Phelps Brown listed below (1658-1661).

(b) Public finance

423 Johnson, C., ed., Dialogus de Scaccario: the Discourse of the Exchequer, by Richard son of Nigel, 1950.
424 —— The De Moneta of Nicholas Oresme, and English Mint Documents, 1956.
425 Brown, R.A., 'The Treasury of the later twelfth century'. In J.C. Davies, ed., Studies Presented to Sir Hilary Jenkinson, 1957, 35-49.
426 Davies, J.C., 'The memoranda rolls of the Exchequer to 1307'. In J.C. Davies, ed., Studies Presented to Sir Hilary Jenkinson, 1957, 97-154.
427 Dowell, S., History of Taxation and Taxes in England, 1884, 2nd ed., 1888. Reprinted, 4 vols., 1965, with a new introduction by A.R. Ilersic. Vol. I.
428 Kaeuper, R.W., Bankers to the Crown. The Riccardi of Lucca and Edward I, Princeton, N.J., 1973.
429 Mitchell, S.K., Studies in Taxation under John and Henry III, New Haven, Conn., 1914.
430 —— Taxation in Medieval England, ed. S. Painter, New Haven, Conn., 1951.
431 Poole, R.L., The Exchequer in the Twelfth Century, 1912.
432 Prestwich, J.O., 'War and finance in the Anglo-Norman state', T.R.H.S., 5th ser., 4, 1954, 19-44.
433 Prestwich, M., 'Edward I's monetary policies and their consequences', Ec.H.R., 2nd ser., XXII, 1969, 406-16.
434 Roseveare, H., The Treasury: The Evolution of a British Institution, 1969.
435 Strayer, J.R., and Rudishill, G., Jnr., 'Taxation and Community in Wales and Ireland, 1272-1327', Speculum, XXIX, 1954, 410-16.
436 White, G.H., 'Financial administration under Henry I', T.R.H.S., 4th ser., 8, 1925, 56-78.
437 Whitwell, R.J., 'Italian bankers and the English Crown', T.R.H.S., n.s., 17, 1903, 175-233. Deals with the thirteenth century.

LABOUR

438 Beveridge, W.H., 'Wages on the Winchester manors', Ec.H.R., VII, 1936, 22-43. Covers the period from the early thirteenth to the mid-fifteenth century.

439 —— 'Westminster wages in the manorial era', Ec.H.R., 2nd ser., VIII, 1955-6, 18-35.

440 Dodwell, Barbara, 'The free tenantry of the hundred rolls', Ec.H.R., XIV, 1944, 163-71.

441 —— 'The free peasantry of East Anglia in Domesday', Norfolk Archaeology, XXVII, 1940, 145-57.

442 Gray, H.L., 'The commutation in villein services in England before the Black Death', E.H.R., XXIX, 1914, 625-56.

443 Hilton, R.H., Bond Men Made Free. Medieval Peasant Movements and the English Rising of 1381, 1973.

444 —— 'Peasant movements in England before 1381', Ec.H.R., 2nd ser., II, 1949, 117-36. Reprinted in Carus-Wilson, ed. (164), listed above, II, 73-90.

445 —— 'Freedom and villeinage in England', P.P., 31, 1965, 3-19. This and the previous article are valuable contributions to medieval labour history.

446 —— 'Lord and peasant in Staffordshire in the Middle Ages', North Staffordshire Jnl. of Field Studies, X, 1970, 1-20.

447 Jones, G.R.J., 'The distribution of bond settlements in N.W. Wales', Welsh Hist. Rev., 2, 1964, 19-36.

448 Knoop, D., and Jones, G.P., The Medieval Mason, 1933.

449 —— 'The impressment of masons in the Middle Ages', Ec.H.R., VIII, 1937-8, 57-67.

450 Kosminsky, E.A., 'Services and money rents in the thirteenth century', Ec.H.R., V, 1935, 24-45. Reprinted in Carus-Wilson, ed. (164), listed above, II, 31-48. Important.

451 Lennard, R.V., 'The economic position of the Domesday villani', Ec.J., LVI, 1946, 244-64.

452 —— 'The economic position of the Domesday sokemen', Ec.J., LVII, 1947, 179-95.

453 —— 'The economic position of the bordars and cottars of Domesday Book', Ec.J., LXI, 1951, 342-71.

454 —— 'The composition of the demesne plough teams in twelfth-century England', E.H.R., LXXV, 1960, 193-207.

455 —— 'Domesday plough teams: the south-west evidence', E.H.R., LXXX, 1965, 217-33.

456 Lloyd, T.H., 'Ploughing services on the demesnes of the Bishop of Worcester in the late thirteenth century', Birm. Hist. Jnl., VIII, 1962, 189-96.

457 Pierce, T.J., 'The growth of commutation in Gwynedd during the thirteenth century', Bulletin of the Board of Celtic Studies, X, 1941, 309-32.

458 Postan, M.M., 'The chronology of labour services', T.R.H.S., 4th ser., 20, 1937, 169-93. Reprinted in a revised form in Minchinton (165), listed above, I, 73-91. A valuable essay by one of the most eminent of economic historians of the Middle Ages.

459 —— The Famulus: The Estate Labourer in the Twelfth and Thirteenth Centuries, supplement to Ec.H.R. 1954. Demonstrates the importance of the hired labourer.

460 —— and Titow, J.Z., 'Heriots and prices on Winchester manors', Ec.H.R., 2nd ser., XI, 1959, 392-411.

461 Richardson, H.G., 'The medieval plough team', History, XXVI, 1942, 287-96.

462 Shelby, L.R., 'The role of the master mason in medieval English building', Speculum, XXXIX, 1964, 387-403. See also the works by Knoop and Jones (448-449), listed above.

463 Stenton, F.M., The Free Peasantry of the Northern Danelaw, 1969.

464 Titow, J.Z., 'Some differences between manors and their effects on the condition of the peasant in the thirteenth century', Ag.H.R., X, 1962, 1-13. Reprinted in Minchinton, (165), listed above, I, 37-51.

465 Vinogradoff, P., Villeinage in England, 1892.

466 —— The Collected Papers of Paul Vinogradoff, ed. Louise Vinogradoff, 2 vols., 1928. Vol.1: Historical. See also the articles by Phelps Brown and Hopkins (1658-1661), listed below.

TOWNS

For older histories of towns the main bibliography is:

467 Gross, C., A Bibliography of British Municipal History, Cambridge, Mass., 1897. Reprinted with a new introduction by G.H. Martin, 1966.

The bibliography by Gross is brought up to date in:

468 Martin, G.H. and MacIntyre, Sylvia, A Bibliography of British and Irish Municipal History 1: General Works, 1971. Subsequent volumes will deal with the history of individual cities and boroughs.

(a) Sources

469 Ballard, A., ed., British Borough Charters, 1042-1216, 1913.

470 —— and Tait, J., eds., British Borough Charters, 1216-1307, 1923.

471 Bateson, Mary, ed., Records of the Borough of Leicester, 1103-1327, 1899.

472 —— Borough Customs, Selden Society, XVIII and XXI, 2 vols., 1904-6.

473 Le Patourel, J., Documents Relating to the Manor and Borough of Leeds, 1066-1400, Thoresby Society publications, 1956.

474 Martin, G.H., The Early Court Rolls of the Borough of Ipswich, University of Leicester Department of English Local History, Occasional Papers, 5, 1954.

475 Palmer, W.M., ed., Cambridge Borough Documents, 1931.

(b) Surveys and monographs

476 Beresford, M. W., New Towns of the Middle Ages: Town Plantation in England, Wales and Gascony, 1967. An important study of a significant aspect of urban history in the medieval period.
477 Billson, C. J., Medieval Leicester, 1920.
478 Carus-Wilson, Eleanora, 'Towns and Trade'. In Poole (222), listed above, I, 209-63.
479 —— 'The first half century of the borough of Stratford upon Avon', Ec.H.R., 2nd ser., XVIII, 1965, 46-63.
480 Finberg, H. P. R., 'The genesis of the Gloucestershire towns'. In Finberg (1051), listed below, 52-88.
481 Fox, L., 'The early history of Coventry', History, XXX, 1945, 21-37.
482 Hibbert, A., 'The economic policies of towns'. In Postan, Rich and Miller (227), listed above, 157-229.
483 Hill, J. W. F., Medieval Lincoln, 1948.
484 Hollaender, A. E. J. and Kellaway, W., eds., Studies in London History Presented to Philip Edmund Jones, 1969. A festschrift which includes essays on London history from medieval to modern times.
485 Hoskins, W. G., 'The origin and rise of Market Harborough', Trans. Leicestershire Archaeological Society, XXV, 1949, 56-68. Reprinted in Hoskins (1053), listed below, 53-67.
486 Lobel, Mary D., The Borough of Bury St. Edmunds: A Study in the Government and Development of a Monastic Town, 1935.
487 Martin, G. H., The Town, 1961 (part of J. Simmons, ed., A Visual History of Modern Britain). A useful introduction to urban history. Well illustrated. A bibliographical note is appended.
488 —— 'The English borough in the thirteenth century', T. R. H. S., 5th ser., 13, 1963, 123-44.
489 Miller, E., 'Medieval York. The twelfth and thirteenth centuries'. In V.C.H. Yorkshire, ed. P. M. Tillott. The City of York, 1961, 25-116.
490 Murray, Katherine M. E., The Constitutional History of the Cinque Ports, 1935.
491 Redford, A., 'The emergence of Manchester', History, XXIV, 1939, 32-49.
492 Reynolds, Susan, 'The rulers of London in the twelfth century', History, LVII, 1972, 337-57.
493 Salter, H. E., Medieval Oxford, 1936.
494 Simmons, J., Leicester Past and Present 1: The Ancient Borough, 1974.
495 Stenton, F. M., 'Norman London'. In Barraclough, ed. (177), listed above, 179-207. Originally issued as an Historical Association pamphlet.
496 Stephenson, C., Borough and Town: A Study of Urban Origins in England, Cambridge, Mass., 1933. Contended that the process of urbanisation was only fully developed in England after 1066.
497 Tait, J., The Medieval English Borough, 1936. An important book which refuted Stephenson's claims (496). Tait demonstrated the importance of towns in the Anglo-Saxon period.
498 —— Medieval Manchester and the Beginnings of Lancashire, 1904.
499 Urry, W., Canterbury under the Angevin Kings, 1967. A significant contribution to urban studies.
500 Werveke, H. van, 'The Rise of the Towns'. In Postan, Rich and Miller (227), listed above, 3-41.
501 Williams, G. A., Medieval London, from Commune to Capital, 1963. A well-documented study of the constitutional and social history of London between c. 1200 and 1337.
502 Young, C. R., The English Borough and Royal Administration 1130-1307, Durham, N. C., 1961.

COMMERCE

503 Baker, J. N. L., 'Medieval trade-routes'. In Barraclough, ed. (177), listed below, 224-46.
504 Brutzkus, J., 'Trade with eastern Europe, 800-1200', Ec.H.R., XIII, 1943, 31-41. For background.
505 Carus-Wilson, Eleanora M., 'The English cloth trade in the late twelfth and early thirteenth centuries', Ec.H.R., XIV, 1944, 32-50.
506 Davies, J. C., 'Shipping and trade in Newcastle upon Tyne, 1294-1296', Archaeologia Aeliana, 4th ser., XXXI, 1953, 175-204.
507 Lopez, R. S., 'The trade of medieval Europe: the south'. In Postan and Rich, eds., (226), listed above, 257-354.
508 Postan, M. M., 'The trade of medieval Europe: the north'. In Postan and Rich, eds. (226), listed above, 119-256.
509 Salzman, L. F., English Trade in the Middle Ages, 1931.
See also Carus-Wilson and Coleman (779), Kerling (789) and Postan (798), listed below.

GOVERNMENT

510 Cam, Helen M., Liberties and Communities in Medieval England, 1944, 2nd ed., corrected, 1963.
511 —— The Hundred and the Hundred Rolls, 1930.
512 Chrimes, S. B., Introduction to the Administrative History of Medieval England, 1952, 3rd ed., 1966.
513 Hoyt, R. S., 'Royal taxation and the growth of the realm in medieval England', Speculum, XXV, 1950, 36-48.
514 Miller, E., 'The economic policies of governments: France and England'. In Postan, Rich and Miller (227), listed above, 290-339.
515 —— 'The state and landed interests in thirteenth century France and England', T. R. H. S., 5th ser., 2, 1952, 109-29.
516 Morris, W. A., The Medieval Sheriff to A.D. 1300, 1927.
517 Richardson, H. G. and Sayles, G. O., The Governance of Medieval England from the

THE JEWS IN ENGLAND

518 Adler, M., The Jews of Medieval England, 1939.
519 Elman, P., 'Jewish finance in thirteenth-century England', Trans. Jewish Historical Society, XVI, 1945-51, 89-96.
520 —— 'Economic causes of the expulsion of the Jews in 1290', Ec.H.R., VII, 1936-7, 145-54.
521 Grayzel, S., The Church and the Jews in the Thirteenth Century, Philadelphia, 1933. Useful for the general background.
522 Lipman, V.D., The Jews of Medieval Ipswich, Jewish Historical Society of England, 1967.
523 Richardson, H.G., The English Jewry under the Angevin Kings, 1960.
524 Roth, C., History of the Jews in England, 1941.

STANDARDS OF LIVING

525 Calthrop, D.C., English Costume from William I to George IV, 1066-1830, 1937.
526 Colvin, H.M., 'Domestic architecture and town planning'. In Poole (222), listed above, I, 37-79.
527 Cunnington, Phillis and Lucas, C., Occupational Dress in England from the Eleventh Century to 1914, 1967.
528 Faulkner, P.A., 'Domestic planning from the twelfth to the fourteenth century', Archaeological Jnl., CXV, 1958, 150-83.
529 Hassall, W.O., How They Lived, 55 B.C.-1485, 1962.
530 Holmes, D.T., Jnr., Daily Living in the Twelfth Century, Madison, Wis., 1962.
531 Labarge, Margaret W., A Baronial Household of the Thirteenth Century, London and N.Y., 1965. Based on the accounts of Eleanor, wife of Simon de Montfort.
532 Nevinson, J.C., 'Civil costume'. In Poole (222), listed above, I, 300-13.
533 Wood, Margaret E., Thirteenth-century Domestic Architecture in England, 1950 (supplement to Archaeological Jnl., CV).

COMMUNICATIONS AND INTERNAL TRADE

534 Coates, B.E., 'The origin and distribution of markets and fairs in medieval Derbyshire', Derbyshire Archaeological Jnl., LXXXV, 1966, 92-111.
535 Lopez, R.S., 'The evolution of land transport in the Middle Ages', P.P., 9, 1956, 17-29. For background.
536 Richardson, H., The Medieval Fairs and Markets of York, Borthwick Papers, 20, 1961.
537 Stenton, Doris M., 'Communications'. In Poole (222), listed above, I, 196-208.
538 Stenton, F.M., 'The road system in medieval England', Ec.H.R., VII, 1936, 1-21. Reprinted in Doris M. Stenton, ed., (236), listed above, 234-52. A useful article.
539 Tupling, G.H., 'The origin of markets and fairs in medieval Lancashire', T.L.C.A.S., XLIX, 1933, 75-94.
540 Verlinden, O., 'Markets and Fairs'. In Postan, Rich and Miller, eds. (227), listed above, 119-53. Useful background.

THE MONASTERIES

No attempt is made here to list the printed sources for this subject. The reader is referred to Altschul's bibliography (166), listed above, 49-56.

541 Cowley, F.G., 'The Cistercian economy in Glamorgan, 1130-1346', Morgannwg, XI, 1967, 5-26.
542 Day, L.J.C., 'The early monastic contribution to medieval farming', Lincolnshire Historian, 5, 1950, 200-14.
543 Dickinson, J.C., Monastic Life in Medieval England, 1961.
544 Donkin, R.A., 'Settlement and depopulation on Cistercian estates during the twelfth and thirteenth centuries, especially in Yorkshire', B.I.H.R., XXXIII, 1960, 141-65.
545 —— 'Cistercian sheep farming and wool sales in the thirteenth century', Ag.H.R., VI, 1958, 2-8.
546 —— 'Cattle on the estates of medieval Cistercian monasteries in England and Wales', Ec.H.R., 2nd ser., XV, 1962, 31-53.
547 —— 'The Cistercian order in medieval England: some conclusions', Trans. of the Institute of British Geographers, 33, 1963, 181-98.
548 —— The Cistercian Settlement and the English Royal Forests, 1960.
549 —— 'The Cistercian Order and the settlement of northern England', Geographical Review, LIX, 1969, 403-16.
550 Hill, B.D., English Cistercian Monasteries and their Patrons in the Twelfth Century, Illinois, 1968.
551 Knowles, D., The Monastic Order in England: A History of its Development, 943-1216, 1940, 2nd ed., 1963. An important and scholarly work.
552 —— The Religious Orders in England, vol. I, 1948. Covers the period 1216-1340.
553 Madden, J.E., 'Business monks, banker monks, bankrupt monks: the English Cistercians in the thirteenth century', Catholic Hist. Rev., XLIX, 1963, 341-64.
554 Matthew, D., The Norman Monasteries and their English Possessions, 1962.
555 Waites, B., Moorland and Vale-land Farming in N.E. Yorkshire: The Monastic Contribution in the Thirteenth and Fourteenth Centuries, Borthwick Papers, 32, 1967.
556 —— 'The monastic grange as a factor in

557 the settlement of N.E. Yorkshire', Yorkshire Archaeological Jnl., XL, 1959-62, 627-56.

— 'The monastic settlement of N.E. Yorkshire', Yorkshire Archaeological Jnl., XL, 1959-62, 478-95.

558 Williams, D.H., The Welsh Cistercians: Aspects of their Economic History, 1969.

559 Wood, S.M., English Monasteries and their Patrons in the Thirteenth Century, 1955.

ENGLAND 1300-1500

GENERAL WORKS

(a) Sources

560 Du Boulay, F. R., ed., Documents Illustrative of Medieval Kentish Society, Kent Archaeological Society, Kent Records, XVIII, 1964.
561 Flemming, Jessie H., ed., England under the Lancastrians, (University of London Intermediate Source Books of History), 1921.
562 Gairdner, J., ed., The Paston Letters, 6 vols., 1904. There is a one-volume selection of the Letters, ed. N. Davis, 1958.
563 Hughes, Dorothy, ed., Illustrations of Chaucer's England (University of London Intermediate Source Books of History), 1919.
564 Jack, I. R., Medieval Wales, 1972 (Sources of History series).
565 Myers, A. R., ed., English Historical Documents IV: 1327-1485, 1969. An invaluable collection. See especially Part 4 on economic and social developments and also Part 2 on the government of the realm, and Part 3 on the Church and education.
566 Thornley, Isobel D., ed., England under the Yorkists (University of London Intermediate Source Books of History), 1920.

(b) General surveys

567 Bean, J. M. W., The Decline of English Feudalism, 1215-1540, 1968. An important contribution to English medieval studies.
568 Beer, M., Early British Economics from the Thirteenth to the Middle of the Eighteenth Century, 1938. Reprinted 1967.
569 Bennett, H. S., The Pastons and their England, 1922, 2nd ed., 1932. Reprinted 1968.
570 Bradac, J., 'Czech visitors to fifteenth-century England', History Today, 15, 1965, 320-7.
571 Bridbury, A. R., Economic Growth: England in the Later Middle Ages, 1962. As its title makes clear, this stimulating little book does not share the traditional view of the period. See also Du Boulay (574), listed below.
572 Cam, Helen M., 'The decline and fall of English Feudalism', History, XXV, 1940, 216-33.
573 Denholm-Young, N., The Country Gentry in the Fourteenth Century, 1969.
574 Du Boulay, F. R. H., An Age of Ambition: English Society in the Late Middle Ages, 1970. The most recent general survey, with a good bibliography. Shares Bridbury's rejection of the traditional view of decline and decay in the later Middle Ages.
575 —— and Barron, Caroline, M., eds., The Reign of Richard II, 1972. A festschrift for Professor May McKisack which includes essays by V. H. Galbraith on the Peasants' Revolt and J. A. Tuck on aspects of the patronage system.
576 Fussell, G. E., 'Social change but static technology: rural England in the fourteenth century', History Studies, I, 1968, 23-32.
577 Hodgett, C. A. J., A Social and Economic History of Medieval Europe, 1972. For background.
578 Holmes, G., The Later Middle Ages, 1272-1485, 1962.
579 Jacob, E. F., The Fifteenth Century, 1399-1485, 1961. A comprehensive study. Good bibliography.
580 Jarrett, B., Social Theories of the Middle Ages, 1200-1500, 1926. Reprinted 1968.
581 Jusserand, J. J., English Wayfaring Life in the Middle Ages, 1889, 2nd ed., 1920. Several times reprinted. Deals for the most part with the fourteenth century.
582 Kingsford, C. L., Prejudice and Promise in Fifteenth England, 1925. Reprinted 1962.
583 Lander, J. R., Conflict and Stability in Fifteenth Century England, 1970.
584 MacFarlane, K. B., 'Bastard feudalism', B.I.H.R., XX, 1945, 161-80.
585 McKisack, May, The Fourteenth Century 1307-1399, 1959. Good bibliography.
586 Myers, A. R., England in the Late Middle Ages, 1307-1536, 1952. Reprinted with revisions 1956, 1959.
586a Pierce, T. J., Medieval Welsh Society: Selected Essays, 1973.
587 Postan, M. M., 'The fifteenth century', Ec.H.R., IX, 1938, 160-7. An important revision article.
588 Raftis, J. A., 'Social structures in five East Midland villages: a study of possibilities in the use of court roll data', Ec.H.R., 2nd ser., XVIII, 1965, 83-99.
589 Rees, W., South Wales and the March, 1234-1415, 1924.
590 Robinson, W. C., 'Money, population and economic change in late medieval Europe', Ec.H.R., 2nd ser., XII, 1959, 63-76. For background.
591 Rosenthal, J. H., The Purchase of Paradise, 1972. An examination of medieval charity highlighting the importance of the self-interest motive.
592 Schofield, R. S., 'The geographical distribution of wealth in England, 1334-1649', Ec.H.R., 2nd ser., XVIII, 1965, 483-510. Suggests that it was mainly concentrated, as in the twentieth century, in the south-east and Midlands.
593 Tuck, J. A., Richard II and the English Nobility, 1974.
594 Ullman, W., The Individual and Society in the Middle Ages, Baltimore, Md., 1966. For background.
595 Watts, D. G., 'A model for the early fourteenth century', Ec.H.R., 2nd ser., XX, 1967, 543-7.

596 Wilkinson, B., The Later Middle Ages in England 1216-1485, 1969. Mainly political in emphasis though social and economic aspects are covered.
See also Clapham (144), Cunningham (145), Lipson (156), and Pollard and Crossley (158), all listed above.

POPULATION

(a) Sources

597 Ekwall, E., ed., Two Early London Subsidy Rolls, Lund, 1951.
598 Erskine, A. M., ed., The Devonshire Lay Subsidy of 1332, Devon and Cornwall Record Society, n.s., XIV, 1969.
599 Hanley, H. A. and Chalklin, C. W., The Kent lay subsidy roll of 1334/5. In Du Boulay, ed. (560), listed above.

(b) Secondary works

600 Bean, J. M. W., 'Plague, population and economic decline in England in the later Middle Ages', Ec.H.R., 2nd ser., XV, 1963, 423-37.
601 Beresford, M. W., Lay Subsidies and Poll Taxes, 1964.
602 ——— 'Dispersed and group settlement in medieval Cornwall', Ag.H.R., XII, 1964, 13-27.
602a Bridbury, A. R., 'The Black Death', Ec.H.R., 2nd ser., XXVI, 1973, 557-92.
603 Boucher, C. E., 'The Black Death in Bristol', Trans. Bristol and Gloucestershire Archaeological Society, LX, 1938, 31-46.
604 Creighton, C., A History of Epidemics in Britain, 2 vols., 1891 and 1894, 2nd ed., 1965, with additional material by D. E. C. Eversley, E. A. Underwood and L. Ovenall.
605 Ekwall, E., Studies on the Population of Medieval London, Stockholm, 1956. Concentrates on the period 1250-1350 and is mainly a detailed study of immigration into the capital.
606 Fraser, C. M., 'Population density in medieval fenland', Ec.H.R., 2nd ser., XIV, 1961, 71-81.
607 Harvey, Barbara, 'The population trend in England, 1300-48', T.R.H.S., 5th ser., 16, 1966, 23-42. Contends that there was no dramatic change during this period.
608 Helleiner, K. F., 'Population movements and agrarian depression in the later Middle Ages', Canadian Jnl. of Economics and Political Science, XV, 1949, 368-77.
609 Langford, A. W., 'The Plague in Herefordshire', Trans. Woolhope Natural History Field Club, XXXV, 1956, 146-53.
610 Levett, Ada E., 'The Black Death on the St Albans manors'. In Levett (360), listed above, 248-86.
611 ———, The Black Death on the Estates of the See of Winchester, 1916.
612 Lucas, H. S., 'The great European famine, 1315, 1316 and 1317', Speculum, V, 1930, 343-77.
613 Mullett, C. F., The Bubonic Plague and England: An Essay in the History of Preventive Medicine, Lexington, Ky., 1956.
614 Nohl, J., The Black Death: A Chronicle of the Plague Compiled from Contemporary Sources, 1961.
615 Pelham, R. A., 'The urban population of Sussex in 1340', Sussex Archaeological Collections, LXXVIII, 1938, 211-23.
616 Postan, M. M., 'Some economic evidence of declining population in the later Middle Ages', Ec.H.R., 2nd ser., II, 1949-50, 221-46. An important article.
617 Raftis, J. A., 'Changes in an English village after the Black Death', Medieval Studies, XXIX, 1967, 158-77. Looks at Upwood, Hampshire.
618 Robo, E., 'The Black Death in the Hundred of Farnham', E.H.R., XLIV, 1929, 560-72.
618a Rubin, S., Medieval English Medicine, 1974.
619 Russell, J. C., 'Late medieval population patterns', Speculum, XX, 1945, 157-71.
620 ——— 'Effects of pestilence and plague, 1315-85', Comparative Studies in Society and History, VIII, 1966, 464-73.
621 Saltmarsh, J., 'Plague and economic decline in England in the later Middle Ages', Cambridge Hist. Jnl., VII, 1941, 23-41.
621a Scammell, Jean, 'Freedom and marriage in medieval England', Ec.H.R., 2nd ser., XXVII, 1974, 523-37.
622 Shrewsbury, J. F. D., A History of Bubonic Plague in the British Isles, 1970.
623 Talbot, C. H., Medicine in Medieval England, 1967.
624 Thrupp, Sylvia, 'The problem of replacement rates in late medieval English population', Ec.H.R., 2nd ser., XVIII, 1965, 101-19. Based mainly on court roll data.
625 ——— 'Plague effects in medieval Europe', Comparative Studies in Society and History, VIII, 1966, 474-83.
626 Ziegler, P., The Black Death, 1969.
See also Hoskins (1053), Hollingsworth (1086) and Wrigley (1096), listed below, and Russell (288), listed above.

AGRICULTURE AND RURAL SOCIETY

(a) General

627 Ault, W. O., The Self-directing Activities of Village Communities in Medieval England, Boston, Mass., 1952.
628 ——— Open Field Farming in Medieval England, 1972.
629 ——— 'By-laws of gleaning and the problem of harvest', Ec.H.R., 2nd ser., XIV, 1961, 210-17. Deals with the situation in England in the fourteenth century.
630 Baker, A. R. H., 'Evidence in the Nonarum Inquisitiones of contracting arable land in the early fourteenth century', Ec.H.R., 2nd ser., XIX, 1966, 518-32.
631 ——— 'Some evidence of a reduction in the acreage of cultivated lands in Sussex during the early fourteenth century',

Sussex Archaeological Collections, CIV, 1966, 1-5.
632 Beresford, M. W., 'The Poll Tax and the census of sheep', Ag.H.R., I, 1953, 9-15; ibid., II, 1954, 15-29.
633 Britnell, R. H., 'Production for the market on a small fourteenth-century estate', Ec.H R., 2nd ser., XIX, 1966, 380-7. Deals with Langenhoe, Essex.
634 Dyer, C., 'A redistribution of incomes in fifteenth-century England', P.P., 39, 1968, 11-33. Explores the relationship between a lord and his tenants as an agency of social and agrarian change in the fifteenth century.
635 Fussell, G. E., 'The classical tradition in west European farming: the fourteenth and fifteenth centuries', Ag.H.R., XVII, 1969, 1-8.
636 Gray, H. L., 'Incomes from land in England in 1436', E.H.R., XLIX, 1934, 607-39.
637 Hilton, R. H., 'The content and sources of English agrarian history before 1500', Ag.H.R., III, 1955, 3-19. See also Thirsk (1182), listed below, a companion article for the later period.
638 Hodgett, C. A. J., Agrarian England in the Later Middle Ages (Historical Association, Aids for Teachers series, 13), 1966. A useful summary with a bibliographical note.
639 Hoskins, W. G., 'Regional farming in England', Ag.H.R., II, 1954, 3-11.
640 Kosminsky, E. A., Studies in the Agrarian History of England in the Thirteenth Century, 1956.
641 Taylor, E. G. R., 'The Surveyor', Ec.H.R., XVII, 1947, 121-33.
642 Trow-Smith, R., A History of British Livestock Husbandry to 1700, 1957. See also Bennett (303), Beveridge (305) Ernle (310), and Slicher van Bath (160), listed above.

(b) Regional studies

643 Cracknell, B. E., Canvey Island: The History of a Marshland Community, University of Leicester, Department of English Local History, Occasional Papers, 12, 1959.
644 Fisher, P. and W. B., 'The medieval land surveys of County Durham', Research Paper No. 2, University of Durham, 1959.
645 Glasscock, R. E., 'The distribution of wealth in East Anglia in the early fourteenth century', Trans. Institute of British Geographers, XXXII, 1963, 113-23.
646 Hallam, H. E., 'The agrarian economy of medieval Lincolnshire before the Black Death', Historical Studies Australia and New Zealand, XI, 1964, 163-69.
647 —— 'The agrarian economy of south Lincolnshire in the mid-fifteenth century', Nottingham Medieval Studies, XI, 1967, 86-95.
648 Halcrow, E. M., 'The decline of demesne farming on the estates of Durham cathedral priory', Ec.H.R., 2nd ser., VII, 1955, 345-56.
649 Hatcher, J., Rural Economy and Society in the Duchy of Cornwall, 1300-1500, 1970.
650 —— 'A diversified economy: later medieval Cornwall', Ec.H.R., 2nd ser., XXII, 1969, 208-27.
651 Hewitt, H. J., Medieval Cheshire. An Economic and Social History of Cheshire in the Reigns of the Three Edwards, Chet. Soc., n.s, 88, 1929.
652 Howells, B., 'The distribution of customary acres in South Wales', National Library of Wales Jnl., XV, 1967, 226-35.
653 Lythe, S. G. E., 'The organisation of drainage and embankment in medieval Holderness', Yorkshire Archaeological Jnl., XXXIV, 1939, 282-95.
654 Newton, K. C., Thaxted in the Fourteenth Century, 1960.
655 Pierce, T. J., 'Some tendencies in the agricultural history of Caernarvonshire during the later Middle Ages', Trans. Caernarvonshire Historical Society, I, 1939, 18-36.
656 Ruston, A. G., and Witney, D., Hooton Pagnell: The Agricultural Evolution of a Yorkshire Village, 1934.
657 Smith, A., 'Regional differences in crop production in medieval Kent', Archaeologia Cantiana, LXXVIII, 1964, 147-60.
658 Smith, R. B., Blackburnshire: A Study in Early Lancashire History, University of Leicester, Department of English Local History, Occasional Papers, 15, 1961. The first part of the essay is a general survey of landholding and of the economy of the area in the early fourteenth century.
659 Spufford, Margaret, A Cambridgeshire Community: Chippenham from Settlement to Enclosure, University of Leicester, Department of English Local History, Occasional Papers, 20, 1965. See also Gras (335), Harvey (336), Hoskins (340) and Postan (223), listed above, and Hoskins (1052), listed below.

(c) The manor

660 Dale, M. K. ed., Court Roll of Chalgrave Manor, 1278-1313, Bedfordshire Historical Record Society, XXVIII, 1948.
661 Salzman, L. F. ed., Ministers' Accounts of the Manor of Petworth, 1347-53, Sussex Record Society, LV, 1955. See also Le Patourel (473), and Bland, Brown and Tawney(141), listed above.
662 Ault, W. O., 'Manor court and parish church in fifteenth-century England: a study of English by-laws', Speculum, XLII, 1967, 53-67. See the other titles by Ault (627-29), listed above.
663 Hatcher, J., 'Non-manorialism in medieval Cornwall', Ag.H.R., XVIII, 1970, 1-16.
664 Lloyd, E., 'The farm accounts of the manor of Hendon 1316-1416', Trans. London and Middlesex Archaeological Society, XXI, 1967, 157-63.
665 Pierce, T. J., 'A Caernarvonshire manorial

borough. Studies in the medieval history of Pwllheli', Trans. Caernarvonshire Historical Society, III, for 1941, 9-32; ibid., IV, for 1942-3, 35-50; ibid., V, for 1944, 12-40.
For other material on this subject, see also Davenport(354) and Hodgett (638), listed above.

(d) Estate management

666 Denney, A. H., ed., The Sibton Abbey Estates: Select Documents, 1325-1509, Suffolk Record Society, II, 1960.
667 Hilton, R. H., ed., Ministers' Accounts of the Warwickshire Estates of the Duke of Clarence, 1479-80, Publications of the Dugdale Society, XXI for 1944, 1952.

668 Bean, J. M. W., The Estates of the Percy Family, 1416-1537, 1958.
669 Denholm-Young, N., Seigneurial Administration in England, 1937.
670 Du Boulay, F. R. H., The Lordship of Canterbury: An Essay on Medieval Society, 1966. A valuable study of the economic, social, legal and military organisation of the lordship.
671 ——— 'Who were farming the English demesnes at the end of the Middle Ages?', Ec.H.R., 2nd ser., XVII, 1965, 443-55.
672 ——— 'A rentier economy in the later Middle Ages: the archbishopric of Canterbury', Ec.H.R., 2nd ser., XVI, 1964, 427-38.
673 Harvey, Barbara, 'The leasing of the Abbot of Westminster's demesnes in the later Middle Ages', Ec.H.R., 2nd ser., XXII, 1969, 17-27.
674 Hilton, R. H., The Economic Development of Some Leicestershire Estates in the Fourteenth and Fifteenth Centuries, 1947.
675 Holmes, G. A., The Estates of the Higher Nobility in Fourteenth-Century England, 1957.
676 Jack, I. R., 'Entail and descent: the Hastings inheritance, 1370-1436', B.I.H.R., XXXVIII, 1965, 1-19.
677 Keil, I., 'Farming on the Dorset estates of Glastonbury Abbey in the early fourteenth century', Proceedings of the Dorset Natural History and Archaeological Society, LXXXVII, 1966, 234-50.
678 Kershaw, I., Bolton Priory: The Economy of a Northern Monastery 1286-1325, 1973.
679 Page, F. M., The Estates of Crowland Abbey, 1934.
680 Plucknett, T. F. T., The Medieval Bailiff (Creighton Lecture in History, 1952), 1954.
681 Raftis, J. A., The Estates of Ramsey Abbey: A Study in Economic Growth and Organisation, Toronto, 1957.
682 Rosenthal, J. T., 'The estates and finances of Richard, Duke of York, 1411-60'. In W. M. Bowsky, ed., Studies in Medieval and Renaissance History, II, Nebraska, 1965, 115-204.
683 Ross, C., The Estates and Finances of Richard Beauchamp, Earl of Warwick, Dugdale Society Occasional Paper No. 12, 1956.
683a Searle, E., Lordship and Community. Battle Abbey and its Banlieue 1066-1538, Toronto, 1974.
684 Smith, R. A. L., Canterbury Cathedral Priory: A Study in Monastic Administration, 1943.
685 Wolffe, B. P., 'The management of English royal estates under the Yorkist kings', E.H.R., LXXI, 1956, 1-27. See also the book by the same author listed below (1220).
686 ——— 'Acts of Resumption in the Lancastrian parliaments, 1399-1456', E.H.R., LXXIII, 1958, 583-613.

(e) Land tenure

687 Dodwell, Barbara, 'Holdings and inheritance in medieval East Anglia', Ec.H.R., 2nd ser., XX, 1967, 53-66.
688 Faith, R. J., 'Peasant families and inheritance customs in medieval England', Ag.H.R., XIV, 1966, 77-95.
689 Pitkin, D. S., 'Partible inheritance and the open fields', Agricultural History, XXXV, 1961, 65-9.
690 Raftis, J. A., Tenure and Mobility: Studies in the Social History of the Medieval English Village, Toronto, 1964.

(f) Field systems

691 Ault, W. O., 'Open field husbandry and the village community: a study of agrarian by-laws in medieval England', Trans. American Philosophical Society, n.s., LV, Pennsylvania, 1965.
692 Baker, A. R. H., 'Open fields and partible inheritance on a Kent manor', Ec.H.R., 2nd ser., XVII, 1964, 1-23. Looks at the manor of Gillingham in 1285 and 1447.
693 Beresford, M. W., 'Glebe terriers and open fields', Yorkshire Archaeological Jnl., XXXVII, 1951, 325-68.
694 ——— 'Ridge and furrow and the open fields', Ec.H.R., 2nd ser., I, 1948, 34-45.
695 ——— 'Lot acres', Ec.H.R., XIII, 1943, 74-9. Discusses the practice of dividing up the arable from the waste by lot.
696 Butler, R. M., 'The common lands of the borough of Nottingham', Trans. Thoroton Society, LIV, 1950, 45-62.
697 Chapman, V., 'Open fields in West Cheshire', T.H.S.L.C., 104, 1952, 35-60.
698 Cromarty, D., The Fields of Saffron Walden in 1400, 1966.
699 Emmison, F. G., Some Types of Common Field Parish, 1965 (Standing Conference for Local History).
700 Finberg, H. P. R., 'The open field in Devon'. In Hoskins and Finberg (1055), listed below, 265-88.
701 Harris, A., The Open Fields of East Yorkshire, East Yorkshire Local Historical Society, pamphlet series, 9, 1959.
702 Hilton, R. H., 'A study in the pre-history of English enclosure in the fifteenth

century'. In Studi in Onore di Armando Sapori, Milan, 1957, I, 675-85.

703   Hoskins, W. G., and Stamp, L. D., The Common Lands of England and Wales, 1963.

704   Lennard, R. V., 'The alleged exhaustion of the soil in medieval England', Ec.J., XXXII, 1922, 12-27. Refuted the views put forward by Harriet Bradley in The Enclosures in England: An Economic Reconstruction, 1918.

705   Orwin, C. S., and Christabel S., The Open Fields, 1954, 3rd ed., 1967, with an introduction by Joan Thirsk.

706   Postgate, M. R., 'The field systems of Breckland', Ag.H.R., X, 1962, 80-101. Points to the variations occurring in traditional field patterns as a response to local soil conditions.

707   Roden, D., 'Field systems in Ibstone: a township of the S. W. Chilterns during the later Middle Ages', Records of Buckinghamshire, XVIII, 1966, 43-57.

708   —— and Baker, A. R. H., 'Field systems of the Chiltern hills and parts of Kent from the late thirteenth to the early seventeenth century', Trans. Institute of British Geographers, XXXVIII, 1966, 73-88.

709   Saltmarsh, J. and Darby, H. C.:'The infield-outfield system on a Norfolk manor' (West Wretham), Ec.J. Economic History Supplement, III, 1935, 30-44.

710   Sylvester, Dorothy, 'The open fields of Cheshire', T.H.S.L.C., 108, 1956, 1-34.

711   Youd, G., 'The common fields of Lancashire', T.H.S.L.C., 113, 1962, 1-42.

(g) Deserted villages

712   Allison, K. J., Beresford, M. W. and Hurst, J. G., The Deserted Villages of Northamptonshire, University of Leicester Department of English Local History, Occasional Papers, 18, 1966.

713   —— The Deserted Villages of Oxfordshire, University of Leicester, Department of English Local History, Occasional Papers, 17, 1965.

714   —— 'The lost villages of Norfolk', Norfolk Archaeology, XXXI, 1955, 116-62.

715   Beresford, M. W., The Lost Villages of England, 1954. The main work on the subject. Beresford stresses the medieval stages in the history of deserted villages and rejects an oversimplified monocausal explanation based on sixteenth-century enclosures. Reprinted 1965.

716   —— and Hurst, J. G., eds., Deserted Medieval Villages, 1971. Brings together essays on the most recent historical and archaeological work on the subject. Gazetteers of deserted sites are appended.

717   Dyer, C., 'Population and agriculture on a Warwickshire manor in the later Middle Ages', Birm. Hist. Jnl., XI, 1968, 113-27. A local study of a village which was only gradually deserted.

718   Gould, J. D., 'Mr Beresford and the lost villages', Ag.H.R., III, 1955, 107-13.

719   Hoskins, W. G., 'The deserted villages of Leicestershire', in Hoskins (1053), listed below, 67-107.

(h) The forests

720   Birrell, J. R., 'The forest economy of the honour of Tutbury in the fourteenth and fifteenth centuries', Birm. Hist. Jnl., VIII, 1962, 114-34.

721   Cantor, L. M., The medieval forests and chases of Staffordshire', North Staffordshire Jnl. of Field Studies, VIII, 1968, 39-53.

722   Husain, B. M. C., 'Delamere forest in later medieval times', T.H.S.L.C., 107, 1955, 23-39.

723   Shaw, R. Cunliffe, The Royal Forest of Lancaster, 1957.

724   Taylor, C. C., 'The pattern of medieval settlement in the Forest of Blackmoor', Proceedings of the Dorset Natural History and Archaeological Society, LXXXVII, 1966, 251-4.

725   —— 'Whiteparish: a study of the development of a forest-edge parish', Wiltshire Archaeological and Natural History Magazine, LXII, 1967, 79-102.
See also Roberts (287), listed above, and Tupling (1057), listed below.

INDUSTRY

(a) General

726   Carus-Wilson, Eleanora M., 'Evidence of industrial growth on some fifteenth-century manors', Ec.H.R., 2nd ser., XII, 1959, 190-205.

727   Lewis, E. A., 'The development of industry and commerce in Wales during the Middle Ages', T.R.H.S., n.s., 17, 1903, 121-73.

728   Salzman, L. F., English Industries of the Middle Ages, 1913, 2nd ed., 1923. Covers— inter al.—mining, building and cloth-making. Illustrated.
See also Chaloner and Musson (393) and White (396), listed above.

(b) Industrial organisation

The literature on individual companies is too enormous to list here. The reader is referred to Kahl's bibliography (1304), and to his introduction to Unwin's Gilds and Companies of London (1321), both of which are listed below.

729   Gross, C., The Gild Merchant, 2 vols., 1890. Reprinted, 1965. Still an important work on the subject.

730   Hibbert, F. A., The Influence and Development of English Gilds, as Illustrated by the History of the Craft Gilds of Shrewsbury, 1891.

731   Imray, Jean M., 'Les Bones Gentes de la Mercerye de Londres: a study of the membership of the medieval Mercers' Company'. In Hollaender and Kellaway (480), listed above, 155-78.

732 Thrupp, Sylvia, 'The gilds'. In Postan, Rich and Miller (227), listed above, 230-80.
733 ——— 'Medieval gilds reconsidered', J.E.H., II, 1942, 164-73.
For source material on this subject, see the useful section on 'Towns and gilds' in Bland, Brown and Tawney (141), listed above, 114-50

(c) Textiles

734 Gray, H. L., 'The production and exportation of English woollens in the fourteenth century', E.H.R., XXXIX, 1924, 13-35.
735 McClenaghan, B., The Springs of Lavenham and the Suffolk Cloth Trade in the Fifteenth and Sixteenth Centuries, 1924.
736 Power, Eileen, The Paycockes of Coggeshall, 1920. A short study of a family of clothiers. See also Carus-Wilson (398), listed above. Studies of the wool trade are listed below under Commerce.

(d) Mining and metallurgy

737 Giuseppi, M. S., 'Some fourteenth-century accounts of iron works at Tudely, Kent', Archaeologia, LXIV, 1912-13, 145-64.
738 Lapsley, G. T., 'The account roll of a fifteenth-century ironmaster', E.H.R., XIV, 1899, 509-28. Contains the text of a long Latin document.
738a Hatcher, J., English Tin Production and Trade Before 1550, 1973.
738b ——— and Barker, T. C., A History of British Pewter, 1974.
739 Mott, R. A., 'English bloomeries, 1329-1589', Jnl. of the Iron and Steel Institute, CXCVIII, 1961, 149-61
740 Nef. J. U., 'Mining and metallurgy in medieval civilisation'. In Postan and Rich (226), listed above, 430-92.
741 Simpson, J. B., 'Coal mining by the monks', Trans. Institute of Mining Engineers, XXXIX, 1910, 572-98.
742 Sprandel, R., 'La Production du fer au moyen age', Annales, 24e année, 1969, 305-21.
See also Fell (1362), Gough (1366), Lewis (1376), Nef (1354), listed below, and Schubert (400) and Waites (401), listed above.

(e) Salt

743 Berry, E. K., 'The borough of Droitwich and its salt industry, 1215-1700', Birm. Hist. Jnl., VI, 1957, 39-61
744 Hallam, H. E., 'Salt making in the Lincolnshire fenlands during the Middle Ages', Lincolnshire Architectural and Archaeological Society, n.s., 8, 1959-60, 85-112.
745 Rudkin, E. H., and Owen, Dorothy M., 'The medieval salt industry in the Lindsey marshland', Lincolnshire Architectural and Archaeological Society, n.s., 8, 1959-60, 76-84.
See also Bridbury's book on the salt trade (773,), listed below.

(f) Miscellaneous

746 Harvey, J., The Master Builders of the Middle Ages, 1972.
747 Salzman, L. F., Building in England down to 1540: A Documentary History, 1952, 3rd ed., 1967.
748 Veale, Elspeth M., 'Craftsmen and the economy of London in the fourteenth century'. In Hollaender and Kellaway (453), listed above, 133-51.
749 Wright, Jane A., Brick Building in England from the Middle Ages to 1550, 1972.
See also Colvin (403), Johnson (405), and Knoop and Junes (448), listed above.

(g) Sources of power for industry

750 Adams, J. W. R., Windmills in Kent, 1955.
751 Atkinson, F., 'The horse as a source of rotary power', Trans. Newcomen Society, XXXIII, 1962, 31-55.
752 Dewar, H. S. L., 'The windmills, watermills and horse mills of Dorset', Proceedings of the Dorset Natural History and Archaeological Society, LXXXII, for 1960, 109-32.
753 ——— 'The windmills, watermills and horsemills of Dorset—new evidence', Proceedings of the Dorset Natural History and Archaeological Society, LXXXVI, 1965, 179-81.
754 Freese, S., Windmills and Millwrighting, 1957. Reprinted 1971
755 Pelham, R.A., Fulling Mills: A Study of the Application of Water Power to the Woollen Industry, 1958 (Society for the Protection of Ancient Buildings: Wind and Watermill section, publications, 5).
756 Pratt, D., 'The medieval watermills of Denbighshire', Denbighshire Historical Society Trans., XIII, 1964, 22-37.
757 Reid, K. C., 'The watermills of London', Trans. London and Middlesex Archaeological Society, n.s., XI, 1954, 227-36.
758 Wailes, R., Windmills in England: A Study of Their Origin, Development and Future, 1948.
759 ——— The English Windmill, 1954.
760 ——— Tidemills, Parts 1 and 2, 1956 (Society for the Protection of Ancient Buildings. Wind and Watermill section, publications 2-3).
761 Wilson, P. N., Watermills: An Introduction, 1956 (Society for the Protection of Ancient Buildings. Wind and Watermill section, publications, 1).
See also Chaloner and Musson (393), listed above.

COMMERCE

(a) Sources

762 Cobb, H.S., ed., The Local Port Book of Southampton, 1439-40, Southampton Records series, V, 1961.
See also Foster (764), listed below.

England 1300-1500

763   Coleman, Olive, ed., The Brokage Book of Southampton, 1443-44, Southampton Records series, IV, 1960.
764   Foster, B., ed., The Local Port Book of Southampton for 1435-6, Southampton Records series, VII, 1963.
765   Lister, J., ed., The Early Yorkshire Woollen Trade: Extracts from the Hull Customs Rolls and Complete Transcripts of the Ulnagers'Rolls, Yorkshire Archaeological Society record series, LXIV, 1924. Deals with the fourteenth and fifteenth centuries.
766   Quinn, D. B., ed., The Port Books or Local Customs Accounts of Southampton for the Reign of Edward IV, vol. 1: 1469-71, Southampton Record Society, XXXVII, 1938.
767   Sellers, Maud, ed., The York Mercers and Merchant Adventurers, 1356-1917, Surtees Society, CXXIX, 1918.
768   Warner, G. F., ed., The Libelle of Englyshe Policye (1436), 1926. A contemporary tract which emphasised the opportunities which English merchants were missing in South-west Europe. See the article by Holmes (787), listed below.
769   Wilson, K. P., Ed., Chester Customs Accounts, 1301-1565, Record Society of Lancashire and Cheshire, CXI, 1969. See the article by Wilson (815), listed below.

(b) General and miscellaneous

770   Baker, R. L., 'The establishment of the English wool staple in 1313', Speculum, XXXI, 1956, 444-53.
771   Blake, J. B., 'The medieval coal trade of N. E. England: some fourteenth-century evidence', Northern History, II, 1967, 1-26.
772   —— 'Medieval smuggling in the N. E. Some fourteenth-century evidence', Archaeologia Aeliana, 4th ser., XLIII, 1965, 243-60. On medieval smuggling, see also Williams (814), listed below.
773   Bridbury, A. R., England and the Salt Trade in the Later Middle Ages, 1965. A valuable study.
774   Carus-Wilson, Eleanora M., 'The ulnage accounts: a criticism', Ec. H. R., II, 1929, 114-23.
775   —— 'Trends in the export of English woollens in the fourteenth century', Ec. H. R., 2nd ser., III, 1950, 162-79.
776   —— 'The effects of the acquisition and of the loss of Gascony on the English wine trade', B. I. H. R., XXI, 1947, 145-54.
777   —— 'The medieval trade of the ports of the Wash', Medieval Archaeology, VI-VII, 1962-3, 182-201.
778   —— The Overseas Trade of Bristol in the Later Middle Ages, 1937, 2nd ed., 1967. The later edition contains a supplement to the bibliography.
779   —— and Coleman, Olive, England's Export Trade, 1275-1547, 1963. An important survey.
780   Dulley, A. J. F., 'The level and port of Pevensey in the Middle Ages', Sussex Archaeological Collections, CIV, 1966, 26-45.

781   Flenley, R., 'London and foreign merchants in the reign of Henry VI', E. H. R., XXV, 1910, 644-55.
782   Fraser, C. M., 'The N. E. coal trade until 1421', Trans. Durham and Northumberland Architectural and Archaeological Society, XI, 1962, 209-20.
783   Fryde, E. B., The Wool Accounts of William de la Pole: A Study of Some Aspects of the English Wool Trade at the Start of the Hundred Years War, St Anthony's Hall publications, 25, 1964.
784   —— Some Business Transactions of York Merchants 1336-49, Borthwick Papers, 29, 1966.
785   —— 'Edward III's wool monopoly of 1337: a fourteenth-century trading venture', History, XXXVII, 1952, 8-24.
786   Girling, F. A., English Merchants' Marks: A Field Survey of Marks Used by Merchants and Tradesmen in England Between 1400 and 1700, 1964.
787   Holmes, G. A., 'The Libel of English Policy', E. H. R., LXXVI, 1961, 193-216. See Warner, ed. (768), listed above.
788   James, Margaret K., Studies in the Medieval Wine Trade, ed. Elspeth Veale, 1971.
789   Kerling, Nellie J. M., Commercial Relations of Holland and Zeeland with England from the Late Thirteenth Century to the Close of the Middle Ages, Leiden, 1954.
790   Kingsford, C. L., 'The beginnings of English maritime enterprise in the fifteenth century', History, XIII, 1928-9, 97-106, 193-203.
791   Lewis, E. A., 'A contribution to the commercial history of medieval Wales, with tabulated accounts from 1301 to 1547', Y Cymmrodor, XXIV, 1913, 86-188.
792   Mace, F. A., 'Devonshire ports in the fourteenth and fifteenth centuries', T. R. H. S., 4th ser., 8, 1925, 98-126.
793   McCusker, J. J., Jnr., 'The wine prise and medieval mercantile shipping', Speculum, XLI, 1966, 279-96.
794   Mallett, M. E., 'Anglo-Florentine commercial relations, 1465-1491', Ec. H. R., 2nd ser., XV, 1962, 250-65.
795   Martin, G. H., 'Shipments of wool from Ipswich to Calais, 1399-1402', Jnl. of Transport History, II, 1956, 177-81.
796   Mollat, M., 'Anglo-Norman trade in the fifteenth century', Ec. H. R., XVII, 1947, 143-50.
796a Munro, J. H. A., Wool, Cloth and Gold: The Struggle for Bullion in Anglo-Burgundian Trade 1340-1478, Brussels and Toronto, 1973.
797   Palais, H., 'England's first attempt to break the commercial monopoly of the Hanseatic League, 1377-80', A. H. R., LXIV, 1959, 852-65.
798   Postan, M. M., Medieval Trade and Finance, 1973. Collected essays.
799   —— 'Credit in medieval trade', Ec. H. R., I, 1927-8, 234-61. Reprinted in Carus-Wilson, ed. (164), listed above, I, 61-87. An important article.
800   —— 'Italy and the economic development

800 of England in the Middle Ages', J.E.H., XI, 1951, 339-46.
801 —— 'The economic and political relations of England and the Hansa from 1400 to 1475', in Power and Postan (804), listed below, 91-153.
802 Pounds, N.J.G., 'The ports of Cornwall in the Middle Ages', Devon and Cornwall Notes and Queries, XXIII, 1947, 65-73.
803 Power, Eileen, The Wool Trade in English Medieval History, 1941. An important study of England's major export in the fourteenth and fifteenth centuries.
804 —— and Postan, M.M., Studies in English Trade in the Fifteenth Century, 1933. Reprinted 1951.
805 Richardson, H., 'Medieval trading restrictions in the N.E.', Archaeologia Aeliana, 4th ser., XXXIX, 1961, 135-50.
806 Ruddock, A.A., Italian Merchants and Shipping in Southampton, 1270-1600, Southampton Records series, 1951.
807 —— 'Italian trading fleets in medieval England', History, XXIX, 1944, 192-202.
808 —— 'John Day of Bristol and the English voyages across the Atlantic before 1497', Geographical Jnl., CXXXII, 1966, 225-32.
809 Sherborne, J.W., The Port of Bristol in the Middle Ages. Bristol branch of the Historical Association, 1965.
810 Simon, A.L., The History of the Wine Trade in England, 3 vols., 1906-9.
811 Usher, G., 'Holyhead as a fourteenth-century port', Bulletin of the Board of Celtic Studies, XV, 1952-4, 209-12.
812 Veale, Elspeth M., The English Fur Trade in the Later Middle Ages, 1966.
813 Wee, H. Van der, The Growth of the Antwerp Market and the European Economy from the Fourteenth to the Sixteenth Centuries, 3 vols., The Hague, 1963. An important study of an entrepôt which was growing in significance throughout this period.
814 Williams, N., Contraband Cargoes: Seven Centuries of Smuggling, 1959.
815 Wilson, K.P., 'The port of Chester in the fifteenth century', T.H.S.L.C., 117, 1966, 1-16. See also Wilson's edition of the Chester customs accounts (769), listed above.
816 Wolff, P., 'English cloth in Toulouse, 1380-1450', Ec. H.R., 2nd ser., II, 1950, 290-4.

(c) **The mercantile community**

817 Carus-Wilson, Eleanora M., Medieval Merchant Venturers, 1954.
818 —— The Merchant Adventurers of Bristol in the Fifteenth Century, Bristol branch of the Historical Association, 1962.
819 —— 'The origins and early development of the Merchant Adventurers' organisation in London as shown in their own medieval records', Ec. H.R., IV, 1932, 147-76.
820 James, Margaret K., 'A London merchant of the fourteenth century', Ec. H.R., 2nd ser., VIII, 1956, 364-76.
821 Postan, M.M., 'Partnership in English medieval commerce'. In Studi in Onore di Armando Sapori, Milan, 1957, I, 522-49.
822 Thrupp, Sylvia, The Merchant Class of Medieval London, 1948. An important study.
823 Ward, G.F., 'The early history of the Merchant Staplers', E.H.R., XXXIII, 1918, 297-319.

PRICES, PUBLIC FINANCE, USURY AND THE ORIGINS OF BANKING

(a) **Prices**

824 Ames, E., 'The sterling crisis of 1337-39', J.E.H., XXV, 1965, 496-522.
825 Burnett, J., History of the Cost of Living, 1969. A work of popularisation.
826 Herlitz, L., 'The medieval theory of the just price', Scandinavian Ec.H.R., VIII, 1960, 71-76. See also Roover (830), listed below.
827 Hughes, A., Crump, C.G. and Johnson, C., 'The debasement of the coinage under Edward III', Ec. J., VII, 1897, 185-97.
828 Miskimin, H.A., 'Monetary movements and market structure forces for contraction in fourteenth- and fifteenth-century England', J.E.H., XXIX, 1964, 470-90.
829 Reddaway, T.F., 'The King's Mint and Exchange in London, 1343-1543', E.H.R., LXXXII, 1967, 1-23.
830 Roover, R. de., 'The concept of the just price', J.E.H., XVIII, 1958, 418-34. See Herlitz (826), listed above.
831 Schreiner, J., 'Wages and prices in England in the later Middle Ages', Scand. Ec.H.R., II, 1954, 61-73.
831*a* Tate, Mavis, 'High prices in fourteenth-century England: causes and consequences', Ec. H.R., 2nd ser., XXVIII, 1975, 1-16. See also Feavearyear (415), and Thorold Rogers (420), listed above, and Beveridge (1652) and Phelps Brown (1658-1661), listed below.

(b) **Public finance**

832 Bryant, W.N., 'The financial dealings of Edward III with the county communities, 1330-60', E.H.R., LXXXIII, 1968, 760-71.
833 Fryde, E.B., 'Materials for the study of Edward III's credit operations, 1327-48', B.I.H.R., XXIII, 1950, 1-30.
834 —— 'Loans to the English Crown, 1328-31', E.H.R., LXIX, 1955, 198-211.
835 MacFarlane, K.B., 'Loans to the Lancastrian kings: the problem of inducement', Cambridge Hist. Jnl., IX, 1947, 51-68.
836 Ramsay, J.H., A History of the Revenues of the Kings of England 1066-1399, 2 vols., 1925.
837 Steel, A., The Receipt of the Exchequer, 1377-1485, 1954.
838 Unwin, G., ed., Finance and Trade under Edward III, 1918. Reprinted 1962.
839 Willard, J.F., Parliamentary Taxes on Personal Property, 1290-1334: A Study in Medieval English Financial Administration, Cambridge, Mass., 1934.
See also Dowell (427) and Roseveare (434), listed above.

England 1300-1500

(c) Usury and the origins of banking

840   Nelson, N., The Idea of Usury, Princeton, N.J., 1949.
841   Noonan, J.T., The Scholastic Analysis of Usury, Cambridge, Mass., 1957.
842   Pugh, R.B., 'Some medieval moneylenders', Speculum, XLIII, 1968, 274-89.
843   Usher, A.P., 'The origins of banking: the primitive bank of deposit, 1200-1600', Ec.H.R., IV, 1932-4, 399-428.
      See also Powell (1712), listed below.

WAR: ITS IMPACT ON MEDIEVAL SOCIETY AND ECONOMY

844   Allmand, C.T., 'War and profit in the late Middle Ages', History Today, 15, 1965, 762-69.
844a Barnie, J., War in Medieval Society, 1974.
845   Fowler, K., ed., The Hundred Years War, 1971. A collection of essays.
846   Hale, J.R., 'War and public opinion in the fifteenth and sixteenth centuries', P.P., 22, 1962, 18-33.
847   Haward, W.I., 'Economic aspects of the Wars of the Roses in East Anglia', E.H.R., XLI, 1926, 170-89.
848   Hay, D., 'The division of the spoils of war in fourteenth-century England', T.R.H.S., 5th ser., 4, 1954, 91-109.
849   Hewitt, H.J., The Organisation of War under Edward III, 1966.
850   Lander, J.R., The Wars of the Roses, 1965.
851   Keen, M., The Laws of War in the Late Middle Ages, 1965.
852   MacFarlane, K.B., 'The investment of Sir John Fastolf's profits in war', T.R.H.S., 5th ser., 7, 1957, 91-116.
853   ——— 'England and the Hundred Years' War', P.P., 22, 1962, 3-13.
854   Nef, J.U., War and Human Progress, Cambridge, Mass., 1950.
855   Postan, M.M., 'Some social consequences of the Hundred Years War', Ec.H.R., XII, 1942, 7-12.
856   ——— 'The costs of the Hundred Years War', P.P., 27, 1964, 34-53.
857   Sherborne, J.W., 'The Hundred Years War: the English navy, shipping and manpower, 1369-89', P.P., 37, 1967, 163-75. Comments on the previous article by Postan (856).
858   Steel, A., 'The financial background of the Wars of the Roses', History, XL, 1955, 18-30.

LABOUR

(a) General and miscellaneous

859   Cheyney, E.P., 'The disappearance of English serfdom', E.H.R., XV, 1900, 20-38.
860   Clark, A., 'Serfdom on an Essex manor, 1308-78', E.H.R., XX, 1905, 479-83.
861   Dale, M.K., 'The London silkwomen of the fifteenth century', Ec.H.R., IV, 1932-3, 324-35.

862   Davenport, F.G., 'The decay of villeinage in East Anglia', T.R.H.S., n.s., XIV, 1900, 123-42.
863   Hilton, R.H., The Decline of Serfdom in Medieval England, 1969. (Studies in Economic History pamphlet series). A very useful survey with a bibliographical guide.
864   Knoop, D., and Jones, G.P., 'Masons' wages in medieval England', Ec.J. Economic History Supplement, II, 1933, 473-99.
865   Ritchie, Nora, 'Labour conditions in Essex in the reign of Richard II', Ec.H.R., IV, 1932-4, 429-51. Reprinted in Carus-Wilson, ed. (164), listed below, II, 91-111.
866   Smith, R.E.F., The Enserfment of the Russian Peasantry, 1968. The introduction by R.H. Hilton and R.E.F. Smith is of general relevance.
      See also Beveridge (438, 439), listed above.

(b) The Peasants' Revolt

867   Dobson, R.B., ed., The Peasants' Revolt of 1381, 1970. A valuable collection of documents.
868   Harvey, Barbara, 'Draft letters patent of manumission and pardon for the men of Somerset in 1381', E.H.R., LXXX, 1965, 89-91.
869   Hilton, R.H. and Fagan, H., The English Rising of 1381, 1950. An interesting Marxist account.
870   Kesteven, G., The Peasants' Revolt, 1964.
871   Lyle, H.M., The Peasants' Revolt, 1381, 1950.
872   Warren, W.L., 'The Peasants' Revolt of 1381', History Today, 12, 1962, 845-53.
873   Wilkinson, B., 'The Peasants' Revolt of 1381', Speculum, XV, 1940, 12-35.
      See also Hilton (443, 444), listed above.

STANDARDS OF LIVING

874   Drummond, J.C. and Wilbraham, Anne, The Englishman's Food. A history of Five Centuries of English Diet, 1939, 2nd ed., revised and enlarged by Dorothy Hollingsworth, 1958.
875   Jope, E.M., 'Cornish houses, 1400-1700'. In E.M. Jope, ed., Studies in Building History, 1961, 192-222.
876   Mead, W.E., The English Medieval Feast, 1931. Reprinted 1968.
877   Pantin, W.A., 'Medieval English town house plans', Medieval Archaeology, VI-VII, for 1962-3, 202-39.
878   ——— 'The merchants' houses and warehouses of King's Lynn', Medieval Archaeology, VI-VII, for 1962-3, 173-81.
879   Thompson, A.H., 'The English house', in Barraclough, ed. (177), listed above, 139-78.
879a Wilson, C. Anne, Food and Drink in Britain from the Stone Age to Recent Times, 1973.
880   Wood, M., The English Medieval House, 1965.
      See also Barley (1885), listed below, and Ashley (302), listed above.

GOVERNMENT AND ADMINISTRATION

881 Baldwin, J. F., The King's Council, 1913.
882 Baker, R. L., The English Customs Service, 1307-43. A study of Medieval administration, Trans. American Philosophical Society, n.s., 56, Part 6, Philadelphia, 1961.
883 Chibnall, A. C., Early Taxation Returns: Taxation of Personal Property in 1332 and Later, Buckinghamshire Record Society, 1967.
884 Coleman, Olive, 'The collectors of customs in London under Richard II'. In Hollaender and Kellaway (486), listed above, 181-94.
885 Fryde, E. B., 'The English farmers of the customs, 1343-51', T. R. H. S., 5th ser., 9, 1959, 1-17.
886 Hunnisett, R. F., The Medieval Coroner, 1961.
887 Lapsley, G. T., Crown, Community and Parliament in the Later Middle Ages, 1951.
888 Levett, Ada E., 'Notes on the Statute of Labourers', Ec.H.R., IV, 1932-4, 77-80.
889 Pelham, R. A., 'The provisioning of the Lincoln parliament of 1301', Birm. Hist. Jnl., III, 1952, 16-32.
890 Prestwich, M., 'Victualling estimates for English garrisons in Scotland during the early fourteenth century', E. H. R., LXXXII, 1967, 536-43.
891 Putnam, Bertha, The Enforcement of the Statute of Labourers, Columbia Studies in History, Economics and Public Law, XXXII, N. Y., 1908.
892 Steel, A., 'The collectors of the customs at Newcastle upon Tyne in the reign of Richard II'. In J. C. Davies, ed., Studies Presented to Sir Hilary Jenkinson, 1957, 390-413.

TOWNS

For fuller bibliographical details, the reader is referred to Gross (467) and to Martin and MacIntyre (468), listed above.
893 Dilks, T. B., ed., Bridgwater Borough Archives, 1445-68, Somerset Record Society Publications, LX, 1947.
894 Weinbaum, M., ed., British Borough Charters, 1307-1660, 1943.
     For further source material on this subject, see the section on 'Towns and gilds' in Bland, Brown and Tawney (141), listed above.

895 Bartlett, J. N., 'The expansion and decline of York in the later Middle Ages', Ec. H. R., 2nd ser., XII, 1965, 17-33.
896 Carus-Wilson, Eleanora M., The Expansion of Exeter at the Close of the Middle Ages, 1963.
897 Cronne, H. A., The Borough of Warwick in the Later Middle Ages, Dugdale Society Occasional Papers, 10, 1951.
898 Dobson, R. B., 'Admissions to the Freedom of the City of York in the Later Middle Ages', Ec. H. R., XXVI, 1973, 1-22.
899 Dulley, A. J. F., 'Four Kent towns at the end of the Middle Ages', Archaeologia Cantiana, LXXXI, 1966, 95-108.
900 Finberg, H. P. R., 'The borough of Tavistock'. In Hoskins and Finberg (1055), listed below, 172-97.
901 Fowler, J., Medieval Sherborne, 1952.
902 Gill, C., 'Coventry in the fifteenth century'. In Gill, Studies in Midland History, 1930, 3-85.
903 Green, Mrs. J. R., Town Life in the Fifteenth Century, 2 vols., 1894.
904 Hilton, R. H., 'Some problems of urban real property in the Middle Ages'. In Feinstein, title cited in (1864), listed below, 326-37.
905 Robertson, D. W., Chaucer's London, N. Y., 1968.
906 Rörig, F., The Medieval Town, English trans., 1967. For background.
907 Salusbury, G. T., Street Life in Medieval England, 1939.
908 Saunders, I. J., 'The boroughs of Aberystwyth and Cardigan in the early fourteenth century', Bulletin of the Board of Celtic Studies, XV, 1952-4, 282-92.
909 Smith, B. S., A History of Malvern, 1964.
910 Tout, T. F., 'The beginnings of a modern capital: London and Westminster in the fourteenth century'. In Tout's Collected Papers, III, 1934, 249-75.
911 Walker, V. W., 'Medieval Nottingham: a topographical study', Trans. Thoroton Society, LXVII, 1963, 28-45.
912 Woledge, G., 'The medieval borough of Leeds', Thoresby Society Publications, XXXVII, 1945, 288-309.
     See also Martin (489), and Williams (501), listed above.

COMMUNICATIONS AND INTERNAL TRADE

(a) Inland transport and communications

913 Barley, M. W., 'Lincolnshire rivers in the Middle Ages', Lincolnshire Architectural and Archaeological Society, n. s., I, 1940, 1-21.
914 Hill, Mary C., The King's Messengers, 1199-1377, 1961.
915 Willard, J. F., 'The use of carts in the fourteenth century', History, n. s., XVII, 1932, 246-50.
916 ——— 'Inland transportation in England during the fourteenth century', Speculum, I, 1926, 361-74.

(b) Markets and fairs

917 Addison, W., English Fairs and Markets, 1953.
918 Oliver, J. G., 'Churches and wool: a study of the wool trade in fifteenth-century England', History Today, 1, 1951, 33-40.
919 Pelham, R. A., 'The early wool trade in Warwickshire and the rise of the merchant middle class', Trans. Birmingham Archaeological Society, LXIII, for 1939-40, 1944, 41-62.

920 —— 'The cloth markets of Warwickshire during the later Middle Ages', Trans. Birmingham Archaeological Society, LXVI, for 1945 and 1946, 1950, 31-41.
921 —— 'The trade relations of Birmingham during the Middle Ages', Trans. Birmingham Archaeological Society, LXII, for 1938, 1943, 32-40.
922 Scarfe, N., 'Markets and fairs in medieval Suffolk', Suffolk Review, III, 1965, 4-11. See also Tupling (539), listed above.

ALIEN IMMIGRANTS IN ENGLAND

923 Allmand, C. T., 'A note on denization in fifteenth-century England', Medievalia et Humanistica, XVII, 1966, 127-8.
924 Beardwood, Alice, Alien Merchants in England, 1350-77, their Legal and Economic Position, Medieval Academy of America Monographs, 3, Cambridge, Mass., 1931.
925 —— 'Alien merchants and the English crown in the later fourteenth century', Ec. H. R., II, 1929-30, 229-60.
926 —— 'Mercantile antecedents of the English naturalisation laws', Medievalia et Humanistica, XVI, 1964, 64-77.
927 Holmes, G. A., 'Florentine merchants in England, 1346-1436', Ec. H. R., 2nd ser., XIII, 1960, 193-208.
928 Kerling, Nellie, J. M., 'Aliens in the county of Norfolk, 1436-1485', Norfolk Archaeology, XXXIII, 1963, 200-15.
929 Ruddock, A. A., 'Alien hosting in Southampton in the fifteenth century', Ec. H. R., XVI, 1946, 30-7.
930 Thrupp, Sylvia, 'A survey of the alien population of England in 1440', Speculum, XXXII, 1957, 262-73.
931 —— 'Aliens in and around London in the fifteenth century'. In Hollaender and Kellaway (484), listed above, 251-72.
932 Wilson, C., 'The immigrant in English history', in Economic Issues in Immigration (Readings in Political Economy No. 5, Institute of Economic Affairs), 1970, 3-16. A very general survey. See also Cunningham (1449), listed below.

RELIGION

933 Aston, Margaret, 'Books and belief in the later Middle Ages', P. P., Conference Papers on Popular Religion, 1966. Separately paginated.
934 —— 'Lollardy and sedition, 1381-1431', P. P., 17, 1960, 1-44.
935 Gilchrist, J., The Church and Economic Activity in the Middle Ages, 1969.
936 Hall, D. J., The English Medieval Pilgrimage, 1965.
937 Leff, G., Heresy in the Later Middle Ages, 2 vols., 1968.
938 MacFarlane, K. B., John Wycliffe and the Beginnings of English Nonconformity, 1952.
939 Owen, Dorothy M., Church and Society in Medieval Lincolnshire, 1971.
940 Southern, R. W., Western Society and the Church in the Middle Ages, 1970 (Pelican History of the Church, II). The most recent addition to the literature of the subject by a leading medievalist.
941 Stacey, J., John Wyclif and Reform, 1964.
942 Thompson, A. H., The English Clergy and their Organisation in the Later Middle Ages, 1947.
943 —— The Later Lollards, 1414-1520, 1965.
944 —— 'Piety and charity in late medieval London', Jnl. of Ecclesiastical History, XVI, 1965, 178-95.
945 Williams, G., The Welsh Church from the Conquest to the Reformation, 1952. The standard work.

THE MONASTERIES

946 Postan, M. M. and Brooke, C. N. L., eds., Carte Nativorum. A Peterborough Abbey Cartulary of the Fourteenth Century, Northamptonshire Record Society, XX, 1950.
946a Dobson, R. B., Durham Priory 1400-1450, 1973.
947 Donnelly, J. S., 'Changes in the grange economy of English and Welsh Cistercian abbeys, 1300-1540', Traditio, X, 1954, 399-458.
948 Finberg, H. P. R., Tavistock Abbey: A Study in the Social and Economic History of Devon, 1951, 2nd ed., 1969, with minor corrections.
949 Furniss, D. A., 'The monastic contribution to medieval medical care: aspects of an earlier welfare state', Jnl. of the Royal College of General Practitioners, 69, 1968, 244-50.
950 Hockey, S. T., Quarr Abbey and its Lands, 1132-1631, 1970.
951 Knowles, D., The Religious Orders in England, vol. II: The End of the Middle Ages, 1955. A work of great scholarship. Vol. I (552), listed above, is also relevant for the early part of this period.
952 Lindley, E. S., 'Kingswood Abbey, its lands and mills', Trans. Bristol and Gloucester Archaeological Society, LXXIII, 1955, 115-91, and ibid., LXXIV, 1956, 36-59.
953 Platt, C., The Monastic Grange in Medieval England: A Re-assessment, 1969. An interesting and original study which makes use of the techniques of the archaeologist. See also Cowley (541), Dickinson (543), and Williams (558), listed above.

EDUCATION AND LEARNING

For source material on this subject, see Sylvester (2074), listed below.

953a Cobban, A. B., The Medieval Universities: Their Origins and Development, 1975.
954 Emden, A. B., 'Learning and education'. In Poole (222), listed above, II, 515-40.

955 Leach, A. F., The Schools of Medieval England, 1915, 2nd ed., 1916. But see Parry (958) and Simon (962), listed below.
956 Leff, G., Paris and Oxford Universities in the Thirteenth and Fourteenth Centuries: An Institutional and Intellectual History, 1968.
957 McMahon, C., Education in Fifteenth-century England, Baltimore, Md., 1947.
958 Orme, N., English Schools in the Middle Ages, 1973.
959 Parry, A. W., Education in England in the Middle Ages, 1920. A corrective to Leach, (955), listed above.
960 Rashdall, H., The Universities of Europe in the Middle Ages, eds. Powicke and Emden, 3 vols., 1936. Vol. 3 deals with the English universities.
961 Robson, J. A., Wyclif and the Oxford Schools, 1961.
962 Simon, Joan, The Social Origins of English Education, 1971. A useful exploration of the medieval social background.
963 Thompson, J. W., The Literacy of the Laity in the Middle Ages, Berkeley, Calif., 1939.

ENGLAND 1500-1700

GENERAL WORKS

(a) Bibliographies

964 Davies, G., ed., Bibliography of British History: Stuart Period 1603-1714, 1928, 2nd ed., revised by Mary F. Keeler, 1970.
965 Grose, C. L., ed., A Select Bibliography of British History 1660-1760, Chicago, 1939. Reprinted N.Y., 1967.
966 Levine, M., ed., Bibliographical Handbooks: Tudor England 1485-1603, 1968.
967 Read, C., ed., Bibliography of British History: Tudor Period 1485-1603, 1933, 2nd ed. 1959.
968 Sachse, W. L., ed., Bibliographical Handbooks: Restoration England 1660-89, 1971.
969 Walcott, R., 'The later Stuarts 1660-1714: significant work of the last twenty years (1939-59)', A.H.R., LXVII, 1962, 352-70.

(b) Source material

970 Browning, A., ed., English Historical Documents, 1660-1714, 1953. Part 3 on public finance, Part 4 on the Church and Part 5 on local government and social life are particularly useful.
971 Burton, Kathleen M., ed., A Dialogue between Reginald Pole and Thomas Lupset by Thomas Starkey, 1948.
972 Dewar, Mary, ed., A Discourse of the Commonweal of this Realm of England, Washington, D.C., 1970. A new edition of the work made known by Lamond (977). The editor argues persuasively that the author of the Discourse was Sir Thomas Smith.
973 Dunham, W. H., Jnr. and Pargellis, S., eds., Complaint and Reform in England 1436-1714, N.Y., 1938. A miscellaneous collection of contemporary writings.
974 Edelen, G., ed., William Harrison's Desscription of England, Folger Shakespeare Library, 1968. A new edition of the work better known in the Furnivall edition listed below.
975 Evelyn, John, Diary, ed. E. S. de Beer, 6 vols., 1955.
976 Furnivall, F. J., ed., Harrison's Description of England in Shakespeare's Youth, New Shakespeare Society, 6th ser., I and VIII, 1877 and 1881.
977 Lamond, Elizabeth, ed., A Discourse of the Commonweal of this Realm of England, 1893. See also Dewar (972), listed above. Lamond attributes the Discourse to John Hales.
978 More, Sir Thomas, Utopia. Numerous editions are available, for example the translation by P. Turner, 1967, and the scholarly edition by E. Surtz and J. H. Hexter, New Haven, Conn., 1965.
979 Morris, C., ed., The Journeys of Celia Fiennes, 1947, 2nd ed., 1949.
980 Pepys, Samuel, Diary. A New and Complete Transcription, ed., R. Latham and W. M. Matthews, 1970-.
981 Stone, T. G., ed., England under the Restoration 1660-1688, (University of London Intermediate Source Books of History, IV), 1923.
982 Tawney, R. H. and Power, Eileen, Tudor Economic Documents, 3 vols., 1924. The standard collection.
983 Thirsk, Joan and Cooper, J. P., eds., Seventeenth-century Economic Documents, 1972. An invaluable source book. Sections on economic crises, agriculture, industries, inland and coastal trade and communications, overseas trade, finance and the coinage, aliens, wealth, population and land: some contemporary statistics.
984 Williams, C. H., ed., English Historical Documents, 1485-1558, 1967. Part 2 on the land, Part 3 on the commonweal, Part 5 on religion and Part 6 on daily life in town and country are particularly useful from the economic and social point of view.
985 Williams, E. N., ed., A Documentary History of England, vol. 2: 1559-1931, 1965. The companion volume to Bagley, listed above, (170).
986 Wilson, J. Dover, Life in Shakespeare's England, 1911. Several times reprinted.
987 Wilson, Thomas, The State of England, 1600, ed. F. J. Fisher, Camden Miscellany, XVI, 1936.
See also Bland, Brown and Tawney (141), Part 2 of which, 231-476, covers the period 1485-1600; and Dunham and Pargellis (973), listed above.

(c) General surveys

988 Ashley, M., England in the Seventeenth Century, 1603-1714, 1952. Reprinted with revisions, 1958, 1960.
989 —— Life in Stuart England, 1964.
990 Aston, T. H., ed., Crisis in Europe, 1560-1660, 1965. A collection of reprinted articles from P.P., several of which are directly concerned with English economic and social history in the period.
991 Bindoff, S. T., Tudor England, 1951. A masterly short survey, useful for social and economic history though the main bias is towards the political aspects of the period.
992 —— Hurstfield, J., and Williams, C. H., eds., Elizabethan Government and Society: Essays Presented to Sir John Neale, 1961.
993 Black, J. B., The Reign of Elizabeth, 1936, 2nd ed., 1960. Good bibliography.
994 Burke, P., ed., Economy and Society in Early Modern Europe. Essays from Annales, 1971. Includes essays by Braudel, Cipolla and Verlinden. For background.
995 Byrne, Muriel St. C., Elizabethan Life in Town and County, 1925, 8th ed., revised, 1961.

995a Chalklin, C. W. and Havinden, M. A., eds., Rural Change and Urban Growth: Essays in Regional History in Honour of W. G. Hoskins, 1974.
996 Chambers, J. D., Population, Economy and Society in Pre-industrial England, 1972.
997 Clark, G. N., The Wealth of England from 1496 to 1760, 1946.
998 —— The Later Stuarts, 1660-1714, 1934, 2nd ed., 1955. Good bibliography.
999 —— War and Society in the Seventeenth Century, 1958.
1000 Clarkson, L. A., The Pre-industrial Economy in England, 1500-1750, 1971. A concise analysis of the changing structure of the economy in this period.
1001 Coate, Mary, Social Life in Stuart England, 1924.
1002 Coleman, D. C., 'Technology and economic history, 1500-1750', Ec.H.R., 2nd ser., XI, 1958-9, 506-14.
1003 Cooper, J. P., 'The social distribution of land and men in England, 1436-1700', Ec.H.R., 2nd ser., XX, 1967, 419-40.
1004 Davies, G., The Earlier Stuarts, 1603-60, 1937, 2nd ed., 1959.
1005 Dodd, A. H., Life in Elizabethan England, 1961.
1006 —— Studies in Stuart Wales, 1952.
1006a Earle, P., ed., Essays in European Economic History 1500-1800, 1974.
1007 Elton, G. R., England under the Tudors, 1955. Mainly political and constitutional in bias. Contains a valuable critical bibliography.
1008 —— ed., New Cambridge Modern History—II: The Reformation, 1958.
1009 Everitt, A. M., Change in the Provinces: The Seventeenth Century, University of Leicester, Department of English Local History, Occasional Papers, 2nd ser., 1, 1969.
1010 Fisher, F. J., ed., Essays in the Economic and Social History of Tudor and Stuart England in Honour of R. H. Tawney, 1961. An invaluable collection of essays.
1011 —— 'The sixteenth and seventeenth centuries: the dark ages in English economic history?', Economica, n.s., XXIV, 1957, 2-18. In Harte, ed. (55), listed below.
1012 Gardiner, S. R., History of England from the Accession of James I to the Outbreak of the Civil War, 10 vols., 1883-4. The major work of one of the greatest of nineteenth-century historians. Unsuperseded as a detailed narrative history of the period.
1013 Hartwell, R. M., 'Economic growth in England before the Industrial Revolution: some methodological issues', J.E.H., XXIX, 1969, 13-31. In Hartwell (2160), listed below.
1014 Hill, C., The Century of Revolution, 1603-1714, 1961. A stimulating textbook, untypical in its method of separating the narrative and analytical chapters.
1015 —— Reformation to Industrial Revolution: A Social and Economic History of Britain, 1530-1780, 1967.
1015a —— Change and Continuity in Seventeenth-century England, 1975. A stimulating collection of (mainly reprinted) essays.
1016 Hurstfield, J. and Smith, A. G. R., Elizabethan People: State and Society, 1972.
1017 Jones, W. R. D., The Tudor Commonwealth, 1529-1559, 1970.
1018 Jordan, W. K., Edward VI: The Young King. The Protectorship of the Duke of Somerset, 1968. A valuable study of this crucial but neglected period of the sixteenth century.
1019 —— Edward VI: The Threshold of Power, 1971. Concludes Jordan's survey of the critical years of the mid-sixteenth century by examining the régime of the Duke of Northumberland.
1020 Lennard, R. V., ed., Englishmen at Rest and Play, 1558-1714, 1931.
1021 Letwin, W., The Origins of Scientific Economics: English Thought, 1660-1776, 1963.
1022 Mackie, J. D., The Earlier Tudors, 1485-1558, 1952. Mainly political in emphasis.
1023 Mathew, D., The Social Structure in Caroline England, 1948.
1024 —— The Age of Charles I, 1951.
1025 Miskimin, H. A., 'Agenda for early modern economic history', J.E.H., XXXI, 1971, 172-83.
1026 Moir, Esther A. L., The Discovery of Britain: The English Tourists 1540-1840, 1964.
1027 Nef, J. U., 'War and economic progress 1540-1640', Ec.H.R., XII, 1942, 13-38.
1028 Ogg, D., England in the Age of Charles II, 2 vols., 1934, 2nd ed., 1955. A useful survey of the reign. Good bibliography.
1029 —— England in the Reigns of James II and William III, 1955.
1030 Ramsey, P., Tudor Economic Problems, 1963. The best short introduction to sixteenth-century English economic history.
1031 Rich, E. E. and Wilson, C., eds., Cambridge Economic History of Europe IV: The Economy of Expanding Europe in the Sixteenth and Seventeenth Centuries, 1967. The contributions are of varying usefulness.
1032 Rowse, A. L., The England of Elizabeth: The Structure of Society, 1951.
1033 Russell, C., The Crisis of Parliaments: English History 1509-1660, 1971. Mainly political, although there is some discussion of economic factors.
1034 Salzman, L. F., England in Tudor Times: An Account of its Social Life and Industries, 1926.
1035 Smith, A. G. R., ed., The Reign of James VI and I, 1973. A collection of essays dealing with various aspects of the reign.
1036 Stoye, J. W., English Travellers Abroad, 1604-67: Their Influence in English Society and Politics, 1952.
1037 Supple, B. E., 'Economic history and economic underdevelopment', Canadian Jnl. of Economics and Political Science, 27, 1961, 460-78.

1038 Tawney, R. H., 'Social history and literature'. In the same author's The Radical Tradition, 1964. Reprinted 1966, 191-219. Deals mainly with the Elizabethan period.

1038a Thompson, R., Women in Stuart England and America. A Comparative Study, 1974. Examines the status and roles of women in the two countries commenting on the implications of sex ratios for the status of women and on the effects of puritanism.

1039 Wernham, R. B., ed., New Cambridge Modern History III: The Counter-Reformation and the Price Revolution, 1559-1610, 1968.

1040 Williams, P., Life in Tudor England, 1964.

1041 Williams, W. O., 'The social order in Tudor Wales', Trans. Honourable Society of Cymmrodorion, 1967, 167-78.

1042 —— Tudor Gwynedd: The Tudor Age in the Principality of Wales, 1958.

1043 Williamson, J. A., The Tudor Age, 1953. Good on maritime affairs.

1044 Wilson, C., England's Apprenticeship, 1603-1763, 1965. An admirably clear and well-argued textbook. Good bibliography.

1045 —— Economic History and the Historian. Collected Essays, 1969. The main part of this useful book consists of reprints of the author's articles on the seventeenth century.

See also Cunningham (145), Lipson (156), Pollard and Crossley (158) and Schofield (592), listed above.

(d) Regional studies

1046 Bouch, C. M. L. and Jones, G. P., A Short Economic and Social History of the Lake Counties, 1500-1830, 1961.

1047 Brears, C., Lincolnshire in the Seventeenth and Eighteenth Centuries, 1940.

1048 Chalklin, C. W., Seventeenth-century Kent, 1965.

1049 Dodd, A. H., A History of Caernarvonshire, 1284-1900, 1968.

1050 Edwards, A. C., English History from Essex Sources, 1550-1750, 1952.

1051 Finberg, H. P. R., ed., Gloucestershire Studies, 1957.

1051a Hey, D., An English Rural Community: Myddle Under the Tudors and Stuarts, 1974.

1052 Hoskins, W. G., The Midland Peasant: The Economic and Social History of a Leicestershire Village, 1957. A study of Wigston Magna.

1053 —— Provincial England: Essays in Social and Economic History, 1963.

1054 —— ed., Essays in Leicestershire History, 1950.

1055 —— and Finberg, H. P. R., Devonshire Studies, 1952.

1055a James, M. E., Family, Lineage, and Civil Society. A Study of Society, Politics and Mentality in the Durham Region 1500-1640, 1974.

1056 Rowse, A. L., Tudor Cornwall, 1941, 2nd ed., 1969.

1057 Tupling, G. H., The Economic History of Rossendale, Chet. Soc., n.s., 87, 1927.

1058 Walker, F., The Historical Geography of South-West Lancashire before the Industrial Revolution, Chet. Soc., n.s., 103, 1939.

(e) Foreigners' views of England

A useful bibliographical introduction to the subject is:

1059 Fussell, G. E., The Exploration of England: A Select Bibliography of Travel and Topography, 1570-1815, 1935.

1060 Ballam, H. and Lewis, R., eds., The Visitors' Book: England and the English as Others Have Seen Them, 1500-1950, 1950.

1061 Bülow, G. von, ed., 'Journey through England and Scotland made by Leopold von Wedel in the years 1584 and 1585', T.R.H.S., n.s., IX, 1895, 223-70.

1062 —— 'Diary of the journey of Philip Julius, Duke of Stettin—Pomerania through England in the year 1602', T.R.H.S., n.s., VI, 1897, 1-67.

1063 Letts, M., As the Foreigner Saw Us, 1935. A survey of foreigners' impressions from c. 1500 to c. 1830. Bibliography, 263-71.

1064 Malfatti, C. V., ed., Two Italian Accounts of Tudor England, Barcelona, 1953.

1065 Palmer, R. E., ed., French Travellers in England, 1600-1900: Selections From Their Writings, 1960.

1066 Rye, W. B., ed., England as Seen by Foreigners in the Days of Elizabeth and James I, 1865. Reprinted 1967.

1067 Salter, E. G., Tudor England Through Venetian Eyes, 1930.

1068 Scott, W. D. Robson, German Travellers in England, 1400-1800, 1953.

1069 Smith, E., Foreign Visitors in England, 1889.

1070 Sneyd, C. A., ed., A Relation, or Rather a True Account of the Island of England... About the Year 1500, Camden Society, o.s., XXXVII, 1847.

1071 Williams, C., ed., Thomas Platter's Travels in England, 1599, 1937.

1072 Wilson, F. M., Strange Island: Britain Through Foreign Eyes, 1395-1940, 1955.

See also Thirsk (1180), listed below, xxix-xxxvi.

POPULATION

(a) Sources

1073 Allison, K. J., ed., 'An Elizabethan village census', B.I.H.R., XXXVI, 1963, 91-103.

1074 Cornwall, J., 'An Elizabethan census', Records of Buckinghamshire, XVI, 1959, 258-73.

1075 Faraday, M. A. (ed.), The Westmorland Protestation Returns 1641-42, Cumberland and Westmorland Antiquarian and Archaeological Society Tract Series, XVII, 1971.

1076 Glass, D. V., ed., London Inhabitants Within the Walls, 1695, London Record Society, 1966. Contains a valuable introduction by Professor Glass.
1077 King, Gregory, Natural and Political Observations Upon the State and Condition of England (1696), in G. Chalmers, ed., Estimate of the Comparative Strength of Great Britain, 1782, new ed., 1802.
1078 Munby, L., ed., Hertfordshire Population Statistics, 1563-1801, 1964.
1079 Petty, William, Political Arithmetick, or a Discourse Concerning the Extent and Value of Lands, People, Buildings, Husbandry, etc., 1690. The work is included in E. A. Aitken, ed., Later Stuart Tracts (An English Garner), 1903, 1-66.

(b) General

1080 Blanchard, I., 'Population change, enclosure and the early Tudor economy', Ec.H.R., 2nd ser., XXIII, 1970, 427-45.
1081 Bonar, J., Theories of Population from Raleigh to Arthur Young, 1931. Reprinted 1966.
1082 Cornwall, J., 'English population in the early sixteenth century', Ec.H.R., 2nd ser., XXIII, 1970, 32-44.
1083 Glass, D. V. and Eversley, D. E. C., eds., Population in History, 1965. An important collection of comparative studies. On English population the book contains 'Two papers on Gregory King' by Professor Glass, 159-220.
1084 Habakkuk, H. J., 'The economic history of modern Britain', J.E.H., XVIII, 1958, 486-501.
1085 Hair, P. E. H., 'Bridal pregnancy in rural England in earlier centuries', Population Studies, XX, 1966, 233-43.
1086 Hollingsworth, T. H., Historical Demography, 1969. A valuable discussion of the present state of historical demography and of the available sources. Excellent bibliography.
1087 —— Demography of the British Peerage, Supplement to Population Studies, XVIII, 1964.
1088 Kerridge, E., 'The returns of the Inquisition of Depopulation', E.H.R., LXX, 1955, 212-28.
1089 Laslett, P., The World We Have Lost, 1965, 2nd ed., 1971. Interesting but it hardly matches up to the author's claims.
1090 Owen, L., 'The population of Wales in the sixteenth and seventeenth centuries', Trans. Honourable Society Cymmrodorion 1959, 99-113.
1091 Patten, J., 'The Hearth Taxes 1662-89', Local Population Studies, 7, 1971, 14-27.
1092 Spengler, J. J., 'Demographic factors and early modern economic development', Daedalus, (Jnl. of the American Academy of Arts and Sciences), XCVII, 1968, 433-46.
1093 Thirsk, Joan, Sources of Information on Population, 1500-1760, and Unexplored Sources in Local Records, 1965.

1094 Tucker, G. S. L., 'English pre-industrial population trends', Ec.H.R., XVI, 1963, 205-18.
1095 Utterström, G., 'Climatic fluctuations and population problems in early modern history', Scand. Ec.H.R., III, 1955, 3-47.
1096 Wrigley, E. A., ed., An Introduction to English Historical Demography, 1966.
1097 —— Population and History, 1969. A very useful general survey. Good bibliography.
1098 —— 'Family limitation in pre-industrial England', Ec.H.R., XIX, 1966, 82-109. An important article using the Colyton evidence.
1099 —— 'Mortality in pre-industrial England: the example of Colyton, Devon, over three centuries', Daedalus, XCVII, 1968, 246-80.
See also F. J. Fisher (1664), listed below.

(c) Internal population mobility and emigration

(1) Internal mobility

1100 Buckatzch, E. J., 'The constancy of local populations and migration in England before 1800', Population Studies, V, 1951-2, 62-9.
1101 —— 'Places of origin of a group of immigrants into Sheffield, 1624-1799', Ec.H.R., 2nd ser., II, 1950, 303-6.
1102 Cornwall, J., 'Evidence of population mobility in the seventeenth century', B.I.H.R., XL, 1967, 143-52. An interesting article which plays down the extent of internal mobility. But the type of source used—the deposition books of an ecclesiastical court—places a strict limit on its value.
1103 Pelham, R. A., 'The immigrant population of Birmingham, 1686-1726', Birmingham Archaeological Society Trans., LX for 1936, 1940, 45-86.
1104 Rich, E. E., 'The population of Elizabethan England', Ec.H.R., 2nd ser., II, 1950, 247-65. Draws attention to the value of muster rolls as a source for the study of population mobility.
1105 Spufford, P., 'Population movement in seventeenth-century England', Local Population Studies, 4, 1970, 41-50.

(2) Emigration

1106 Banks, C. E. and Morison, S. E., 'Persecution as a factor in emigration', Massachusetts Historical Society Proceedings, LXIII, 1930, 136-54.
1107 Bridenbaugh, C., Vexed and Troubled Englishmen, 1590-1642, 1968. An important book. Its footnotes are a mine of information.
1108 Campbell, Mildred, 'Of people either too few or too many. The conflict of opinion on population and its relation to emigration'. In W. A. Aiken, and B. D. Henning, eds., (1907), listed below, 169-202.
1109 Crouse, N. M., 'Causes of the great migration, 1630-40', New England Quarterly, V, 1932, 3-36.

32   England 1500-1700

1110 Newton, A. P., The Colonizing Activities of English Puritans, 1914. Reprinted 1966. See also Knorr (1560) and Quinn (1564), listed under the section on Colonisation.

(d) Disease

1111 Appleby, A. B., 'Disease or famine? Mortality in Cumberland and Westmorland 1580-1640', Ec.H.R., 2nd ser., XXVI, 1973, 403-32.
1112 Bell, W. G., The Great Plague in London in 1665, 1924, 2nd rev. ed., 1951.
1113 Copeman, W. S. C., Doctors and Disease in Tudor Times, 1960.
1113a Debus, A. G., ed., Medicine in Seventeenth-century England, Berkeley, Calif., 1974.
1114 Levy, H., 'The economic history of sickness and medical benefit before the Puritan Revolution', Ec.H.R., XIII, 1943, 42-57.
1115 —— 'The economic history of sickness and medical benefit since the Puritan Revolution', Ec.H.R., XIV, 1944, 135-60.
1116 Mullett, C. F., 'Some neglected aspects of plague medicine in sixteenth-century England', Scientific Monthly, 44, 1937, 325-37.
1117 —— 'The plague of 1603 in England', Annals of Medical History, n.s., 9, 1937, 230-47.
1118 Roberts, R. S., 'The personnel and practice of medicine in Tudor and Stuart England. Parts I and 2', Medical History, 6, 1962, 363-82, ibid., 8, 1964, 217-34.
1119 Wilshore, J. E. O., 'Plague in Leicester, 1558-1665', Trans. Leicestershire Archaeological and Historical Society, XLIV, for 1968-9, 1970, 45-71.

(e) The family

1120 Macfarlane, A., The Family Life of Ralph Josselin, a Seventeenth-century Clergyman: An Essay in Historical Anthropology, 1970. An important contribution to seventeenth-century social history.
1121 Morgan, E. S., The Puritan Family, Boston, Mass., 1944. Based on New England evidence.
1122 Powell, C. L., English Domestic Relations, 1487-1653, N.Y., 1917.
1123 Schücking, L. L., The Puritan Family: A Study from the Literary Sources, 1929, English trans., 1969.
1124 Thirsk, Joan, 'The family', P.P., 27, 1964, 116-22. A useful review article.
1125 —— 'Younger sons in the seventeenth century', History, LIV, 1969, 358-78. See also Hill (2025), listed below ch. 13 on 'The spiritualization of the household', 443-81.

(f) Local and regional studies

1126 Chalklin, C. W., 'The Compton Census of 1676: the diocese of Canterbury and Rochester', Kent Records, A Seventeenth-Century Miscellany, Kent Archaeological Society, 17, 1960, 153-83.
1127 Meekings, C. A. F., ed., Dorset Hearth Tax Assessments, 1662-64, Dorset Natural History and Archaeological Society, Occasional Publications, 1951.
1128 —— Surrey Hearth Tax, 1664, Surrey Record Society, XVII, 1940.
1129 Watkins-Pritchard, W., ed., Shropshire Hearth Tax Roll of 1672, Shropshire Archaeological Society Publications, 1949.
1130 Weinstock, Maureen, ed., Hearth Tax Returns, Oxfordshire, 1665, Oxfordshire Record Society, 21, 1940. As an introduction to this class of archive material the following can be recommended:
1131 Howell, R., 'Short guides to records. 7; Hearth Tax Returns', History, XLIX, 1964, 42-5.
1132 Cornwall, J., 'A Tudor Domesday. The musters of 1522', Jnl. Society of Archivists, III, 1965, 19-24.
1133 —— 'The people of Rutland in 1522', Trans. Leicestershire Archaeological and Historical Society, XXXVII, 1961-2, 7-28.
1134 Cowgill, Ursula M., 'Life and death in the sixteenth century in the city of York', Population Studies, XXI, 1967, 53-62.
1135 Dymond, D. P., 'Suffolk and the Compton Census of 1676', Suffolk Review, III, 1966, 103-18.
1136 Eversley, D. E. C., 'A survey of population in an area of Worcestershire, 1660-1850', Population Studies, X, 1957, 253-79.
1137 Glass, D. V., 'Notes on the demography of London at the end of the seventeenth century', Daedalus, XCVII, 1968, 581-92.
1138 Gould, J. D., 'The inquisition of depopulation of 1607 in Lincolnshire', E.H.R., LXVII, 1952, 392-6.
1139 Hoskins, W. G., 'The population of an English village, 1086-1801: a study of Wigston Magna (Leics)', in Hoskins (1053), listed above, 181-208.
1140 Howson, W. G., 'Plague, poverty and population in parts of N. W. England, 1580-1720', T.H.S.L.C., CXII, 1960, 29-56
1141 James, F. G., 'The population of the diocese of Carlisle in 1676', Trans. Cumberland and Westmorland Antiquarian and Archaeological Society, LI, 1951, 137-41.
1142 Jones, P. E. and Judges, A. V., 'London's population in the late seventeenth century', Ec.H.R., VI, 1935, 45-63.
1143 Laslett, P. and Harrison, J., 'Clayworth and Cogenhoe'. In H. F. Bell and R. L. Ollard, eds., Historical Essays 1600-1750 presented to David Ogg, 1962, 157-84. A pioneer English study of population and social structure using seventeenth-century census material.
1144 Marshall, Lydia M., The Rural Population of Bedfordshire, 1671-1921, Bedfordshire Historic Record Society, XVI, 1934.
1145 —— 'The levying of the Hearth Tax, 1662-88'. E.H.R., LI, 1936, 628-46.
1146 Morrison, E. J. D., 'The Hearth Tax in Chester', Jnl. Chester and North Wales Architectural, Archaeological and Historical Society, XXXVI, 1946, 31-43.

1146a Palliser, D. M., 'Epidemics in Tudor York', Northern History, VII, 1973, 45-63.
1147 Parker, L. A., 'Depopulation returns for Leicestershire in 1607', Leicestershire Archaeological and Historical Society Trans., XXIII, 1947, 231-91.
1148 Parry, O., 'The Hearth Tax of 1662 in Merioneth', Jnl. Merioneth Historical Record Society, II, 1953-4, 16-38.
1149 Pickard, R., The Population and Epidemics of Exeter in Pre-Census Times, 1947.
1150 Ralph, E., and Williams, M. E., The Inhabitants of Bristol in 1696, Bristol Record Society, XXV, 1968.
1151 Richards, T., The Religious Census of 1676: An Enquiry Into Its Historical Value Mainly in Reference to Wales, 1927 (Honourable Society of Cymmrodorion publications).
1151a Richardson, R. C., 'Wills and will-makers in the sixteenth and seventeenth centuries', Local Population Studies, 9, 1972, 33-42.
1152 Smith, C. T., 'Population'. In V.C.H. Leicestershire, ed. W. G. Hoskins and R. A. McKinley, III, 1955, 129-75.
1153 Spufford, Margaret, 'The significance of the Cambridgeshire Hearth Tax', Cambridge Antiquarian Society Proceedings, LV, 1962, 53-64.
1154 Styles, P., 'A census of a Warwickshire village in 1698', Birm. Hist. Jnl., III, 1951, 33-51.

AGRICULTURE AND RURAL SOCIETY

(a) Sources

1155 Bankes, Joyce and Kerridge, E., eds., The Early Records of the Bankes Family at Winstanley, Chet. Soc., 3rd ser., 21, 1973. Contains the Memoranda book of James Bankes together with accounts and rentals.
1156 Eyre, Adam, A Dyurnall, or Catalogue of all my Accions and Expenses, etc. In Yorkshire Diaries, Surtees Society, LXV, 1877
1157 Fussell, G. E., ed., Robert Loder's Farm Accounts 1610-1620, Camden Society, 3rd ser., LIII, 1936.
1158 Hartley, Dorothy, ed., Thomas Tusser: His Good Points of Husbandry, 1931.
1159 Lodge, Eleanor, The Account Book of a Kentish Estate, 1616-1704 (Godminton), 1927.
1160 Robinson, C. B., ed., Rural Economy in Yorkshire in 1641: Being the Farming and Account Books of Henry Best of Elmeswell in the East Riding, Surtees Society, XXXIII, 1857.
1161 Skeat, W. W., ed., Fitzherbert's Book of Husbandry, English Dialect Society, XIII, 1882.
See also Lamond (977) and Dewar (972) listed above. Additional source material will be found in Tawney and Power (982), listed above, Vol. 1, Section 1, 'Agriculture and rural society', 1-90 and Vol. III, section 1, 'Enclosures and the countryside', 12-81.

(b) General

1162 Allison, K. J., 'Flock management in the sixteenth and seventeenth centuries', Ec.H.R., 2nd ser., XI, 1959, 98-112.
1163 Amherst, Alicia, A History of Gardening in England, 1895, 3rd ed., enlarged, 1910.
1163a Bridbury, A. R., 'Sixteenth-century farming', Ec.H.R., 2nd ser., XXVII, 1974, 538-56.
1164 Fussell, G. E., The England Diary Farmer, 1500-1900, 1966.
1165 —— The Classical Tradition in West European Farming, 1972. A collection of the author's essays.
1166 —— 'Agriculture from the Restoration to Anne', Ec.H.R., IX, 1938-9, 68-74.
1167 —— 'Crop nutrition in Tudor and Stuart England', Ag.H.R., III, 1955, 95-106.
1168 —— 'Crop nutrition in the late Stuart Age, 1660-1714', Annals of Science, XIV, 1958, 173-84.
1169 —— and K. R., The English Countrywoman: A Farmhouse Social History, 1500-1900, 1953.
1170 —— and K. R., The English Countryman: His Life and Work, 1500-1900, 1955.
1171 Hoskins, W. G., 'Harvest fluctuations and English economic history, 1480-1619', Ag.H.R., XII, 1964, 28-46, reprinted in Minchinton (165), listed above, I, 93-115.
1172 —— 'Harvest fluctuations and English economic history, 1620-1759', Ag.H.R., XVI, 1968, 13-31. Two useful articles which emphasise the crucial importance of the harvest in the pre-industrial economy.
1173 Jones, E. L., ed., Agriculture and Economic Growth in England, 1650-1815, 1967. A useful collection of reprinted articles with an introduction and bibliography.
1174 Kerridge, E., Agrarian Problems in the Sixteenth Century and After, 1969. An attack on Tawney (1179), listed below. Half the book consists of documents.
1175 —— The Farmers of Old England, 1973.
1176 —— Ridge and furrow in agrarian history', Ec.H.R., 2nd ser., IV, 1951, 14-36.
1177 Lennard, R. V., 'English agriculture under Charles II', Ec.H.R., IV, 1932, 23-45. Reprinted in Minchinton (165), listed above, I, 161-85.
1178 Smith, R. B., Land and Politics in the England of Henry VIII, 1970.
1178a Spufford, Margaret, Contrasting Communities: English Villagers in the Sixteenth and Seventeenth Centuries, 1974.
1179 Tawney, R. H., The Agrarian Problem in the Sixteenth Century, 1912. Reprinted, N.Y., 1967, with an introduction by Lawrence Stone. A landmark in the writing of agrarian history.
1180 Thirsk, Joan, ed., The Agrarian History of England and Wales IV: 1500-1640, 1967. A massive but stimulating book. Excellent bibliography.
1181 —— ed., Land Church and People. Essays

Presented to Professor H. P. R. Finberg, 1970. The collection contains an important and wide-ranging article by Dr Thirsk on 'Seventeenth-century agriculture and social change', 148-77, which attempts to place agricultural developments within the framework of the economic crises of the seventeenth century.

1182 —— 'The content and sources of English agrarian history after 1500', Ag. H.R., III, 1955, 66-79.

1183 Webber, R., The Early Horticulturalists, 1968.
See also Barnes (3403) and Russell (2355), listed below, and Slicher van Bath (160) and Trow-Smith (642), listed above.

(c) Miscellaneous

1184 Chilton, D., 'Land measurement in the sixteenth century', Trans. Newcomen Society, XXXI, 1957-9, 111-29.

1185 Fussell, G. E., The Old English Farming Books from Fitzherbert to Tull, 1947.

1186 —— The Farmer's Tools, 1500-1900: The History of British Farm Implements, Tools, and Machinery Before the Tractor Came, 1952.

1187 Hallam, H. E., 'Fen by-laws of Spalding and Pinchbeck', Lincolnshire Architectural and Archaeological Society Trans., X, 1967, 40-56. Includes the text of by-laws of 1591.

1188 Hammersley, G., 'The Crown Woods and their exploitation in the sixteenth and seventeenth centuries', B.I.H.R., XXX, 1957, 136-61.

1189 Skipp, V. H. T., 'Economic and social change in the Forest of Arden, 1530-1649'. In Thirsk (1181), listed above, 84-111.

(d) Regional studies

1189a Havinden, M. A., ed., Husbandry and Marketing in the South-West 1500-1800, 1973.

1190 Hoskins, W. G., ed., Studies in Leicestershire Agrarian History, 1949.

1191 Kerridge, E., 'Agriculture, 1500-1793', V. C. H. Wiltshire, ed. E. Crittall, IV, 1959, 43-64.

1192 Pettit, P. A. J., The Royal Forests of Northamptonshire: A Study in Their Economy, 1558-1714, Northamptonshire Record Society Publications, XXIII, 1968.

1193 Rodgers, H. B., 'Land use in Tudor Lancashire', Trans. Institute of British Geographers, XXVII, 1955, 79-98.

1194 Thirsk, Joan, English Peasant Farming: The Agrarian History of Lincolnshire from Tudor to Recent Times, 1957.

1195 —— 'The Isle of Axholme before Vermuyden', Ag. H. R., I, 1953, 16-28.

1196 —— 'Agrarian history, 1540-1950', In V. C. H. Leicestershire, ed. W. G. Hoskins and R. A. McKinley, II, 1954, 199-264.

1197 —— 'Horn and thorn in Staffordshire. The economy of a pastoral county', North Staffordshire Jnl. of Field Studies, IX, 1969, 1-16.

(e) Marketing

1198 Bowden, P. J., The Wool Trade in Tudor and Stuart England, 1962.

1199 Everitt, A. M., 'The marketing of agricultural produce'. In Thirsk (1120), listed above, 466-592. An important general survey of the subject.

1200 —— 'The food market of the English town, 1660-1760', Third International Conference of Economic History, Paris, 1968, 57-71.

1201 Fisher, F. J., 'The development of the London food market, 1540-1640', Ec. H. R., V, 1935, 46-64. Reprinted in Carus-Wilson, (164), listed above, I, 135-151.

1202 Gras, N. S. B., The Evolution of the English Corn Market, Cambridge, Mass., 1915.

1203 Kneisel, E., 'The evolution of the English corn market', J. E. H., XIV, 1954, 46-52.

1204 Ponko, V., Jnr., 'N. S. B. Gras and Elizabethan corn policy: a re-examination of the problem', Ec. H. R., 2nd ser., XVII, 1964, 24-42. A critique of Gras's book, listed above.

1205 Skeel, Caroline A. J., 'The cattle trade between Wales and England from the fifteenth to the nineteenth centuries', T.R.H.S., 4th ser., 9, 1926, 135-58.
See also the section on Communications and internal trade.

(f) The manor

1206 Kerridge, E., ed., Surveys of the Manors of Philip, First Earl of Pembroke, 1631-32, Wiltshire Archaeological and Natural History Society, Records Branch, IX, 1953.

1207 Ellis, M. J., 'A study in the manorial history of Halifax parish in the sixteenth and early seventeenth centuries', Yorkshire Archaeological Jnl., XL, 1960-1, 250-64, 420-42.

1208 Hill, C., 'Professor Lavrovsky's study of a seventeenth-century manor', Ec. H. R., XVI, 1946, 125-9.

1209 Leconfield, Lord, Petworth Manor in the Seventeenth Century, 1954.

1210 —— Sutton and Duncton Manors, 1956.
See also Davenport (354), and Kerridge (1174), 17-31, listed above.

(g) Landholding (including Crown lands)

See also the separate section on The gentry and their estates (1785-1805).

(1) Landholding

1211 Batho, G. R., 'Landlords in England: noblemen, gentlemen and yeomen'. In Thirsk (1180), listed above, 276-305. A convenient survey.

1212 Cross, M. Claire, 'The economic problems of the see of York: decline and recovery in the sixteenth century'. In Thirsk (1181), listed above, 64-83.

1213 Habakkuk, H. J., 'Economic functions of English landowners in the seventeenth and eighteenth centuries', Explorations in

Entrepreneurial History, VI, 1953, 92-102. Reprinted in Minchinton (165), listed above, I, 187-201.

1214 Heal, Felicity, 'The Tudors and church lands: economic problems of the bishopric of Ely during the sixteenth century', Ec. H. R., XXVI, 1973, 198-217.

1215 Pierce, T. J., 'Landlords in Wales: nobility and gentry'. In Thirsk (1180), listed above, 357-80.

1216 Thompson, F. M. L., 'The social distribution of landed property in England since the sixteenth century', Ec. H. R. 2nd ser., XIX, 1966, 505-17.
See also Stone (1777), and Campbell (1768), listed below.

(2) The Crown lands

1217 Batho, G. R., 'Landlords in England: the Crown', in Thirsk (1180), listed above, 256-76.

1218 Gentles, I., 'The management of the Crown lands, 1649-60', Ag. H. R., XIX, 1971, 25-41.

1218a —— 'The sales of Crown lands during the English Revolution', Ec. H. R., 2nd ser., XXVI, 1973, 614-35.

1219 Pugh, R. B., The Crown Estate: An Historical Essay, 1960.

1220 Wolffe, B. P., The Crown Lands, 1461-1536, 1970. A valuable examination of the subject. Half the book consists of documents.

1221 —— 'Henry VIII's land revenues and chamber finance', E. H. R., LXXIX, 1964, 225-54.
Material relating to the disposal of the dissolved monastic land is listed below in the sections on The Land market and on The dissolution of the monasteries.

(h) The land market

1222 Clay, C., 'The price of freehold land in the later seventeenth and eighteenth centuries', Ec. H. R., 2nd ser., XXVII, 1974, 173-89.

1222a Coleman, D. C., 'London scriveners and the estate market in the later seventeenth century', Ec. H. R., 2nd ser., IV, 1951, 221-30.

1223 Habakkuk, H. J., 'The market for monastic property', Ec. H. R., 2nd ser., X, 1957-8, 362-80. See also the article by Outhwaite (1225), listed below.

1224 —— 'The long-term rate of interest and the price of land in the seventeenth century', Ec. H. R., 2nd ser., V, 1952, 26-45.

1225 Outhwaite, R. B., 'The price of Crown land at the turn of the sixteenth century', Ec. H. R., 2nd ser., XX, 1967, 229-40. See also Habakkuk (1213), listed above.

1226 —— 'Who bought Crown lands? The pattern of purchases 1589-1603', B. I. H. R., XLIV, 1971, 18-33.

1227 Richardson, W. C., History of the Court of Augmentations, 1536-1554, 1962. An authoritative study of the institution which handled the sales of monastic lands.

1228 Woodward, G. W. O., 'A speculation in monastic lands', E. H. R., LXXIX, 1964, 778-83.
See also Thirsk (1954), listed below.

(i) Rent

1229 Jones, T. I. G., 'A study of rents and fines in South Wales in the sixteenth and early seventeenth centuries'. In Harlech Studies, ed. B. B. Thomas, 1938, 215-44.

1230 Kerridge, E., 'The movement of rent, 1540-1640', Ec. H. R., 2nd ser., VI, 1953-4, 16-34. Reprinted in Carus-Wilson, ed. (164), listed above, II, 208-26. An important article.
See also Bowden (1653), listed under the section on Prices.

(j) Field systems and enclosures

For bibliographical guidance on this subject, the reader is referred to:

1231 Chaloner, W. H., 'Recent work on enclosure, the open fields and related topics', Ag. H. R., II, 1954, 48-52.

1232 Brewer, J. G., Enclosures and the Open Fields: A Bibliography, 1972. Lists 355 items. Supplements the article by W. H. Chaloner.
See also the two items by Thirsk (1248, 1249), listed below. For details of tracts and sermons on enclosures, see the list in Read (967), listed above, 169 et. seq.

1233 Hosford, W. A., 'An eye witness's account of a seventeenth-century enclosure', Ec. H. R., 2nd ser., IV, 1951, 215-20.

1234 Leadam, I. S., ed., The Domesday of Inclosures, 1517-18, 2 vols, 1892. The information gathered by Wolsey's commission.

1235 Baker, A. R. H., 'Field systems in the Vale of Holmesdale', Ag. H. R., XIV, 1966, 1-24.

1236 —— 'Howard Levi Gray and English field systems: an evaluation, Agricultural History, XXXIX, 1965, 86-91. Gray's book is listed below (1243).

1237 Beresford, M. W., 'Habitation versus improvement: the debate on enclosure by agreement'. In Fisher (1010), listed above, 40-69.

1238 Butlin, R. A., 'Northumberland field systems', Ag. H. R., XII, 1964, 99-120.

1239 —— 'Enclosure and improvement in Northumberland in the sixteenth century', Archaeologia Aeliana, 3rd ser., XLV, 1967, 149-60.

1240 Curtler, W. H., The Enclosure and Redistribution of Our Land, 1920.

1241 Elliott, G., 'The system of cultivation and evidence of enclosure in the Cumberland open fields in the sixteenth century', Trans. Cumberland and Westmorland Antiquarian and Archaeological Soc., n.s., LIX, 1959, 85-104.

1242 Gay, E. F., 'Inquisitions of depopulation in 1517 and the Domesday of Inclosures', T. R. H. S., n.s. 14, 1900, 231-303.

1243 Gray, H. L., English Field Systems, Harvard

England 1500-1700

Historical Studies, XXII, Cambridge, Mass., 1915, reprinted 1959.

1244 Johnson, A. H., The Disappearance of the Small Landowner, 1909. Reprinted with an introductory note by Joan Thirsk, 1963.

1245 Leonard, Elizabeth M., 'The enclosure of common fields in the seventeenth century', T. R. H. S., n.s., 19, 1905, 101-46. Reprinted in Carus-Wilson, (164), listed above, II, 227-56.

1246 Parker, L. A., 'The agrarian revolution at Cotesbach (Leics.)'. In Hoskins (1190), listed above, 41-76.

1247 Tate, W. E., 'An early record of open-field agriculture in Nottinghamshire', Thoroton Society Trans. XLIII, for 1939, 1940, 33-48.

1248 Thirsk, Joan, Tudor Enclosures, Historical Association pamphlet, 1959.

1249 ——— 'Enclosing and engrossing'. In Thirsk (1180), listed above, 200-55. The most recent and balanced survey of the problem. See also Kerridge's article (1088), listed above, and Gonner (2364) and Tate (2369), listed below.

(k) Agricultural improvements

1250 Wood, E. B., ed., Rowland Vaughan, His Booke (1610), 1897. A seventeenth-century description by a pioneer of the floating of water-meadows.

1251 Allison, K. J., 'The sheep-corn husbandry of Norfolk in the sixteenth and seventeenth centuries', Ag. H. R., V, 1957, 12-30.

1252 Cornwall, J., 'Agricultural improvement, 1560-1640', Sussex Archaeological Collections, XCVIII, 1960, 118-32.

1253 Darby, H. C., The Draining of the Fens, 1956.

1254 Fussell, G. E., 'The Low Countries' influence on English farming', E. H. R., LXXIV, 1959, 611-22.

1255 Harris, L. E., Vermuyden and the Fens, 1953.

1256 Havinden, M. A., 'Agricultural progress in open-field Oxfordshire', Ag. H. R., IX, 1961, 73-83. Reprinted in Minchinton (165), listed above, I, 147-59. Argues against the traditional view that open-field agriculture was backward and static.

1256a ——— 'Lime as a means of agricultural improvement: the Devon example'. In Chalklin and Havinden (995a), listed above, 104-34.

1257 Hoskins, W. G., 'The reclamation of the waste in Devon, 1550-1800', Ec. H. R., XIII, 1943, 80-92.

1258 Kerridge, E., The Agricultural Revolution, 1967. An important and provocative book which argues that the main agricultural innovations belong, not to the eighteenth century, but to the period from about 1560 to 1690. For a balanced criticism of the book, see the review by Joan Thirsk in History, LV, 1970, 259-62.

1259 ——— 'The sheepfold in Wiltshire and the floating of the water-meadows', Ec. H. R., 2nd ser., VI, 1954, 282-9.

1260 ——— 'A reconsideration of some former husbandry practices', Ag. H. R., III, 1955, 26-40.

1261 Simpson, A., 'The East Anglian Foldcourse: some queries', Ag. H. R., VI, 1958, 87-96. Comments on the article by Allison (1251), listed above.

1262 Thirsk, Joan, 'Farming techniques'. In Thirsk (1180), listed above, 161-99. Dr Thirsk's essay on 'Seventeenth-century agriculture and social change' (1181), listed above, is also very relevant in this connection.

1262a ——— 'New crops and their diffusion: tobacco-growing in seventeenth-century England'. In Chalklin and Havinden (995a), listed above, 76-103.

1263 Williams, M., The Draining of the Somerset Levels, 1970.

1264 Yelling, J., 'The combination and rotation of crops in east Worcestershire, 1540-1660', Ag. H. R., XVII, 1969, 24-43.

(l) The dissolution of the monasteries

(1) Sources

1265 Hibbert, F. A., The Dissolution of the Monasteries, as illustrated by the Suppression of the Religious Houses of Staffordshire, 1910. Documentary appendices.

1266 Mellows, W. T., ed., The Last Days of Peterborough Monastery, Northamptonshire Record Society, XII, 1947.

1267 Purvis, J. S., A Selection of Monastic Records and Dissolution Papers, Yorkshire Archaeological Society, Record Series, LXXX, 1931.

1268 Youings, Joyce, ed., Devon Monastic Lands: Calendar of Particulars for Grants, 1536-1558, Devon and Cornwall Record Society, n.s., I, 1955.

(2) Studies

1269 Baskerville, G., English Monks and the Suppression of the Monasteries, 1937. Takes a hostile view of the monks.

1270 Haigh, C., The Last Days of the Lancashire Monasteries and the Pilgrimage of Grace, Chet. Soc., 3rd ser., 17, 1969. The most recent addition to the regional literature of the subject.

1271 Hodgett, C. A. J., 'The dissolution of the religious houses in Lincolnshire and the changing structure of society', Lincolnshire Architectural and Archaeological Society Report and Papers, IV, 1951, 83-99.

1272 Jack, S., 'Monastic lands in Leicestershire and their administration on the eve of the Dissolution', Leicestershire Archaeological and Historical Society Trans., XLI, 1967, 9-40.

1273 Kew, J., 'The disposal of crown lands and the Devon land market, 1536-58', Ag. H. R., XVIII, 1970, 93-105.

1274 Knowles, D., The Religious Orders in England III: The Tudor Age, 1959. A scholarly account.

1275 Oxley, J. E., The Reformation in Essex to the Death of Mary, 1965. Chapters 6 and 7 deal with the Dissolution and its aftermath.
1276 Savine, A., English Monasteries on the Eve of the Dissolution, Oxford Studies in Social and Legal History, 1909. An important study based mainly on the Valor Ecclesiasticus.
1277 Snell, L. S., The Suppression of the Religious Foundations of Devon and Cornwall, 1967.
1278 Swales, T. H., 'The re-distribution of the monastic lands in Norfolk at the Dissolution. 1: Value, gifts, leases and sales', Norfolk Archaeology, XXXIV, 1966, 14-44.
1279 Williams, G., 'The dissolution of the monasteries in Glamorgan', Welsh Hist. Rev., III, 1966, 23-43.
1280 —— 'Landlords in Wales: the Church'. In Thirsk (1180), listed above, 381-95.
1281 Woodward, G. W. O., The Dissolution of the Monasteries, 1966. A clear and concise survey.
1282 Youings, Joyce, 'The terms of the disposal of the Devon monastic lands, 1536-58', E.H.R., LXIX, 1954, 18-38. Reprinted in Minchinton (165), listed above, I, 117-40.
1283 —— 'Landlords in England: the Church'. In Thirsk (1180), listed above, 306-56. A useful exploration of the subject. See also Finberg (1051), listed above, 265-77, and Richardson (1227), listed above.

(m) Risings and riots

1284 Allan, D. G. C., 'The rising in the west, 1628-31', Ec. H.R., 2nd ser., V, 1952, 76-85.
1285 Bindoff, S. T., Ket's Rebellion, 1549, Historical Association pamphlet, 1949, reprinted 1968.
1286 Davies, C. S. L., 'The Pilgrimage of Grace reconsidered', P.P., 41, 1968, 54-76.
1287 —— 'Les révoltes populaires en Angleterre, 1500-1700', Annales, 24e année, 1969, 24-60.
1288 Gay, E. F., 'The Midland Revolt and the Inquisitions of Depopulation of 1607', T.R.H.S., n.s., 18, 1904, 195-244.
1289 James, M. E., 'Obedience and dissent in Henrician England: the Lincolnshire Rebellion, 1536', P.P., 48, 1970, 3-78.
1289a —— 'The concept of order and the Northern Rising of 1569', P.P., 60, 1973, 49-83.
1290 Kerridge, E., 'The revolts in Wiltshire against Charles I', Wiltshire Archaeological and Natural History Magazine, LVII, 1958-9, 64-75.
1291 Williams, N., 'The risings in Norfolk, 1569 and 1570', Norfolk Archaeology, XXXII, 1959, 73-81.

INDUSTRY

(a) General

1292 Burstall, A. F., History of Mechanical Engineering, 1963. A very general survey from prehistoric to modern times. Chapters 4 and 5 cover the period from 400 to 1750.
1293 Court, W. H. B., The Rise of the Midland Industries, 1600-1838, 1938. An important regional study.
1294 Jenkins, R., Links in the History of Engineering and Technology from Tudor Times, 1936. A useful collection of miscellaneous papers.
1295 Jones, E. L., 'The agricultural origins of industry', P.P., 40, 1968, 58-71.
1296 Kellenbenz, H., 'Industries rurales en occident de la fin du moyen age au xviiie siècle', Annales, 18e année, 1963, 833-82. Translated in Earle (1006a), listed above.
1297 Nef, J. U., 'English and French industry after 1540 in relation to the constitution'. In Conyers Read, ed., The Constitution Reconsidered, N.Y., 1938, 79-103.
1298 Sella, D., European Industries, 1500-1700, 1970. Fontana Economic History of Europe, II, Section 5. Like Kellenbenz (1296), listed above, this provides useful background.
1299 Thirsk, Joan, 'Industries in the countryside'. In Fisher, ed. (1010), listed above, 70-88.
1300 —— 'Roots of industrial England', Geographical Magazine, XLII, 1970, 816-26. See also Chaloner and Musson (393), listed above.

(b) Industrial growth

1301 Coleman, D. C., 'Industrial growth and industrial revolutions', Economica, n.s., XXIII, 1956, 1-20.
1302 Nef, J. U., 'The progress of technology and the growth of large-scale industry in Great Britain, 1540-1640', Ec. H.R., V, 1934, 3-24. Reprinted in Carus-Wilson, ed. (164), listed above, I, 88-107. Presents the famous 'Industrial Revolution' thesis.
1303 —— 'A comparison of industrial growth in France and England from 1540 to 1640', Jnl. of Political Economy, XLIV, 1936, 289-317; 505-33; 643-66.

(c) Industrial organisation

Histories of individual companies are too numerous to list in full and only a selection is given here. The reader is referred to the following, which provides a comprehensive bibliography of the subject:

1304 Kahl, W. F., The Development of the London Livery Companies: a bibliographical essay, 1960.
1305 Alford, B. W. E. and Barker, T. C., A History of the Carpenters' Company, 1968.
1306 Bindoff, S. T., 'The making of the Statute of Artificers'. In Bindoff, Hurstfield and Williams, (992), listed above, 59-94.
1307 Blagden, C., The Stationers' Company: A History, 1403-1959, 1960. An interesting and well-documented study. Chapters 1-11 deal with the pre-1700 period.
1308 Coleman, D. C., The Domestic System in Industry, Historical Association, Aids for Teachers series, 6, 1960.

38   England 1500-1700

1309 Consitt, F., The London Weavers' Company. Vol. I: From the Twelfth Century to the Close of the Sixteenth, 1933.
1310 Fisher, F. J., 'Some experiments in company organisation in the early seventeenth century', Ec. H.R., IV, 1932-4, 177-94.
1311 Foster, E. R., 'The procedure of the House of Commons against Patents and Monopolies, 1621-24'. In Aiken and Henning, eds. (1907), listed below, 57-87.
1312 Kellett, J. R., 'The break-down of gild and corporation control over the handicraft and retail trade in London' (in the seventeenth and eighteenth centuries), Ec. H.R., 2nd ser., X, 1958, 381-94.
1313 Kramer, Stella, The English Craft Gilds and the Government, Columbia University Studies in History, Economics and Public Law, 23, N.Y., 1905.
1314 —— The English Craft Gilds: Studies in Their Progress and Decline, N.Y., 1927.
1315 Marshall, T. H., 'Capitalism and the decline of the English gilds', Cambridge Hist. Jnl., III, 1929, 23-33.
1316 Ramsay, G. D., 'Industrial laissez-faire and the policy of Cromwell', Ec. H.R., XVI, 1946, 93-110.
1317 Reddaway, T. F., 'The Livery Companies of Tudor London', History, LI, 1966, 287-99.
1318 —— 'The London Goldsmiths c. 1500', T.R.H.S., 5th ser., 12, 1962, 49-62.
1319 Thrupp, Sylvia L., A Short History of the Worshipful Company of Bakers, 1933.
1320 Unwin, G., Industrial Organisation in the Sixteenth and Seventeenth Centuries, 1904, new ed., 1957, with an introduction by T. S. Ashton.
1321 —— The Gilds and Companies of London, 1908. New ed., 1966.
1322 Youings, Joyce, Tuckers Hall, Exeter: The History of a Provincial City Company Through Five Centuries, 1968. See also W. R. Scott (1507), listed below.

(d) Investment

1323 Coleman, D. C., Sir John Banks, Baronet and Businessman: A Study of Business, Politics and Society in Later Stuart England, 1963. Banks (1627-99) was one of the richest businessmen of his day.
1324 Davies, K. G., 'Joint stock investment in the later seventeenth century', Ec. H.R., 2nd ser., IV, 1952, 283-301.
1325 Davis, R., 'The earnings of capital in the English shipping industry, 1670-1730', J.E.H., XVII, 1957, 409-25.
1326 Gough, J. W., Sir Hugh Myddleton: Entrepreneur and Engineer, 1964. Not a biography of Myddleton (c. 1560-1631) but a study of aspects of his career including his part in the New River project.
1327 —— The Rise of the Entrepreneur, 1969. Somewhat old-fashioned in approach, but the book usefully gathers together much material on the subject.
1328 —— The Superlative Prodigall: A Life of Thomas Bushell, 1932. A case study of entrepreneurship.
1329 Robertson, H. M., 'Sir Bevis Bulmer, a large-scale speculator of Elizabethan and Jacobean times', Jnl. of Economic and Business History, 4, 1931, 99-120.
1330 Stone, L., 'The Nobility in business'. In The Entrepreneur, Cambridge, Mass., 1957, 14-21. See also Stone (1777), listed below.

(e) Textiles

1331 Williams, N. J., 'Two documents concerning the New Draperies', Ec. H.R., 2nd ser., IV, 1952, 353-8.
1332 Allison, K. J., 'The Norfolk worsted industry in the sixteenth and seventeenth centuries. 1: The traditional industry', Yorks. Bull., 12, 1960, 73-83.
1333 —— 'The Norfolk worsted industry in the sixteenth and seventeenth centuries. 2: The New Draperies', Yorks. Bull., 13, 1961, 61-77.
1333a Chapman, S. D., 'The genesis of the British hosiery industry 1600-1750', Textile History, III, 1972, 7-50.
1334 Coleman, D. C., 'An innovation and its diffusion: the New Draperies', Ec. H.R., 2nd ser., XXII, 1969, 417-29.
1335 Elliott, G., 'The decline of the woollen trade in Cumberland, Westmorland and Northumberland in the late sixteenth century', Trans. Cumberland and Westmorland Antiquarian and Archaeological Society, LXI, 1961, 112-19.
1336 Heaton, H., The Yorkshire Woollen and Worsted Industries, 1920, 2nd ed., 1965. The standard work.
1337 James, J., History of the Worsted Manufacture in England from the Earliest Times, 1857. Reprinted 1968. Chapters 2-6 deal with the Middle Ages and early modern period.
1338 Jenkins, J. G., The Welsh Woollen Industry, 1969.
1339 Lipson, E., The History of the Woollen and Worsted Industries, 1921. Reprinted 1965.
1340 Lowe, N., The Lancashire Textile Industry in the Sixteenth Century, Chet. Soc., 3rd ser., 20, 1972.
1341 Mann, Julia de L., 'A Wiltshire family of clothiers: George and Hester Wansey, 1683-1714', Ec. H.R., 2nd ser., IX, 1956, 241-53.
1342 Mendenhall, T. C., The Shrewsbury Drapers and the Welsh Wool Trade, 1953.
1343 Moir, Esther A. L., 'Benedict Webb, clothier', Ec. H.R., 2nd ser., X, 1957, 256-64.
1344 Pilgrim, J. E., 'The rise of the New Draperies in Essex', Birm. Hist. Jnl., 7, 1959, 36-59.
1345 Ramsay, G. D., 'The distribution of the cloth industry in 1561-2', E.H.R., LVII, 1942, 361-9.
1346 —— 'The report of the Royal Commission on the clothing industry, 1640', E.H.R., LVII, 1942, 482-93.
1347 —— The Wiltshire Woollen Industry in the Sixteenth and Seventeenth Centuries, 1943.

Reprinted 1965. Contains an additional bibliographical note.
1348 Skeel, Caroline A. J., 'The Welsh woollen industry in the sixteenth and seventeenth centuries', Archaeologia Cambrensis, series 7, II, 1922, 220-57.
1349 Tann, Jennifer, Gloucestershire Woollen Mills, 1967. The first three chapters are relevant to this period. The main part of the book consists of a gazetteer of woollen mills in the county.
1349a Thirsk, Joan, 'The fantastical folly of fashion; the English stocking knitting industry 1500-1700'. In Harte and Ponting (2672), listed below, 50-73.
1350 Wadsworth, A. P. and Mann, Julia de L., The Cotton Trade and Industrial Lancashire, 1600-1780, 1931. Reprinted 1965. See also Bowden (1198), and Thirsk (1299), listed above.

(f) Coal

1351 Galloway, R. L., Annals of Coalmining and the Coal Trade, 1898, 1904, 2nd ed., with new introduction by B. F. Duckham, 1970.
1352 —— A History of Coalmining in Great Britain, 1882. Reprinted with an extremely useful bibliographical introduction by B. F. Duckham, 1969.
1353 Hopkinson, G. G., 'The development of the South Yorkshire coalfield, 1500-1775', Trans. Hunter Archaeological Society, VII, 1957, 295-319.
1354 Nef, J. U., The Rise of the British Coal Industry, 1550-1700, 2 vols, 1932. Reprinted 1966. The standard work.
1355 Stone, L., 'An Elizabethan coalmine', Ec.H.R., 2nd ser., III, 1950-1, 97-106. Stone stresses the very modest scale of the undertaking and so questions Nef's claims for an Industrial Revolution in this period.

(g) Metals

1356 Agricola, G., De Re Metallica (1556), ed. H. and L. Hoover, 1912.
1357 France, R. S. ed., The Thieveley Lead Mines, 1629-1635, Record Society of Lancashire and Cheshire, CII, 1947.
1358 Andrews, C. B., The Story of Wortley Iron Works: a record of its History, Traditions and eight centuries of Yorkshire Iron-Making, 1950, 2nd rev. ed., 1956.
1359 Crossley, D. W., 'The management of a sixteenth-century iron works', Ec.H.R., 2nd ser., XIX, 1966, 273-88.
1360 Donald, M. B., Elizabethan Copper, 1955.
1361 —— Elizabethan Monopolies: The History of the Company of Mineral and Battery Works, 1961.
1362 Fell, A., The Early Iron Industry of Furness and District: an historical and descriptive account from Earliest Times to the end of the eighteenth century, 1908. Reprinted 1968.

1363 Flinn, M. W., 'Sir Ambrose Crowley, ironmonger, 1658-1713', Explorations in Entrepreneurial History, V, 1953, 162-80.
1364 —— 'The growth of the English iron industry, 1660-1760', Ec.H.R., 2nd ser., XI, 1958, 144-53. Bibliography.
1365 —— 'Timber and the advance of technology: a reconsideration', Annals of Science, XV, 1959, 109-20. An important article which takes a critical look at the so-called timber 'famine' of this period. The conclusion is that its nature and extent have been much exaggerated.
1366 Gough, J. W., The Mines of Mendip, 1930, rev. ed., 1967.
1367 Hamilton, H., The English Brass and Copper Industries to 1800, 1926. Reprinted with a bibliographical introduction by J. R. Harris, 1967.
1367a Hammersley, G., 'The charcoal iron industry and its fuel 1540-1750', Ec.H.R., XXVI, 1973, 593-613.
1368 Hopkinson, G. G., 'The charcoal iron industry in the Sheffield region, 1588-1755', Trans. Hunter Archaeological Society, VIII, 1961, 122-51.
1369 Jenkins, R., 'Notes on the early history of steelmaking in England', Newcomen Society Trans., III, for 1922-3, 1924, 16-40.
1370 —— 'Copper smelting in England: revival at the end of the seventeenth century', Newcomen Society Trans., XXIV, for 1943-5, 1949, 73-80.
1371 —— 'Ironfounding in England, 1490-1603', Newcomen Society Trans., XIX, for 1938-9, 1940, 35-49.
1372 Johnson, B. L. C., 'The Stour Valley iron industry in the late seventeenth century', Trans. Worcestershire Archaeological Society, n.s. XXVII, 1950, 35-46.
1373 —— 'The Foley partnerships: the iron industry at the end of the Charcoal era', Ec.H.R., 2nd ser., IV, 1952, 322-40.
1374 —— 'The Iron industry of Cheshire and North Staffordshire, 1688-1712', Trans. North Staffordshire Field Club, LXXXVIII, 1953-4, 32-55.
1375 —— 'New light on the iron industry in the Forest of Dean', Trans. Bristol and Gloucester Archaeological Society, 72, for 1953, 1954, 129-43.
1376 Lewis, G. R., The Stannaries: A Study of the English Tin Miner, Harvard Economic Series, III, Cambridge, Mass., 1906. See also Hatcher (738a), listed above.
1377 Lewis, W. J., Leadmining in Wales, 1967. The first four chapters deal with the pre-1700 period.
1378 Pelham, R. A., 'The migration of the iron industry towards Birmingham during the sixteenth century', Trans. Birmingham Archaeological Society, 66, 1950, 192-9.
1379 —— 'The establishment of the Willoughby iron works in N. Warwickshire in the sixteenth century', Birm. Hist. Jnl., 4, 1953, 18-29.
1380 Raistrick, A. and Jennings, B., A History of Leadmining in the Pennines, 1965.

1381 Rees, W., Industry before the Industrial Revolution, 2 vols., 1968. Has chapters on coal and metal mining, on the Mines Royal and on the Mineral and Battery works.
1382 Smith, R. S., 'Sir Francis Willoughby's ironworks, 1570-1610', Renaissance and Modern Studies, XI, 1967, 90-140.
1383 Straker, E., Wealden Iron, 1931. Reprinted 1969.
1384 Williams, L. J., 'A Welsh iron works at the close of the seventeenth century', National Library of Wales Jnl., XI, 1959-60, 266-84.

(h) Salt, leather, paper and glass

(1) Salt

1385 Calvert, A. F., Salt in Cheshire, 1915.
1386 Chaloner, W. H., 'Salt in Cheshire, 1600-1870', T.L.C.A.S., LXXI, for 1961, 1963, 58-74.
1387 Laver, H., 'Salt works in Essex', Essex Review, LII, 1943, 184-8.
1388 Lewis, W. J., 'A Welsh salt-mining venture of the sixteenth century', Jnl. National Library of Wales, VIII, 1953-4, 419-25. See also Berry (743), listed above.

(2) Leather

1389 Clarkson, L. A., 'English economic policy in the sixteenth and seventeenth centuries: the case of the leather industry', B.I.H.R., 38, 1965, 149-62.
1390 —— 'The leather crafts in Tudor and Stuart England', Ag.H.R., XIV, 1966, 23-39.
1391 —— 'The organisation of the English leather industry in the late sixteenth and seventeenth centuries', Ec.H.R., 2nd ser., XIII, 1960, 245-56.
1392 Woodward, D. M., 'The Chester leather industry, 1558-1625', T.H.S.L.C., 119, 1968, 65-112.

(3) Paper

1393 Coleman, D. C., The British Paper Industry, 1495-1860: A study in industrial Growth, 1958. The standard work on the subject.
1394 Shorter, A. H., Paper Mills and Paper Makers in England 1495-1800, Hilversum, 1957. Chapter 1 deals with the period 1495-1700. A full list of known paper mills is given.

(4) Glass

1395 Crossley, D. W., 'The performance of the glass industry in sixteenth-century England', Ec.H.R., XXV, 1972, 421-33.
1396 Kenyon, G. H., The Glass Industry of the Weald, 1967.
1397 Smith, R. S., 'Glass-making at Wollaton in the early seventeenth century', Trans. Thoroton Society, LXVI, 1963, 24-34.

(i) Shipping

1398 Albion, R. G., Forests and Sea Power: The Timber problem of the Royal Navy, 1652-1862, Harvard Economic Studies, 29, Cambridge, Mass., 1926.
1399 Barbour, V., 'Dutch and English merchant shipping in the seventeenth century', Ec.H.R., II, 1930, 261-90. Reprinted in Carus-Wilson, ed. (164), listed above, I, 227-53.
1400 Burwash, Dorothy, English Merchant Shipping, 1460-1540, Toronto, 1947. Reprinted 1969.
1401 Coleman, D. C., 'The naval dockyards under the later Stuarts', Ec.H.R., 2nd ser., VI, 1953, 134-155.
1402 Davis, R., The Rise of the English Shipping Industry in the Seventeenth and Eighteenth Centuries, 1962. An excellent example of the writing of industrial history and the standard work on the shipping industry.
1403 Lane, F. C., 'Tonnages, medieval and modern', Ec.H.R., 2nd ser., XVII, 1964, 213-33.
1404 Scammell, G. V., 'Ship-owning in England, 1450-1550', T.R.H.S., 5th ser., 12, 1962, 105-22.
1405 —— 'English merchant shipping at the end of the Middle Ages: some East Coast evidence', Ec.H.R., 2nd ser., XIII, 1960-1, 327-41.

(j) Miscellaneous

1406 Cheke, V., The Story of Cheesemaking in Britain, 1959.
1407 Cutting, C. L., Fish Saving: A History of fish processing from Ancient to Modern Times, 1955.
1408 Hogg, O. F. G., The Royal Arsenal: its Background, Origin and Subsequent History, 2 vols., 1963. Chapter 1 is relevant for this period.
1409 Lloyd, G. I. H., The Cutlery Trades: an Historical Essay in the Economics of Small-scale Production, 1913. Reprinted 1968.
1410 Rowlands, Marie B., 'Industry and Social change in Staffordshire, 1660-1760', Lichfield and South Staffordshire Archaeological and Historical Society, IX, 1967-8, 37-58.
1411 Singer, C. J., The Earliest Chemical Industry: an Essay in the Historical Relations of Economics and Technology Illustrated from the Alum Trade, 1948. For developments in England, see 182-202. See also Salzman (747), listed above, on the building industry, and Brace (2786), listed below.

TOWNS

Urban history has a voluminous literature. For a comprehensive guide to older histories of towns, see Gross (467), and Martin and MacIntyre (468), listed above.

(a) General

1412 Clark, P. and Slack, P., eds., Crisis and Order in English Towns, 1500-1700: Essays in Urban History, 1971.
1413 Cornwall, J., 'English country towns in the 1520s', Ec.H.R., 2nd ser., XV, 1962, 54-69.

1414 Dodd, A. H., 'Elizabethan towns and cities', History Today, 11, 1961, 136-44.
1414a Everitt, A. M., ed., Perspectives on English Urban History, 1973. An interesting collection of essays, including one by the editor on 'The English urban inn, 1560-1760'.
1415 Hoskins, W. G., 'English provincial towns in the early sixteenth century', T.R.H.S., 5th ser., 6, 1956, 1-19. Reprinted in Hoskins (1053), listed above, 68-85. See also Dyos (3577), listed below.

(b) Specialised studies

1416 Martin, G. H., ed., The Royal Charters of Grantham, 1463-1688, 1963.
1417 Atkinson, T., Elizabethan Winchester, 1963.
1418 Brett-James, N. G., The Growth of Stuart London, 1935.
1419 Davies, C. Stella, ed., A History of Macclesfield, 1961.
1420 Dickens, A. G., 'Tudor York'. In V.C.H. Yorkshire. The City of York, ed. P. M. Tillott, 1961, 117-59. See also Forster (1426), listed below.
1421 Dodd, A. H., ed., A History of Wrexham, Denbighshire, 1957.
1422 Dyer, A. D., The City of Worcester in the Sixteenth Century, 1973.
1423 Edie, C. A., 'New buildings, new taxes and old interests: an urban problem of the 1670s', Jnl. of British Studies, VI, 1967, 35-63.
1424 Fisher, F. J., 'The development of London as a centre of conspicuous consumption in the sixteenth and seventeenth centuries', T.R.H.S., 4th ser., 30, 1948, 37-50. Reprinted in Carus-Wilson, ed. (164), listed above, II, 197-207.
1425 ——— 'The growth of London', in Ives (1940), listed below, 76-86. See also Fisher's article on the London food market (164), and Wrigley (1440), listed below.
1426 Forster, G. C. F., 'York in the seventeenth century'. In V.C.H. Yorkshire. The City of York, ed. P. M Tillott, 1961, 160-206. See also Dickens (1420), listed above.
1427 François, M. E., 'The social and economic development of Halifax, 1558-1640', Proceedings of the Leeds Philosophical and Literary Society, XI, 1966, 217-80.
1428 Gill, C., History of Birmingham 1: Manor and Borough to 1865, 1952.
1429 Hill, J. W. F., Tudor and Stuart Lincoln, 1956.
1430 Holmes, M., Elizabethan London, 1969.
1431 Hoskins, W. G., 'An Elizabethan provincial town: Leicester'. In J. H. Plumb, ed., Studies in Social History, 1955, 33-67. Reprinted in Hoskins (1053), listed above, 86-114.
1432 Kerridge, E., 'Social and economic history of Leicester, 1509-1660'. In V.C.H., Leicestershire, ed. W. G. Hoskins and R. I. McKinley, IV, 1958, 76-109.
1433 MacCaffrey, W. T., Exeter, 1540-1640: The Growth of an English County Town, Cambridge, Mass., 1958.
1434 Pound, J. F., 'The social and trade structure of Norwich, 1525-75', P.P., 34, 1966, 49-69.
1435 Reddaway, T. F., The Rebuilding of London after the Great Fire, 1940. Reprinted 1951.
1436 Rimmer, W. G., 'The evolution of Leeds to 1700', Thoresby Society Publications, 50, Part 2, 1967, 91-129.
1437 Stephens, W. B., ed., A History of Congleton, 1970. A recent and good example of urban history.
1438 Thirsk, Joan, 'Stamford in the sixteenth and seventeenth centuries'. In A. Rogers, ed., The Making of Stamford, 1965, 58-76.
1439 Woodhead, J. R., The Rulers of London, 1660-1689: a Biographical Record of the Aldermen and Common Councilmen of the City of London, London and Middlesex Archaeological Society Publications, 1966.
1440 Wrigley, E. A., 'A simple model of London's importance in changing English society and economy, 1650-1750', P.P., 37, 1967, 44-70. An important article. See also Redford on Manchester (3627). listed below.

ALIEN IMMIGRANTS

The two specialised journals dealing with Huguenot and Jewish immigration are:

Proceedings of the Huguenot Society of London

Transactions of the Jewish Historical Society

(a) Dutch, Huguenots and Germans

1441 Cross, F. W., ed., History of the Walloon and Huguenot Church at Canterbury, Huguenot Society, 1898.
1442 Kirk, R. E. G. and E. F., eds., Returns of Aliens Dwelling in the City and Suburbs of London from the Reign of Henry VIII to that of James I, Huguenot Society, 4 vols., 1900-1908.
1443 Moens, W. J. C., ed., The Walloons and their Church at Norwich: Their History and Registers, 1565-1832, Huguenot Society, 1888.
1444 ——— Register of Baptisms in the Dutch Church at Colchester from 1645 to 1728, Huguenot Society, 1905.
1445 Carter, Alice C., 'The Huguenot contribution to the early years of the Funded Debt, 1694-1714', Proc. Hug. Soc., XIX, 1955, 21-41.
1446 Chitty, C. W., 'Aliens in England in the sixteenth century', Race, VIII, 1966, 129-45.
1447 ——— 'Aliens in England in the seventeenth century to 1660', Race, XI, 1969, 189-201.
1448 Coleman, D. C., 'The early British paper industry and the Huguenots', Proc. Hug. Soc., XIX, 1959, 210-25.
1449 Cunningham, W., Alien Immigrants to England, 1897. Reprinted with a new introduction by C. Wilson, 1969. The best general

survey of the period from the late fifteenth to the eighteenth century. The opening and closing sections of the book, however, are less valuable.

1450 Girouard, M., 'Some alien craftsmen in sixteenth- and seventeenth-century England', Proc.Hug.Soc., XX, 1959, 26-35.

1451 Gwynn, R.D., 'The arrival of the Huguenot refugees in England, 1680-1705', Proc.Hug.Soc., XXI, for 1969, 1970 404-36.

1452 Hayward, J.F., 'The Huguenot gunmakers of London', Proc.Hug.Soc., XX, 1963-4, 649-63.

1453 Holmes, M., 'Evil May Day 1517: the story of a riot', History Today, 15, 1965, 642-50.

1454 Le Fanu, W.R., 'Huguenot refugee doctors in England', Proc.Hug.Soc., XIX, 1956, 113-27.

1455 Morant, Valerie, 'The settlement of Protestant refugees in Maidstone during the sixteenth century', Ec.H.R., 2nd ser., IV, 1951, 210-14.

1456 Murray, J.J., 'The cultural impact of the Flemish Low Countries on sixteenth and seventeenth-century England', A.H.R., LXII, 1957, 837-54.

1457 Ransome, D.R., 'The struggle of the Glaziers' Company with foreign glaziers, 1500-1550', Guildhall Miscellany, II, 1960, 12-20.

1458 Rye, W.B., The Dutch Refugees in Norwich, 1887.

1459 Scouloudi, Irene, 'Alien immigration into and alien communities in London, 1558-1640', Proc.Hug.Soc., XVI, 1938, 27-49.

1460 Scoville, W.C., 'The Huguenots and the diffusion of technology', Jnl. of Political Economy, LX, 1952, 294-311, 392-411.

1461 Shears, P.J., 'Huguenot connections with the clockmaking trade in England', Proc. Hug.Soc., XX, 1960, 158-76.

1462 Sheppard, F.H.W., 'The Huguenots in Spitalfields and Soho', Proc.Hug.Soc., XXI, 1969, 355-65.

1463 Taube, E., 'German craftsmen in Tudor England', Ec.J.Economic History Supplement, 3, 1939, 167-78.

1464 Williams, L., 'Alien immigrants in relation to industry and society in Tudor England', Proc.Hug.Soc., XIX, 1956, 146-69.

1465 Wyatt, T., 'Aliens in England before the Huguenots', Proc.Hug.Soc., XIX, 1953, 74-94.
See also Consitt (1309), listed above, 33-60, on the Flemish weavers.

(b) Jews

1466 Giuseppi, J.A., 'Sephardic Jews and the early years of the Bank of England', Trans. Jewish Historical Society, XIX, 1960, 53-64.

1467 Hyamson, A.M., The Sephardim of England: a History of the Spanish and Portuguese Jewish Community, 1492-1951, 1951.

1468 Osterman, N., 'The controversy over the proposed readmission of the Jews to England (1655)', Jewish Society Studies, III, 1941, 301-28.

1469 Rubens, A., 'Portrait of Anglo-Jewry, 1656-1836. 1: The Anglo-Jewish community, source material', Trans. Jewish Historical Society, XIX, 1960, 13-52.

1470 Samuel, E.R., 'Portuguese Jews in Jacobean London', Trans. Jewish Historical Society, XVIII, sessions 1953-5, 1958, 171-230.

1471 Wolf, L., 'The Jews in Tudor England'. In C.Roth, ed., Essays in Jewish History, 1934, 73-90.
See also Roth (574), listed above.

COMMERCE AND COLONISATION

1472 McCulloch, J.R., ed., Early English Tracts on Commerce, 1856. Reprinted 1952. A very valuable collection which includes Lewes Roberts' The Treasure of Traffike; or, A Discourse of Forraigne Trade (1641) and Thomas Mun's England's Treasure by Forraign Trade (1664).

1473 Willan, T.S., ed., A Tudor Book of Rates, 1962.

For other documentary material on this subject, see Bland, Brown and Tawney (141), and Tawney and Power, (982), II, 1-89, listed above.

(a) General

1474 Bindoff, S.T., 'The greatness of Antwerp'. In G.R.Elton, ed., New Cambridge Modern History, II, 1958, 50-69.

1475 Bridenbaugh, C. and Roberta, No Peace Beyond the Line: The English and the Caribbean 1624-1690, 1972.

1476 Connell-Smith, G., Forerunners of Drake: A Study of English Trade With Spain in the Early Tudor Period, 1954.

1477 Davis, R., English Overseas Trade 1500-1700, 1973.

1478 ——— 'English foreign trade, 1660-1700', Ec.H.R., 2nd ser., VII, 1954, 150-166. Reprinted in Minchinton (1487), listed below, 99-120.

1479 ——— A Commercial Revolution: English Overseas Trade in the seventeenth and eighteenth Centuries, Historical Association pamphlet, 1967. A valuable short survey.

1480 Fisher, F.J., 'London's export trade in the early seventeenth century', Ec.H.R., 2nd ser.,III, 1950, 151-61. Reprinted in Minchinton (1487), listed below, 64-77.

1481 ——— 'Commercial trends and policy in sixteenth-century England', Ec.H.R., X, 1940, 95-117. Reprinted in Carus-Wilson, ed., (164), listed above, I, 152-72. A valuable article.

1482 Friis, Astrid, Alderman Cockayne's Project: the commercial policy of England in its main aspects, 1603-25, Copenhagen, 1927. A useful book. The subtitle is justified.

1483 Gould, J.D., 'Cloth exports, 1600-1640', Ec.H.R., 2nd ser., XXIV, 1971, 249-52. A comment on W.B.Stephens's article (1493),

1484 Harper, L.A., The English Navigation Laws, N.Y., 1939.
1485 Kepler, J.S., 'Fiscal aspects of the English carrying trade during the Thirty Years War', Ec.H.R., 2nd ser., XXV, 1972, 261-83.
1486 McLachlan, Jean M.O., Trade and Peace with Old Spain, 1607-1750, 1940.
1487 Minchinton, W.E., ed., The Growth of English Overseas Trade in the Seventeenth and Eighteenth Centuries, 1969. A collection of reprinted articles, with a valuable introduction and critical bibliography.
1488 Price, J.M., 'Multilateralism and/or bilateralism. The settlement of English trade balance with "the North" c. 1700', Ec.H.R., 2nd ser., XIV, 1961, 254-74.
1489 Priestley, M., 'Anglo-French trade and the "unfavourable balance" controversy, 1660-1685', Ec.H.R., 2nd ser., IV, 1951, 37-52.
1490 Rabb, T.K., Enterprise and Empire: Merchant and Gentry investment in the expansion of England, 1575-1630, Cambridge, Mass., 1967. An important study of the financial backing which made possible the commercial development of England in the late sixteenth and early seventeenth centuries. Much of the book is devoted to a discussion of the assembling of the data and of its processing by computer. The book contains a very good bibliography.
1491 Ramsay, G.D., English Overseas Trade during the Centuries of Emergence, 1957. A good survey.
1492 Ramsey, P., 'Overseas trade in the reign of Henry VII: the evidence of customs accounts', Ec.H.R., 2nd ser., VI, 1953, 173-82.
1493 Stephens, W.B., 'The cloth exports of the provincial ports, 1600-1640', Ec.H.R., 2nd ser., XXII, 1969, 228-48.
1494 Stone, L., 'Elizabethan overseas trade', Ec.H.R., 2nd ser., II, 1949, 30-58.
1495 Supple, B.E., Commercial Crisis and Change in England 1600-1642: A Study in the Instability of a Mercantile Economy, 1959. A very important contribution to seventeenth-century English economic and social history.
1496 Taylor, H., 'Trade, neutrality and the "English road", 1630-1648', Ec.H.R., 2nd ser., XXV, 1972, 236-60.
1497 Waters, D.W., The Art of Navigation in England in Elizabethan and Early Stuart Times, 1958.
1498 Willan, T.S., Studies in Elizabethan Foreign Trade, 1959. An important collection of essays, particularly useful for English trade with Morocco.
See also Carus-Wilson and Coleman (779), listed above.

(b) **England and the age of discovery**

Many contemporary accounts of voyages of discovery have been published in modern editions. The reader is referred to the publications of the Hakluyt Society, London.

1499 Cipolla, C.M., Guns and Sails in the Early Phase of European Expansion, 1400-1700, 1966. A general survey of the European background.
1500 Parry, J.H., The Age of Reconnaissance, 1963. The best general introduction.
1501 Scammell, G.V., 'The New Worlds and Europe in the sixteenth century', Hist.Jnl., XII, 1969, 389-412.
1502 Williamson, J.A., A Short History of British Expansion, 1945.
1503 —— Maritime Enterprise, 1485-1558, 1913.

(c) **Trading companies and their organisation**

1504 Carr, C.T., ed., Select Charters of Trading Companies, 1530-1707, Selden Society, XXVIII, 1913. A very useful collection which includes the charters of the Levant, Newfoundland and African Companies (1600, 1610 and 1618 respectively), and also the charters of major industrial undertakings.
1505 Rich, E.E., ed., Hudson's Bay Company Minutes (1671-84), 3 vols., 1942-60.
1506 Davies, K.G., 'Joint stock investment in the late seventeenth century', Ec.H.R., 2nd ser., IV, 1952, 283-301. Reprinted in Carus-Wilson, ed. (164), listed above, II, 273-90.
1507 Scott, W.R., The Constitution and Finance of English, Scottish and Irish Joint Stock Companies to 1720, 3 vols., 1910-12. The scope of the work is as follows: volume 1 deals with the general development of the joint stock system to 1720; volume 2 surveys companies for foreign trade, colonization, fishing and mining; volume 3 covers water supply, postal arrangements, street lighting, manufacturing, banking, finance and insurance.

(1) The Merchant Adventurers

1508 Lingelbach, W.E., ed., The Merchant Adventurers of England: Their Laws and Ordinances, With Other Documents, Philadelphia, 1902.
1509 McGrath, P.V., ed., Records Relating to the Society of Merchant Venturers of Bristol in the Seventeenth Century, Bristol Record Society, XVII, 1952.
1510 Wheeler, J., A Treatise of Commerce (1601), ed. G.B. Hotchkiss, N.Y., 1931. Designed as a defence of the Merchant Adventurers' Company.
1511 Lingelbach, W.E., 'The internal organisation of the Merchant Adventurers of England', T.R.H.S., 2nd ser., 16, 1902, 19-67.
1512 Unwin, G., 'The Merchant Adventurers' Company in the reign of Elizabeth'. In Unwin's Collected Papers (126), listed above, 133-220.

(2) The Russia Company

1513 Willan, T.S., The Muscovy Merchants of 1555, 1953.

1514 —— The Early History of the Russia Company, 1553-1603, 1956. The standard works on the subject.

(3) The Eastland Company and trade with the Baltic

1515 Sellers, Maud, ed., The Acts and Ordinances of the Eastland Company of York, Camden Society, 3rd ser., XI, 1906.

1516 Aström, S.E., From Stockholm to St. Petersburg: Commercial Factors in the Political Relations between England and Sweden, 1675-1700, Finnish Historical Society, Studia Historica, II, Helsinki, 1962.

1517 —— From Cloth to Iron: The Anglo-Baltic Trade in the Late Seventeenth Century. Part Two, Helsinki, 1965.

1518 —— 'The English Navigation Laws and the Baltic trade 1660-1700', Scand. Ec. H. R., VIII, 1960, 3-18.

1519 Deardorff, N.R., 'English trade in the Baltic during the reign of Elizabeth', in Studies in the History of English Commerce in the Tudor Period, N.Y., 1912.

1520 Hinton, R.W.K., The Eastland Trade and the Commonweal in the Seventeenth Century, 1959. The main work on England's trade with the Baltic. See the review article by R.H. Tawney, Ec.H.R., 2nd ser., XII, 1959, 280-82.

1520a Zins, H., England and the Baltic in the Elizabethan Era, 1972.

(4) The Levant

1521 Davis, R., 'England and the Mediterranean, 1570-1670', in Fisher, ed. (1010), listed above, 117-37.

1522 Foster, W., England's Quest of Eastern Trade, 1933.

1523 Horniker, A.L., 'Anglo-French rivalry in the Levant from 1583 to 1612', Jnl. Mod. Hist., XVIII, 1946, 289-305.

1524 Willan, T.S., 'Some aspects of English trade with the Levant in the sixteenth century', E.H.R., LXX, 1955, 399-410.

1525 Wood, A.C., A History of the Levant Company, 1935. Reprinted 1964.

(5) The East India Company

1526 Stevens, H., ed., The Dawn of British Trade to the East Indies as Recorded in the Minutes of the East India Company, 1599-1603, 1886.

1527 Bassett, D.K., 'The trade of the East India Company in the Far East, 1623-1684', Jnl. Royal Asiatic Society, 1960, 32-47

1528 Chaudhuri, K.N., The English East India Company: The Study of an Early Joint Stock Company, 1600-1640, 1965. A valuable study.

1529 —— 'The East India Company and the export of treasure in the early seventeenth century', Ec.H.R., 2nd ser., XVI, 1963, 23-38.

1530 —— 'Treasure and trade balances: the East India Company's export trade', Ec.H.R., 2nd ser., XXI, 1968, 480-502.

1531 Krishna, B., Commercial Relations Between India and England, 1601-1757, 1924.

1532 Thomas, P.J., Mercantilism and the East India Trade, 1926. Reprinted 1963.

(6) Miscellaneous

1533 Davies, K.G., The Royal Africa Company, 1957.

1534 Preston, R.A., 'The Laconia Company of 1629: an English attempt to intercept the fur trade', Canadian Historical Review, XXXI, 1950, 125-44.

1535 Rich, E.E., The History of the Hudson's Bay Company I: 1670-1763, Hudson's Bay Record Society, 1958.

1536 Robbins, W.G., 'The Massachusetts Bay Company: an analysis of motives', Historian, XXXII, 1969, 83-98.
See also Rose-Troup (1566), listed below.

(d) The mercantile community

1537 Dodd, A.H., 'Mr Myddleton, the merchant of Tower St.', In Bindoff, Hurstfield and Williams, eds., (992), listed above, 249-81.

1538 Grassby, R., 'The personal wealth of the business community in seventeenth-century England', Ec.H.R., 2nd ser., XXIII, 1970, 220-34.

1539 —— 'English merchant capitalism in the late seventeenth century: the composition of business fortunes', P.P., 46, 1970, 87-107.

1540 Hoskins, W.G., 'The Elizabethan merchants of Exeter'. In Bindoff, Hurstfield and Williams, eds., (992), listed above, 163-87.

1540a Lang, R.G., 'Social origins and social aspirations of Jacobean London merchants', Ec.H.R., 2nd ser., XXVII, 1974, 28-47.

1541 Ramsay, G.D., ed., John Isham: Mercer and Merchant Adventurer. Two Account Books of a London Merchant in the Reign of Elizabeth I, Northamptonshire Record Society, XXI, 1962.

1542 Ramsay, P., 'Some Tudor merchants' accounts'. In A.C. Littleton and B.S. Yamey, eds., Studies in the History of Accounting, Homewood, Ill., 1956, 185-201.

1543 Webb, J., Great Tooley of Ipswich: A Portrait of an Early Tudor Merchant, Suffolk Record Society, 1963.

(e) Anglo-Dutch commercial relations

1544 Boxer, C.R., The Dutch Seaborne Empire, 1600-1800, 1965.

1545 —— 'Some second thoughts on the third Anglo-Dutch War, 1672-74', T.R.H.S., 5th ser., 19, 1969, 67-94.

1546 Clark, G.N., The Dutch Alliance and the War Against French Trade, 1688-1697, 1923.

1547 Farnell, J.E., 'The Navigation Act of 1651, the first Dutch War and the London merchant community', Ec.H.R., 2nd ser., XVI, 1964, 439-54.

1548 Wilson, C., Profit and Power: A Study of England and the Dutch Wars, 1957. The main work on the subject. For eighteenth-century developments in Anglo-Dutch relations, see (1044), listed above, by the same author.
1549 —— 'Cloth production and international competition in the seventeenth century', Ec.H.R., 2nd ser., XIII, 1960, 209-21. See also Barbour (1399), listed above.

(f) Coastal trade

1550 Smith, R.A., Sea Coal for London: History of the Coal Factors in the London Market, 1961. Nef (1354), listed above, is also useful on this aspect.
1551 Willan, T.S., The English Coasting Trade, 1600-1750, 1938. Reprinted with new preface, 1967. The standard work.

(g) Smuggling

1552 Ramsay, G.D., 'The smugglers' trade: a neglected aspect of English commercial development', T.R.H.S., 5th ser., 2, 1952, 131-57.
1553 Rive, A., 'A short history of tobacco smuggling', Ec.J. Economic History Supplement, I, 1929, 554-69.
See also Williams (814), listed above.

(h) Colonies

Only a brief selection of titles is given below. For further information on the subject, the reader is referred to:

1554 Morrell, W.P., British Overseas Expansion and the History of the Commonwealth: A Select Bibliography, Historical Association Helps for Students of History series, 63, 1961, rev. ed., 1970.
1555 Andrews, C.M., The Colonial Period of American History, 4 vols., 1934.
1556 —— British Committees, Commissions and Councils of Trade and Plantations, 1622-1675, Baltimore, Md., 1908.
1557 Bailyn, B., The New England Merchants in the Seventeenth Century, Harvard, Mass., 1955.
1558 Cell, G.T., 'The Newfoundland Company: a study of subscribers to a colonizing venture', William and Mary Quarterly, XXII, 1965, 611-25.
1559 Gillespie, J.E., The Influence of Overseas Expansion on England to 1700, Columbia University Studies in History, Economics and Public Law, N.Y., 1920.
1560 Knorr, K.E., British Colonial Theories, 1570-1850, 1944. Reprinted 1963.
1561 Lucas, C.P., Religion, Colonising and Trade: The Driving Forces of the Old Empire, 1930.
1562 Newton, A.P., The European Nations in the West Indies, 1933.
1563 Quinn, D.B.,"The first Pilgrims', William and Mary Quarterly, 3rd ser., XXIII, 1966, 359-90.

1564 —— 'The failure of Raleigh's American colonies'. In H.A. Cronne, T.W. Moody and D.B. Quinn, eds., Essays in British and Irish History in Honour of James Eadie Todd, 1949, 61-85.
1565 Rose, J.H., Newton, A.P. and Benians, E.A., eds., Cambridge History of the British Empire I: The Old Empire from the Beginnings to 1783, 1929.
1566 Rose-Troup, Frances, The Massachusetts Bay Company and its Predecessors, 1930.
1567 Rowse, A.L., The Elizabethans and America, 1959.
1568 Wright, L.B., Religion and Empire: The Alliance Between Piety and Commerce in English Expansion, 1558-1625, Chapel Hill N.C., 1943.

(i) Miscellaneous

1569 Hinton, R.W.K., ed., The Port Books of Boston, 1601-1640, Lincoln Record Society, 50, 1956.
1570 Lewis, E.A., ed., The Welsh Port Books, 1550-1603, Cymmrodorion Record series, XII, 1927.
1571 See also:
Jarvis, R.C., 'Sources for the history of ports', Jnl. of Transport History, III, 1957-8, 76-93.
1572 Andrews, K.R., Elizabethan Privateering. English Privateering During the Spanish War, 1585-1603, 1964.
1573 Ashton, R., 'The parliamentary agitation for free trade in the opening years of the reign of James I', P.P., 38, 1967, 40-55.
1573a Croft, Pauline, 'Free trade and the House of Commons 1605-1606', Ec.H.R., 2nd ser., XXVIII, 1975, 17-27.
1574 Cullen, L.M., Anglo-Irish Trade, 1660-1800, 1968. Extensive bibliography, 221-42.
See also Longfield (1587), listed below.
1575 Davis, R., The Trade and Shipping of Hull, 1500-1700, East Yorkshire Local History Society, pamphlet series, 17, 1964.
1576 Edler, F., 'Winchcombe kerseys in Antwerp, 1538-44', Ec.H.R., VII, 1936, 57-62.
1577 Gould, J.D., 'The crisis in the export trade, 1586-7', E.H.R., LXXI, 1956, 212-22.
1578 —— 'The trade depression of the early 1620s', Ec.H.R., 2nd ser., VII, 1954, 81-90.
1579 —— 'The trade crisis of the early 1620s and English economic thought', J.E.H., XV, 1955, 121-33.
1580 Gravil, R., 'Trading to Spain and Portugal, 1670-1700', Business History, X, 1968, 69-88.
1581 Innis, H.A., The Cod Fisheries, 1940. Chapter 3 deals with the Spanish and English fisheries, 1550-1600, 30-51.
1582 Jenkins, J.T., The Herring and the Herring Industries, 1927. See 80-90 for some account of Stuart fishery companies.
1583 Jones, D.W., 'The "Hallage" receipts of the London cloth markets 1562-c.1720', Ec.H.R., 2nd ser., XXV, 1972, 567-87.

1584 Jones, J.R., 'Some aspects of London mercantile activity during the reign of Queen Elizabeth'. In N. Downes, ed., Essays in Honour of Conyers Read, Chicago, Ill., 1953, 186-99.

1585 Jones, W.J., 'Elizabethan marine insurance—the judicial undergrowth', Business History, II, 1959, 53-66.

1586 Koenigsberger, H., 'English merchants in Naples and Sicily in the seventeenth century', E.H.R., LXII, 1947, 304-26.

1587 Longfield, Ada K., Anglo-Irish Trade in the Sixteenth Century, 1929. See also Cullen (1574), listed above.

1588 Loomie, A.J., 'Religion and Elizabethan commerce with Spain', Catholic Historical Review, 50, 1964, 27-51.

1589 Lounsbury, R.G., The British Fishery at Newfoundland, 1634-1763, New Haven, Conn., 1934.

1590 MacInnes, C.M., The Early English Tobacco Trade, 1926.

1591 McGrath, P.V., Merchants and Merchandise in Seventeenth-Century Bristol, Bristol Record Society, 1955.

1592 Maloney, F.X., The Fur Trade in New England, 1620-1676, 1931. Reprinted 1967.

1593 Miller, L.R., 'New evidence on the shipping and imports of London, 1601-1602', Quarterly Jnl. of Economics, 1927, 740-60.

1594 Nettels, C.P., 'England and the Spanish-American trade, 1680-1715', Jnl. Mod.Hist., III, 1931, 1-32.

1595 Parkinson, C.N., The Rise of the Port of Liverpool, 1952.

1596 Rabb, T.K., 'Free trade and the gentry in the parliament of 1604', P.P., 40, 1968, 165-73. A rejoinder to Ashton (1573), listed above.

1597 Reynolds, P., 'Elizabethan traders in Normandy', Jnl. Mod. Hist., IX, 1937, 289-303.

1598 Ruddock, A.A., 'London capitalists and the decline of Southampton in the early Tudor period', Ec.H.R., 2nd ser., II, 1949, 137-51.

1599 Stephens, W.B., 'The overseas trade of Chester in the early seventeenth century', T.H.S.L.C., 120, 1968, 23-34.

1600 —— 'The West Country ports and the struggle for the Newfoundland fisheries in the seventeenth century', Trans. Devonshire Association, LXXXVIII, 1956, 90-101.

1601 —— 'The foreign trade of Plymouth and the Cornish ports in the early seventeenth century', Trans. Devonshire Association, CI, 1969, 125-37.

1602 Tawney, R.H., Business and Politics in the Reign of James I: Lionel Cranfield as Merchant and Statesman, 1958. Though not Tawney's best book this is still an important one.

1603 Williams, N., 'England's tobacco trade in the reign of Charles I', Virginia Magazine of History and Biography, LXV, 1957, 403-49.

1604 Woodward, D.M., The Trade of Elizabethan Chester, University of Hull Occasional Papers in Economic and Social History, No.4, 1970. Deals with the port's overseas, coastal and home trade.
See also Ruddock (806) and van der Wee (813), listed above. For the English customs in this period, see Atton and Holland (1725), listed in the section on Government policy and administration.

THE CONCEPT OF MERCANTILISM

1605 Biltz, R.C., 'Mercantilist policies and the pattern of world trade, 1500-1750', J.E.H., XXVII, 1967, 39-55.

1606 Coats, A.W., 'In defence of Heckscher and the idea of Mercantilism', Scand. Ec.H.R., V, 1957, 173-87. See Heckscher (1610) and Coleman (1607), listed below.

1607 Coleman, D.C., ed., Revisions in Mercantilism, 1969. A useful collection of reprinted articles, including Coleman's own essay 'Eli Heckscher and the idea of mercantilism', 92-117. Bibliography.

1608 Grampp, W.D., 'The liberal elements in English Mercantilism', Quarterly Jnl. of Economics, 66, 1952, 456-501.

1609 Heaton, H., 'Heckscher on mercantilism', Jnl. of Political Economy, 45, 1937, 370-93.

1610 Heckscher, E.F., Mercantilism, 2 vols. English trans., 1935, 2nd ed., London and N.Y. 1956. A major work though one which has been criticised for its failure to distinguish between economic theory and economic practice. See Coleman (1607), listed above.

1611 —— 'Revisions in economic history: mercantilism', Ec.H.R., VII, 1936-7, 44-54. Reprinted in Coleman (1607), 19-34. Heckscher's second thoughts on the subject.

1612 Herlitz, L., 'The concept of mercantilism', Scand. Ec.H.R., XII, 1964, 101-20.

1613 Hinton, R.W.K., 'The mercantile system in the time of Mun', Ec.H.R., 2nd ser., VII, 1954-5, 277-90.

1614 Judges, A.V., 'The idea of a mercantile state', T.R.H.S., 4th ser., 21, 1939, 41-70. Reprinted in Coleman (1607), listed above 35-60.

1615 Minchinton, W.E., ed., Mercantilism: system or expediency?, Boston, Mass., 1969. A collection of brief extracts from the main contributions to the debate on the subject.

1616 Viner, J., 'Power versus plenty as objectives of foreign policy in the seventeenth and eighteenth centuries', World Politics, I, 1948, 1-29. Reprinted in Coleman (1607), listed above, 61-91.

1617 Wilson, C., Mercantilism, Historical Association pamphlet, 1958.

1618 —— 'The other face of Mercantilism', T.R.H.S., 5th ser., 9, 1959, 81-101. Reprinted in Wilson (1045), listed above, 73-93.

1619 —— 'Mercantilism. Some vicissitudes of an idea', Ec.H.R., 2nd ser., X, 1957, 181-88. Reprinted in Wilson (1045), listed above, 62-72.

1620 —— 'Treasure and trade balances: the Mercantilist problem', Ec.H.R., 2nd ser., II, 1949, 152-61. Reprinted in Wilson (1045), listed above 48-61.
1621 —— 'Treasure and trade balances: further evidence', Ec.H.R., 2nd ser., IV, 1951, 231-42.
1622 —— 'Trade, society and the state'. In Wilson (1045), listed above, 487-576.

COMMUNICATIONS AND INTERNAL TRADE

For fuller details of the literature of the subject, the reader is referred to the extensive bibliographies contained in Dyos and Aldcroft (3268) and Jackman (3269), listed below.

(a) River navigation

1623 Chalklin, C. W., 'Navigation schemes of the Upper Medway, 1600-1665', Jnl. of Transport History, V, 1961, 105-15.
1623a Duckham, B. F., The Yorkshire Ouse. The History of a River Navigation, 1967.
1624 Skempton, A. W., 'The engineers of the English river navigations, 1620-1760', Trans Newcomen Society, XXIX, 1953-5, 24-54.
1625 Stephens, W. B., 'The Exeter Lighter Canal, 1566-1698', Jnl. of Transport History III, 1957, 1-11.
1625a Summers, Dorothy, The Great Ouse: The History of a River Navigation, 1973.
1626 Willan, T. S., River Navigation in England, 1600-1750, 1936. Reprinted 1964. The standard work.
1627 —— The Navigation of the Great Ouse between St Ives and Bedford in the Seventeenth Century, Bedfordshire Historical Record Society Publications, 1946.
1628 —— 'The navigation of the Thames and Kennet, 1600-1750', Berkshire Archaeological Jnl., XL, 1936, 144-56.
1629 —— 'Yorkshire river navigation, 1600-1750', Geography, XXII, 1937, 189-99.
1630 —— 'River navigation and trade from the Witham to the Yare, 1600-1750', Norfolk Archaeology, XXVI, 1938, 296-309.
1631 —— 'The river navigation and trade of the Severn Valley, 1600-1750', Ec.H.R., VIII, 1937-8, 68-79.
1632 —— 'Salisbury and the navigation of the Avon', Wiltshire Archaeological and Natural History Magazine, XLVII, 1937, 592-4.
1633 Wood, A. C., 'The history of the trade and transport on the river Trent', Trans. Thoroton Society, LIV, 1950, 1-44.

(b) Roads and their traffic

1634 Cossons, A., 'Warwickshire turnpikes', Trans. Birmingham Archaeological Society, LXIX, for 1941-2, 1946, 53-100.
1635 Crofts, J. E. W., Packhorse, Waggon and Post: Land Carriage and Communications under the Tudors and Stuarts, 1967. A rather unsystematic treatment of the subject, based on literary evidence.
1636 Emmison, F. G., 'The earliest Turnpike Bill (Biggleswade to Baldock road), 1622', B.I.H.R., XII, 1935, 108-22.
1637 —— '1555 and all that: a milestone in the history of the English road', Essex Review, 64, 1955, 15-25.
1638 —— 'Was the Highways Act of 1555 a success?', Essex Review, 64, 1955, 221-34.
1639 Fordham, H. G., The Road Books and Itineraries of Great Britain, 1570-1850, 1924.
1640 Guttery, D. R., 'Stourbridge market in Tudor times', Trans. Worcester Archaeological Society, n.s., XXX, 1954, 16-38.
1641 La Mar, Virginia, Travel and Roads in Tudor England (Folger Booklets on Tudor and Stuart Civilisation), Washington, D.C., 1960.
1642 Parkes, Joan, Travel in England in the Seventeenth Century, 1925. Reprinted 1968.
1643 Thomson, Gladys Scott, 'Roads in England and Wales in 1603', E.H.R., XXXIII, 1918, 234-43.

(c) Internal trade

See also the section on Marketing under Agriculture

1644 Lewis, E. A., 'The toll books of some North Pembrokeshire fairs, 1599-1603', Bulletin of the Board of Celtic Studies, VII, 1934, 283-318.
1645 Rodgers, H. B., 'The market area of Preston in the sixteenth and seventeenth centuries', Geographical Studies, III, 1956, 46-55.
1646 Simpson, A., 'Thomas Cullum, draper, 1587-1664', Ec.H.R., 2nd ser., XI, 1958, 19-34.
1647 Tupling, G. H., 'Lancashire markets in the sixteenth and seventeenth centuries, Parts 1 and 2', T.L.C.A.S., LVIII, 1947, 1-34; ibid., LIX, 1948, 1-34.
1648 Westerfield, R. B., Middlemen in English Business, Particularly between 1660 and 1760, Trans. Connecticut Academy of Arts and Sciences, XIX, Connecticut, 1915. Reprinted N.Y. 1969. A useful book.
1649 Williams, N., Tradesmen in Early Stuart Wiltshire, Wiltshire Archaeological and Natural History Society, Records branch, XV, 1960.
See also Everitt (1199-1200), Fisher (1201) and Gras (1202), listed above.

PRICES, PUBLIC FINANCE, BANKING AND FINANCIAL DEALINGS

(a) Prices

1650 McCulloch, J. R., ed., A Select Collection of Scarce and Valuable Tracts on Money (and Metallic Currency), 1856. Reprinted 1966.
1651 Shaw, W. A., ed., Select Tracts and Documents Illustrative of English Monetary

History, 1626-1730, 1896. Reprinted 1967. See also the sections on credit and money lending, high prices and the coinage and on taxation in Tawney and Power (982), listed above, II, 133-245.

1652 Beveridge, W. H., Prices and Wages in England from the Twelfth to the Nineteenth Century I: Prices Tables: The Mercantile Era, 1939. Reprinted 1966.

1653 Bowden, P. J., 'Agricultural prices, farm profits and rents'. In Thirsk (1180), listed above, 593-695. An important 'physical' interpretation of trends in agricultural prices.

1654 Braudel, F. P. and Spooner, F., 'Prices in Europe from 1450 to 1750'. In Rich and Wilson, eds. (1031), listed above, 378-486.

1655 Brenner Y. S., 'The inflation of prices in early sixteenth-century England', Ec.H.R., 2nd ser., XIV, 1961, 225-39.

1656 ——— 'The inflation of prices in England, 1551-1650', Ec.H.R., XV, 1962, 266-84.

1657 ———, 'The price revolution reconsidered: a reply', Ec.H.R., 2nd ser., XVIII, 1965, 392-6. A reply to Gould (1667), listed below.

1658 Brown, E. H. Phelps and Hopkins, Sheila, 'Seven centuries of building wages', Economica, XXII, 1955, 195-206. Reprinted in Carus-Wilson, ed. (164), listed above, II, 168-78.

1659 ——— 'Seven centuries of the prices of consumables, compared with builders' wage-rates', Economica, XXIII, 1956, 296-314. Reprinted in Carus-Wilson, ed. (164), listed above, II, 179-96.

1660 ——— 'Wage-rates and prices: evidence for population pressure in the sixteenth century', Economica, XXIV, 1957, 289-306.

1661 ——— 'Builders' wage-rates, prices and population: some further evidence', Economica, XXVI, 1959, 18-38. Influential articles. Although—as the titles make clear—their relevance extends beyond the period and subject of this present subsection, it has been thought most useful to group the articles together in series.

1662 Challis, C. E., 'The debasement of the coinage, 1542-1551', Ec.H.R., 2nd ser., XX, 1967, 441-66.

1663 ——— 'Currency and the economy in mid-Tudor England', Ec.H.R., 2nd ser., XXV, 1972, 313-22.

1664 Fisher, F. J., 'Influenza and inflation in Tudor England', Ec.H.R., 2nd ser., XVIII, 1965, 120-29. Argues that a sharp fall in prices in 1558 was possibly the result of an influenza epidemic in the preceding year.

1665 Gould, J. D., The Great Debasement: currency and the economy in mid-Tudor England, 1970. The most recent contribution in this field.

1666 ——— 'The Royal Mint in the early seventeenth century', Ec.H.R., 2nd ser., V, 1952, 240-8.

1667 ——— 'Y. S. Brenner on prices: a comment', Ec.H.R., 2nd ser., XVI, 1963, 351-60.

1668 ——— 'The price revolution reconsidered', Ec.H.R., 2nd ser., XVII, 1964, 249-66.

1669 Hamilton, E. J., 'American treasure and Andalusian prices, 1503-1660', Jnl. of Economic and Business History, I, 1928, 1-35. Related inflation to the influx of specie from the New World.

1670 Horsefield, J. K., British Monetary Experiments, 1650-1710, 1960.

1671 Li, Ming-Hsun, The Great Recoinage of 1696-9, 1963.

1672 Monroe, A. E., Monetary Theory before Adam Smith, 1923. Reprinted N.Y., 1966.

1673 Nef, J. U., 'Prices and industrial capitalism in France and England, 1540-1640', Ec.H.R., VII, 1937, 155-85. Reprinted in Carus-Wilson, ed. (164), listed above, I, 108-34.

1674 Outhwaite, R. B., Inflation in Tudor and Early Stuart England, 1969, Studies in Economic History series (pamphlet). A valuable summary, with a bibliographical guide to the growing literature of the subject.

1675 Price, J. M., 'Notes on some London price currents, 1667-1715', Ec.H.R., 2nd ser., VII, 1954, 240-50.

1676 Ramsey, P., ed., The Price Revolution in Sixteenth-Century England, 1971.

1677 Schumpeter, Elizabeth, 'English prices and public finance, 1660-1682', Review of Economics and Statistics, XX, 1938, 21-37.

1678 Supple, B. E., 'Currency and commerce in the early seventeenth century', Ec.H.R., 2nd ser., X, 1957, 239-55.

1679 Taylor, H., 'Price revolution or price revision? The English and Spanish trade after 1604', Renaissance and Modern Studies, XII, 1968, 5-32.

See also Burnett (825), Craig (410), Feavearyear (415), Thorold Rogers (419) and Shaw (421), listed above.

(b) Public finance: income and management

1680 Ashton, R., The Crown and the Money Market, 1603-40, 1960.

1681 ——— 'Charles I and the City'. In Fisher (1010), listed above, 138-63.

1682 ——— 'Revenue farming under the early Stuarts', Ec.H.R., 2nd ser., VIII, 1956, 310-22.

1683 ——— 'Deficit finance in the reign of James I', Ec.H.R., 2nd ser., X, 1957, 15-29.

1684 Aylmer, G. E., 'The last years of purveyance, 1610-60', Ec.H.R., 2nd ser., X, 1957, 81-93.

1685 ——— 'Attempts at administrative reform, 1625-40', E.H.R., LXXII, 1957, 229-59. See also Aylmer's detailed books (1726-1727), listed in the section on Government and administration

1686 Baxter, S. B., The Development of the Treasury, 1660-1702, 1957.

1687 Dietz, F., English Government Finance, 1485-1558, Urbana, Ill., 1920. Reprinted, with corrections, 1964.

Government Policy and Administration 49

1688 —— English Public Finance, 1558-1641, N.Y., 1932. Reprinted 1964.
1689 Elton, G. R., 'The Elizabethan Exchequer: war in the receipt'. In Bindoff, Hurstfield and Williams (992), listed above, 213-48.
1690 Harriss, G. L., 'Aids, loans and benevolences', Hist. Jnl., VI, 1963, 1-19.
1691 —— 'Fictitious loans', Ec.H.R., 2nd ser., VIII, 1955-56, 187-99.
1692 Hurstfield, J., The Queen's Wards: Wardship and Marriage under Elizabeth I, 1958. A scholarly investigation of the administration of wardships by the Court of Wards.
1693 —— 'The profits of fiscal feudalism', Ec.H.R., 2nd ser., VIII, 1955, 53-61.
1694 Mayes, L. R., 'The sale of peerages in early Stuart England', Jnl. Mod. Hist., XXIX, 1957, 21-37.
1695 Richards, R. D., 'The Exchequer in Cromwellian times', Ec.J. Economic History Supplement, II, 1931, 213-33.
1696 —— 'The stop of the Exchequer', Ec.J. Economic History Supplement, II, 1930, 45-62.
1697 Richardson, W. C., 'Some financial expedients of Henry VIII', Ec.H.R., 2nd ser., VII, 1954, 33-58.
1698 Stone, L., 'The inflation of honours, 1558-1641', P.P., 14, 1958, 45-70. See also Dickson (2823), listed below. The books by Dowell (427) and Roseveare (434) listed above, are also relevant in this connection. See also the section on Crown Lands listed under Agriculture and rural society.

(c) Banking and financial dealings

1699 Tawney, R. H., ed. Thomas Wilson's Discourse on Usury, 1572, 1925. Reprinted 1962. An interesting text with a very valuable historical introduction by Professor Tawney.
1700 Andréades, A. M., History of the Bank of England, 1640-1903, 1909, 4th ed., with an introduction by P. Einzig, 1966.
1701 Ashton, R., 'Usury and high finance in the age of Shakespeare and Jonson', Renaissance and Modern Studies, IV, 1960, 14-43.
1701a Bindoff, S. T., The Fame of Sir Thomas Gresham, 1973.
1702 Bisschop, W. R., The Rise of the London Money Market, 1640-1826, 1910. Reprinted 1968.
1703 Buckley, H., 'Sir Thomas Gresham and the foreign exchanges', Ec.J., 34, 1924, 589-601.
1704 Ehrenberg, R., Capital and Finance in the Age of the Renaissance, N.Y., 1928.
1705 Grassby, R., 'The rate of profit in seventeenth-century England', E.H.R., LXXXIV, 1969, 721-51.
1706 Holden J. M., 'Bills of exchange in the seventeenth century', Law Quarterly Review, LXVII, 1951, 230-48.
1707 Horsefield, J. K., 'The Bank of England as mentor', Ec.H.R., 2nd ser., II, 1949, 80-108.
1708 Lane, N., 'The origins of Lloyd's', History Today, 7, 1957, 848-53.
1709 —— 'The years before the Stock Exchange', History Today, 7, 1957, 760-5.
1710 Outhwaite, R. B., 'The trials of foreign borrowing: the English Crown and the Antwerp Money Market in the mid-sixteenth century', Ec.H.R., 2nd ser., XIX, 1966, 289-305.
1711 —— 'Royal borrowing in the reign of Elizabeth I: the Aftermath of Antwerp', E.H.R., LXXXVI, 1971, 251-63.
1712 Powell, E. T., The Evolution of the Money Market, 1385-1915, 1915. Reprinted 1966.
1713 Richards, R. D., The Early History of Banking in England, 1928. Reprinted 1958.
1714 —— 'The pioneers of banking in England', Ec.J. Economic History Supplement, I, 1929, 485-502.
1715 Roover, R. de, Gresham on Foreign Exchange: An Essay on Early English Mercantilism, With the Text of Sir Thomas Gresham's Memorandum for the Understanding of the Exchange, Cambridge, Mass., 1949. While the book as a whole is of considerable value, the question of the authorship of the Memorandum is less clear-cut than is suggested here.
1716 Rubini, D., 'Politics and the battle for the banks, 1688-1697', E.H.R., LXXXV, 1970, 693-714.
1717 Stone, L., An Elizabethan: Sir Horatio Palavicino, 1956. Palavicino was an important source of loans to the crown.
1718 Tucker, G. S. L., Progress and Profits in British Economic Thought, 1650-1850, 1960. Chapter 2 deals with 'The problem of interest in the seventeenth century'.
1719 Yamey, B. S., Edey, H. C. and Thomson H. W., Accounting in England and Scotland, 1543-1800, 1963.
1720 Yamey, B. S., 'Scientific book-keeping and the rise of capitalism', Ec.H.R., 2nd ser., I, 1948, 99-113.

GOVERNMENT POLICY AND ADMINISTRATION

(a) The central government

1721 Elton, G. R., ed., The Tudor Constitution: Documents and Commentary, 1960.
1722 Hughes, P. L. and Larkin, J. F., eds., Tudor Royal Proclamations, 1485-1603, 3 vols., New Haven and London, 1964-9.
1723 Kenyon, J. P., ed., The Stuart Constitution: Documents and Commentary, 1966.
1724 Ashley, M., Financial and Commercial Policy under the Cromwellian Protectorate, 1934, 2nd ed., 1962.
1725 Atton, H. and Holland, H. H., The King's Customs, 1600-1706, 2 vols., 1908-10. Reprinted 1968.
1726 Aylmer, G. E., The King's Servants: The Civil Service of Charles I, 1625-42, 1961, 2nd ed., 1974. An important and detailed investigation of the subject

50   England 1500-1700

1726a —— The State's Servants. The Civil Service of the English Republic 1649-1660, 1973.
1727 Baldwin, F. E., Sumptuary Legislation and Personal Regulation in England, John Hopkins University Studies in Historical and Political Science, ser. 44, No. 1, Baltimore, Md., 1926.
1728 Beresford, M. W., 'The common informer, the penal statutes and economic regulation', Ec.H.R., 2nd ser., X, 1957-8, 221-38.
1729 Bindoff, S. T., 'The making of the Statute of Artificers'. In Bindoff, Hurstfield and Williams, ed., (992), listed above, 59-94.
1730 Boynton, L., The Elizabethan Militia, 1966.
1731 Colvin, H. M., 'Castles and government in Tudor England', E.H.R., LXXXIII, 1968, 225-34.
1732 Cooper, J. P., 'Economic regulation and the cloth industry in seventeenth-century England', T. R.H.S., 5th ser., 20, 1970, 73-99.
1733 Davies, C. S. L., 'The administration of the royal navy under Henry VIII', E.H.R., LXXX, 1966, 268-86.
1734 —— 'Provisions for armies, 1509-60: a study in the effectiveness of early Tudor government', Ec.H.R., 2nd ser, XVII, 1964, 234-48.
1735 Davis, R., 'The rise of Protection in England, 1669-1786', Ec.H.R., XIX, 1966, 306-17.
1736 Elton, G. R., 'State planning in early Tudor England', Ec.H.R., 2nd ser., XIII, 1961, 433-9.
1737 —— The Tudor Revolution in Government, 1953. A controversial study which concentrates on Thomas Cromwell's administrative reforms and argues that they marked the end of the Middle Ages.
1737a —— Reform and Renewal: Thomas Cromwell and the Commonweal, 1973.
1738 —— Policy and Police, 1972. A study of the enforcement of the Henrican Reformation.
1739 —— Star Chamber Stories, 1958.
1740 —— 'Informing for profit: a sidelight on Tudor methods of law enforcement', Cambridge Hist. Jnl., XI, 1954, 149-67.
1741 Fox, H. G., Monopolies and Patents: A Study in the History and Future of the Patent Monopoly, Toronto and London, 1947.
1742 Harriss, G. L., 'Medieval government and statecraft', P.P., 25, 1963, 8-38. A criticism of the Tudor Revolution thesis. See also Williams (1756), listed below.
1743 Hughes, E., Studies in Administration and Finance, 1558-1825, With Special Reference to the History of Salt Taxation in England, 1934.
1744 —— 'The English Stamp Duties, 1664-1764', E.H.R., XVI, 1941, 234-64.
1745 Hurstfield, J., 'Was there a Tudor despotism after all?', T.R.H.S., 5th ser., XVII, 1967, 83-108.
1746 —— 'Political corruption in modern England: the historian's problem', History, LII, 1967, 16-34.
1747 Nef, J. U., Industry and Government in France and England, 1540-1640, Memoirs of the American Philosophical Society, XV, Philadelphia, 1940. Reprinted Ithaca, N.Y., 1957.
1748 Pearce, B., 'Elizabethan food policy and the armed forces', Ec.H.R., XII, 1942, 39-46.
1749 Pickthorn, K., Early Tudor Government I: Henry VII, 1934, revised 1949; II: Henry VIII, 1934.
1750 Prestwich, Menna, 'Diplomacy and trade in the Protectorate', Jnl. Mod. Hist., XXII, 1950, 103-21.
1751 Price, W. H., The English Patents of Monopoly, Boston and London, 1906. Documentary appendix.
1752 Read, C., 'Tudor economic policy', in R. L. Schuyler and H. Ausubel, eds., The Making of English History, N.Y., 1952, 195-201.
1753 Riemersma, J. C., 'Government influence on company organisation in Holland and England, 1550-1650', J.E.H., supplement 10, 1950, 31-9.
1754 Smith, A. G. R., The Government of Elizabethan England, 1967. A brief general survey with a guide to further reading.
1755 Stone, L., 'State control in sixteenth-century England', Ec.H.R., XVII, 1947, 103-20.
1756 Williams, P., 'The Tudor State', P.P., 25, 1963, 39-58. Takes a critical look at Elton's Tudor Revolution thesis. See also Harriss (1742), listed above.
1757 Wilson, C., 'Government policy and private interest in modern English history'. In Wilson (1045), listed above, 129-39. See also Margaret G. Davies (1854) and A. A. Gomme (2494), listed below.

(b) Local government

1758 Barnes, T. G., Somerset, 1625-40: A County's Government During the 'Personal Rule', 1961.
1759 Forster, G. C. F., The East Riding J.P. s in the Seventeenth Century, 1973.
1760 Gleason, J. H., The Justices of the Peace in England, 1558-1640, 1969.
1761 Moir, Esther A., The Justice of the Peace, 1969.
1762 Tate, W. E., The Parish Chest, 1946, 3rd ed., 1969. The best introduction to the records of parochial government.
1763 Trotter, Eleanor, Seventeenth-century Life in the Country Parish, With Special Reference to Local Government, 1919. Reprinted 1968.
1764 Webb, S. and Beatrice, English Local Government, 11 vols., 1906-29. Reprinted 1963, with new introductions. The Webbs' major work.
1765 Willcox, W. B., Gloucestershire: A Study in Local Government, 1590-1640, New Haven, Conn., 1940.

CLASSES AND SOCIAL GROUPS

(a) General and miscellaneous

1766 Ashley, M., 'Ordinary people in Stuart

England', History Today, 14, 1964, 192-201.
1767 Batho, G. R., 'The finances of an Elizabethan nobleman: Henry Percy, ninth Earl of Northumberland (1564-1631)', Ec.H.R., 2nd ser., IX, 1957, 433-50.
1768 Campbell, Mildred, The English Yeoman in the Tudor and Early Stuart Age, New Haven, Conn., 1942. Reprinted 1960. A valuable and well-documented treatment of the subject.
1769 Davies, K. G., 'The mess of the middle class', P.P., 22, 1962, 77-83.
1770 Everitt, A. M., 'Social mobility in England, 1500-1700', P.P., 33, 1966, 56-73. See also Stone (1781), listed below. An important article.
1771 Hexter, J. H., 'The myth of the middle class in Tudor England'. In the same author's Reappraisals in History, 1961, 71-116.
1772 —— 'The English aristocracy: its crises and the English Revolution', Jnl. of British Studies, VIII, 1968, 22-78.
1773 Hill, C., 'The many-headed monster in late Tudor and early Stuart political thinking'. In C. H. Carter, ed., From Renaissance to Counter-Reformation, 1966, 296-324.
1774 Ives, E. W., 'The reputation of the common lawyer in English society 1450-1550', Birm. Hist. Jnl., VII, 1960, 130-61.
1775 Ross, D., 'Class privilege in seventeenth-century England', History, XXVIII, 1943, 148-55.
1776 Speck, W. A., 'Social status in late Stuart England', P.P., 34, 1966, 127-129. A comment on Stone's article on social mobility (1781), listed below.
1777 Stone, L., The Crisis of the Aristocracy, 1558-1641, 1965. A massive study which not only presents the 'crisis' thesis, but also comprehensively surveys the whole socio-economic setting and activities of the aristocracy. See the review articles on this book by D. C. Coleman in History, LI, 1966, 165-78; by R. Ashton in Ec.H.R., 2nd ser., XXII, 308-22; and by A. M. Everitt in Ag.H.R., XVI, 1968, 60-7.
1778 —— Family and Fortune. Studies in Aristocratic Finance in the Sixteenth and Seventeenth Centuries, 1973. A series of case studies which supplement Stone's Crisis of the Aristocracy.
1779 —— 'The anatomy of the Elizabethan aristocracy', Ec.H.R., XVIII, 1948, 1-53.
1780 —— 'The Elizabethan aristocracy—a restatement', Ec.H.R., 2nd ser., IV, 1952, 302-21.
1781 —— 'Social mobility in England, 1500-1700', P.P., 33, 1966, 16-55. See also Everitt (1770) and Speck (1776), listed above. Stone's book Social Change and Revolution (1798), listed below, is also relevant in this connection.
1782 Styles, P., 'The social structure of Kineton hundred in the reign of Charles II', Trans. Birmingham Archaeological Society, LXXVIII, 1962, 96-117.

1783 Supple, B. E., 'Class and social tension: the case of the merchant', in Ives (1910), listed below, 131-43.
1784 Trevor-Roper, H. R., 'The Elizabethan aristocracy: an anatomy anatomized', Ec.H.R., 2nd ser., III, 1951, 279-98. A highly critical examination of Stone's article (1779), listed above.
See also the articles by Ashton (1910) and Manning (1954), listed below, on social tensions in the Civil War.

(b) **The gentry and their estates**

This section is not intended to be self-contained. It should, for example, be seen in conjunction with those on Landholding and the Land market.

1785 Clay, C., 'Marriage, inheritance and the rise of large estates in England, 1660-1815', Ec.H.R., 2nd ser., XXI, 1968, 503-18.
1786 Cliffe, J. T., The Yorkshire Gentry from the Reformation to the Civil War, 1969. An important regional study.
1787 Cooper, J. P., 'The counting of manors', Ec.H.R., 2nd ser., VIII, 1956, 377-89. A significant contribution to the debate on the gentry which pointed out the statistical errors underlying Tawney's thesis (1800), listed below.
1788 Cornwall, J., 'The early Tudor gentry', Ec.H.R., 2nd ser., XVII, 1965, 456-71.
1789 Finch, Mary E., The Wealth of Five Northamptonshire Families, Northamptonshire Record Society, XIX, 1956. An interesting and valuable book. One of the first real attempts to approach the gentry controversy using the method of case-study rather than that of generalisation.
1790 Hexter, J. H., 'Storm over the gentry'. In the same author's Reappraisals in History, 1961, 117-62. A very good—and witty—summary of the gentry controversy.
1791 Hoskins, W. G., 'The estates of the Caroline gentry'. In Hoskins and Finberg, eds., (1055), listed above, 334-65.
1792 Laslett, P., 'The gentry of Kent in 1640', Cambridge Historical Jnl., IX, 1948, 148-64. See also the book by Everitt (1977), listed below.
1793 Lavrovsky, V. M., 'The Great Estate in England from the sixteenth to the eighteenth centuries', First International Conference of Economic History, Contributions and Communications, Stockholm, 1960, 353-65.
1794 Lloyd, H. A., The Gentry of South-west Wales, 1540-1640, 1968.
1795 Mousley, J. E., 'The fortunes of some gentry families of Elizabethan Sussex', Ec.H.R., 2nd ser., XI, 1958, 467-83.
1796 Roots, I., 'Gentlemen and others', History, XLVII, 1962, 233-8.
1797 Simpson, A., The Wealth of the Gentry, 1540-1660, Chicago and Cambridge, 1961.
1798 Stone, L., Social Change and Revolution in England, 1540-1640, 1965. Summarises the gentry controversy, providing extracts from contemporary sources and from the main contributions to the historical debate. Useful bibliography.

England 1500-1700

1799 ——— 'The fruits of office: the case of Robert Cecil, first Earl of Salisbury, 1596-1612'. In Fisher (1010), listed above, 89-116.
1800 Tawney, R. H., 'The rise of the gentry, 1558-1640', Ec.H.R., XI, 1941, 1-38. The famous article which initiated the gentry controversy. See also Tawney's 'Postscript', Ec.H.R., 2nd ser., VII, 1954, 91-7. Both are reprinted in Carus-Wilson, ed. (164), listed above, I, 173-214.
1801 ——— 'Harrington's interpretation of his age', Proceedings of the British Academy, XXVII, 1941, 199-223.
1802 Trevor-Roper, H. R., The Gentry, 1540-1640 (Ec.H.R. supplements, I), 1953. A vigorous attack on the Tawney thesis, arguing that the 'mere gentry', who lacked access to profitable offices in royal administration and whose income was derived entirely from the land, actually declined during this period.
1803 Upton, A. P., Sir Arthur Ingram, c. 1565-1642: A Study of the Origins of an English Landed Family, 1961.
1804 Williams, W. O., 'The Anglesey gentry as businessmen in Tudor and Stuart times', Anglesey Antiquarian Society and Field Club Trans., 1948, 100-14.
1805 Wood, A. C., 'The Holles Family', T.R.H.S., 4th ser., 19, 1936, 145-65.

POOR RELIEF: CHARITY AND THE POOR LAW

For the medieval background, see:
1806 Clay, Rotha M., The Medieval Hospitals of England, 1909. Reprinted, 1966.
1807 Tierney, B., Medieval Poor Law: A Sketch of Canonical Theory and its Application in England, Berkeley and Los Angeles, 1959.

1808 Cutlack, S. A., ed., The Gnosall Records, 1679-1837, Staffordshire Record Society, I, 1936.
1809 Emmison, F. G., 'The care of the poor in Elizabethan Essex: recently discovered records', Essex Review, LXII, 1953, 7-28.
1810 ——— 'Poor relief accounts of two rural parishes in Bedfordshire, 1563-98', Ec.H.R., III, 1931, 102-16.
1811 Fish, Simon, A Supplication for the Beggars (1528). An extract is printed in G. R. Elton, ed., The Tudor Constitution, 1960, 322-4.
1812 Fry, A. Ruth, Ed., John Bellers, 1654-1725: Quaker, Economist and Social Reformer, 1935. Contains, inter al., extracts from Bellers's Proposals for Raising a College of Industry (1696) and from his Essays about the Poor, Manufacturers, Trade, Plantations and Immorality (1699).
1813 Melling, Elizabeth ed., The Poor: A Collection of Examples from Original Sources in the Kent Archives Office from the Sixteenth to the Nineteenth Century, 1964.
1814 Salter, F. R., ed., Some Early Tracts on Poor Relief, 1926. Mainly a collection of early European treatises and ordinances, but the text of the English legislation of 1531 and 1536 is included.
1815 Tanner, J. R., ed., Tudor Constitutional Documents, 1485-1603, 1922, 2nd ed., 1930. Has a section on vagabonds, beggars and poor relief, 469-95.
1816 Webb, J., ed., Poor Relief in Elizabethan Ipswich, Suffolk Record Society, IX, 1966. A collection of documents with an introduction.
1817 Wilkins, H. J., ed., Transcription of the Poor Book of the Tithings of Westbury on Trym, Stoke Bishop and Shirehampton from 1656-1698, 1910.
1818 Williams, E. N., ed., A Documentary History of England 2: 1558-1931. Contains the text of the 1598 act and a commentary. See also Bland, Brown and Tawney (141), listed above, Part II, section IV, 366-96, and Tawney and Power (982), listed above, II, 296-369, III, 405-58, for other source material on this subject.
1819 Aydelotte, F., Elizabethan Rogues and Vagabonds, 1913. Reprinted 1967.
1820 Bagley, J. J. and A. J., The English Poor Law, 1968. A short introduction with suggestions for further reading.
1821 Beier, A. L., 'Poor relief in Warwickshire, 1630-1660', P.P., 35, 1966, 77-100. Argues that the Civil War did not bring about a general breakdown in poor relief.
1822 Cannan, E., History of Local Rates in England, 1896, 4th ed., 1927.
1823 Davies, C. S. L., 'Slavery and Protector Somerset: the Vagrancy Act of 1547', Ec.H.R., 2nd ser., XIX, 1966, 533-49.
1824 Eden, F. M., The State of the Poor; or, A History of the Labouring Classes in England from the Conquest to the Present Period, 3 vols., 1797. Reprinted 1966.
1825 Elton, G. R., 'An early Tudor Poor Law', Ec.H.R., 2nd ser., VI, 1953, 55-67.
1826 Fessler, A., 'The official attitude towards the sick poor in seventeenth-century Lancashire', T.H.S.L.C., 102, 1951, 85-114.
1827 Gray, B. K., A History of English Philanthropy from the Dissolution of the Monasteries to the Taking of the First Census, 1905. Reprinted 1967.
1828 Hampson, Ethel M., The Treatment of Poverty in Cambridgeshire, 1597-1834, 1934. An important regional study.
1829 Hill, C., 'Puritans and the poor', P.P., 2, 1952, 32-50. Reprinted in Hill (1932), listed below, as 'William Perkins and the poor', 215-38.
1830 ——— 'The Poor and the parish'. In Hill (2025), listed below, 259-97.
1831 James, Margaret, Social Problems and Policy During the Puritan Revolution, 1930. Reprinted 1966.
1832 Jones, G. H., History of the Law of Charity, 1532-1827, 1969. The first five chapters deal with the pre-1700 period.
1833 Jones, G. P., 'The poverty of Cumberland and Westmorland', Trans. Cumberland and Westmorland Antiquarian and Archaeological Society, LV, 1956, 198-208.

1834 Jordan, W. K., Philanthropy in England: A study of the Changing Pattern of English Social Aspirations, 1480-1660, 1959.
1835 ——— The Charities of Rural England, 1480-1660, 1961.
1836 ——— The Charities of London, 1480-1660, 1961.
1837 ——— The Social Institutions of Lancashire, Chet. Soc., 3rd ser., 11, 1962.
1838 ——— Social institutions in Kent, 1480-1660, Archaeologia Cantiana, 75, 1961.
1839 ——— The Forming of the Charitable Institutions of the West of England, American Philosophical Society Trans., n.s., 50, Part 8, Philadelphia, 1960. Altogether, Jordan's work amounts to a monumental study of the patterns of charitable giving in the early modern period. From a quantitative point of view, however, Jordan is less useful, since the Price Rise is not taken into account.
1840 Judges, A. V., The Elizabethan Underworld, 1930. Reprinted 1965.
1841 Kiernan, V. G., 'Puritanism and the poor', P.P., 3, 1953, 45-54. A comment on Hill (1829), listed above.
1842 Leonard, Elizabeth M., The Early History of English Poor Relief, 1900. Reprinted 1965. Still the standard work though largely by default.
1843 Marshall, Dorothy, 'The old Poor Law, 1662-1795', Ec.H.R., VIII, 1937, 38-47. Reprinted in Carus-Wilson, ed. (164), listed above, I, 295-305.
1844 Nicholls, G. and MacKay, T., A History of the English Poor Law, 3 vols., 1854, new edition 1898-1904. Reprinted 1968.
1845 Pinchbeck, Ivy and Hewitt, Margaret, Children in English Society I: From Tudor Times to the Eighteenth Century, 1969. Chapters 5-9 are particularly relevant in this connection. Good bibliography.
1846 Pound, J. F., Poverty and Vagrancy in Tudor England, 1971.
1847 ——— 'An Elizabethan census of the poor. The treatment of vagrancy in Norwich, 1570-80', Birm. Hist. Jnl., VIII, 1962, 135-61.
1848 Rodgers, B., The Battle against Poverty I: From Pauperism to Human Rights, 1969.
1849 Steinbicker, C. R., Poor Relief in the Sixteenth Century, Studia Facultas Theologica, Washington, D.C., 1937. A Roman Catholic attempt to show that Catholic countries excelled Protestant in providing for the poor.
1850 Styles, P., 'The evolution of the Law of Settlement', Birm. Hist. Jnl., IX, 1963, 33-63. See also the Webbs (3746), Bruce (2230) and Owen (3756), listed below.

LABOUR

1851 Buckatzsch, E. J., 'Occupations in the parish registers of Sheffield, 1655-1719', Ec.H.R., 2nd ser., I, 1948-9, 145-50.
1852 Clark, Alice, The Working Life of Women in the Seventeenth Century, 1919. Reprinted 1968. A useful study.
1853 Coleman, D. C., 'Labour in the English economy in the seventeenth century', Ec.H.R., 2nd ser., VIII, 1956, 280-95. Reprinted in Carus-Wilson, ed. (164), listed above, II, 291-308. An important and wide-ranging article.
1854 Davies, Margaret G., The Enforcement of English Apprenticeship 1563-1642: A Study in Applied Mercantilism, Harvard, Mass., 1956. A useful study showing the gulf between the theory and practice of Tudor economic legislation.
1855 Dunlop, O. J. and Denham, R. D., English Apprenticeship and Child Labour, 1912.
1856 Everitt, A. M., 'Farm labourers'. In Thirsk (1180), listed above, 396-465. A very valuable study of a neglected subject.
1857 Furniss, E. S., The Position of the Labourer in a System of Nationalism, Boston and N.Y., 1920. Reprinted N.Y., 1957.
1858 Fussell, G. E., The English Rural Labourer, 1949.
1859 Glass, D. V., 'Socio-economic status and occupations in the city of London at the end of the seventeenth century'. In Hollaender and Kellaway (486), listed above, 373-89.
1860 Gregory, T. E., 'The economics of employment in England, 1660-1713', Economica, I, 1921, 37-51.
1861 Habakkuk, H. J., 'La disparition du paysan anglais', Annales, 20e année, 1965, 649-63.
1862 Hart, C. E., The Free Miners of the Forest of Dean, 1953.
1863 Hasbach, W., History of the English Agricultural Labourer, 1908. Reprinted 1966.
1864 Hill, C., 'Pottage for free-born Englishmen: attitudes to wage labour in the sixteenth and seventeenth centuries'. In C.H. Feinstein, ed., Socialism, Capitalism and Economic Growth, 1967, 338-50. Considers the stigma which was attached to wage labour in the sixteenth and seventeenth centuries and suggests that this helps explain working class reluctance to enter the early factories of the Industrial Revolution.
1865 Hole, Christina, The English Housewife in the Seventeenth Century, 1953. See also Clark (1852), listed above in this section.
1866 Hoskins, W. G., 'The farm labourer through four centuries'. In Hoskins and Finberg (1055), listed above, 419-41.
1867 Jenkin, A. K. Hamilton, The Cornish Miner, 1927, 3rd. ed., 1962.
1868 Kelsall, R. K., Wage Regulation under the Statute of Artificers, 1938. The standard work. See Minchinton (1874), listed below.
1869 ——— 'A century of wage assessment in Herefordshire', E.H.R., LVII, 1942, 115-19.
1870 ——— 'Statute wages during a Yorkshire epidemic 1679-81', Yorkshire Archaeological Jnl., 34, 1939, 310-19.
1871 Knoop, D. and Jones, G. P., The Sixteenth-century Mason, 1937.
1872 ——— The London Mason in the Seventeenth Century, 1935.
1873 ——— 'Overtime in the age of Henry VIII',

Ec.J. Economic History Supplement, 3, 1938, 13-20.

1874 Minchinton, W. E., ed., Wage Regulation in Pre-industrial England, 1971. A valuable reprint of the works by Tawney (1877) and Kelsall (1868), listed above, with a new introductory essay.

1875 Norman, F. A. and Lee, L. G., 'Labour exchanges in the seventeenth century', Ec.J. Economic History Supplement, 1, 1928, 399-404.

1876 Ransome, D. R., 'Artisan dynasties in London and Westminster in the sixteenth century', Guildhall Miscellany, II, 1964, 236-47.

1877 Tawney, R. H., 'The assessment of wages in England by the justices of the peace', Vierteljahrschrift für Sozial- und Wirtschaftsgeschichte, 11, 1913, 307-37, 533-64. See Minchinton (1874), listed above.

1878 —— 'An occupational census of the seventeenth century', Ec.H.R., V, 1934-5, 25-64. An important article, analysing the occupational structure of Gloucestershire as revealed in the muster roll of 1608. Shows the intertwining of agriculture and industry.

1879 Woodward, D. M., 'The assessment of wages by justices of the peace, 1563-1813', The Local Historian, VIII, 1969, 293-9. See also the articles by Phelps Brown and Hopkins (1658-1661), and Tanner (1815), listed above, who has a section on the regulation of wages and labour, 502-6.

STANDARDS OF LIVING

1880 Batho, G. R., ed., The Household Papers of Henry Percy, Ninth Earl of Northumberland, Camden Society, 3rd ser., XCIII, 1962.

1881 Cash, M., Devon Inventories of the Sixteenth and Seventeenth Centuries, Devon and Cornwall Record Society, n.s. XI, 1966.

1882 Harland, J., ed., The Household and Farm Accounts of the Shuttleworths of Gawthorpe Hall from September 1582 to October 1621, Chet. Soc., o.s., 35, 41, 43, 46, 1856-8.

1883 Havinden, M. A., ed., Household and Farm Inventories in Oxfordshire, 1550-1590, 1965.

1884 Ashmore, O., 'Household inventories of the Lancashire gentry, 1550-1700', T.H.S.L.C., 110, 1958, 59-105.

1885 Barley, M. W., The English Farmhouse and Cottage, 1961. A valuable study. Well illustrated.

1886 —— 'Rural housing in England'. In Thirsk (1180), listed above, 696-766.

1887 Cunnington, C. W. and Phillis, Handbook of English Costume in the sixteenth Century, 1954, 2nd rev. ed., 1970.

1888 Emmison, F. G., Tudor Food and Pastimes, 1964.

1889 Hole, Christina, English Home Life, 1500-1800, 1947.

1890 Hoskins, W. G., 'The rebuilding of rural England, 1570-1640', P.P., 4, 1953, 44-59 Reprinted in Hoskins (1053), listed above, 131-48. An important article.

1891 Mercer, E., 'The houses of the gentry', P.P., 5, 1954, 11-32.

1892 Rive, A., 'The consumption of tobacco since 1600', Ec. J. Economic History Supplements, I, 1926, 57-75.

1893 Smith, J. T., 'The evolution of the English peasant house in the late seventeenth century', Jnl. British Archaeological Association, XXXIII, 1970, 122-47.

1894 Smith, P., 'Rural housing in Wales'. In Thirsk (1180), listed above, 767-813.

1895 Thomas, K., 'Work and Leisure in pre-industrial society. Conference paper and discussion', P.P., 29, 1964, 50-66.

1896 Thomson, Gladys Scott, Life in a Noble Household, 1641-1700, 1937.

1897 Willan, T. S., 'Sugar and the Elizabethans', In Willan (1498), listed above, 313-32. See also Phelps Brown and Hopkins (1658-1661), Harrison (977), Dover Wilson (986), Stone (1777) and Campbell (1768), listed above, all of which are relevant in this connection.

CIVIL WAR, INTERREGNUM, RESTORATION AND REVOLUTION, 1640-89

What follows is only a selection—though, it is hoped, a representative one—on the period 1640-89. It should, for example, be seen in conjunction with the sections on Classes and social groups and on Religion. For further bibliographical guidance on the English Civil War, the reader is referred to Roots (1950), Manning (1943) and Ives (1941), listed below.

(a) Sources

1898 Bamford, F., ed., A Royalist's Notebook: the Commonplace Book of Sir John Oglander, Knight, 1936. The archetype of the grumbling 'mere gentleman'.

1899 Baxter, Richard, Autobiography, ed. J. M. Lloyd-Thomas, Everyman ed., 1931, new edition 1974. Baxter—1615-91—was a puritan divine; his autobiography forms a valuable contemporary account of the troubles of the mid-seventeenth century and provides some revealing insights into the line-up of society in the Civil War.

1900 Clarendon, Earl of, History of the Rebellion, ed. W. D. Macray, 6 vols., 1888. There is also a one-volume edition of Selections from Clarendon, ed. G. Huenns, 1955. Clarendon's History is the classic Royalist account of the Civil War.

1901 Gardiner, Dorothy, ed., Oxinden Letters, 1607-42, 1933; Peyton Letters, 1642-70, 1937.

1902 Hill, C. and Dell, E. M., The Good Old Cause, 1949, 2nd ed., 1969. A useful collection of documents.

1903 Hutchinson, Lucy, Memoirs of the Life of Colonel Hutchinson, ed. C. H. Firth, 2 vols., 1885. Other editions are available in the

Bohn's Library series, 1904, and in Everyman's Library, 1936.
1904 James, Margaret and Weinstock, Maureen, England During the Interregnum, 1642-60. (University of London Intermediate Source Books of History), 1935.
1905 Prall, S. E., ed., The Puritan Revolution, A Documentary History, 1969. A well-chosen selection.
1906 Woodhouse, A. S. P., ed., Puritanism and Liberty, Being the Army Debates, 1647-49. 1938, 3rd ed., 1974.

(b) General

1907 Aiken, W. A. and Henning, B. D., eds., Conflict in Stuart England, Essays in honour of Wallace Notestein, 1960.
1908 Allan, D. G. C., 'Politics and the climate of economic opinion, 1660-88', Notes and Queries, n.s., III, 1956, 254-58.
1909 Ashton, R., 'Cavaliers and capitalists', Renaissance and Modern Studies, V, 1961, 149-75.
1910 ——— 'The Civil War and the class struggle', in Parry (1945), listed below, 93-110. See also Manning (1944), listed below.
1911 Aylmer, G. E., ed., The Interregnum: The Quest for Settlement 1646-60, 1972. Includes an important essay by J. P. Cooper on social and economic policy.
1912 Brinton, C., The Anatomy of Revolution, N.Y., 1938, 2nd ed., N.Y., 1952, London, 1953.
1913 Brunton, D. and Pennington, D. H., Members of the Long Parliament, 1954. Reprinted 1968. An analysis—on Namierite lines—of the social composition of the Long Parliament. The book threw doubts on some well-known generalisations about Royalists and Roundheads, but was itself much criticised. See Hill (1932), listed below, and
1914 Manning, B., 'The Long Parliament', P.P., 5, 1954, 71-6. See also Keeler (1941), listed below.
1915 Coates, W. H., 'An analysis of major conflicts in seventeenth-century England'. In Aiken and Henning (1907), listed above, 15-40.
1916 Davies, G., The Restoration of Charles II, 1658-1660, 1955.
1917 Elton, G. R., 'A high road to Civil War', in C. H. Carter, ed., From Renaissance to Counter-Reformation, 1966, 325-47.
1918 Engberg, J., 'Royalist finances during the English Civil War, 1642-46', Scand. Ec.H.R., XIV, 1966, 73-96.
1919 Everitt, A. M., 'The county community'. In Ives (1941), listed below.
1920 ——— The Local Community and the Great Rebellion, Historical Association pamphlet, 1969. A valuable short essay. See also the two specialised studies by Everitt (1976-1977), listed below.
1921 Firth, C., The Last Years of the Protectorate, 1656-58, 2 vols., 1909. A continuation of Gardiner (1924), listed below.
1922 French, A., Charles I and the Puritan Upheaval: A Study of the Causes of the Great Migration, 1955.
1923 Gardiner, S. R., History of the Great Civil War, 1642-49, 4 vols., 1893.
1924 ——— History of the Commonwealth and Protectorate, 4 vols., 1893. Continued by Firth (1921), listed above. As a detailed narrative, Gardiner remains unsuperseded.
1925 Habakkuk, H. J., 'Landowners and the Civil War', Ec.H.R., 2nd ser., XVIII, 1965, 130-51. See also Thirsk (1954), listed below.
1926 ——— 'Public finance and the sale of confiscated property during the Interregnum', Ec.H.R., 2nd ser., XV, 1962-3, 70-88.
1927 ——— 'The Parliamentary army and the crown lands', Welsh History Review, 3, 1966-7, 403-26.
1928 ——— 'English landownership, 1680-1740', Ec.H.R., X, 1940, 2-17.
1929 Hammersley, G., 'The revival of the Forest laws under Charles I', History, XLV, 1960 85-102.
1930 Hardacre, P. H., The Royalists during the Puritan Revolution, The Hague, 1956.
1931 Hill, C., The English Revolution, 1948, revised 1955.
1932 ——— Puritanism and Revolution: Studies in the Interpretation of the English Revolution of the Seventeenth Century, 1958.
1933 ——— The Intellectual Origins of the English Revolution, 1965.
1934 ——— God's Englishman: Oliver Cromwell and the English Revolution, 1970.
1935 ——— The World Turned Upside Down. Radical Ideas During the English Revolution, 1972.
1936 ——— 'Soviet interpretations of the English Interregnum', Ec.H.R., VIII, 1937-8, 159-67.
1937 ——— 'Cavaliers, Roundheads or neither?', Amateur Historian, I, 1952, 13-17.
1938 Hobsbawm, E. J., 'The crisis of the seventeenth century', P.P., 5, 6, 1954, 33-53, 44-65. Reprinted in Aston (990), listed above, 5-58. See also Trevor-Roper (1958), listed below.
1939 Holiday, P. G., 'Land sales and repurchases in Yorkshire after the Civil Wars, 1650-1670', Northern History, V, 1970, 67-92.
1940 Ives, E. W., ed., The English Revolution, 1600-1660, 1968. A useful collection of short essays, originally broadcast talks, with guides to further reading.
1941 Keeler, Mary F., The Long Parliament: A Biographical Study of its Members, American Philosophical Society, Philadelphia, 1954. See also Brunton and Pennington (1913), listed above.
1942 Madge, S. J., The Domesday of Crown Lands: A Study of the Legislation, Surveys and Sales of Royal Estates Under the Commonwealth, 1938. See also Thirsk (1954), listed below.
1943 Manning, B., ed., Politics, Religion and the English Civil War, 1973.
1944 ——— 'The outbreak of the English Civil War'. In Parry (1958), listed below, 1-21. A stimulating article.

1945 Parry, R. H., ed., The English Civil War and After, 1642-1658, 1970.
1946 Pearl, Valerie, 'The Royal Independents' in the English Civil War', T.R.H.S., 5th ser., 18, 1968, 69-96.
1947 —— 'London's Counter-revolution'. In Aylmer (1911), listed above, 29-56.
1948 Pennington, D. H., 'The cost of the English Civil War', History Today, 7, 1958, 126-33.
1949 —— 'The accounts of the Kingdom'. In Fisher (1010), listed above, 182-203.
1949a Richardson, R. C., 'The English Revolution and the historians', Literature and History, 1, 1975, 28-48. Surveys the historiography from the seventeenth century to the present day.
1950 Roots, I., The Great Rebellion, 1640-60, 1966. A brave attempt at a one-volume history, mainly political in scope. Good bibliography.
1951 Russell, C., ed., The Origins of the English Civil War, 1973. Includes essays by Conrad Russell, 'Parliament and the King's finances', and by Penelope Corfield, 'Economic issues and ideologies'.
1952 Stone, L., The Causes of the English Revolution, 1529-1642, 1972. A useful and stimulating group of studies of the period. The longest section is on the causes of the Revolution which are sensibly discussed under the headings presuppositions, preconditions, precipitants, and triggers.
1953 Taylor, P. A. M., ed., The Origins of the English Civil War: Conspiracy, Crusade or Class Conflict?, Boston, Mass., 1960. A collection of extracts.
1954 Thirsk, Joan, 'The sale of Royalist lands during the Interregnum', Ec.H.R., 2nd ser., V, 1952, 188-207. An important article which shows that the confiscated lands of royalists were commonly being re-acquired by their former owners before the Restoration.
1955 —— 'The Restoration land settlement', Jnl. Mod. Hist., XXVI, 1954, 315-28.
1956 Trevelyan, G. M., England under the Stuarts, 1904, 12th rev. ed., 1925. An elderly textbook though not without its uses.
1957 Trevor-Roper, H. R., 'The social origins of the Great Rebellion', History Today, 5, 1955, 376-82.
1958 —— 'The general crisis of the seventeenth century', P.P., 16, 1959, 31-64. Reprinted in Aston (990), listed above, 59-96.
1959 Underdown, D., Royalist Conspiracy in England, 1649-1660, New Haven, Conn., 1960.
1960 —— 'The Independents again', Jnl. of British Studies, VIII, 1968, 83-93. Part of a debate on the subject. See Yule (2002), listed below.
1961 Walzer, M., The Revolution of the Saints, 1966. A sociological study which analyses the role of puritan ideology in the English Revolution.
1962 Wedgwood, C. Veronica, The King's Peace, 1637-41, 1955.
1963 —— The King's War, 1641-47, 1958. Mainly political narrative.
1964 —— 'The causes of the English Civil War', History Today, 5, 1955, 670-76. Deals with an aspect which was largely omitted from her books on the Civil War and its background.
1965 Wilson, C. 'Economics and politics in the seventeenth century', Hist. Jnl., V, 1962, 80-92. Reprinted in Wilson (1045), listed above, 1-21.
1966 Woolrych, A., 'The English Revolution: an introduction'. In Ives (1940), listed above, 1-33.
1967 —— 'Puritanism, politics and society'. In ibid., 87-100.
1968 Yule, G., The Independents in the English Civil War, 1957.
1969 —— 'Independents and revolutionaries', Jnl. of British Studies, VII, 1967, 11-32.
1970 Zagorin, P., The Court and the Country. The Beginning of the English Revolution, 1969. Stresses the constitutional aspect of the Rebellion, but at the same time places it firmly in its socio-economic setting.
1971 —— 'The social interpretation of the English Revolution', J.E.H., XIX, 1959, 376-401.
1972 —— 'The English Revolution', Jnl. of World History, II, 1955, 668-81.
See also Stone (1777), listed above.

(c) Regional studies

1973 Blackwood, B. G., 'The Lancashire cavaliers and their tenants', T.H.S.L.C., 117, 1965, 17-32.
1974 Coate, Mary, Cornwall in the Great Civil War and Interregnum, 1642-1660, 1933. Reprinted 1963.
1975 Dore, R. N., The Civil Wars in Cheshire, 1966.
1976 Everitt, A. M., Suffolk and the Great Rebellion, Suffolk Record Society, III, 1960.
1977 —— The Community of Kent and the Great Rebellion, 1640-60, 1966. See the two shorter and more general works by Everitt on the same subject (1919-1920), listed above.
1978 Farrar, W. J., The Great Civil War in Shropshire, 1642-49, 1926.
1979 Guttery, D. R., The Great Civil War in Midland Parishes, 1950.
1979a Holmes, C., The Eastern Association in the English Civil War, 1974. An interesting analysis of the interaction between local and national issues.
1980 Howell, R., Jnr., Newcastle-upon-Tyne and the Puritan Revolution: A Study of the Civil War in Northern England, 1967.
1981 Ketton-Cremer, R. W., Norfolk in the Civil War, 1969. Looks solid and old-fashioned in comparison with Everitt (1977), listed above.
1982 Leach, A. L., The History of the Civil War, 1642-49, in Pembrokeshire and on its Borders, 1937.
1983 Lennard, R. V., Rural Northamptonshire under the Commonwealth, Oxford Studies in Social and Legal History, 1916.

1983a Morrill, J. S., Cheshire 1630-1660: County Government and Society During the English Revolution, 1974.
1984 Pearl, Valerie, London and the Outbreak of the Puritan Revolution, 1961.
1985 Pennington, D. H., and Roots, I., The Committee at Stafford, 1643-45: The Order Book of the Staffordshire County Committee, 1957.
1986 Tupling, G. H., 'The causes of the Civil War in Lancashire', T.L.C.A.S., LXV, 1955, 1-32.
1987 Underdown, D., Somerset in the Civil War and Interregnum, 1973.
1988 Wood, A. C., Nottinghamshire in the Civil War, 1937.

(d) Miscellaneous

1989 Berens, C. H., The Digger Movement in the Days of the Commonwealth, 1906. Reprinted 1961.
1990 Brailsford, H. N., The Levellers and the English Revolution, 1961.
1991 Cole, W. A., 'The Quakers and the English Revolution', P.P., 9, 1956, 39-54. Reprinted in Aston (990), listed above, 341-58.
1992 Davis, J. C., 'The Levellers and Democracy', P.P., 40, 1968, 174-80.
1993 Gordon, M. D., 'The collection of Ship Money in the reign of Charles I', T.R.H.S., 3rd ser., 4, 1910, 141-62.
1994 Gregg, Pauline, Free-born John: A Biography of John Lilburne, 1961.
1995 Lamont, W. M., Marginal Prynne, 1600-1669, 1963.
1996 Manning, B., 'The Levellers'. In Ives (1940), listed above, 144-57. Contains a bibliographical note on the subject.
1997 Petegorsky, D. W., Left-wing Democracy in the English Civil War: A Study of the Social Philosophy of Gerrard Winstanley, 1940.
1998 Prall, S. E., The Agitation for Law Reform During the Puritan Revolution, 1640-60, 1966. See Veall (2001), listed below.
1999 Thomas, K., 'Women and the Civil War sects', P.P., 13, 1958, 42-62. Reprinted in Aston (990), listed above, 317-40.
2000 —— 'The social origins of Hobbes' political thought'. In K. Brown, ed., Hobbes Studies, 1965, 185-236.
2001 Veall, D., The Popular Movement for Law Reform, 1640-1660, 1970. See also Prall (1998), listed above.
2002 Yule, G., The Independents in the Civil War, Melbourne and Cambridge, 1958.

RELIGION

(a) General and miscellaneous

2003 Ashton, R., 'Puritanism and progress', Ec.H.R., 2nd ser., XVII, 1965, 579-87. A review article on Hill (2025), listed below.
2004 Barbour, H., The Quakers in Puritan England, Yale, 1964.
2005 Bebb, E. D., Nonconformity and Social Life, 1660-1800, 1935.
2006 Blackwood, B. G., 'Agrarian unrest and the early Lancashire Quakers', Jnl. Friends' Historical Society, LI, 1966, 72-6.
2007 Bossy, J., 'The character of Elizabethan Catholicism', P.P., 21, 1962, 39-59. Reprinted in T. H. Aston, ed., Crisis in Europe, 1965, 223-46. An important article presenting a social interpretation of Catholicism in the period.
2008 Bouch, C. M. L., Prelates and People of the Lake Counties: A History of the Diocese of Carlisle, 1133-1933, 1948.
2009 Breslow, M. A., A Mirror of England. English Puritan Views of Foreign Nations 1618-40, Cambridge, Mass., 1970.
2010 Capp, B. S., The Fifth Monarchy Men, 1972.
2011 Cole, W. A., 'The social origins of the early Friends', Jnl. Friends' Historical Society, XLVIII, 1957, 99-118. See also Vann (1952), listed below.
2012 Collinson, P., The Elizabethan Puritan Movement, 1967. A very important book. The most recent and most comprehensive treatment of the subject.
2013 —— 'The godly: aspects of popular Protestantism in Elizabethan England', P.P. Conference Papers, 1966, separately paginated.
2014 —— 'The beginnings of English Sabbatariansim'. In C. W. Dugmore and C. Duggan, eds., Studies in Church History, I, 1964, 207-21.
2015 Cross, M. Claire, The Puritan Earl: The Life of Henry Hastings, Third Earl of Huntingdon, 1536-1595, 1966. A study of influence and patronage.
2016 Dickens, A. G., The English Reformation, 1964.
2017 Everitt, A. M., 'Nonconformity in country parishes'. In Joan Thirsk, ed., Land, Church and People: Essays Presented to Professor H. P. R. Finberg, 1970, 178-99. An interesting survey which examines the social and economic factors affecting the distribution of nonconformity.
2018 Hall, B., 'Puritanism: the problem of definition'. In C. J. Cuming, ed., Studies in Church History, II, 1965, 283-96.
2019 Haller, W., The Rise of Puritanism, N.Y., 1938. A classic work by the doyen of historians of puritanism.
2020 —— Liberty and Reformation in the Puritan Revolution, N.Y., 1955. Reprinted 1963.
2021 Hart, A. T., The Country Clergy in Elizabethan and Stuart Times, 1958.
2022 —— The Man in the Pew, 1966.
2023 Hembry, Pauline M., The Bishops of Bath and Wells, 1540-1640: Social and Economic Problems, 1967.
2024 Hill, C., Economic Problems of the Church from Archbishop Whitgift to the Long Parliament, 1956.
2025 —— Society and Puritanism in Prerevolutionary England, 1964. This and the previous book are essential reading on the social history of religion in the first half of the seventeenth century.
2026 —— Antichrist in Seventeenth-century England, 1971.

2027 —— 'Propagating the Gospel'. In H. E. Bell and R. L. Ollard, eds., title cited in (1108), listed above, 35-59.
2028 —— 'Puritans and the "Dark corners of the land", T.R.H.S., 5th ser., 13, 1962. 77-102.
2029 Jordan, W. K., The Development of Religious Toleration in England, 4 vols., 1932-40.
2030 Knappen, M. M., Tudor Puritanism, Chicago, Ill., 1939. Reprinted 1965. A standard work, which still supplements, and is not made redundant by, Collinson (2012), listed above.
2031 Lamont, W. M., Godly Rule: Politics and Religion, 1603-60, 1969.
2032 Leys, Mary D. R., Catholics in England, 1559-1829: A Social History, 1961.
2033 Lloyd, A., Quaker Social History, 1669-1738, 1950.
2034 McGrath, P. V., Papists and Puritans under Elizabeth I, 1967. A clear survey with a useful bibliography.
2035 Morton, A. L., The World of the Ranters, 1971. See also Hill (1935), listed above.
2036 Richards, T., The Puritan Movement in Wales, 1639-53, 1920.
2037 —— Religious Developments in Wales, 1654-62, 1923.
2038 —— Wales under the Penal Code, 1662-87, 1925.
2039 —— Wales under the Indulgence, 1672-75, 1928.
2040 Richardson, R. C., Puritanism in Northwest England: A Regional Study of the Diocese of Chester to 1642, 1972. A social approach examining the structure of puritanism in the region and the forces at work within it.
2041 Schlatter, R. B., The Social Ideas of Religious Leaders, 1660-1688, 1940.
2042 Seaver, P. S., The Puritan Lectureships: The Politics of Religious Dissent, 1560-1662, Stanford, Calif., 1970.
2043 Solt, L. F., Saints in Arms: Puritanism and Democracy in Cromwell's Army, Stanford, Calif., 1959.
2044 Steffan, T. G., 'The social argument against Enthusiasm, 1650-60', Studies in English (Texas), Calif., 21, 1941, 39-63.
2045 Trevor-Roper, H. R., Religion, the Reformation and Social Change, 1967. A collection of masterly essays.
2046 Trimble, W. R., The Catholic Laity in Elizabethan England, Cambridge, Mass., 1964.
2047 Tyacke, N., 'Puritanism, Arminianism and Counter-Revolution'. In Russell (1951), listed above, 119-43.
2048 Underdown, D., Pride's Purge, 1971. Argues that the Purge involved a deeper division than that between Presbyterian and Independent, i.e. that between gentry constitutionalism and radical puritanism.
2049 Vann, R. T., The Social Development of English Quakerism, 1655-1755, Harvard, Mass., 1969.
2050 —— 'Quakerism and the social structure in the Interregnum', P.P., 43, 1969, 71-91.
2051 Whitaker, W. B., Sunday in Tudor and Stuart Times, 1933.
2052 Whitney, Dorothy Williams, 'London puritanism: the Haberdashers' Company', Church History, XXXII, 1963, 298-321. A case study of the patronage wielded by bodies of merchants and tradesmen. See also Walzer (1961), listed above.

(b) **Religion and economic development**

2053 Birnbaum, N., 'Conflicting interpretations of the rise of capitalism: Marx and Weber', British Jnl. of Sociology, IV, 1953, 125-41.
2054 Breen, T. H., 'The non-existent controversy. Puritan and Anglican attitudes to work and wealth, 1600-1640', Church History, XXXV, 1966, 273-87. See also the book by the Georges (2059), listed below.
2055 Burrell, S. A., 'Calvinism, capitalism and the middle classes: some afterthoughts on an old problem', Jnl. Mod. Hist., 32, 1960, 129-41.
2056 Fanfani, A., Catholicism, Protestantism and Capitalism, N.Y., 1935.
2057 Fischoff, E., 'The Protestant ethic and the spirit of capitalism; the history of a controversy', Social Research, XI, 1944, 61-77.
2058 George, C. H., 'English Calvinist opinion on usury, 1600-1640', Jnl. of the History of Ideas, XVIII, 1957, 455-74.
2059 —— and K., The Protestant Mind of the English Reformation, 1570-1640, Princeton, N.J., 1961. A useful book but by no means wholly convincing in its attempts to play down the distinctiveness of puritanism.
2060 Green R. W., ed., Protestantism and Capitalism: The Weber Thesis and its Critics, Boston, Mass., 1959. A collection of extracts from the main contributions to the debate.
2061 Hill, C., 'Protestantism and the rise of capitalism', in Fisher, ed. (1010), listed above, 29-39. A stimulating essay by a distinguished defender of the Weber Thesis.
2062 Hudson, W. S., 'Puritanism and the spirit of capitalism', Church History, XVIII, 1949, 3-16.
2063 Kearney, H., 'Puritanism, capitalism and the scientific revolution', P.P., 28, 1964, 81-101.
2064 Kitch, M. J., ed., Capitalism and the Reformation, 1967. A collection of extracts from contemporary writings and from historians' interpretations, with an introduction and bibliography.
2065 Luethy, M., 'Once again: Calvinism and capitalism', Encounter, XXII, 1964, 26-38.
2066 Robertson, H. M., Aspects of the Rise of Economic Individualism, 1933. Reprinted N.Y., 1959. A hostile criticism of the Weber thesis.
2067 Samuelsson, K., Religion and Economic Action, 1961. A more recent attack on the Weber thesis.
2068 Sombart, W., The Quintessence of Capitalism, London and N.Y., 1915. The work of one of Weber's earliest opponents.

2069 Supple, B. E., 'The great capitalist manhunt', Business History, VI, 1963, 48-62.
2070 Tawney, R. H., Religion and the Rise of Capitalism, 1926. Several times reprinted. A profound and wide-ranging study. One of the masterpieces of English historical writing.
2071 Trevor-Roper, H. R., 'The bishopric of Durham and the capitalist Reformation', Durham University Jnl., XXXVIII, 1946, 45-58.
2072 Troeltsch, E., The Social Teaching of the Christian Churches, English trans., 2 vols, 1931. An important work which lent support to the Weber thesis.
2073 Weber, M., The Protestant Ethic and the Spirit of Capitalism, 1904, English trans., N.Y. and London, 1930. One of the earliest attempts to explore the relationship between reformed religion and economic development. Its publication initiated a controversy amongst historians, economists, sociologists and theologians which has lasted for over sixty years.

See also the chapter "Religion and the social environment" in Thompson (2173), listed below.

EDUCATION AND LEARNING

(a) Schools and schooling

2074 Sylvester, D. W., ed., Educational Documents, 800-1816, 1970. See also Maclure (3848), listed below.
2075 Adamson, J. W., A Short History of Education, 1919.
2076 ——— The Illiterate Anglo-Saxon and Other Essays on Education Medieval and Modern, 1946.
2077 ——— 'The extent of literacy in England in the fifteenth and sixteenth centuries: notes and conjectures', The Library, 4th ser., X, 1929-30, 163-93.
2078 Axtell, J. L., 'Education and status in Stuart England: the London physician', History of Education Quarterly, X, 1970, 141-59.
2079 Beales, A. C. F., Education under Penalty: English Catholic Education from the Reformation of the Fall of James II, 1963.
2080 Bennett, H. S., English Books and Readers, 1475-1640, 3 vols., 1952-70. A scholarly treatment of the subject.
2081 Brauer, G. C., The Education of a Gentleman: Theories of Gentlemanly Education in England, 1660-1775, N.Y., 1959.
2082 Brown, J. H., Elizabethan Schooldays, 1933.
2083 Caspari, F., Humanism and the Social Order in Tudor England, Chicago and Cambridge, 1955.
2084 Charlton, K., Education in Renaissance England, 1965.
2085 Conant, J. B., 'The advancement of learning during the Puritan Commonwealth', Massachusetts Historical Society Proceedings, LXVI, for 1936-41, 1942, 3-31.

2086 Costello, W. T., The Scholastic Curriculum at Early Seventeenth-century Cambridge, Cambridge, Mass., 1958.
2087 Cressy, D., 'The social composition of Caius College, Cambridge, 1580-1640', P.P., 47, 1970, 113-15.
2088 Curtis, M. H., Oxford and Cambridge in Transition, 1959. A valuable study of the two universities in the early modern period.
2089 ——— 'The alienated intellectuals of early Stuart England', P.P., 23, 1962, 25-43. Reprinted in Aston (990), listed above, 295-316.
2089a Greaves, R. L., The Puritan Revolution and Educational Thought, New Jersey, 1969.
2090 Green, V. H. H., The Universities, 1969. A competent and readable general outline of their development.
2091 Hexter, J. H., 'The education of the aristocracy in the Renaissance'. In the same author's Reappraisals in History, 1961, 45-70.
2092 Howell, W. S., Logic and Rhetoric in England, 1500-1700, Princeton, N.J., 1958.
2093 Kearney, H., Scholars and Gentlemen: Universities and Society in Pre-industrial Britain, 1500-1700, 1970. An important recent addition to the literature on the subject.
2094 Lawson, J., A Town Grammar School Through Six Centuries (Hull), 1963. One of the best examples of the large crop of local studies.
2095 Prest, W. R., The Inns of Court under Elizabeth I and the Early Stuarts, 1590-1640, 1972.
2095a ——— 'The legal education of the gentry at the Inns of Court, 1560-1640', P.P., 38, 1967, 20-39.
2096 Schofield, R. S., 'The measurement of literacy in pre-industrial England'. In J. Goody, ed., Literacy in Traditional Societies, 1968, 311-25.
2097 Simon, B., ed., Education in Leicestershire, 1540-1940, 1968.
2098 Simon, Joan, Education and Society in Tudor England, 1966. An authoritative study. Thorough bibliography.
2099 ——— 'A. F. Leach and the Reformation', British Jnl. of Educational Studies, 3, 1955, 128-43; ibid., 4, 1956, 32-48. An effective criticism of the chief authority on the history of education in the early modern period.
2100 ——— 'The Reformation and English education', P.P., 2, 1957, 48-65. Rejects the view—associated with Leach—that the dissolution of the chantries had widespread destructive consequences for English education.
2101 ——— 'The social origins of Cambridge students, 1603-40', P.P., 26, 1963, 58-67.
2102 Spufford, Margaret, 'The schooling of the peasantry in Cambridgeshire, 1575-1700'. In Joan Thirsk, ed., Land, Church and People: Essays Presented to Professor H. P. R. Finberg, 1970, 112-47. An interesting local study of the availability of educational facilities and of the extent of literacy.

2103 Stone, L., 'The educational revolution in England, 1560-1640', P.P., 28, 1964, 41-80.
2104 —— 'Literacy and education in England, 1640-1900', P.P., 42, 1969, 69-139. These two articles, along with Simon (2098), listed above, are essential reading on the history of education in this period.
2104a Vincent, W. A. L., The State and School Education 1640-1660 in England and Wales, 1950.
2104b —— The Grammar Schools. Their Continuing Tradition 1660-1714, 1969.
2105 Wright, L. B., Middle Class Culture in Elizabethan England, Chapel Hill, N.C., 1935. Reprinted Washington, D.C., 1958, and in Britain in 1964. An important work. The bibliography, unfortunately, was not brought up to date for the reprint.

The various books by Professor Jordan on English philanthropy (1834-1839), listed above, are also relevant in this connection. See also Lawson and Silver (3860) listed below.

(b) The book trade and the newspaper press

2106 Beer, E. S. de., 'The English newspapers from 1695 to 1702'. In Ragnild Hatton and J. S. Bromley, eds., William III and Louis XIV: Essays by and for Mark Thomson, 1968, 117-29.
2107 Clyde, W. M., The Struggle for the Freedom of the Press from Caxton to Cromwell, 1934.
2108 Dukes, G., 'The beginnings of the English newspaper', History Today, 4, 1954, 197-204.
2109 Frank, J., The Beginnings of the English Newspaper, 1620-1660, Cambridge, Mass., 1961.
2110 Fraser, P., The Intelligence of the Secretaries of State and their Monopoly of Licensed News, 1660-1688, 1956.
2110a Myers, R., The British Book Trade from Caxton to the Present Day, 1973.
2110b Rostenberg, L., The Minority Press and the English Crown 1558-1625, Nieuwkoop, 1971.
2111 Shaaber, M. A., Some Forerunners of the Newspaper in England, 1476-1622, 1929. Reprinted 1966.
2112 Varley, F. J., ed., Mercurius Aulicus, 1948. Extracts from the Royalist newspaper published at Oxford, 1643-5.

ENGLAND 1700-1970

BIBLIOGRAPHICAL AND STATISTICAL GUIDES, DOCUMENTARY COMPILATIONS AND GENERAL WORKS

(a) Bibliographical and statistical guides

As a guide to directions in current research in the field, the following publication will be found useful:

2113 Social Science Research Council, Research in Economic and Social History, 1971.

2114 Ashton, T.S., The Industrial Revolution: A Study in Bibliography, 1937.

2115 Beales, H.L. and Cole, G.D.H., A Select List of Books on Economic and Social History, 1700-1850, 1927.

2116 Black, R.D.C., A Catalogue of Pamphlets on Economic Subjects Published between 1750 and 1900 and Now Housed in Irish Libraries, Belfast, 1969.

2117 Cannery, Margaret and Knott, D., eds., Catalogue of Goldsmiths' Library of Economic Literature, I, 1970.

2118 Clark, G.N., The Idea of the Industrial Revolution, 1953.

2119 Deane, Phyllis and Cole, W.A., British Economic Growth 1688-1959: Trends and Structure, 1962, 2nd ed., 1967.

2120 Hanson, L.W., ed., Contemporary Printed Sources for British and Irish Economic History, 1701-1750, 1963.

2121 Mitchell, B.R. and Deane, Phyllis, Abstract of British Historical Statistics, 1962. Covers the period from 1697 to the 1950s.

2122 —— and Jones, H.G., Second Abstract of British Historical Statistics, 1971.

2123 Power, Eileen, The Industrial Revolution 1750-1850: A Select Bibliography, 1927.

2124 Williams, Judith B., A Guide to the Printed Materials for English Social and Economic History 1750-1850, N.Y., 2 vols., 1926.

(b) Documentary compilations and readings

2125 Bowditch, J. and Ramsland, C., eds., Voices of the Industrial Revolution. Selected Readings from the Liberal Economists and their Critics. Ann Arbor, Mich., 1961.

2126 Breach, R.W. and Hartwell, R.M., British Economy and Society, 1870-1970: Documents, Descriptions, Statistics, 1972.

2127 Brown, A.F.J., ed., English History from Essex Sources, 1750-1900, 1952. Useful book of documents on many aspects of economic and social life.

2128 Court, W.H.B., ed., British Economic History, 1870-1914: Commentary and Documents, 1965. Extracts from contemporary and secondary sources with useful bibliographical notes.

2129 Harrison, J.F.C., Society and Politics in England, 1780-1960: A Selection of Readings and Comments, 1965. Largely economic in content.

2130 Harvie, C., Martin, G. and Scharf, A., Industrialisation and Culture, 1830-1914, 1970. Documentary material with comments.

2130a Pike, E.R., ed., Human Documents of Adam Smith's Time, 1974.

2131 —— Human Documents of the Industrial Revolution in Britain, 1966. Editorial comments not well informed and often flippant; the extracts from documents are useful.

2132 —— Human Documents of the Victorian Golden Age (1850-75), 1967.

2133 —— Human Documents of the Age of the Forsytes, 1969.

2134 —— Human Documents of the Lloyd George Era, 1972. Suffers from the same defects as its predecessors.

2135 Read, D., Documents from Edwardian England, 1901-1915, 1973.

2136 Tames, R.L., ed., Documents of the Industrial Revolution, 1750-1850, 1971. The extracts tend to be short.

2137 Taylor, P.A.M., ed., The Industrial Revolution in Britain: Triumph or Disaster?, Boston, Mass., 1958, 2nd rev. ed., 1970. A collection of extracts from the writings of famous economic historians and Karl Marx.

2138 Warburg, J., ed., The Industrial Muse: The Industrial Revolution in English Poetry, 1958.

(c) General works

2139 Ashton, T.S., The Industrial Revolution, 1760-1830, 1948.

2140 —— An Economic History of England: The Eighteenth Century, 1955.

2141 Beales, H.L., The Industrial Revolution, 1750-1850: An Introductory Essay, 1928, reissue with new introduction, 1958.

2142 Best, G.F.A., Mid-Victorian Britain, 1851-75, 1971.

2143 Butt, J. and Clarke, I.F., eds., The Victorians and Social Protest, 1973. Contains chapters by H.J. Perkin on land reform and class conflict in Victorian Britain, and J.H. Treble on Irish immigrant attitudes to north of England Chartism. See Hollis (2162a), listed below.

2144 Chambers, J.D., The Workshop of the World: British Economic History from 1820-1880, 2nd rev. ed., 1968.

2145 Chapman, S.D. and Chambers, J.D., The Beginnings of Industrial Britain, 1970. Covers the period c. 1700-1830; good illustrations.

2146 Checkland, S.G., The Rise of Industrial Society in England, 1815-1885, 1964. Particularly valuable for footnote references to theses; good bibliography, 413-54.

2147 Clapham, J.H., An Economic History of Modern Britain: Vol. I, The Early Railway Age, 1820-1850, 1926; Vol. II, Free Trade

and Steel, 1850-1886, 1932; Vol. III, Machines and National Rivalries (1886-1914) with an Epilogue (1914-29), 1938.
2148 Clark, G. Kitson, The Making of Victorian England (Covers the period 1830-60), 1962.
2149 Court, W. H. B., A Concise Economic History of Britain from 1750 to Recent Times, 1954.
2150 Deane, Phyllis, The First Industrial Revolution, 1965.
2151 Fay, C. R., Great Britain from Adam Smith to the Present Day, 1928 and subsequent editions
2152 —— English Economic History, Mainly Since 1700, 1940.
2153 Flinn, M. W., The Origins of the Industrial Revolution, 1966.
2154 Halévy, E., A History of the English People in 1815, 1st ed. in 1 vol., 1924, 2nd ed. in 3 vols., 1938. Vol. 2 of 1938 ed. (i.e. Book II of 1st ed.) deals with economic life.
2155 Hammond, J. L. and Barbara, The Rise of Modern Industry, 1925. Many times reprinted. The 9th ed., 1965, with new introduction by R. M. Hartwell, XV-XXI, should be used.
2156 Harrison, J. F. C., The Early Victorians, 1832-51, 1971.
2157 Hartwell, R. M., ed., The Industrial Revolution, 1970. A collection of essays.
2158 —— The Causes of the Industrial Revolution in England, 1967. A collection of articles on various aspects of the subject by eminent economic historians.
2159 —— The Industrial Revolution. Historical Association Pamphlet, 1965.
2160 —— The Industrial Revolution and Economic Growth, 1972. Collected essays.
2161 Hobsbawm, E. J., Industry and Empire: An Economic History of Britain, 1968.
2162 Hoffmann, W. G., British Industry, 1700-1950, 1955.
2162a Hollis, Patricia M. (ed.), Pressure from Without in Early Victorian England, 1974. See also Butt and Clarke (2143), listed above.
2163 Klingender, F. D., Art and the Industrial Revolution, 1947. 2nd rev. and enlarged ed., 1968, by Sir Arthur Elton.
2164 Landes, D. S., The Unbound Prometheus: Technological Change and Industrial Development in Western Europe from 1750 to the Present, 1969. Mainly about Britain.
2165 Mantoux, P., The Industrial Revolution in the Eighteenth Century, 1st English trans., 1928, rev. ed. with fuller bibliography, 1961.
2166 Marshall, Dorothy, English People in the Eighteenth Century, 1956.
2167 Mathias, P., The First Industrial Nation, 1969.
2168 Moffit, L. W., England on the Eve of the Industrial Revolution: A Study of Economic and Social Conditions from 1740 to 1760, 1925.
2169 Perkin, H. J., The Origins of Modern English Society, 1780-1880, 1969.
2170 Pressnell, L. S., ed., Studies in the Industrial Revolution Presented to T. S. Ashton, 1960.

2171 Smart, W., Economic Annals of the Nineteenth Century, 1910-17. Reprinted 1964. Vol. I covers 1801-20, Vol. II, 1821-30. An economic epitome of Hansard's Parliamentary Debates and The Annual Register.
2172 Sussmann, H. L., Victorians and the Machine: The Literary Response to Technology, Cambridge, Mass., 1968. See also Warburg (2138), listed above.
2173 Thompson, A., The Dynamics of the Industrial Revolution, 1973. Considers the interaction between the various factors which produced the industrial changes.
2174 Toynbee, A., The Industrial Revolution of the Eighteenth Century in England, 1st ed., 1884, latest ed., with introductory note by T. S. Ashton, 1968.
2175 Young, G. M., Victorian England: Portrait of an Age, 1936.
2176 —— Early Victorian England, 1830-1865, 2 vols., 1934. Articles by specialists on many aspects of economic and social life.

(d) Regional and county studies

2177 Ashmore, O., The Industrial Archaeology of Lancashire, 1969.
2178 Aspin, C., Lancashire, the First Industrial Society, 1969.
2179 Booker, F., The Industrial Archaeology of the Tamar Valley, 1967.
2180 Buchanan, R. A. and Cossons, N., The Industrial Archaeology of the Bristol Region, 1969.
2181 Burt, R., ed., Industry and Society in the South West, 1970. Useful for Cornwall during the Industrial Revolution.
2182 Chambers, J. D., The Vale of Trent, 1670-1800: A Regional Study of Economic Change, Ec. H. R. Supplement, 3, 1957.
2183 Harris, Helen, The Industrial Archaeology of Dartmoor, 1968.
2184 Hudson, K., The Industrial Archaeology of Southern England (Hampshire, Wiltshire, Dorset, Somerset and Gloucestershire and the Severn), 1965.
2185 Marshall, J. D., Furness and the Industrial Revolution, 1958.
2186 Nixon, F., The Industrial Archaeology of Derbyshire, 1969.
2187 Rowe, J., Cornwall in the Age of the Industrial Revolution, 1953. See also Todd and Laws (2190), listed below.
2188 Singleton, F., The Industrial Revolution in Yorkshire, 1970.
2189 Smith, D. M., The Industrial Archaeology of the East Midlands (Nottinghamshire, Leicestershire and the Adjoining parts of Derbyshire), 1965.
2190 Todd, A. C. and Laws, P., The Industrial Archaeology of Cornwall, 1972. See also Rowe (2187), listed above.
2191 Trinder, B., The Industrial Revolution in Shropshire, 1973.

ECONOMIC AND SOCIAL CHANGES FROM THE 1880s INTO THE TWENTIETH CENTURY

(a) The changing structure of the economy

2192 Aldcroft, D.H., The Inter-War Economy 1919-1939, 1970.
2193 —— and Fearon P., eds., Economic Growth in Twentieth Century Britain, 1969. Thirteen articles by various hands with an introduction and bibliographical guide, 233-7.
2194 —— and Richardson, H.W., The British Economy 1870-1939, 1969.
2195 Allen, G.C., British Industries and their Organisation, 2nd ed., 1935, 3rd ed., 1951.
2196 Armitage, Susan M.H., The Politics of Decontrol of Industry: Britain and the United States, 1969.
2197 Ashworth, W., An Economic History of England, 1870-1939, 1960.
2198 Barry, E.E., Nationalisation in British Politics, 1965 (Begins with the 1890s).
2199 Beales, H.L., 'The "basic industries" of England, 1850-1914', Ec.H.R., V, 1935, 99-112.
2200 Beckerman, W., The Labour Government's Economic Record, 1964-1970, 1972.
2201 British Association, Britain in Depression: A Review of British Industries since 1929, 1935.
2202 —— Britain in Recovery, 1938.
2203 Broadway, F., State Intervention in British Industry 1964-68, 1969.
2204 Dow, J.C.R., The Management of the British Economy, 1945-60, 1968.
2205 Jones, G.P. and Pool, A.G., A Hundred Years of Economic Development in Great Britain, 1939. Covers the period 1837-1937.
2206 Kahn, A.E., Great Britain in the World Economy, 1946.
2207 Kelf-Cohen, R., British Nationalisation, 1945-1973, 1974.
2208 Kindleberger, C.P., Economic Growth in France and Britain, 1851-1950, 1964. One of the few comparative studies; bibliography, 341-66.
2208a Lee, C.H., Regional Economic Growth in the United Kingdom since the 1880s, 1971.
2209 McCloskey, D.N., ed., Essays on a Mature Economy: Britain after 1840, 1971 (mainly industrial, with a strong bias towards the 'new economic history', but includes a chapter on agriculture).
2210 Phillips, G.A. and Madocks, R.T., The Growth of the British Economy, 1918-1968, 1973.
2211 Pigou, A.C., Aspects of British Economic History, 1918-1925, 1947.
2212 Plummer, A., New British Industries in the Twentieth Century, 1937.
2213 Pollard, S., The Development of the British Economy, 1914-1967, 2nd ed., 1969.
2214 Saul, S.B., The Myth of the Great Depression, 1873-1896, 1969. Excellent bibliography, 56-62.
2215 Saville, J., ed., 'The British economy, 1870-1914', Yorks Bull., XVII, No. 1, 1965, 1-112.
2216 Williams, L.J., Britain and the World Economy, 1919-1970, 1971.
2217 Worswick, G.D.N. and Tipping, D.G., Profits in the British Economy 1909-1938, 1967.
2218 Youngson, A.J., Britain's Economic Growth, 1920-1966, 2nd ed., 1968.

(b) Social conditions and social policy

2219 Baily, L.W.A., Scrapbook for the Twenties, 1959.
2220 —— Scrapbook, 1900 to 1914, 1957.
2221 Beales, H.L. and Lambert, R.S., Memoirs of the Unemployed, 1934.
2222 Beveridge, W.H., Unemployment: A Problem of Industry, 1st ed., 1909, 2nd ed., with new material, 1930.
2223 Blair, E. (pseud. G. Orwell), The Road to Wigan Pier, 1937.
2224 Blythe, R., The Age of Illusion: England in the Twenties and Thirties, 1919-1940, 1963.
2225 Bogdanov, V. and Skidelsky, R.W., eds., The Age of Affluence, 1951-1964, 1970.
2226 Bott, A., Our Fathers (1870-1900): Manners and Customs of the Ancient Victorians, n.d. (c. 1930).
2227 Branson, Noreen and Heinemann, Margot, Britain in the Nineteen Thirties, 1971. The Marxist view.
2228 Briggs, A., ed., They Saw It Happen: An Anthology of Eye-witnesses' Accounts of Events in British History 1897-1940. 1962.
2229 Brown, K.D., Labour and Unemployment, 1900-1914, 1971, bibliography, 203-13. See Harris (2250), listed below.
2230 Bruce, M., The Coming of the Welfare State, 1st ed., 1961, 4th rev. ed., 1968. Extensive bibliographical references from Tudor to modern times.
2231 Burns, Eveline M., British Unemployment Programs, 1920-1938, Washington, D.C., 1941.
2232 Carney, J.J., Institutional Change and the Level of Employment: A Study of British Unemployment, 1918-1929, Coral Gables, Fla., 1956.
2233 Carr-Saunders, A.M. and Jones, D.C., A Survey of the Social Structure of England and Wales, 1927, 2nd rev. ed., 1937.
2234 —— and Moser, C.A., A Survey of Social Conditions in England and Wales as illustrated by Statistics, 1958.
2235 Clephane, Irene, Ourselves, 1900-1930, 1933.
2236 Cohen, P., The British System of Social Insurance: A History and Description, 1932.
2237 Cole, G.D.H. and Margaret, I., The Condition of Britain, 1937.
2238 Davison, R.C., The Unemployed: Old Policies and New, 1929.
2239 —— British Unemployment Policy: The Modern Phase since 1930, 1938.
2240 Fraser, D., The Evolution of the British Welfare State: A History of Social Policy since the Industrial Revolution, 1973.
2241 Gilbert, B.B., The Evolution of National Insurance in Great Britain: The Origins of the Welfare State, 1966.
2242 —— British Social Policy, 1914-1939,

1970. Better on the period 1914-31 than on the 1930s; critical bibliography, 325-36.
2243 Goldring, D., The Nineteen Twenties: A General Survey and some Personal Memories, 1945.
2244 Graves, R. and Hodge, A., The Long Weekend: A Social History of Great Britain 1918-1939, 1941, latest ed., 1971.
2245 Gregg, Pauline, The Welfare State: An Economic and Social History of Britain from 1945 to the Present Day, 1967. Useful select bibliography, 368-76.
2246 Hannington, W., The Problem of the Distressed Areas, 1937.
2247 —— A Short History of the Unemployed, 1938.
2248 —— Ten Lean Years: An Examination of the Record of the National Government in the Field of Unemployment, 1940.
2249 —— Unemployed Struggles, 1919-1936, 1937.
2250 Harris, José, Unemployment and Politics: A Study in English Social Policy, 1886-1914, 1972. Better than Brown (2229), listed above.
2251 Harris, R. W., National Health Insurance in Great Britain, 1911-1946, 1946.
2252 Hutt, A., The Post-War History of the British Working Class, 1937.
2253 Hynes, S., The Edwardian Turn of Mind, 1968.
2254 Lynd, Helen M., England in the Eighteen-eighties: Towards a Social Basis for Freedom, 1945. Reprinted 1968.
2255 McElwee, W., Britain's Locust Years, 1918-1940, 1962.
2256 Marsh, D. C., The Changing Social Structure of England and Wales, 1871-1961, rev. ed., 1965.
2257 Marwick, A., The Explosion of British Society, 1914-62, 1963, 2nd ed., 1971.
2258 Montgomery, J., The Twenties, 1st ed., 1957, 2nd rev. ed., 1970.
2259 —— The Fifties, 1965.
2260 Mowat, C. L., Britain Between the Wars, 1918-1940, 1955.
2261 Muggeridge, M., The Thirties: 1930-1940 in Great Britain, 1940.
2262 Nowell-Smith, S., ed., Edwardian England 1901-1914, 1964. Chapters on the economy (A. J. Taylor) and domestic life (Marghanita Laski).
2263 Peel, Dorothy C., A Hundred Wonderful Years: Social and Domestic Life of a Century, 1820-1920, 1926.
2264 Raymond, J., ed., The Baldwin Age, 1960. A collection of essays on various topics of the inter-war period.
2265 Read, D., Edwardian England, 1901-15: Society and Politics, 1973. See also Read (2135), listed above.
2266 Ryder, Judith and Silver, H., Modern English Society: History and Structure, 1850-1970, 1970. Attempts to marry history and sociology.
2267 Sissons, M. and French, P., eds., The Age of Austerity, 1945-51, 1963.

(c) The World Wars and their effects

2268 Abrams, P., 'The failure of social reform, 1918-20', P.P., 24, 1963, 43-64.
2269 Bowley, A. L., Some Economic Consequences of the Great War, 1930. Mainly the effects on Great Britain.
2270 Calder, A., The People's War: Britain 1939-45, 1969. Critical bibliography, 624-39.
2271 Fitzgibbon, C., The Blitz, 1970.
2272 Johnson, P. B., Land Fit for Heroes: The Planning of British Reconstruction, 1916-1919, Chicago, Ill., 1968.
2273 Longmate, N., How We Lived Then: A History of English Life During the Second World War, 1971.
2274 Marwick, A., Britain in the Century of Total War, 1968. Extensive bibliography.
2275 —— The Deluge: British Society and the First World War, 1965.
2276 Milward, A. S., The Economic Effects of the World Wars on Britain, 1970. Critical bibliography, 53-7.
2277 Mosley, L., Backs to the Wall, 1971. Life in London, 1939-45.
2278 Peel, Dorothy C., How We Lived Then, 1914-1918: A Sketch of Social and Domestic Life in England During the War, 1929.
2279 Pelling, H. M., Britain and the Second World War, 1970.
2280 Playne, Caroline E., Society at War, 1914-1916, 1931.
2281 —— Britain Holds On, 1917, 1918, 1933.
2282 Woodward, L., Great Britain and the War of 1914-1918, 1967. Chapter XII deals with economic matters.

POPULATION

(a) General works

2283 Population Studies (I, 1947-8 to date) contains numerous articles on British population history.
2284 Nottingham University, Department of Adult Education, ed., Local Population Studies, No. 1, Autumn 1968 to date.
2285 Abel-Smith, B. and Pinker, R., The Hospitals, 1800-1948: A Study in Social Administration in England and Wales, 1964.
2286 Banks, J. A., Prosperity and Parenthood, 1954. Family limitation among the late nineteenth-century British middle classes.
2287 Buer, M. C., Health, Wealth and Population in the Early Days of the Industrial Revolution, 1926. See also Chambers (996), listed above.
2288 Connell, K. H., 'Some unsettled problems in English and Irish population history, 1750-1845', Irish Historical Studies, VII, 1951.
2289 Drake, M., ed., Population in Industrialisation, 1969. Reprints eight articles on the subject. Good bibliography.
2290 Eversley, D. E. C., 'Population and economic growth in England before the "Take Off" ', Communications of the First International Conference of Economic History, Stockholm, Paris, 1960, 457-73.

2291 Flinn, M.W., British Population Growth, 1700-1850, 1970. The best introduction to the study of this subject; critical bibliography, 59-64; glossary, 65.
2292 Glass, D.V., 'Population and population movements in England and Wales, 1700-1850'. In Glass and Eversley, eds., (1083), listed above, 221-46.
2293 ——— ed., Introduction to Malthus, 1953. Essays, bibliography (84-112) and reprints of two scarce Malthus items.
2294 Griffith, G.T., Population Problems of the Age of Malthus, 1926. Reprinted 1967, with new bibliographical introduction, V-XVII, and bibliography of recent work, 277-80.
2295 Habakkuk, H.J., 'English population in the eighteenth century'. In Glass and Eversley, eds., (1083), listed above, 269-84.
2296 ——— Population Growth and Economic Development since 1750, 1971.
2297 Himes, N.E., Medical History of Contraception, 1st ed., 1936. Reprinted New York, 1963.
2298 Krause, J.T., 'Changes in English fertility and mortality, 1781-1850', Ec.H.R., 2nd ser., XI, 1958, 52-70.
2299 ——— 'Some neglected factors in the English Industrial Revolution'. Reprinted in Drake (2289), listed above, 103-17.
2300 ——— 'Some aspects of population change, 1690-1790'. In Jones and Mingay (2346), listed below, 187-205.
2301 ——— 'The changing adequacy of English registration, 1690-1837'. In Glass and Eversley, eds., (1083), listed above, 379-93.
2302 McKeown, T. and Brown, R.G., 'Medical evidence related to English population changes in the eighteenth century'. In Glass and Eversley, eds., (1083), listed above, 285-307.
2303 ——— and Record, R.G., 'Reasons for the decline of mortality in England and Wales during the nineteenth century', Population Studies, XVI, 1962-3, 94-122. Covers mainly the period 1851-1900.
2304 Marshall, T.H., 'The population of England and Wales from the Industrial Revolution to the First World War', Ec.H.R., V, 1934, 65-78.
2305 ——— 'The population problem during the Industrial Revolution: a note on the present state of the controversy'. In Carus-Wilson, ed., (164), listed above, I, 306-30.
2306 Poynter, F.N.L., ed., The Evolution of Hospitals in Britain, 1964.
2307 Razzell, P.E., 'Population change in eighteenth-century England: a re-interpretation'. In Jones and Mingay (2345), listed below, 260-81. Importance of mass inoculations against smallpox from 1760s.
2308 ——— 'Population growth and economic change in eighteenth and early nineteenth-century England and Ireland'. In Jones and Mingay (2346), listed below, 260-81.
2309 Sigsworth, E.M., 'Gateways to death? Medicines, hospitals and mortality, 1700-1850'. In Mathias, ed. (2497), listed below, 97-110.
2310 ——— 'A provincial hospital [York County] in the eighteenth and early nineteenth centuries', College of General Practitioners Yorkshire Faculty Journal, June 1966, 1-8.
2311 Tranter, N.L., Population and Industrialization, 1973. Extracts from British writers on population problems between 1680 and 1967.
2311a ——— Population since the Industrial Revolution: The Case of England and Wales, 1973.
2312 Woodward, J.H., To Do The Sick No Harm: A Study of the British Voluntary Hospital System to 1875, 1974.

(b) **Regional studies**

2313 Chambers, J.D., 'Population change in a provincial town: Nottingham, 1700-1800'. See Pressnell (2170), listed above, 97-124.
2314 Beckwith, F., 'The population of Leeds during the Industrial Revolution', Thoresby Soc. Pubns., XII, 1948, 118-96.
2315 Lawton, R., 'Population trends in Lancashire and Cheshire from 1801', T.H.S.L.C., CXIV, 1962, 189-213.
2316 Sogner, S., 'Aspects of the demographic situation in seventeen parishes in Shropshire, 1711-1760: an exercise based on parish registers', Population Studies, XVII, 1963-4, 126-46.
See also Hoskins (1053), listed above, 181-208.

(c) **Internal migration**

2317 Cairncross, A.K., 'Internal migration in Victorian England', Manchester School, XVII, 1949, 67-81. Reprinted in Cairncross (3453), listed below, 65-83.
2318 Redford, A., Labour Migration in England 1800-1850, 1926, 2nd rev. ed., 1963.
2319 Saville, J., Rural Depopulation in England and Wales, 1851-1951, 1957.

(d) **Immigration**

2320 Gainer, B., The Alien Invasion: The Origins of the Aliens Act of 1905, 1972.
2321 Gartner, L.P., The Jewish Immigrant in England, 1870-1914, 1960.
2322 Gerrard, J.A., The English and Immigration, 1880-1910, 1971.
2322a Jackson, J.A., The Irish in Britain, 1963.
2323 Kerr, Barbara M., 'Irish seasonal migration to Great Britain 1800-38', Irish Historical Studies, III, 1942, 365-80.
2324 Lawton, R., 'Irish immigration to England and Wales in the mid-nineteenth century', Irish Geography, IV, 1959, 35-54.

AGRICULTURE AND RURAL SOCIETY

(a) **Bibliographies**

2325 Fussell, G.E., More Old English Farming Books from Tull to the Board of Agriculture, 1731-1793, 1950.

England 1700-1970

2326 Harvey, N., ed., G. E. Fussell: A Bibliography of his Writings on Agricultural History, 1967.
See also Brewer (1232), listed above.

(b) General works dealing with the process of agricultural change

2327 Adams, L. P., Agricultural Depression and Farm Relief in England 1813-1852, 1932, new impression, 1965.
2328 Beer, M., ed., The Pioneers of Land Reform: Thomas Spence, William Ogilvie, Thomas Parrie, 1920.
2329 Caird, J., English Agriculture in 1850-51, 1st ed., 1852, 2nd ed., 1968 with important new introduction by G. E. Mingay, 1968.
2330 Carter, H. B., His Majesty's Spanish Flock, 1964. The building up of George III's flock of merino sheep.
2331 Chambers, J. D. and Mingay, G. E., The Agricultural Revolution 1750-1880, 1966.
2332 Collins, E. J. T., 'Harvest technology and labour supply in Britain, 1790-1870', Ec. H. R., 2nd ser., XXII, 1969, 453-73.
2333 Drescher, L., 'The development of agricultural production in Great Britain and Ireland from the early nineteenth century', Manchester School, 1955, 153-83. Translation of an attempt to construct an index of agricultural production, first published in 1935.
2334 Fletcher, T. W., 'The Great Depression of English Agriculture 1873-96', in (165), listed above, II, 239-58.
2335 Fussell, G. E., Jethro Tull: His Influence on Mechanized Agriculture, 1973. See also Marshall (2348) and Wicker (2361), listed below.
2336 —— 'The size of English cattle in the eighteenth century', Agricultural History (Chicago), III, 1929, 160-81. Criticises the view that the average weight of cattle and sheep increased considerably.
2337 —— and Goodman, Constance, 'Eighteenth-century estimates of sheep and wool production', Agricultural History (Chicago), IV, 1930, 131-51.
2338 —— and Goodman, Constance, 'The eighteenth-century traffic in milk products', Ec. H. Supplement, III, No. 12, February 1937, 380-7.
2339 Galpin, W. F., The Grain Supply of England during the Napoleonic Period, N.Y., 1925.
2340 Gould, J. D., 'Agricultural fluctuations and the English economy in the eighteenth century', J. Ec. H., XX, 1962, 313-33.
2341 Habakkuk, H. J., 'Economic functions of English landowners in the seventeenth and eighteenth centuries'. Reprinted in Carus-Wilson, ed. (164), listed above, I, 187-201.
2342 John, A. H., 'The course of agricultural change 1660-1760', reprinted in Carus-Wilson, ed. (164), listed above, I, 221-53.
2343 —— 'Farming in war-time: 1793-1815'. In Jones and Mingay (2346), listed below, 28-47.
2344 Jones, E. L., The Development of English Agriculture, 1815-1873, 1968. Useful pamphlet, with select bibliography, 35-7.
2345 Jones, E. L., 'Industrial capital and landed investment: the Arkwrights in Herefordshire, 1809-43'. In (2346), listed below, 48-71.
2346 Jones, E. L. and Mingay, G. E., Land, Labour and Population in the Industrial Revolution: Essays Presented to J. D. Chambers, 1967.
2347 —— 'Agriculture and economic growth in England, 1660-1750: agricultural change'. Reprinted in Carus-Wilson, ed. (164), listed above, I, 203-19.
2348 Marshall, T. H., 'Jethro Tull and the "New Husbandry" of the eighteenth century', Ec. H. R., II, No. 1, January 1929, 41-60.
2349 Mingay, G. E., 'The agricultural depression 1730-1750', Ec. H. R., 2nd ser., 1956, 323-38.
2350 —— 'The "Agricultural Revolution" in English history: a reconsideration', Agricultural History (Chicago), XXXVII, 1963, 123-33.
2351 Orwin, Christabel S. and Whetham, Edith H., History of British Agriculture, 1846-1914, 1964.
2352 Parker, R. A. C., 'Coke of Norfolk and the agrarian revolution', Ec. H. R., 2nd ser., VIII, 1955, 156-66.
2353 Pawson, H. C., Robert Bakewell, Pioneer Livestock Breeder, 1957. A disappointing book.
2354 Perry, P. J., ed., British Agriculture, 1873-1914, 1973 (a collection of essays on various aspects of this historical problem).
2354a —— British Agriculture in the Great Depression, 1870-1914: An Historical Geography, 1974.
2355 Russell, E. J., A History of Agricultural Science in Great Britain 1620-1954, 1966.
2356 —— British Agricultural Research: Rothamsted, 1st ed., 1942, 2nd rev. ed., 1946.
2357 Thompson, F. M. L., 'Landownership and economic growth in England in the eighteenth century'. In Agrarian Change and Economic Development, ed. E. L. Jones and S. J. Woolf, 1969, 41-60.
2358 Trow-Smith, R., A History of British Livestock Husbandry 1700-1900, 1959.
2359 Wallace, A. R., Land Nationalisation, 1892. Useful bibliography on the land question, 253-6.
2360 Whetham, Edith H., British Farming, 1939-49, 1952.
2361 Wicker, E. R., 'Jethro Tull, innovator or crank?', Agricultural History (Chicago), XXXI, 1957, 46-8.
2362 Woodward, D. M., 'Agricultural revolution in England, 1500-1900: a survey', The Local Historian, IX, 1971, 323-33.

(c) Enclosures

2363 Collins, K., 'Marx on the English agricultural revolution: theory and evidence', History and Theory, Middleton, Conn., VI, 1967, 351-81.

2364 Gonner, E.C.K., Common Land and Inclosure, 1912, 2nd ed. with introduction by G.E. Mingay, 1966.
2365 Levy, H., Land and Small Holdings: A Study of English Agricultural Economics, 1st ed., 1911, new impression, 1966.
2366 McCloskey, D.N., 'The enclosure of openfields: preface to the study of its impact on the efficiency of English agriculture in the eighteenth century', J.E.H. (New York), XXXII, 1972, 15-35.
2367 Mingay, G.E., Enclosure and the Small Farmer in the Age of the Industrial Revolution, 1968.
2368 Slater, G., The English Peasantry and the Enclosure of the Common Fields, 1909. Inaccurate.
2369 Tate, W.E., The English Village Community and the Enclosure Movements, 1967. See in particular Appendix II on the historiography of the enclosure movements.

(d) Landed society

2370 Bateman, J., The Great Landowners of Great Britain and Ireland, 4th ed., 1883, 5th ed., with introduction by D. Spring, 1971.
2371 Brodrick, G.C., English Land and English Landlords, 1st ed., 1881. Reprinted 1968.
2372 Caird, J., The Landed Interest and the Supply of Food, 1st ed., 1878, 5th ed., 1968, with introduction by G.E. Mingay.
2373 Mingay, G.E., English Landed Society in the Eighteenth Century, 1963.
2374 ───── 'The eighteenth-century land steward'. In Jones and Mingay (2346), listed above, 3-27.
2375 Spring, D., The English Landed Estate in the Nineteenth Century: Its Administration, Baltimore, Md., 1963.
2376 Thompson, F.M.L., English Landed Society in the Nineteenth Century, 1963. The final chapter deals with the period 1914-39; excellent bibliography.
2377 Ward, J.T. and Wilson, R.G., eds., Land and Industry: The Landed Estate and the Industrial Revolution, 1971.

(e) The drovers

2378 Bonser, K.J., The Drovers: Who They Were and How They Went. An Epic of the English Countryside, 1970.
2379 Cregeen, E., 'Recollections of an Argyllshire drover, with historical notes on the West Highland cattle trade', Scottish Studies, III, 1959, 143-62.
2380 Haldane, A.R.B., The Drove Roads of Scotland, 1952. See also Skeel (1205), listed above.

(f) Farm labourers

2381 Barnett, D.C., 'Allotments and the problem of rural poverty, 1780-1840'. In Jones and Mingay (2345), listed above, 162-83.
2381a Dunbabin, J.P.D., Rural Discontent in Nineteenth-century Britain, 1973 (with chapters by A.J. Peacock and Pamela R.L. Horn).

2382 Gash, N., 'Rural unemployment, 1815-34', Ec.H.R., VI, 1935, 90-3.
2383 Hammond, J.L. and Barbara, The Village Labourer, 1760-1832: A Study in the Government of England before the Reform Bill, 1st ed., 1911, 5th ed., 1948. Well-written, sentimental and misleading; Gonner's book (2364), although dull and difficult to read, is more valuable than the Hammonds' work.
2384 Hobsbawm, E.J. and Rudé, G., Captain Swing, 1969, 2nd ed., 1973 with new introduction (The agrarian riots of 1830). See bibliography, 367-71.
2385 Kerr, Barbara, M., Bound to the Soil: A Social History of Dorset, 1750-1918, 1968.
2386 Peacock, A.J., Bread or Blood: The Agrarian Riots in East Anglia, 1816, 1965.
2387 Rogers, P.G., The Battle in Bossenden Wood: The Strange Story of Sir William Courtenay, 1961.
2388 Springall, L. Marion, Labouring Life in Norfolk Villages, 1834-1914, 1936. See also Hasbach (1863) and Fussell (1858), listed above.

(g) William Cobbett

2389 Cobbett, W., The Progress of a Ploughboy to a Seat in Parliament, 1933, ed. W. Reitzel.
2390 Cole, G.D.H., The Life of William Cobbett, 1927. Includes a chapter on his Rural Rides by F.E. Green.
2391 Osborne, J.W., William Cobbett: His Thought and his Times, New Brunswick, N.J., 1964.
2392 Pearl, M., ed., William Cobbett: A Bibliographical Account of his Life and Times, 1953.
2393 Sambrook, J., William Cobbett, 1973.

(h) Regional and local studies

2393a Ambrose, P., The Quiet Revolution: Social Changes in a Sussex Village, 1871-1971, 1974 (Ringmer).
2394 Ashby, Mabel K., Joseph Ashby of Tysoe, 1859-1919: A Study of English Village Life, 1961.
2395 Branch, Johnson W., The Carrington Diary, 1797-1810, 1956. Based on the papers of John Carrington, a Hertfordshire farmer.
2396 Davies, C. Stella, The Agricultural History of Cheshire, 1750-1850, Chet. Soc., 3rd ser., 10, 1960.
2397 Fletcher, T.W., 'The agrarian revolution in arable Lancashire', T.L.C.A.S., LXXII, 1965, 93-122.
2398 ───── 'Lancashire livestock farming during the Great Depression', in Perry, ed. (2354), listed above.
2399 Garnett, F.W., Westmorland Agriculture, 1800-1900, 1912.
2400 Gaut, R.C., A History of Worcestershire Agriculture and Rural Evolution, 1939.
2401 Grigg, D.B., The Agricultural Revolution in South Lincolnshire, 1966.

2402 Havinden, M.A. and others, Estate Villages: A Study of the Berkshire Villages of Ardington and Lockinge, 1966. Study in depth of a Victorian landed estate.
2403 Hoskins, W.G., ed., History from the Farm, 1970. Historical studies of a number of individual farms in Great Britain.
2404 Melling, Elizabeth, ed., Kentish Sources III: Aspects of Agriculture and Industry, 1961. 1-90 deal with Kentish agriculture.
2405 Riches, Naomi, The Agricultural Revolution in Norfolk, 1937, 2nd ed., 1967, with bibliographical note.
2406 Tyrer, F., ed., The Great Diurnal of Nicholas Blundell of Little Crosby, Lancashire I: 1702-11, 1968; II: 1712-19, 1970; III: 1720-8, 1972.
2407 Ward, J.T., East Yorkshire Landed Estates in the Nineteenth Century, 1967.
2408 Winter, G., A Country Camera, 1844-1914: Rural Life as Depicted in Photographs, 1966.

ECONOMIC FLUCTUATIONS

As a brief general introduction, see:

2409 Morgan, E.V., The Study of Prices and the Value of Money, 1950.

(a) 1700-1800

2410 Ashton, T.S., Economic Fluctuations in England, 1700-1800, 1959.

(b) 1800-1913

2411 Aldcroft, D.H. and Fearon, P., eds., British Economic Fluctuations, 1790-1939, 1972. A selection of key articles.
2412 Gayer, A.D., Rostow, W.W. and Schwartz, Anna J., The Growth and Fluctuation of the British Economy, 1790-1850, 2 vols., 1953.
2413 Hughes, J.R.T., Fluctuations in Trade, Industry and Finance: A Study of British Economic Development, 1850-1860, 1960.
2414 Layton, W.T. and Crowther, G., An Introduction to the Study of Prices, 3rd rev. ed., 1938. Useful charts and tables of prices since 1820.
2415 Link, R.G., English Theories of Economic Fluctuations, 1815-1848, 1959.
2416 Matthews, R.C.O., A Study in Trade-Cycle History: Economic Fluctuations in Great Britain, 1833-1842, 1954.
2417 Rostow, W.W., British Economy of the Nineteenth Century, 1948. A classic treatment.
2418 Rousseaux, P., Les Mouvements de fond de l'économie anglaise, 1800-1913, Louvain, 1938.
2419 Ward-Perkins, C.N., 'The commercial crisis of 1847' in Carus-Wilson, ed. (164), listed above, III, 263-79.

(c) 1918-1939

2420 Alford, B.W.E., Depression and Recovery? British Economic Growth 1918-1939, 1972.
2421 Rees, G., The Great Slump: Capitalism in Crisis, 1929-33, 1970.
2422 Richardson, H.W., Economic Recovery in Britain, 1932-39, 1967.

FOOD AND DRINK

See also Ashley (302), Drummond and Wilbraham (874), Wilson (874a) and Cheke (1406), listed above.

(a) General

2423 Barker, T.C., McKenzie, J.C. and Yudkin, J., Our Changing Fare: Two Hundred Years of British Food Habits, 1966. Contains chapters on marketing, bread, meat, fish and fruit consumption and Scots diet, with detailed references.
2424 ——, Oddy, D.J. and Yudkin, J., The Dietary Surveys of Dr Edward Smith, 1862-3: A New Assessment, 1970.
2425 Blackman, Janet, 'The food supply of an industrial town: a study of Sheffield's public markets, 1780-1900', Business History, V, 1963, 82-97.
2426 Burnett, J., Plenty and Want: A Social History of Diet in England from 1815 to the Present Day, 1966.
2427 Chivers, K., 'Henry Jones versus the Admiralty', History Today, X, 1960, 247-54 (the invention of self-raising flour).
2428 Corley, T.E.B., Quaker Enterprise in Biscuits: Huntley and Palmers of Reading, 1822-1972, 1972.
2429 Crawford, W. and Broadley, H., The People's Food, 1938.
2430 Curtis-Bennett, N., The Food of the People: Being the History of Industrial Feeding, 1949.
2431 Deerr, N., The History of Sugar, 2 vols., 1949-50.
2432 Filby, F.A., History of Food Adulteration and Analysis, 1934.
2433 Hyde, H.M., Mr and Mrs Beeton, 1951.
2434 Kirby, C., 'The English game law system', A.H.R., XXXVIII, 1932-3, 240-62.
2435 —— 'The attack on the English game laws in the Forties', Jnl. Mod. Hist., IV, 1932, 18-37.
2436 Morris, Helen, Portrait of a Chef: The Life of Alexis Soyer, 1938.
2437 Palmer, A., Movable Feasts, 1952. Reprinted 1953. Changing English mealtimes.
2438 Salaman, R.N., The History and Social Influence of the Potato, 1949.
2439 Spain, Nancy, Mrs Beeton and her Husband, 1948. Reissued as The Beeton Story, 1956.
2440 Stuyvenberg, J.H. van, ed., Margarine: An Economic, Social and Scientific History, 1869-1969, 1969.
2441 Twining, S., The House of Twining, 1706-1956, 1956. Tea and coffee.
2442 Unwin, Jane C., ed., The Hungry Forties, or Life under the Bread Tax, 1904.

2443   Webber, R., Covent Garden: Mud Salad Market, 1969.

(b) Fish

2444   Barker, T. C. and Yudkin, J., eds., Fish in Britain: Trends in its Supply, Distribution and Consumption During the Past Two Centuries, 1971.
2445   Chaloner, W. H., 'Trends in fish consumption', in Barker et al. (2423), listed above, 94-114.
2446   Gray, M., 'Organisation and growth in the East-coast herring fishing, 1800-1885', in Payne (87), listed above, 187-216.
2447   Samuel, A. M., The Herring: Its Effect on the History of Britain, 1918.
2448   Stern, W., 'Fish supplies for London in the 1760s: an experiment in overland transport', parts I and II, Jnl. Royal Society of Arts, CXVIII, May 1970, 360-5; June 1970, 430-5.
See also Cutting (1407), listed above.

(c) Drink and the temperance movement

2449   French, R. V., Nineteen Centuries of Drink in England, 1886.
2450   Harrison, B., Drink and the Victorians: The Temperance Question in England 1815-1872, 1971.
2451   Harrison, B., Dictionary of British Temperance Biography, 1973.
2452   ——— 'The British prohibitionists, 1853-1872: a biographical analysis', International Review of Social History, XV, 1970, 375-467.
2453   Longmate, N., The Waterdrinkers: A History of Temperance, 1968.
2454   Mathias, P., The Brewing Industry in England 1700-1830, 1959.
2455   Sigsworth, E. M., The Brewing Trade During the Industrial Revolution: The Case of Yorkshire, 1967.
2456   Vaizey, J., The Brewing Industry, 1886-1951: An Economic Study, 1960.
2457   Wilson, G. B., Alcohol and the Nation, 1800-1935, 1940.

HOME MARKET, INCLUDING SHOPPING AND THE CO-OPERATIVE MOVEMENT

(a) Developments to 1850

2458   Alexander, D., Retailing in England during the Industrial Revolution, 1970.
2459   Davis, Dorothy, A History of Shopping, 1965.
2460   Eversley, D. E. C., 'The home market and economic growth in England 1750-80'. In Jones and Mingay (2346), listed above, 206-59.
2461   Gilboy, Elizabeth W., 'Demand as a factor in the Industrial Revolution', in A. H. Cole, ed., Facts and Factors in Economic History, Cambridge, Mass., 1932. Reprinted in Hartwell, ed. (2158), listed above, 121-38.
2462   Marshall, J. D., ed., The Autobiography of William Stout of Lancaster, 1665-1752, 1967.
2463   Robinson, E. H., 'Eighteenth-century commerce and fashion: Matthew Boulton's marketing techniques', Ec.H.R., 2nd ser., XVI, 1963, 39-60.
2464   Willan, T. S., An Eighteenth-century Shopkeeper: Abraham Dent of Kirkby Stephen, 1970.

(b) Co-operation

2465   Barou, N., ed., The Co-operative Movement in Labour Britain, 1948.
2466   Car-Saunders, A. M., Florence, P. Sargant, and Peers, R., eds., Consumers' Co-operation in Great Britain, 1933, 3rd rev. ed., 1942.
2467   Cole, G. D. H., A Century of Co-operation, 1945. A history of the co-operative movement in Great Britain and Ireland.
2468   Flanagan, D., 1869-1969: The Centenary Story of the Co-operative Union of Great Britain and Ireland, 1969.
2469   Holyoake, G. J., The History of Co-operation, 2 vols., 1875-79, 2nd rev. ed., 2 vols., 1906.
2470   Mercer, T. W., ed., Dr William King and the Co-operator, 1828-1830, 1922. Reprinted 1947.
2471   Musson, A. E., 'The ideology of early co-operation in Lancashire and Cheshire', T.L.C.A.S., LXVIII, 1959, 117-38. Reprinted in Musson (3055a), listed below.
2472   Pollard, S., 'Nineteenth century co-operation: from community-building to shop-keeping'. In Briggs and Saville (2989), listed below, 74-112.
2473   Redfern, P., The Story of the C.W.S.: the Jubilee History of the Co-operative Wholesale Society Ltd., 1863-1913, 1913.
2474   ——— The New History of the C.W.S., 1938.
2475   Webb, Catherine, ed., Industrial Co-operation: The Story of a Peaceful Revolution, Being an Account of the History, Theory and Practice of the Co-operative Movement in Great Britain, 2nd ed., 1906.

(c) Developments since 1850

2476   Adburgham, Alison, Shops and Shopping, 1800-1914: Where and in What Manner the Well-Dressed Englishwoman Bought her Clothes, 1964.
2477   Corina, M., Pile it High, Sell it Cheap: The Authorised Biography of Sir John Cohen, Founder of Tesco, 1971.
2478   Grether, E. T., Resale Price Maintenance in Great Britain, University of California Publications in Economics, XI (for 1932-5), 1942.
2479   Harrison, G. and Mitchell, F. C., The Home Market: A Handbook of Statistics, 1936, 2nd rev. ed., 1939.
2480   Jeffreys, J. B., Retail Trading in Britain, 1850-1950, 1954.
2481   Lambert, R. S., The Universal Provider: A Study of William Whiteley and the Rise of the London Department Store, 1938.

70   *England 1700-1970*

2482 Mathias, P., Retailing Revolution: A History of Multiple Retailing in the Food Trades, Based on the Allied Suppliers Group of Companies, 1967. Useful bibliography, 402-5. A history of the group built up around Maypole, Home and Colonial, and Lipton.
2483 Perkins, H. E., A Treatise on Haberdashery, Hosiery and General Drapery, 8th ed., 1853, 9th ed., 1874.
2484 Pound, R., Selfridge: A Biography, 1960.
2485 Rees, G., St Michael: A History of Marks and Spencer, 1969.
2486 Willcock, H. D., ed., Browns and Chester: Portrait of a Shop 1780-1946, 1946.

(d) Advertising

2487 Darwin, B., The Dickens Advertiser, 1930 (a collection of the advertisements in the original parts of Dickens's novels).
2487a Elliott, Blanche B., A History of English Advertising, 1962.
2488 Field, E., Advertising: The Forgotten Years, 1959 (the inter-war period).
2489 Mills, G. H. Saxon, There is a Tide, 1954. Life of Sir William Crawford (1878-1950), pioneer of modern advertising: some details about general advertising history.
2490 Sampson, H., A History of Advertising from the Earliest Times, 1875.
2491 Turner, E. S., The Shocking History of Advertising, 1952.
2492 Vries, L. de, Victorian Advertisements, 1968.

SCIENCE AND INVENTION

2493 Clark, G. N., Science and Social Welfare in the Age of Newton, 2nd rev. ed., 1949.
2494 Gomme, A. A., Patents of Invention: Origins and Growth of the Patent System in Britain, 1946.
2495 Habakkuk, H.J., American and British Technology in the Nineteenth Century: The Search for Labour-saving Inventions, 1962.
2496 Hatfield, H. S., The Inventor and his World 1933, 2nd rev. ed., 1948, with useful bibliography, 242-52.
2497 Mathias, P., ed., Science and Society, 1660-1900, 1972. Essays by various hands. See also Sigsworth (2309-2310), listed above.
2498 Musson, A. E., ed., Science, Technology and Economic Growth in the Eighteenth Century, 1972. Assembles eight key articles.
2499 Musson, A. E., and Robinson, E. H., Science and Technology in the Industrial Revolution, 1969. Also contains important material on the rise of the British chemical industry.
2500 Robinson, E. H., 'The Lunar Society: its membership and organisation', Trans. Newcomen Society, XXXV, 1964, 153-77.
2501 Saul, S. B., ed., Technological Change: The United States and Britain in the Nineteenth Century, 1970. Six essays by H. J. Habakkuk, D. L. Burn and others.
2502 Schofield, R. E., The Lunar Society of Birmingham: A Social History of Provincial Science and Industry in Eighteenth-century England, 1963.
2503 Woodcroft, B., Alphabetical List of Patentees of Inventions, 1854. Reprinted 1969 with new introduction and corrections.

TRUSTS, CARTELS AND COMPETITION

2504 Aldcroft, D. H., ed., The Development of British Industry and Foreign Competition, 1875-1914, 1968.
2505 Carter, G.R., Tendencies towards Industrial Combination, 1913.
2506 Fitzgerald, P., Industrial Combination in England, 1927.
2507 Levine, A. L., Industrial Retardation in Britain, 1880-1914, 1967.
2508 Levy, H., Monopolies, Cartels and Trusts in British Industry, 1927.
2509 Lucas, A. F., Industrial Reconstruction and the Control of Competition: The British Experiment, 1937.
2510 Macrosty, H. W., The Trust Movement in British Industry, 1907.

BUSINESS HISTORY

2511 Barker, T. C. et al., Business History, 2nd rev. ed., 1971. Useful bibliography, 27-32.
2512 Bellamy, Joyce, ed., Yorkshire Business Histories: A Bibliography, 1970.
2513 Business History, I, 1958-9 (now issued twice yearly).
2514 Horrocks, S., ed., Lancashire Business Histories, 1971. Part III of The Lancashire Bibliography (in progress). For Scottish business history see Payne [87] above.

POWER AND LIGHT

(a) Wind and water mills

2515 Bennett, R. and Elton, J., History of Corn Milling, 4 vols., 1898-1904.
2516 Ellis, C. M., 'A gazetteer of the water, wind and tide mills of Hampshire', Proceedings of the Hampshire Field Club, XXV, 1968, 119-40.
2517 Farriers, K. G. and Mason, M. G., The Windmills of Surrey and Inner London, 1966.
2518 Hillier, J., Old Surrey Watermills, 1951.
2519 Norris, J. H., 'The water-powered corn mills of Cheshire', T.L.C.A.S., LXXV and LXXVI, 1968, 33-71.
2520 Pelham, R. A., The Old Mills of Southampton, 1963.
2521 Syson, L., British Water Mills, 1965. Contains a good bibliography.

(b) The steam engine

2522 Barton, D. B., The Cornish Beam Engine, 1965, 2nd ed., 1966.

2523 Cardwell, D. S. L., Steam Power in the Eighteenth Century, 1963. The scientific background.
2524 Cule, J. E., 'Finance and industry in the eighteenth century: the firm of Boulton and Watt', Econ. Hist., IV, No. 15, February 1940, 319-25.
2525 Dickinson, H. W., The Cornish Engine, 1950.
2526 ——— James Watt, Craftsman and Engineer, 1935.
2527 ——— Matthew Boulton, 1936.
2528 ——— A Short History of the Steam Engine, 1st ed, 1938, 2nd ed., with corrections and new bibliographical introduction by A. E. Musson, 1963.
2529 ——— and Jenkins, R., James Watt and the Steam Engine, 1927.
2530 ——— and Titley, A., Richard Trevithick: The Engineer and the Man, 1934.
2531 Gale, W. K. V., 'Soho Foundry: Some Facts and Fallacies', Trans. Newcomen Society, XXXIV, 1963, 73-87.
2532 Harris, J. R., 'The employment of steam power in the eighteenth century', History, LII, 1967, 133-48.
2533 Hills, R. L., Power in the Industrial Revolution, 1970.
2534 Lord, J., Capital and Steam Power, 1750-1800, 1st ed. 1923, 2nd ed., with corrections and bibliographical introduction by W. H. Chaloner, 1966.
2535 Musson, A. E. and Robinson, E. H., 'The early growth of steam power', Ec.H.R. 2nd ser., XI, 1959, 418-39. Reprinted with additions in Musson and Robinson (2499), listed above.
2536 Roll, E., An Early Experiment in Industrial Organisation: Being a History of the Firm of Boulton & Watt, 1775-1805, 1930. Reprinted 1968.
2537 Rolt, L. T. C., Thomas Newcomen: The Prehistory of the Steam Engine, 1963.
2538 Robinson, E. H. and Musson, A. E., James Watt and the Steam Revolution: A Documentary History, 1969.
2539 Tunzelmann, G. N. von 'Technological diffusion during the Industrial Revolution: the case of the Cornish pumping engine'. In Hartwell, ed. (2157), listed above, 77-98.
2540 Watkins, G., The Stationary Beam Engine, 1968.
2541 ——— The Textile Mill Engine, I, 1970, II, 1971.

(c) Light

(1) General

2542 O'Dea, W. T., The Social History of Lighting, 1958.

(2) Gas

2543 Chandler, D. and Lacey, A. D., The Rise of the Gas Industry in Britain, 1949.
2544 Everard, S., History of the Gas Light and and Coke Company, 1812-1949, 1949.
2545 Falkus, M., 'The British gas industry before 1850', Ec.H.R., 2nd ser., XX, 1967, 494-508.
2546 Harris, S. A., The Development of Gas Supply on North Merseyside, 1815-1949, 1956.

(3) Electricity

2547 Ballin, H. H., The Organisation of Electricity Supply in Great Britain, 1946 (covers the period 1879-1944).
2548 Dunsheath, P., A History of Electrical Engineering, 1962.
2549 Parsons, R. H., A Short History of the Power Station Industry, 1939.
2550 Swale, W. E., Forerunners of the North Western Electricity Board, 1963.

ENGINEERING

2551 Armytage, W. H. G., A Social History of Engineering, 1st ed. 1961, 3rd rev. ed., 1969.
2552 Boucher, C. T. G., James Brindley, Engineer, 1716-1772, 1968.
2553 ——— John Rennie, 1761-1821: The Life and Work of a Great Engineer, 1963.
2554 Bracegirdle, B. and Miles, Patricia H., Thomas Telford, 1973. See also Burstall (1292), listed above.
2555 Clements, P., Marc Isambard Brunel, 1769-1849, 1970.
2556 Dougan, D., The Great Gun Maker, 1971. A biography of Sir William, later Lord, Armstrong.
2557 Gibb, A., The Story of Telford, 1934. Still valuable on engineering aspects.
2558 Harris, T. R., Arthur Woolf: The Cornish Engineer, 1766-1837, 1966.
2559 McNeil, I., Joseph Bramah: A Century of Invention, 1749-1851, 1968.
2560 Pole, W., ed., The Life of Sir William Fairbairn, Bart., Partly Written by Himself, 1st ed., 1877, 2nd ed., 1970 with new introduction by A. E. Musson.
2561 Roe, J. W., English and American Tool Builders, New Haven, Conn., 1916.
2562 Rolt, L. T. C., Great Engineers, 1962. Short studies of A. Darby, T. Newcomen, W. Jessop, M. Murray, H. Maudslay, J. Locke, J. Fowler, B. Baker, R. E. Crompton and F. W. Lanchester.
2563 ——— Thomas Telford, 1958.
2564 ——— Tools for the Job: A Short History of Machine Tools, 1965.
2565 ——— Victorian Engineering, 1970.
2566 ——— Waterloo Ironworks: A History of Taskers of Andover, 1809-1968, 1969.
2567 Saul, S. B., 'The machine tool industry in Britain to 1914', Business History, X, 1968, 22-43.
2568 ——— 'The market and the development of the mechanical engineering industries in Britain, 1860-1914', Ec.H.R., 2nd ser., XX, 1967, 111-30.
2569 Scott, J. D., Siemens Brothers, 1858-1958: An Essay in the History of Industry, 1958.

2570 Semler, E. G., ed., Engineering Heritage, 2 vols., 1963, 1966. Short biographies of eminent British engineers and industrial innovators.
2571 Simmons, J., 'William Jessop, civil engineer'. In Parish and Empire, 1952, 146-54.
2572 Smiles, S., The Lives of the Engineers, 5 vols., 1874.
2573 Sturt, G. (pseud. George Bourne), The Wheelwrights' Shop, 1st ed., 1923. Reprinted 1934, 1948. A business history, Farnham, Hampshire.
2574 Todd, A. C., Beyond the Blaze: A Biography of Davies Gilbert, 1967.
2575 Wilson, C. and Reader, W. J., Men and Machines: A History of D. Napier & Son, Engineers, Limited, 1808-1958, 1958.

COAL

2576 Anderson, D., 'Blundell's Wigan Collieries' (Parts, I, II, III, T.H.S.L.C., CXVI, 1964, 69-115; 117, 1965, 109-43: 119, 1967, 113-79.
2577 Ashton, T. S. and Sykes, J., The Coal Industry of the Eighteenth Century, 1929, 2nd rev. ed., 1964, with additions to the bibliography, 255-62.
2578 Atkinson, F., The Great Northern Coalfield, 1700-1900. Illustrated Notes on the Durham and Northumberland Coalfield, 1966.
2579 Banks, A. G. and Schofield, R. B., Brindley at Wet Earth Colliery: An Engineering Study, 1968. Reconstruction of James Brindley's work at a colliery near Manchester.
2580 Bulley, J. A., '"To Mendip for coal": A Study of the Somerset Coalfield before 1830', Proceedings of the Somersetshire Archaeological and Natural Historical Society, Part I, XCVII, 1952, 46-78; Part II, XCVIII, 1953, 46-78.
2581 Butt, J., 'Legends of the coal-oil industry, 1847-64', Explorations in Entrepreneurial History, 2nd ser., II, 1964, 16-30.
2582 ——— 'Technical change and the growth of the British shale-oil industry, 1680-1870', Ec.H.R., 2nd ser., XVII, 1965, 511-21.
2583 Down, C. G. and Warrington, A. J., The History of the Somerset Coalfield, 1971.
2584 Duckham, B. F., A History of the Scottish Coal Industry I: 1700-1815, 1970.
2585 Duckham, B. F. and H., Great Pit Disasters: Great Britain 1700 to the Present Day, 1973.
2586 ——— 'The emergence of the professional manager in the Scottish coal industry, 1760-1815', Business History Review, XLIII, 1969, 21-38.
2587 ——— 'Life and labour in a Scottish colliery, 1698-1755', Scot. H.R., XLVII, 1968, 109-28.
2588 ——— 'Some eighteenth-century Scottish coal mining methods: the 'Dissertation of Sir John Clerk', Industrial Archaeology, V, 1968, 217-32.
2589 Fraser-Stephen, Elspet, Two Centuries in the London Coal Trade: The Story of Charringtons, 1950.
2590 Griffin, A. R., Mining in the East Midlands, 1550-1947, 1971. Deals with production and unionism.
2591 Hair, P. E. H., 'The Lancashire collier girl, 1795', T.H.S.L.C., CXX, 1968, 63-86.
2592 Hair, T. H., A Series of Views of the Collieries in the Counties of Northumberland and Durham, 1844, 2nd ed., with new introduction, 1969.
2593 Hare, A. E. C., The Anthracite Coal Industry of the Swansea District, 1940.
2594 Holland, J., The History and Description of Fossil Fuel, the Collieries and Coal Trade of Great Britain, 1835, 2nd ed., 1841, new impression, 1968.
2595 Hughes, E., 'The coal trade', in North Country Life in the Eighteenth Century: The North East, 1700-1750, 1952, 151-257.
2596 ——— 'The collieries' and 'The coal trade'. In North Country Life in the Eighteenth Century: Cumberland and Westmorland, 1700-1830, 1965, 133-99.
2597 Jevons, H. S., The British Coal Trade, 1915, 2nd ed., with new introduction 1969.
2598 Jevons, W. S., The Coal Question, 1865.
2599 Leifchild, J. R., Our Coal and Our Coal Pits, the People in Them and the Scenes around Them, 2nd ed., 1856, new impression, 1968.
2600 Lerry, G. G., The Collieries of Denbighshire, 1946.
2601 Lloyd, A. L. (compiler), Come all ye Bold Miners: Ballads and Songs of the Coalfields, 1952.
2602 Mining Association of Great Britain, Historical Review of Coal Mining, 1924.
2603 Morris, J. H. and Williams, L. J., The South Wales Coal Industry, 1841-1875, 1958.
2604 Mott, R. A., 'The London and Newcastle chaldron for measuring coal', Archaeologia Aeliana, 4th ser., XL, 1962, 227-39.
2605 Sweezy, P. M., Monopoly and Competition in the English Coal Trade, 1550-1850, Cambridge, Mass., 1938.
2606 Taylor, A. J., 'The coal industry'. In Aldcroft, ed. (2504), listed above, 37-70.
2607 ——— 'Combination in the mid-eighteenth-century coal industry', T.R.H.S., 5th ser., III, 1953, 23-39.
2608 ——— 'Labour productivity and technological innovation in the British coal industry, 1850-1914', Ec.H.R., 2nd ser., XIV, 1961, 48-70.
2609 ——— 'The third marquis of Londonderry and the north-eastern coal trade', Durham University Jnl., 1955, 21-7.
2610 ——— 'The Wigan coalfield in 1851', T.H.S.L.C., 106, 1954, 117-26.
2611 Walker, S. F., Coal Cutting by Machinery in the United Kingdom, 1902.
2612 White, A. W. A., Men and Mining in Warwickshire, 1970.
2613 Wood, O., 'A Cumberland colliery during the Napoleonic War', Economica, XXI, 1954, 54-63.

COPPER AND BRASS

2614 Burt, R., ed., Cornish Mining: Essays on the Organisation of the Cornish Mines and the Cornish Mining Economy, 1969.
2614a Day, Joan, Bristol Brass: The History of the Industry, 1973.
2615 Harris, J. R., The Copper King: A Biography of Thomas Williams of Llanidan, 1964.
2616 Leifchild, J. R., Cornwall: Its Mines and Miners, 1853. Reprinted 1968.
2617 Roberts, R. O., 'Copper and economic growth in Britain, 1729-84', National Library of Wales Jnl. X, 1957, 1-10.
See also Hamilton (1367) and Jenkin (1867), listed above.

LEAD MINING

2618 Bevan-Evans, M., 'Gadlys and Flintshire lead-mining in the eighteenth century', Parts I, II, III, Flintshire Historical Society Publications, XVIII, 1960, 75-130; XIX, 1961, 32-60; XX, 1962, 58-89.
2619 Clough, R. T., The Lead Smelting Mills of the Yorkshire Dales: Their Architectural Character, Construction and Place in the European Tradition, 1962; bibliography, 169-72.
2620 Ford, T. D. and Nieuwerts, J. H., eds., Lead Mining in the Peak District, 1968; bibliography, 123-4.
2621 Hunt, C. J., The Lead Miners of the Northern Pennines in the Eighteenth and Nineteenth Centuries, 1970.
2622 Jennings, B., ed., A History of Nidderdale, 1967, 151-61, 266-325.
2623 Kirkham, Nellie, Derbyshire Lead-mining through the Centuries, 1968.
2624 O'Neal, R., A Bibliography of Derbyshire Lead Mining, 1961.
2625 Raistrick, A., Miners and Miners of Swaledale, 1955.
2626 —— Two Centuries of Industrial Welfare: The London (Quaker) Lead Company, 1692-1905, 1938.
See also Raistrick and Jennings (1380), listed above.

IRON AND STEEL

2627 Addis, J. P., The Crawshay Dynasty: A Study in Industrial Organisation and Development, 1765-1867, 1957.
2627a Allen, G. C., The Industrial Development of Birmingham and the Black Country 1860-1927, 1929.
2628 Andrews, P. W. S. and Brunner, Elizabeth, Capital Development in Steel: A Study of the United Steel Companies, Ltd., 1951.
2629 Ashton, T. S., An Eighteenth-century Industrialist: Peter Stubs of Warrington, 1756-1806, 1939, 2nd ed., 1961.
See also (2640a), listed below.
2630 —— Iron and Steel in the Industrial Revolution, 1st ed., 1924, 2nd rev. ed., 1951, 3rd ed., with new bibliographical introduction, 1963.
2631 Bessemer, H., Autobiography, 1905.
2632 Birch, A., The Economic History of the British Iron and Steel Industry, 1784-1879, 1967.
2633 —— and Flinn, M. W., 'The English steel industry before 1856 with special reference to the development of the Yorkshire Steel industry', Yorks. Bull., VI, 1954, 163-77.
2634 Burn, D. L., The Economic History of Steelmaking, 1867-1939, 1940, 2nd rev. ed., 1961.
2635 —— The Steel Industry, 1939-1959, 1961.
2636 Butler, R. F., The History of Kirkstall Forge Through Seven Centuries, 1200-1945, A.D., 1945, 2nd rev. ed., 1954.
2637 Campbell, R. H., Carron Company, 1961.
2638 Carr, J. C., Taplin, W. and Wright, A. E. G., History of the British Steel Industry, 1962.
2639 Chaloner, W. H., 'Isaac Wilkinson, potfounder'. In Pressnell (2170), listed above.
2640 Chappell, E. L., Historic Melingriffith: An Account of the Pentyrch Iron Works, 1940.
2640a Dane, E. S., Peter Stubs and the Lancashire Hand Tool Industry, 1973.
2641 Elsas, Madeleine, Iron in the Making: Dowlais Iron Company Letters, 1782-1860, 1960.
2642 Evans, J. D., 'The uncrowned Iron King (the first William Crawshay)', National Library of Wales Jnl., VII, 1951, 12-32.
See also Fell (1362), listed above.
2643 Fereday, R. P., The Career of Richard Smith 1783-1868, Round Oak Steel Works Ltd., 1966 (Smith was mineral agent to the Earl of Dudley).
2644 Flinn, M. W., The Law Book of the Crowley Iron Works, Surtees Society, 1957.
2645 —— Men of Iron: The Crowleys in the Early Iron Industry, 1962.
See also Birch and Flinn (2633), listed above.
2646 Gale, W. K. V., The Black Country Iron Industry: A Technical History, 1966 (mainly 1700 to 1960s).
2647 —— The British Iron and Steel Industry: A Technical History, 1967.
2648 —— The Coneygre Story (Tipton, Staffordshire), 1954.
2649 Gloag, J. and Bridgwater, D., A History of Cast Iron in Architecture, 1948.
2650 Griffiths, S., Guide to the Iron Trade of Great Britain, 1873, 2nd ed., with new introduction, 1967.
2651 Harris, A., Cumberland Iron: The Story of Hodbarrow Mine, 1855-1968, 1971.
2651a Hey, D., The Rural Metalworkers of the Sheffield Region, 1972.
2652 Hulme, E. W., 'Henry Cort, founder of the iron puddling process and his family', Notes and Queries, CXCVII, 77-82.

2653 —— 'The pedigree and career of Benjamin Huntsman, inventor in Europe of crucible steel', Trans. Newcomen Society, XXIV, 1943-5, 37-48.
2654 —— 'A statistical history of the iron trade in England and Wales, 1717-1750', Trans. Newcomen Society, IX, 1928-9, 12-35
2655 John, A. H., ed., Minutes Relating to Messrs. Samuel Walker & Co., Rotherham, Iron Founders and Steel Refiners, 1741-1829, 1951.
2656 Johnson, B. L. C., 'The Midland iron industry in the early eighteenth century: the background to the first successful use of coke in iron smelting', Business History, II, 1960, 67-74.
2656a McCloskey, D., Economic Maturity and Enterpreneurial Decline: British Iron and Steel, 1870-1913, 1974.
2657 Minchinton, W. E., The British Tinplate Industry: A History, 1957.
2658 Mottram, R. H. and Coote, C., Through Five Generations: The History of the Butterley Company, 1950.
2659 Musgrave, P. W., Technical Change, the Labour Force and Education: A Study of the British and German Iron and Steel Industries, 1860-1964, 1967. Deals mainly with technical evolution; should be used with great caution.
2660 Namier, L. B., 'Anthony Bacon, M.P., an eighteenth-century merchant'. In Minchinton, ed. (3902), listed below, 59-106.
2661 Osborn, F. M., The Story of the Mushets, 1952.
2662 Pollard, S., Three Centuries of Sheffield Steel: The Story of a Family Business (Marsh Bros. & Co.), 1954.
2663 Scrivenor, H., History of the Iron Trade, 1st ed., 1841, 2nd rev. ed., 1854. Reprinted 1967.
2664 Raistrick, A., Dynasty of Ironfounders: The Darbys and Coalbrookdale, 1953.
2665 —— and Allen, E., 'The South Yorkshire ironmasters, 1690-1750', Ec.H.R., IX, 1939, 168-85.
2666 Raybould, T. J., The Economic Emergence of the Black Country: A Study of the Dudley Estate, 1973.
2667 Robinson, P., The Smiths of Chesterfield: A History of the Griffin Foundry, Brampton, 1775-1833, 1957.
2668 Roepke, H., Movements of the British Iron and Steel Industry, 1720-1951, Urbana, Ill., 1956. See Schubert (400), listed above.
2669 Warren, K., The British Iron and Steel Sheet Industry since 1840, 1970.
2670 Williams, L. J., 'A Carmarthenshire ironmaster and the Seven Years War', Business History, II, 1959-60, 32-43.

TEXTILES

(a) General

2671 Textile History, I, Nos. 1-3, 1968-70; II, No. 1, 1971 (all published); III, 1972 (continuing).
2672 Harte, N. B. and Ponting, K. G., eds., Textile History and Economic History: Essays in Honour of Miss Julia de Lacy Mann, 1973. Essays on aspects of the stocking-knitting, wollen, worsted, linen and cotton trades from 1500 to 1867.

(b) Cotton

2673 Anderson, M., Family Structure in Nineteenth-century Lancashire, 1971. Excellent bibliography. Largely based on Preston.
2674 Aspin, C., James Hargreaves and the Spinning Jenny, 1964.
2675 Baines, E., History of the Cotton Manufacture in Great Britain, 1835, 2nd ed., 1966, with bibliographical introduction, 5-14.
2676 Bowker, B., Lancashire under the Hammer, 1928.
2677 Boyson, R., The Ashworth Cotton Enterprise: The Rise and Fall of a Family Firm, 1818-1880, 1970.
2678 Bythell, D., The Handloom Weavers: A Study in the English Cotton Industry During the Industrial Revolution, 1969.
2679 Catling, H., The Spinning Mule, 1970.
2680 Chapman, S. D., The Early Factory Masters: The Transition to the Factory System in the Midlands Textile Industry, 1967.
2680a ——, The Cotton Industry in the Industrial Revolution, 1972 (excellent summary).
2681 Chapman, S. J., The Lancashire Cotton Industry: A Study in Economic Development, 1904. Select bibliography, 277-304.
2682 —— and Ashton, T. S., 'The sizes of businesses, mainly in the textile industries', Jnl. Royal Stat. Soc., LXXVII, Part V, 1914, 469-555.
2683 —— and Kemp, D., 'The war and the textile industries', Jnl. Royal Stat. Soc., LXXVIII, Part II, 1915, 157-237.
2684 Clapp, B. W., John Owens, Manchester Merchant, 1965. Covers period 1790-1846.
2685 Collier, Frances, The Family Economy of the Working Classes in the Cotton Industry, 1784-1833, 1964.
2686 Daniels, G. W., The Early English Cotton Industry, 1920.
2687 Edwards, M. M., The Growth of the British Cotton Trade, 1780-1815, 1967.
2688 Ellison, Mary, Support for Secession: Lancashire and the American Civil War, Chicago, Ill., 1972.
2689 Ellison, T., The Cotton Trade of Great Britain: Including a History of the Liverpool Cotton Market, 1886.
2690 English, W., The Textile Industry: An Account of the Early Inventions of Spinning, Weaving and Knitting Machines, 1969. Useful glossary of technical terms and bibliography, 225-35.
2690a Farnie, D. A., 'John Rylands of Manchester', Bulletin of the John Rylands University Library of Manchester, LVI, No. 1, 1973, 93-129.

2691 Fitton, R. S. and Wadsworth, A. P., The Strutts and the Arkwrights, 1758-1830, 1958.

2692 Henderson, W. O., The Lancashire Cotton Famine, 1861-1865, 1934, 2nd rev. and enlarged ed., 1969, with bibliography, 157-94.

2693 Jewkes, J. and Gray, E. M., Wages and Labour in the Lancashire Cotton Spinning Industry, 1935.

2694 Jones, G. T., 'The Lancashire cotton industry, 1845-1913'. In Increasing Return, 1933, 100-19.

2695 Lee, C. H., A Cotton Enterprise, 1795-1840: A History of McConnel and Kennedy, Fine Cotton Spinners, 1972.

2696 Muir, A., The Kenyon Tradition: The History of James Kenyon and Son, Ltd., 1664-1964, 1964.

2697 Pigott, S. C., Hollins: A Study of Industry, 1784-1949, 1949.

2698 Political and Economic Planning, Report on the British Cotton Industry, 1934.

2699 Prest, J., The Industrial Revolution in Coventry, 1960.

2700 Robson, R., The Cotton Industry in Britain, 1957.

2701 Sandberg, L. G., 'American rings and English mules: the role of economic rationality'. In S. B. Saul, ed., Technological Change: The United States and Britain in the Nineteenth Century, 1970, 120-40.

2701a —— Lancashire in Decline: A Study in Entrepreneurship Technology and International Trade, Columbus, Ohio, 1974.

2702 Shapiro, S., Capital and the Cotton Industry in the Industrial Revolution, Ithaca, N.Y., 1967.

2703 Silver, A., Manchester Men and Indian Cotton, 1847-1872, 1966.

2704 Smelser, N. J., Social Change in the Industrial Revolution: An Application of Theory to the Lancashire Cotton Industry, 1770-1840, 1959; bibliography, 411-40.

2705 Tewson, W. F., The British Cotton Growing Association: Golden Jubilee, 1904-1954, 1954.

2706 Tippett, L. H. C., A Portrait of the Lancashire Textile Industry, 1969. Covers the period 1919-69.

2707 Unwin, G., et al., Samuel Oldknow and the Arkwrights; The Industrial Revolution at Stockport and Marple, 1st ed., 1924, 2nd rev. ed., 1968.

2708 Utley, F., Lancashire and the Far East, 1931.
See also Bowker (1676) and Sandberg (2701a), listed above.

2709 Wells, F. A., Hollins and Viyella: A Study in Business History, 1968.

(c) Woollens and worsteds

2710 Atkinson, F., ed., Some Aspects of the Eighteenth Century Woollen and Worsted Trade in Halifax, 1956.

2711 Beckinsale, R. P., ed., The Trowbridge Woollen Industry as Illustrated by the Stock Books of John and Thomas Clark, 1804-1824, 1951.

2712 —— 'The plush industry of Oxfordshire', Oxoniensa, XXVIII, 1963, 53-67.

2713 Bischoff, J., A Comprehensive History of the Woollen and Worsted Manufactures, 2 vols., 1942. Reprinted 1968.

2714 Clapham, J. H., 'The transference of the worsted industry from Norfolk to the West Riding', Ec.J., XX, 1910, 195-210.

2715 Coleman, D. C., 'Growth and decay during the Industrial Revolution: the case of East Anglia', Scand. Ec.H.R., X, Stockholm, 1962, 115-27.

2716 Crump, W. B., The Leeds Woollen Industry, 1780-1820, 1931.

2717 —— and Ghorbal, Gertrude, History of the Huddersfield Woollen Industry, 1935. Reprinted 1967.

2718 Hartley, Marie and Ingilby, Joan, The Old Hand-knitters of the Yorkshire Dales, 1951.

2719 Hunter, D. M., The West of England Woollen Industry, 1910.
See also James (1337) and Jenkins (1338), listed above.

2720 Lipson, E., A History of Wool and Wool Manufacture, 1953.
See also Lipson (1339) listed above.

2721 Mann, Julia de L., The Cloth Industry in the West of England, 1640-1880, 1971.

2722 —— 'Clothiers and weavers in Wiltshire during the eighteenth century'. In Pressnell, ed. (2170), listed above.

2723 —— ed., Documents Illustrating the Wiltshire Woollen Trades in the Eighteenth Century, 1964.

2724 Moir, Esther, A. L., 'The gentlemen clothiers; a study of the organisation of the Gloucestershire cloth industry, 1750-1835'. In H. P. R. Finberg, ed., Gloucestershire Studies, 1957.

2725 Plummer, A., The Witney Blanket Industry: The Records of the Witney Blanket Weavers, 1934.

2726 —— and Early, R. E., The Blanket Makers, 1669-1969: A History of Charles Early and Marriot (Witney) Ltd., 1969.

2727 Ponting, K. G., ed., Baines's Account of the Woollen Industry of England, 1970. Text of E. Baines' article on the subject from T. Baines's Yorkshire Past and Present, 1875; useful glossary, 145-65, and bibliography, 60-5.

2728 —— A History of the West of England Cloth Industry, 1957.

2729 —— The Woollen Industry of South-West England, 1971.

2730 Prichard, M. F. Lloyd, 'The decline of Norwich', Ec.H.R., 2nd ser., III, 1951, 371-7.

2731 Sigsworth, E. M., Black Dyke Mills: A History, 1958. Contains useful introductory chapters on the development of the worsted industry in the nineteenth century. See also Tann (1349), listed above.

2732 Wilson, R. G., Gentlemen Merchants: The Merchant Community in Leeds, 1700-1830, 1971.

76 England 1700-1970

(d) Clothing industry

2733 Thomas, Joan, A History of the Leeds Clothing Industry, 1955.
2734 Wray, Margaret, The Women's Outerwear Industry, 1957.

(e) Silk

2735 Chaloner, W. H., 'Sir Thomas Lombe (1685-1739) and the British silk industry'. In People and Industries, 1963, 8-20.
2736 Clapham, J. H., 'The Spitalfields Acts, 1773-1824', Ec.J., XXVI, 1916, 459-71.
2737 Coleman, D. C., Courtaulds: An Economic and Social History, 2 vols., 1969.
2738 Hertz (later Hurst), G. B., 'The English silk industry in the eighteenth century', E.H.R., XXIV, 1909, 710-27.
2739 Warner, F., The Silk Industry of the United Kingdom, 1921.
2740 Weinstock, Maureen, 'Portrait of an eighteenth-century Sherborne silk mill owner'. In Studies in Dorset History, 1953, 83-102.

(f) Linen and flax

2741 Gill, C., The Rise of the Irish Linen Industry, 1925. Reprinted 1964.
2742 Horner, J., The Linen Trade of Europe During the Spinning-Wheel Period, 1920. Contains useful trade statistics.
2743 Rimmer, W. G., Marshalls of Leeds, Flax-Spinners, 1788-1886, 1960. Excellent bibliography, 327-35.
2744 Warden, A. J., The Linen Trade, Ancient and Modern, 1864, 3rd impression, 1967.

(g) Hatting

2745 Dony, J. G., A History of the Straw Hat Industry, 1942 (South Midlands, Essex and Suffolk). Covers the period 1680-1939.
2746 Giles, Phyllis M., 'The felt-hatting industry, c. 1500-1800, with particular reference to Lancashire and Cheshire', T.L.C.A.S., LXIX, 1960, 104-32.

(h) Hosiery

2747 Felkin, W., History of the Machine-wrought Hosiery and Lace Manufactures, 1867. 2nd ed., with introduction by S. D. Chapman, 1967, v-xxxviii; select bibliography of books, articles and theses since 1867, xxxix-xliii.
2748 Wells, F. A., The British Hosiery Trade, 1935; 2nd, rev. and enlarged edn., 1972.

CHEMICALS AND SOAP

2749 Barker, T.C., 'Lancashire coal, Cheshire salt and the rise of Liverpool', T.H.S.L.C., CIII, 1951, 83-101.
2750 Bolitho, H., Alfred Mond, First Lord Melchett, 1933.
2751 Clow, A. and Nan L., The Chemical Revolution: A Contribution to Social Technology, 1952.
2752 Cohen, J. M., The Life of Ludwig Mond, 1956.
2753 Crathorne, Nancy, Tennant's Stalk: The Story of the Tennants of the Green, 1973.
2754 Haber, L. F., The Chemical Industry During the Nineteenth Century: A Study of the Economic Aspect of Applied Chemistry in Europe and North America, 1958.
2755 ——— The Chemical Industry, 1900-1930: International Growth and Technological Change, 1971.
2756 Hardie, D. W. F., A History of the Chemical Industry in Widnes, 1950.
2757 ——— 'The Macintoshes and the origins of the chemical industry', Chemistry and Industry, 1952, 606-13.
2758 ——— and Pratt, J.D., A History of the Modern British Chemical Industry, 1966.
2759 Iredale, D. A., 'John and Thomas Marshall and the Society for improving the British Salt Trade', Ec.H.R. 2nd ser., XX, 1967, 79-93.
2760 ——— 'The rise and fall of the Marshalls of Northwich, salt proprietors, 1720-1917', T.H.S.L.C., CXVII, 1965, 59-82.
2761 Koss, S. E., Sir John Brunner, Radical Plutocrat, 1842-1919, 1970.
2762 Musson, A. E., Enterprise in Soap and Chemicals: Joseph Crosfield and Sons, Ltd., 1815-1865, 1965. The soap industry in Warrington.
2763 Padley, R., 'The beginnings of the British alkali industry', Birm.Hist.Jnl., III, 1951, 64-78.
2764 Reader, W. J., Imperial Chemical Industries: A History I: The Forerunners, 1870-1926, 1970. Excellent bibliography, 524-34.
2765 Wilson, C. H., The History of Unilever: A Study in Economic Growth and Social Change, 2 vols., 1954.
2766 ——— Unilever, 1945-1965: Challenge and Response in the Post-war Industrial Revolution, 1968.

POTTERY

2767 Anon., Some Descriptions of Pottery Making and Working Conditions, 1557-1844, 1970.
2768 Barton, R. M., A History of the Cornish China-clay Industry, 1966.
2769 Bladen, V. W., 'The Potteries in the Industrial Revolution', Ec. J. Economic History Supplement, I, No. 1, 1926, 117-30.
2770 Finer, Ann and Savage, G., eds., The Selected Letters of Josiah Wedgwood, 1965.
2771 Hower, R. M., 'The Wedgwoods: ten generations of potters', Jnl. of Economic and Business History, IV, No. 2, 1932, 281-313, LV, No. 4, 1932, 665-90.
2772 Jewitt, Ll., The Wedgwoods: Being a Life of Josiah Wedgwood: With Notices of his Works and their Productions, Memoir of the Wedgwoods and Other Families and a History of the Early Potteries of Staffordshire, 1865.
2773 Mackenzie, C., The House of Coalport, 1750-1950, 1951.
2774 Meteyard, Eliza, Life of Josiah Wedgwood from his Private Correspondence, 2 vols., 1865-66.

2774a Rolt, L. T. C., Potters' Field: A History of the South Devon Ball Clay Industry, 1974.
2775 Thomas, J., 'The pottery industry and the Industrial Revolution', Ec. J. Economic History Supplement, III, No. 12, Feb. 1937, 399-414.
2776 —— The Rise of the Staffordshire Potteries, 1971.
2777 Owen, H., The Staffordshire Potter, with a Chapter on the Dangerous Processes in the Potting Industry by the Duchess of Sutherland, 1901.
2778 Weatherill, Lorna, The Pottery Trade and North Staffordshire, 1660-1760, 1971.
2779 Whiter, L., Spode: A History of the Family, Factory and Wares from 1733 to 1833, 1970.

GLASS

2780 Barker, T. C., Pilkington Brothers and the Glass Industry, 1960.
2781 Harris, J. R., 'Origins of the St. Helens glass industry', Northern History, III, 1968, 105-17.

RUBBER

2782 Payne, P. L., Rubber and Railways in the Nineteenth Century: A Study of the Spencer Papers, 1961.
2783 Schidrowitz, P., and Dawson, T. R., eds., History of the Rubber Industry, 1952.
2784 Woodruff, W., The Rise of the British Rubber Industry During the Nineteenth Century, 1958.

MISCELLANEOUS

2785 Alford, B. W. E., W. D. and H. O. Wills and the Development of the U. K. Tobacco Trade, 1786-1965, 1973.
2786 Brace, H. W., History of Seed Crushing in Great Britain, 1960.
2786a Chapman, S. D., Jesse Boot of Boots the Chemists, 1974.

PRINTING AND NEWSPAPERS

2787 Adburgham, Alison, Women in Print, 1972. Covers women authors and women's magazines from 1660 to 1837.
2788 Altick, R. D., The English Common Reader: A Social History of the Mass Reading Public 1800-1900, Chicago, Ill., 1957.
2789 Anon., History of the Times, 4 vols., 1935-52.
2790 Aspinall, A., Politics and the Press, 1780-1850, 1949.
2791 Ayerst, D., Guardian: Biography of a Newspaper, 1971.
2792 Camrose, Lord, London Newspapers: Their Owners and Controllers, 1939.
2793 Clair, C., A History of Printing in Britain, 1965.
2794 Collet, C. D., History of the Taxes on Knowledge: Their Origin and Repeal, 2 vols., 1899, 2nd abridged ed., 1933.
2795 Cranfield, G. A., The Development of the Provincial Newspaper, 1700-1760, 1962. Bibliography, 274-8.
2796 Ewald, W. B., The Newsmen of Queen Anne, 1956.
2797 Ffrench, Yvonne, ed., News from the Past, 1805-1887: The Autobiography of the Nineteenth Century, 1934. Extracts from the newspaper press.
2798 Handover, P. M., Printing in London from 1476 to Modern Times, 1960.
2799 Hanson, L., Government and the Press, 1695-1763, 1936.
2800 Hollis, Patricia, The Pauper Press: A Study in Working-class Radicalism of the 1830s, 1970.
2801 James, L., Fiction for the Working Man, 1830-1850, 1963.
2802 Knight, C., Passages of a Working Life during half a century, 1864-5. Reprinted 1971.
2803 Mills, W. H., The Manchester Guardian: A Century of History, 1921.
2804 Milne, M., Newspapers of Northumberland and Durham in the Nineteenth Century, 1971.
2805 Plant, Marjorie, The English Book Trade, 1939. Reprinted 1974.
2806 Political and Economic Planning, Report on the British Press, 1938.
2807 Price, R. G. G., A History of Punch, 1957.
2808 Read, D., Press and People, 1790-1850: Opinion in Three English Cities (Manchester, Leeds and Sheffield), 1961.
2809 Siebert, F. S., Freedom of the Press in England, 1476-1776: The Rise and Decline of Government Control, Urbana, Ill., 1965.
2810 Webb, R. K., The British Working-Class Reader, 1790-1848: Literary and Social Tension, 1955.
2811 Weed, K. K., and Bond, R. P., 'Studies of British newspapers and periodicals from their beginning to 1800: a bibliography'. In Studies in Philology, Durham, N. C., 1946.
2812 White, Cynthia, L., Women's Magazines, 1693-1968, 1970.
2813 Wickwar, W. H., The Struggle for the Freedom of the Press, 1819-1832, 1928.
2814 Wiener, J. H., A Descriptive Finding List of Unstamped British Periodicals, 1830-1836, 1970.
2815 —— The War of the Unstamped: A History of the Movement to Repeal the British Newspaper Tax, 1830-1836, 1970.
2816 Wiles, R. M., Freshest Advices: Early Provincial Newspapers in England, Columbus, Ohio, 1965.

PAPERMAKING

2816a Shorter, A. H., Paper Making in the British Isles, 1971.
See Coleman (1393) and Shorter (1394), listed above.

BANKING, CURRENCY AND PUBLIC FINANCE

2817 Clapham, J. H., 'Modern bibliography of banking and currency (British Empire) from the fifteenth century to 1815'. In J. G. Van Dillen, History of the Principal Public Banks, 1934, 449-56.

2817a Fetter, F. W. and Gregory, D., Monetary and Financial Policy, 1973 (a guide to nineteenth century Blue Books).

(a) Currency

2818 Dalton, R. and Hamer, S. H., The Provincial Token Coinage of the Eighteenth Century, 4 vols., 1910-18. Reissued in one vol., 1967.

2819 Davis, W. J., The Nineteenth-Century Token Coinage of Great Britain and Ireland, 1904, 2nd ed., 1969.

2820 Holden, J. M., The History of Negotiable Instruments in English Law, 1955.

2821 Mathias, P., English Trade Tokens: The Industrial Revolution Illustrated, 1962.

(b) Public finance

(1) The National Debt

2822 Carter, Alice C., The English Public Debt in the Eighteenth Century, 1968.

2823 Dickson, P. G. M., The Financial Revolution in England: A Study in the Development of Public Credit, 1688-1756, 1967.

2824 Hargreaves, E. L., The National Debt, 1930, 2nd ed., 1966.

(2) South Sea Bubble

2825 Carswell, J., The South Sea Bubble, 1960.

2826 Sperling, J. G., The South Sea Company: An Historical Essay and Bibliographical Finding List, Boston, Mass., 1962.

(3) Taxes

2827 Dowell, S., A History of Taxes and Taxation in England from the Earliest Times to the Present Day, 1884, 2nd ed., 1888, 3rd ed., 1965. Vol. II: Taxes from the Civil War to 1883. Vol. III: Direct and Stamp Duties. Vol. IV: Articles of Consumption.

2828 Kennedy, W., English Taxation, 1640-1799: An Essay on Policy and Opinion, 1913, 2nd ed., 1964.

(i) Income Tax

2829 Farnsworth, A., Addington, Author of the Modern Income Tax, 1951.

2830 Hope-Jones, A., Income Tax in the Napoleonic Wars, 1939.

2831 Sabine, B. E. V., A History of Income Tax, 1966. Covers the modern period.

2832 Shehab, F. A., Progressive Taxation: A Study of the Progressive Principle in the British Income Tax, 1953.

(ii) Land Tax

2833 Ward, W. R., The English Land Tax in the Eighteenth Century, 1953.

2834 ——— 'The Land Tax in Scotland, 1707-98', Bulletin of the John Rylands Library, XXXVII, 1954, 288-308.

(iii) Salt Tax

See Hughes (1743), listed above.

(4) Administration and budgetary control

2835 Baker, N., Government and Contractors: The British Treasury and War Supplies, 1775-1783, 1971.

2836 Binney, J. E. D., British Public Finance and Administration, 1774-1792, 1958.

2837 Hicks, Ursula K., British Public Finances: Their Structure and Development, 1880-1952, 1954.

2838 ——— The Finance of British Government, 1920-36, 1938.

2839 Hirst, F. W., Gladstone as Financier and Economist, 1931.

2840 ——— and Allen, J. E., British War Budgets, 1926. Goes up to the budget of 1924.

2841 Kirkcaldy, A. W., British Finance During and After the War, 1914-21, 1921.

2842 Mallet, B., British Budgets, 1887-88 to 1912-13, 1913.

2843 ——— and George, C. O., British Budgets: Second Series, 1913-14 to 1920-21, 1929.

2844 ——— and George, C. O., British Budgets: Third Series, 1921-22 to 1932-33, 1933.

2845 Morton, W. A., British Finance, 1930-1940, Madison, Wis., 1943.

2846 Nevin, E., The Mechanism of Cheap Money: A Study of British Monetary Policy, 1931-39, 1955.

2847 Sabine, B. E. V., British Budgets in Peace and War, 1932-1945, 1970.

2848 Sayers, R. S., Financial Policy, 1939-45, 1956. Part of the British official civil history of the war.

(c) Banking and the London money market

2849 Acworth, A. W., Financial Reconstruction in England, 1815-1822, 1925. See also Andréades (1700), listed above.

2850 Ashton, T. S. and Sayers, R. S., eds., Papers in English Monetary History, 1953.

2851 Balogh, T., Studies in Financial Organisation, 1947. See Bisschop (1702), listed above.

2852 Boyle, A., Montagu Norman, 1967.

2853 Cannan, E., ed., The Paper Pound of 1797-1821: A Reprint of the Bullion Report (of 1810), 1st ed., 1919, 2nd ed., 1925, 3rd ed., with new introduction by B. A. Corry, 1969.

2854 Clapham, J. H., The Bank of England: A History, 2 vols., 1944. Reprinted 1958 (Vol. I: 1694-1797, Vol. II: 1797-1914).

2855 Clay, H., Lord Norman, 1957, especially Chapter VIII on banks and the finance of industry.

2856 Coppieters, E., English Bank Note Circulation, 1694-1954, The Hague, 1955.

2857 Cramp, A. B., Opinion on Bank Rate, 1822-1860, 1962.

2858 Dacey, H. M., The British Banking Mechanism, 1951. Outlines the working of the financial system since 1931.
2859 Fetter, F. W., The Development of British Monetary Orthodoxy, 1797-1875, Cambridge, Mass., 1965.
2860 Flinn, M. W., 'The Poor Employment Act of 1817', Ec. H. R., 2nd ser., XIV, 1961, 82-92.
2861 Giuseppi, J., The Bank of England: A History from its Foundation in 1694, 1966. A much slighter work than Clapham's.
2862 Goetschin, P., L'Evolution du marché monetaire de Londres (1931-1952), Geneva and Paris, 1963.
2863 Goodhart, C. A. E., The Business of Banking, 1891-1914, 1972.
2864 Graham, W., The One Pound Note in the History of Banking in Great Britain, 1911.
2865 Grant, A. T. K., A Study of the Capital Market in Britain from 1919-1936 2nd ed., 1967, of book originally published 1937 under slightly different title.
2866 Gregory, T. E., ed., Select Statutes, Documents and Reports Relating to British Banking, 1832-1928, 2 vols., 1st ed., 1929, 2nd ed., 1964 (vol. I: 1832-44; vol. II: 1847-1928).
2867 Hawtrey, R. G., A Century of Bank Rate, 1938.
2868 Horsefield, J. K., 'The origins of the Bank Charter Act, 1844'. In Ashton and Sayers, eds. (2850), listed above, 109-25.
2869 King, W. T. C., The History of the London Discount Market, 1936.
2870 Lavington, E., The English Capital Market, 1921. Reprinted 1969.
2871 Moggridge, D. E., The Return to Gold, 1925, 1969.
2872 —— British Monetary Policy, 1924-1931: The Norman Conquest of $4.86, 1972.
2873 Morgan, E. V., The Theory and Practice of Central Banking, 1797-1913, 1st ed., 1943, 2nd ed., 1965.
2874 —— Studies in British Financial Policy, 1914-1925, 1952.
2875 —— and Thomas, W. A., The Stock Exchange: Its History and Functions, 1962.
2876 Pollard, S., ed., The Gold Standard and Employment Policies between the Wars, 1970. Seven essays by Keynes, R. S. Sayers and others.
2877 Pressnell, L. S., 'Gold reserves, banking reserves and the Baring Crisis of 1890'. In Essays in Money and Banking in Honour of R. S. Sayers, eds. C. R. Whittlesey and J. S. G. Wilson, 1968, 167-78.
2878 Rees, J. F., A Short Fiscal and Financial History of England, 1815-1918, 1921.
2879 Richards, R. D., 'The first fifty years of the Bank of England, 1694-1744'. In J. G. van Dillen, History of the Principal Public Banks, 1st ed., 1934, 2nd ed., 1964, 201-72.
2880 Sayers, R. S., Bank of England Operations, 1890-1914, 1936.
2881 —— Central Banking after Bagehot, 1957.
2882 —— Gilletts in the London Money Market, 1867-1967, 1968.
2883 Sheppard, D. K., The Growth and Role of U. K. Financial Institutions, 1880-1962, 1971.
2884 Silberling, N. J., 'Financial and monetary policy in Great Britain during the Napoleonic Wars', Quarterly Jnl. of Economics, LXXIII, February 1924, 145-68.
2885 Thomas, S. E., British Banks and the Finance of Industry, 1931.
2886 Thornton, H., An Enquiry into the Nature and Effects of the Paper Credit of Great Britain, 1802, ed. F. A. von Hayek, 1st ed., 1939, 2nd ed., 1962.
2887 Tooke, T., An Inquiry into the Currency Principle, 2nd ed., 1844. Reprinted 1959.
2888 Truptil, R. J., British Banks and the London Money Market, 1936.
2889 Whale, P. B., 'A retrospective view of the Bank Charter Act, 1844'. In Ashton and Sayers, eds. (2850), listed above, 126-31.
2890 Wood, E., English Theories of Central Banking Control, 1819-1858, With Some Account of Contemporary Procedure, Cambridge, Mass., 1939.

(d) The exchange equalisation account

2891 Hall, N. F., The Exchange Equalization Account, 1935.
2892 Waight, L., The History and Mechanism of the Exchange Equalisation Account, 1939.

(e) Country banking

(1) General

2893 Gillett, W., History of the Clearing for Country Bankers' Cheques and Notes, 1925.
2894 Horne, H. O., A History of Savings Banks, 1947.
2895 Pressnell, L. S., Country Banking in the Industrial Revolution, 1956. Those beginning research into local banking history should consult this book first.
2896 Sykes, J., The Amalgamation movement in English Banking, 1926.
2897 Thomas, S. E., The Rise and Growth of Joint Stock Banking, 2 vols., 1934.

(2) Regional and local studies

2897a Allman, A. H. et al., Williams Deacon's, 1771-1970, 1971.
2898 Ashton, T. S., 'The bill of exchange and private banks in Lancashire, 1790-1830'. In Ashton and Sayers, eds. (2850), listed above, 37-50.
2899 Bidwell, W. H., Annals of an East Anglian Bank, 1900.
2900 Cave, C. H., A History of Banking in Bristol, from 1750 to 1899, 1899.
2901 Chandler, G., Four Centuries of Banking, as Illustrated by the Bankers, Customers, and Staff Associated with the Constituent Banks of Martins Bank Ltd., 2 vols., 1964-8. Vol. I: The Grasshopper and the Liver-Bird—Liverpool and London. Vol. II: The Northern Constituent Banks.
2902 Christy, M., 'The history of banks and banking in Essex', Journal of the Institute of Bankers, XXVII, 1906, 319-30.

2903 Crick, W. F. and Wadsworth, J. E., A Hundred Years of Joint Stock Banking, 1936. A history of the Midland Bank.
2904 Davies, A. S., The Early Banks of Mid-Wales, 1935.
2905 Dodd, A. H., 'The beginnings of banking in North Wales', Economica, VI, 1926, 16-30.
2906 Green, F., 'Early banks in West Wales', Historical Society of West Wales, VI, 1916.
2907 Grindon, L. H., Manchester Banks and Bankers, 1st ed., 1877, 2nd ed., 1878.
2908 Hoare, H. P. R., Hoare's Bank: A Record, 1673-1932, 1932.
2909 Hughes, J., Liverpool Banks and Bankers, 1916.
2910 Hyde, F. E. et al., 'The port of Liverpool and the crisis of 1793', Economica, new ser., XVIII, 1951, 363-78.
2911 Isaac, A. W., The Worcestershire Old Bank, n.d. (privately printed).
2912 Jones, A. G. E., 'Early banking in Ipswich', Notes and Queries, CXCVI, 1951, 402-5.
2913 Leader, R. E., The Sheffield Banking Company Ltd., 1916.
2914 Leighton-Boyce, J. A. S. L., Smiths the Bankers [of Nottingham] 1658-1958, 1958.
2915 Matthews, P. W. and Tuke, A. W., A History of Barclays Bank Ltd., 1928.
2916 Perkins, M., Dudley Tradesmen's Tokens and History of Dudley Banks, Bankers and Bank Notes, 1905.
2917 Phillips, M., A History of Banks, Bankers and Banking in Northumberland, Durham and North Yorkshire, 1894.
2918 Porter, J., 'Lincolnshire private bankers', Parts I and II, The Lincolnshire Magazine, July-August 1937.
2919 Roth, H. L., The Genesis of Banking in Halifax, 1914.
2920 Saunders, P. T., Stuckey's Bank, 1926. A famous Somerset bank.
2921 Sayers, R. S., Lloyds Bank in the History of English Banking, 1957.
2922 Smith, T. J., Banks and Bankers of Leek, 1891.
2923 Taylor, Audrey M., Gilletts, Bankers at Banbury and Oxford: A Study in Local Economic History, 1964.
For Scottish and Irish banking see Payne (87), listed above, and (4220a-4227), listed below.

ACCOUNTANCY

2924 Brown, R., ed., A History of Accounting and Accountants, 1st ed., 1905, 2nd ed., 1968. Particularly valuable for Scotland.
2925 Littleton, A. C. and Yamey, B. S., Studies in the History of Accounting, 1956. Contains a number of articles on various aspects of British accountancy history.
2926 Stacey, N. A. H., English Accountancy: A Study in Social and Economic History, 1800-1954, 1954.
See also Yamey, Edey, and Thomson (1719), listed above.

INSURANCE

2927 Dickson, P. G. M., The Sun Insurance Office, 1710-1960: The History of Two Hundred and Fifty Years of British Insurance, 1960.
2928 Drew, B., The London Assurance: A Second Chronicle, 1949. Much enlarged version of a 'first chronicle' published in 1927.
2929 Garnett, R. G., A Century of Co-operative Insurance: The Co-operative Insurance Society 1867-1967, 1968.
2930 Morrah, D., A History of Industrial Life Assurance, 1955.
2931 Supple, B. E., The Royal Exchange Assurance: A History of British Insurance, 1970 (the best treatment of the subject).
2932 Withers, H., Pioneers of British Life Assurance, 1951.

THE PROFESSIONS

2933 Armytage, W. H. G., The Rise of the Technocrats: A Social History, 1965. Contains important material on connections between British industrialists and scientists.
2934 Carr-Saunders, A. M., and Wilson, P., The Professions, 1933.
2935 Lewis, R. and Maude, A., The English Middle Classes, 1949.
2936 Reader, W. J., Professional Men: The Rise of the Professional Classes in Nineteenth-century England, 1966.
2937 Robson, R., The Attorney in Eighteenth-century England, 1959.
2938 Thompson, F. M. L., Chartered Surveyors: The Growth of a Profession, 1968. With the exception of the first two chapters the book is concerned with developments after 1700.
2939 Wade, J., History of the Middle and Working Classes, 1833. Reprinted N. Y., 1966.

MANAGEMENT AND MASTERS' ORGANISATIONS

2940 Aldcroft, D. H., 'The entrepreneur and the British economy, 1870-1914'. In Aldcroft (2504), listed above.
2940a Bell, S. P., ed., Victorian Lancashire, 1973.
2941 Beresford, M. W., The Leeds Chambers of Commerce, 1951.
2942 Bowden, W., Industrial Society in England Towards the End of the Eighteenth Century, 1st ed., 1925, 2nd ed., with new introduction and bibliography, 1965.
2942a [Burnley, J.], Fortunes Made in Business, 3 vols., 1884-6.
2943 Erickson, Charlotte, British Industrialists: Steel and Hosiery, 1850-1950, 1959.
2944 Hartwell, R. M., 'Business management in England during the period of early industrialization: inducements and obstacles'. In Hartwell, ed. (2157), listed above, 28-41.
2945 Hobsbawm, E. J., 'Custom, wages and workload', in Hobsbawm (3036), listed below.
2946 Howe, E., The British Federation of Master Printers, 1900-1950, 1950.

2947 Hudson, K., Working to Rule: Railway Workshop Rules: A Study of Industrial Discipline, 1970.
2948 Mackay, T., ed., The Autobiography of Samuel Smiles, LL.D., 1905.
2949 McKendrick, N., 'Josiah Wedgwood and factory discipline', Hist. Jnl., IV, 1961, 30-55.
2949a Payne, P. L., British Entrepreneurship in the Nineteenth Century, 1974.
2950 Pollard, S., The Genesis of Modern Management: A Study of the Industrial Revolution in Great Britain, 1965.
2951 Smiles, Aileen, Samuel Smiles and his Surroundings, 1956.
2952 Thompson, E. P., 'Time, work-discipline and industrial capitalism', P. P., 38, 1967, 56-97.

CAPITAL FORMATION

2952a Anderson, B. L., ed., Capital Accumulation in the Industrial Revolution, 1974 (selected readings from Adam Smith to Giffen).
2953 Crouzet, F., intro. and ed., Capital Formation in the Industrial Revolution, 1972 (a symposium of essays by various hands).
2954 Higgins, J. P. R. and Pollard, S., eds., Aspects of Capital Investment in Great Britain, 1750-1850: A Preliminary Survey, 1971.
2955 Pollard, S., 'Fixed capital in the industrial Revolution in Britain', J. E. H., XXIV, 1964.
2956 Thomas, W. A., The Provincial Stock Exchanges (mainly 1800-1914), 1973.

JOINT STOCK COMPANIES

2957 Campbell, R. H., 'The law and the joint-stock company in Scotland'. In Payne (87), listed above, 136-51.
2958 Cooke, C. A., Corporation, Trust and Company: An Essay in Legal History, 1950.
2959 Du Bois, A. B., The English Business Company After the Bubble Act, 1720-1800, N.Y., 1938.
2960 Evans, G. H., British Corporation Finance, 1775-1800, Baltimore, Md., 1936. The evolution of the preference share in the canal age.
2961 Formoy, R. R., Historical Foundations of Modern Company Law, 1923.
2962 Hunt, B. C., The Development of the Business Corporation in England, 1800-1867, Cambridge, Mass., 1936.
2963 Jefferys, J. B., 'The denomination and character of shares, 1855-1885'. In Carus-Wilson, ed. (164), listed above, I, 344-57.
2964 Shannon, H. A., 'The coming of general limited liability'. In Carus-Wilson, ed., (164), listed above, I, 358-79.
2965 —— 'The first five thousand limited companies and their duration', Ec. H., II, No. 7, January 1932, 396-424.
2966 —— 'The limited companies of 1866-1883'. In Carus-Wilson, ed. (164), listed above, I, 380-405.
2967 Welbourne, E., 'Bankruptcy before the era of Victorian reform', Cambridge Hist. Jnl., IV, 1932, 51-62.

THE WORKING CLASSES

Attention is drawn to:
2968 Bulletin of the Society for the Study of Labour History, 1960–, issued twice yearly
2969 Llafur, 1972–, issued yearly as the bulletin of the Welsh Labour History Society.
2969a Bellamy, Joyce M. and Saville, J., eds., Dictionary of Labour Biography, I, 1972; II, 1974.

(a) Bibliographical studies and statistics

2970 Department of Labour and Productivity, British Labour Statistics: Historical Abstract, 1886-1968, 1971.
2971 Maehl, W. H., '"Jerusalem deferred": recent writing in the history of the British labour movement', Jnl. Mod. Hist. (Chicago), 41, 1969, 335-67.
2972 Mowat, C. L., 'The history of the Labour Party: the Coles, the Webbs, and some others', Jnl. Mod. Hist. (Chicago), 23, 1951, 146-53.
2973 —— 'Some recent books on the British Labour movement', Jnl. Mod. Hist. (Chicago), 17, 1945, 356-66.

(b) Documentary collections

2974 Cole, G. D. H., and Filson, A. W., British Working Class Movements: Select Documents, 1789-1875, 1951. Reprinted 1965.
2975 Hobsbawm, E. J., ed., Labour's Turning Point . . . 1880-1900: Extracts from Contemporary Sources, 1948.
2976 Jeffreys, J. B., ed., Labour's Formative Years . . . 1849-1879: Extracts from Contemporary Sources, 1948.
2977 Morris, M., ed., From Cobbett to the Chartists . . . 1815-1848: Extracts from Contemporary Sources, 1948.

(c) Socialist theories and theorists

2978 Beales, H. L., The Early English Socialists, 1933.
2979 Beer, M., A History of British Socialism, 1st ed., 2 vols., 1919, 2nd, rev. and enlarged ed., in 1 vol., 1940.
2980 Bray, J. F., A Voyage from Utopia, ed. M. F. Lloyd-Prichard, 1957.
2981 —— Labour's Wrongs and Labour's Remedy, 1st ed., 1839. Reprinted 1931.
2982 Gray, A., The Socialist Tradition: Moses to Lenin, 3rd rev. impression, 1948. 'The pre-Marxians', 262-96.
2983 Halévy, E., Thomas Hodgskin, trans. and ed. A. J. Taylor, 1956.
2984 Hodgskin, T., Labour Defended Against the Claims of Capital, 1825. Reprinted 1922 and 1964, with introduction by G. D. H. Cole.
2985 Kimball, Janet, The Economic Doctrines of John Gray, 1799-1883, Washington, D. C., 1948.
2986 Pankhurst, R. K. P., William Thompson, 1775-1833: Britain's Pioneer Socialist, Feminist and Co-operator, 1954.

(d) General studies

2987 Cole, G. D. H. and Postgate, R., The Common People, 1746-1946, 1946.
2988 Briggs, A. and Saville, J., eds., Essays in Labour History: In Memory of G. D. H. Cole, 1st ed., 1960, 2nd rev. ed., 1967.
2989 ——— and Saville, J., eds., Essays in Labour History, 1886-1923, 1971.
2989a Brown, K. D., ed., Essays in Anti-Labour History: Responses to the Rise of Labour in Britain, 1974.
2990 Day, C., 'The distribution of industrial occupations in England 1841-1861', Trans. Connecticut Academy of Arts and Sciences, New Haven, Conn., XXVIII, March 1927, 79-235.
2991 Engels, F., The Condition of the Working Class in England (originally published in 1845), trans. and ed. by W. O. Henderson and W. H. Chaloner, 1958, 2nd rev. ed., 1971.
2991a Foster, J., Class Struggle and the Industrial Revolution: Early Industrial Capitalism in Three English Towns (Oldham, Northampton and South Shields), 1974.
2992 Hammond, J. L. and Barbara, The Skilled Labourer, 1760-1832, 1919. Last reprinted 1965 (the best of the 'labourer' trilogy).
2993 ——— The Town Labourer, 1760-1832: The New Civilisation, 1917. Many times reprinted; editions from 1947 have a rewritten chapter XIII.
2994 Hollis, Patricia M., ed., Class and Conflict in Nineteenth-century England, 1815-50, 1973. A collection of documents largely from Radical sources; guides to further reading are unsatisfactory.
2995 Neale, R. S., Class and Ideology in the Nineteenth Century, 1972.
2996 Saville, J., ed., Democracy and the Labour Movement, 1955.
2997 Simon, Daphne, 'Master and servant'. In Saville, ed. (2996), listed above, 160-200. The historical development of the laws affecting employers and employed in mid-nineteenth century England.
2997a Thomis, M. I., The Town Labourer and the Industrial Revolution, 1974.
2998 Thompson, E. P., The Making of the English Working Class, 1963, 2nd ed., with critical appendix, 916-39.

(e) Trade unionism and labour

(1) Documentary and general studies

2999 Frow, Ruth and E. and Katanka, M., The History of British Trade Unionism: A Select Bibliography, Historical Association, 1969 (extremely useful, and should be used to supplement this section).
3000 Aspinall, A., ed., The Early English Trade Unions: Documents from the Home Office Papers in the Public Record Office, 1949. Covers the period 1791-1825.
3001 Bailey, W. Milne, Trade Union Documents: Compiled and Edited with an Introduction, 1929. Documents and extracts ranging from 1841 to 1928 but mostly 1913-28.
3002 Clegg, H. A., Fox, A. and Thompson, A. F., A History of British Trade Unions since 1889, I (1889-1910), 1964.
3003 Coates, K. and Topham, T., Workers' Control: A Book of Readings and Witnesses for Workers' Control, 1970. Documents and extracts from books relative to anarcho-syndicalism in the British labour movement from 1910 to 1969.
3004 Cole, G. D. H., Attempts at General Union: A Study in British Trade Union History, 1818-1834, 1953. Should be used with caution; many inaccuracies.
3005 Frow, Ruth and E. and Katanka, M., Strikes: A Documentary History, 1971. Collection of contemporary or near-contemporary accounts of strikes in Britain, 1812-1926.
3006 George, M. Dorothy, 'The Combination Laws reconsidered', Ec. J. Economic History Supplement, I, No. 2, May 1927, 214-28. Essential for any real understanding of the laws relating to early trade unions.
3007 ——— 'The Combination Laws', Ec. H. R., VI, 1936, 172-8. See remarks on previous entry.
3008 Hedges, R. Y., and Winterbottom, A., The Legal History of Trade Unionism, 1930.
3009 Howell, G., Trade Unionism Old and New. Reprint of 4th ed., 1907, with introduction by F. M. Leventhal, 1973.
3010 Musson, A. E., British Trade Unions, 1800-1875, 1972. Excellent bibliography.
3011 Pelling, H. M., A History of British Trade Unionism, 1963.
3012 Pollard, S., ed., The Sheffield Outrages: Report Presented to the Trades Union Commissioners in 1867, 1971.
3013 Robertson, N. and Sams, K. I., British Trade Unionism: Select Documents, 2 vols., 1972.
3014 Webb, S. and Beatrice, The History of Trade Unionism, 1894 (bibliography), 2nd enlarged ed., 1920 (no bibliography).

(2) Working-class autobiographies

3015 Bamford, S., The Autobiography of Samuel Bamford, ed. W. H. Chaloner, 2 vols., 1967.
3015a Burnett, J., ed., Useful Toil: Autobiographies of Working People from the 1820s to the 1920s, 1974.
3016 Carter, T., Memoirs of a Working Man, 1846.
3017 Chancellor, Valerie E., ed., Master and Artisan in Victorian England: The Diary of William Andrews and the Autobiography of William Gutteridge, 1969.
3018 Herbert, G., Shoemaker's Window: Recollection of Banbury Before the Railway Age, 1972.
3019 Holloway, J., ed., The Journals of Two Poor Dissenters, 1786-1880, 1970. A bricklayer and baker named Swan.
3020 Hopkinson, J., Memoirs of a Victoria Cabinet Maker, 1968, ed. Jocelyne B. Goodman.
3021 Lovett, W., The Life and Struggles of William Lovett, 1st ed., 1876, 2nd ed., introduction by R. H. Tawney, 1920.
3022 Smith, C. Manby, The Working Man's Way in the World, ed. E. Howe, 1968.

3023 Somerville, A., The Autobiography of a Working Man, 1848, 2nd ed., ed. J. Carswell, 1951.
3024 Thale, Mary, ed., The Autobiography of Francis Place, (1771-1854), 1972. See also Howe (3242) and Wallas (3251), listed below.
3025 Thomson, C., The Autobiography of an Artisan, 1847.

(3) The labour aristocracy controversy

3026 Banks, J. A., 'Imperialism and the aristocracy of labour'. In Marxist Sociology in Action, 1970, 218-37.
3027 Chaloner, W. H., The Skilled Artisan During the Industrial Revolution, 1750-1850, 1969.
3028 Hobsbawm, E. J., 'The labour aristocracy in nineteenth-century Britain'. In Hobsbawm (3046), listed below, 272-315.
3029 —— 'The tramping artisan'. In Hobsbawm (3046), listed below, 34-63.
3030 Pelling, H. M., 'The concept of the labour aristocracy'. In Popular Politics and Society in Late Victorian Britain, 1968, 37-61.
3031 Price, R., An Imperial War and the British Working Class: Working Class Attitudes and Reactions to the Boer War, 1899-1902, 1972.

(4) Miscellaneous, including the Labour Party and the history of the Trades Union Congress

3031a Bagwell, P., Industrial Relations, 1974. Guide to British Parliamentary Papers on this subject.
3032 Barou, N. I., British Trade Unions, 1947.
3033 Bealey, F. and Pelling, H. M., Labour and Politics, 1900-1906: A History of the Labour Representation Committee, 1958.
3034 Birch, L., ed., The History of the Trades Union Congress, 1868-1968, 1968.
3035 Brand, C. F., 'The conversion of British trade unions to political action', A.H.R., XXX, 1924, 251-70.
3036 Brown, E. H. Phelps, The Growth of British Industrial Relations from the Standpoint of 1906-14, 1959.
3037 Cole. G. H. D., 'Some notes on British trade unionism in the third quarter of the nineteenth century'. In Carus-Wilson, ed. (164), listed above, 144, III, 202-21.
3038 Davis, W. J., The British Trades Union Congress: History and Recollections, 2 vols., 1910, 1916.
3039 Duffy, A. E. P., 'New Unionism in Britain, 1889-90: a reappraisal', Ec.H.R., 2nd ser., XIV, 1961, 306-19.
3040 Fraser, W. H., Trade Unions and Society: The Struggle for Acceptance, 1850-1880, 1974.
3041 Frow, E. and Katanka, M., 1868: Year of the Unions, 1968.
3042 Garbati, J., 'British trade unionism in the mid-Victorian era', University of Toronto Quarterly, XX, 1950-51, 69-84.
3043 Gillespie, F. E., Labor and Politics in England, 1850-1867, Durham, N.C., 1927.
3044 Harrison, M., Trade Unions and the Labour Party since 1945, 1960.

3045 Harrison, R., Before the Socialists: Studies in Labour and Politics, 1861-1881, 1965.
3045a Hinton, J., The First Shop Stewards' Movement, 1973. See also Pribicevic (3052), listed below.
3046 Hobsbawm, E. J., Labouring Men: Studies in the History of Labour, 1964. Reprints eighteen articles on working-class subjects.
3047 —— 'General labour unions in Britain, 1889-1914'. In Hobsbawm (3046), listed above, 179-203.
3048 Knowles, K. G. J. C., Strikes: A Study of Industrial Conflict, with Special Reference to British Experience between 1911 and 1947, 1952.
3049 Leventhal, F. M., Respectable Radical: George Howell and Victorian Working-class Politics, 1971.
3050 London Trades Council, The First Annual Trades Union Directory of the United Kingdom, 1861. Reprinted 1968.
3051 Lovell, J. and Roberts, B. C., A Short History of the T.U.C., 1968.
3052 Maccoby, S., English Radicalism, 6 vols., 1935-61. I: 1762-1785, 1955; II: 1786-1832, 1955; III: 1832-1852, 1935; IV: 1953-1886, 1938; V: 1886-1914, 1953; VI: The End?, 1961.
3053 Macdonald, D. F., The State and the Trade Unions, 1960.
3053a McKibbin, R., The Evolution of the Labour Party, 1910-1924, 1975.
3054 Martin, R., Communism and the British Trade Unions, 1924-1933: A Study of the National Minority Movement, 1969.
3055 Musson, A. E., The Congress of 1868: The Origins and Establishment of the Trades Union Congress, 1955, 2nd rev. ed., 1968.
3055a —— Trade Union and Social History, 1974.
3056 National Association for the Promotion of Social Science, Trades' Societies and Strikes, 1860. Reprinted 1968.
3057 Orton, W. A., Labour in Transition: A survey of British Industrial History since 1914, 1921.
3058 Pelling, H. M., A Short History of the bour Party, 1961, 3rd rev. ed., 1968. Useful guides to further reading at end of each chapter.
3059 —— The Origins of the Labour Party, 1880-1900, 1954, 2nd ed., 1965, with excellent bibliographical essay, 234-45.
3060 —— Social Geography of British Elections 1885-1910, 1967.
3061 Poirier, P. P., The Advent of the Labour Party, 1958. History of the Labour Representation Committee.
3062 Pribicevic, B., The Shop Stewards' Movement and Workers' Control, 1910-1922, 1959. See also Hinton (3045a), listed above.
3063 Roberts, B. C., The Trades Union Congress, 1868-1921, 1958.
3064 Sharp, I. G., Industrial Conciliation and Arbitration in Great Britain, 1950.
3065 Trades Union Congress, Seventy Years of Trade Unionism, 1938.

(5) Histories of unionism in particular industries

(i) Agriculture

3066 Dunbabin, J. P. D., 'The "Revolt of the Field": the agricultural labourers' movement in the 1870s', P. P., 26, 1963, 68-97, (see also P. P. 27, 1964, 109-13 for further discussion). See also Dunbabin (2381a), listed above.

3067 Edwards, G., From Crow-scaring to Westminster: An Autobiography, 1st ed., 1922, 2nd ed., 1957.

3068 Fussell, G. E., From Tolpuddle to T. U. C.: A Century of Farm Labourers' Politics, 1948.

3069 Green, F. E., A History of the English Agricultural Labourer, 1870-1920, 1920. Mainly about agricultural trade unionism.

3070 Groves, R., Sharpen the Sickle! The History of the Farm Workers' Union, 1949.

3071 Horn, Pamela L. R., Joseph Arch (1826-1919), the Farm Workers' Leader, 1971. A model biography with abundant documentation.

3072 Marlow, Joyce, The Tolpuddle Martyrs, 1972. See also Trades Union Congress (3075), listed below.

3073 Russell, R. C., The 'Revolt of the Field' in Lincs.: The Origins and Early History of Farm Workers' Trade Unions, 1956.

3074 Selley, E., Village Trade Unions in Two Centuries, 1919.

3075 Trades Union Congress, The Book of the Martyrs of Tolpuddle, 1934. See also Marlow (3072), listed above.

(ii) Engineering and metalworkers

3076 Allen, E., Clarke, J. F., McCord, N., and Rowe, D. J., eds, The North-East Engineers' Strikes of 1871, 1971.

3077 Fyrth, H. J., and Collins, H., The Foundry Workers: A Trade Union History, 1959.

3078 Jeffreys, J. B., The Story of the Engineers, 1800-1945, 1946. The Amalgamated Society of Engineers and the Amalgamated Engineering Union.

3079 Kidd, A. T., History of the Tin-Plate Workers' and Sheet-Metal Workers' and Braziers' Societies, 1949.

3080 Mortimer, J. E., A History of the Association of Engineering and Shipbuilding Draughtsmen, 1960.

3081 —— The Boilermakers, vol. I, 1973.

3082 Owen, J., Ironmen: Short History of the National Union of Blastfurnacemen, 1878-1935, 1935, 2nd rev. ed. 1953.

3083 Pugh, A., Men of Steel, by One of Them: A Chronicle of Eighty-eight Years of Trade Unionism, 1952.

(iii) Builders and woodworkers

3084 Connelly, T. J., The Woodworkers, 1860-1960, 1960.

3085 French, J. O., Plumbers in Unity: History of the Plumbing Trades Union, 1865-1965, 1965.

3086 Heginbotham, S., Our Society's History.

1939. The Amalgamated Society of Woodworkers.

3087 Hilton, W. S., Foes to Tyranny: A History of the Amalgamated Union of Building Trade Workers, 1963.

3088 Newman, J. R., The N.A.O.P. Heritage: A Short Historical Review of the Development of the National Association of Operative Plasterers 1860-1960, 1961.

3089 Postgate, R. W., The Builders' History, 1923.

(iv) Railway labour

3090 Bagwell, P. S., The Railwaymen: The History of the National Union of Railwaymen, 1963.

3091 Coleman, T., The Railway Navvies, 1965, 2nd rev. ed., 1968. Excellent guide to sources and selected bibliography, 238-46 of 2nd ed.

3092 Kingsford, P. W., Victorian Railwaymen: The Emergence and Growth of Railway Labour, 1830-1870, 1970.

3093 Lewis, R. A., 'Edwin Chadwick and the railway labourers', Ec. H. R., 2nd ser., III, 1950, 107-18.

3094 McKillop, N., The Lighted Flame: A History of the Associated Society of Locomotive Engineers and Firemen, 1950.

3095 Simmons, J., 'The building of the Woodhead Tunnel'. In Parish and Empire, 1952, 155-65.

(v) Coal mining

3096 Arnot, R. P., The Miners: A History of the Miners' Federation of Great Britain, 1889-1910, 1949.

3097 —— The Miners: Years of Struggle: A History of the Miners' Federation of Great Britain from 1910 onwards, 1953.

3098 —— The Miners in Crisis and War: A History of the Miners' Federation of Great Britain from 1930 onwards, 1961.

3099 —— A History of the Scottish Miners from the Earliest Times, 1955.

3100 —— South Wales Miners ... A History of the South Wales Miners' Federation, 1898-1914, 1967.

3101 Challinor R., The Lancashire and Cheshire Miners, 1972 (a study in trade union history from the 1840s onwards).

3102 —— and Ripley, B., The Miners Association: A Trade Union in the age of the Chartists, 1969.

3103 Gregory, R., The Miners and British Politics, 1906-14, 1968.

3104 Griffin, A. R., The Miners of Nottinghamshire A History of the Nottinghamshire Miners' Association, I, 1956.

3105 —— The Miners of Nottinghamshire, 1914-1944: A History of the Nottinghamshire Miners' Union, II, 1962.

3106 Machin, F., The Yorkshire Miners: A History, I, 1958.

3107 Taylor, A. J., 'The Miners' Association of Great Britain and Ireland, 1842-48 ...'. Economica, XXII, 1955, 45-60.

3108 Webb, S., The Story of the Durham Miners, 1662-1921, 1921.

3109 Welbourne, E., The Miners' Unions of Northumberland and Durham, 1923.

3110 Williams, J. E., The Derbyshire Miners: A Study in Industrial and Social History, 1962.

(vi) Printing and publishing

3111 Bundock, C.J., The National Union of Journalists: A Jubilee History, 1907-1957, 1957.
3112 Healey, H.A.H. (pseud. T.N. Shane), Passed for Press: A Centenary History of the Association of the Correctors of the Press, 1954.
3113 Howe, E., ed., The London Compositor: Documents Relating to Wages, Working Conditions and Customs of the London Printing Trade, 1785-1900, 1947.
3114 ——— and Waite, H.H., The London Society of Compositors: A Centenary History, 1948.
3115 ——— and Child, J., The Society of London Bookbinders, 1780-1951, 1952.
3116 Moran, J., Natsopa Seventy-five Years: The National Society of Operative Printers and Assistants, 1889-1964, 1964.
3116a Musson, A.E., The Typographical Association: Origins and History up to 1949, 1954.

(vii) White-collar and service workers

3117 Bain, G.S., The Growth of White Collar Unionism, 1970.
3118 Hoffman, P.C., They also Serve: The Story of the Shop Worker, 1950. See also Whitaker (3127), listed below.
3119 Hughes, F., By Hand and Brain: The story of the Clerical and Administrative Workers' Union, 1953.
3120 Humphreys, B.V., Clerical Unions in the Civil Service, 1958.
3121 Perkin, H.J., Key Profession: The History of the Association of University Teachers, 1969.
3122 Radford, F.H., 'Fetch the Engine ...': The Official History of the Fire Brigades Union, 1951.
3123 Reynolds, G.W., and Judge, A., The Night the Police Went on Strike, 1969.
3124 Spoor, A., White-collar Union: Sixty Years of N.A.L.G.O., 1967 (National Association of Local Government Officers).
3125 Swift, H.G., A History of Postal Agitation from Fifty Years Ago till the Present Day, 1st ed., 1900, 2nd ed., 1929.
3126 Tropp, A., The School Teachers: The Growth of the Teaching Profession in England and Wales from 1800 to the Present Day, 1957.
3127 Whitaker, W.B., Victorian and Edwardian Shopworkers: The Struggle to Obtain Better Conditions and a Half-holiday, 1973.

(viii) Cotton unions

3128 Hopwood, E., A History of the Lancashire Cotton Industry and the Amalgamated Weavers' Association, 1969.
3129 Turner, H.A., Trade Union Growth Structure and Policy: A Comparative Study of the Cotton Unions, 1962.

(ix) Dockers

3129a Brown, R., Waterfront Organisation In Hull, 1870-1900, 1972.

3130 Lovell, J., Stevedores and Dockers, 1969. (London waterside unionism c. 1870-1914).
3131 Pedlar, Ann (pseud. Stafford), A Match to Fire the Thames, 1961. The London matchgirls, dockers and gas workers' strikes of 1888-9.
3132 Smith, H.L., and Nash, V., The Story of the Dockers' Strike, 1889.

(x) Footwear and clothing

3133 Cuthbert, N.H., The Lace Makers' Society: A Study of Trade Unionism in the British Lace Industry, 1760-1960, 1960.
3134 Fox, A., A History of the National Union of Boot and Shoe Operatives, 1874-1957, 1958.
3135 Galton, F.W., ed., Select Documents, Illustrating the History of Trade Unionism. I: The Tailoring Trade, 1896.
3136 Kiddier, W., The Old Trade Unions: From Unprinted Records of the Brushmakers, 1930, 2nd ed., 1932.
3137 Stewart, Margaret and Hunter, L., The Needle is Threaded: The History of an Industry. (National Union of Tailors and Garment Workers), 1964.

(xi) Miscellaneous

3138 Lyman, R., The Workers' Union, 1971.

(6) Local studies

3138a [Bennett, A.,] Oldham Trades and Labour Council ... 1867-1967, 1967.
3138b Corbett, J., The Birmingham Trades Council, 1866-1966, 1966
3139 Hambling, W., A Short History of the Liverpool Trades Council 1848-1948, 1948.
3139a Large, D. and Whitfield, R., The Bristol Trades Council, 1873-1973, 1973.
3140 Pollard, S., A History of Labour in Sheffield, 1959.
3140a [Tate, G.K.], London Trades Council, 1860-1950: A History 1950.
3141 Warburton, W.H., The History of Trade Union Organisation in the North Staffordshire Potteries, 1931.

(7) Wages

3142 Brown, E. H. Phelps and Browne, Margaret, H., A Century of Pay, 1968.
3143 Hilton, G.W., The Truck System, Including a History of the British Truck Acts, 1465-1960, 1960.
3144 Hines, A.G., 'Trade unions and wage inflation in the United Kingdom, 1893-1961', Review of Economic Studies, XXXI, 1964, 221-52.
3145 Hunt, E. H., Regional Wage Variations in Britain, 1850-1914, 1973.
3146 Lipsey, R. G., 'The relation between unemployment and the rate of change of money wage rates in the United Kingdom 1862-1957: a further analysis', Economica, XXVII, 1960, 1-31.
3147 Phillips, A.W., 'The relation between unemployment and the rate of change of money wages in the United Kingdom, 1861-1957', Economica, XXV, 1958, 283-99.

(8) The General Strike of 1926

3148 Blaxland, G., J.H. Thomas: A Life for Unity, 1964, 179-203.
3149 Bullock, A., The Life and Times of Ernest Bevin, I, 1960, 248-390.
3150 Clegg, H.A., 'Some consequences of the General Strike', Proceedings of the Manchester Statistical Society, 1954, 1-29.
3151 Crook, W.H., The General Strike: A Study Of Labour's Tragic Weapon in Theory and Practice, Chapel Hill, N.C., 1931, 233-495.
3152 ——— Communism and the General Strike, 1960.
3152a Farman, C., The General Strike, 1973.
3153 Glasgow, G., General Strikes and Road Transport, Being an Account of the Road Transport Organisation Prepared by the British Government to Meet National Emergencies, 1926.
3154 Hughes, M., ed., Cartoons from the General Strike, 1968.
3155 Martin, K., The British Public and the General Strike, 1926.
3156 Mason, A., The General Strike in the North East, 1970.
3157 Morris, Margaret, The British General Strike, 1926, 1973. (Useful footnotes and bibliography, 36-40).
3157a Renshaw, P., The General Strike, 1975.
3158 Simon, J., Three Speeches on the General Strike, 1926.
3159 Sitwell, O., 'The General Strike' In Laughter in the Next Room, 1949, 199-243.
3160 Symons, J., The General Strike: A Historical Portrait, 1957.

(9) The Communist Party, the I.L.P. and the Fabian Society

3161 Collins, H., and Abramsky, C., Karl Marx and the British Labour Movement: The Years of the First International, 1965.
3162 Dowse, R.E., Left in the Centre, 1966. History of the Independent Labour Party.
3163 Klugmann, J., History of the Communist Party of Great Britain, Vol. I (1919-1924), 1968. Vol. II (1925-1927: The General Strike), 1969. (The official history, with all that implies).
3164 McBriar, A. M., Fabian Socialism and English Politics, 1884-1918, 1962. Excellent bibliography, 350-74.
3165 MacFarlane, L.J., The British Communist Party: Its Origin and Development until 1929, 1966.
3166 Pease, E.R., The History of the Fabian Society, 1918, 3rd ed., 1963.
3167 Pelling, H.M., The British Communist Party: A Historical Profile, 1958.

(f) Friendly Societies, etc.

3168 Baernreither, J.M., English Associations of Working Men, 1889.
3169 Fuller, Margaret, D., West Country Friendly Societies, 1964.

3170 Gosden, P.H.J.H., The Friendly Societies in England, 1815-75, 1961.
3171 ——— Self-Help: Voluntary Associations in the Nineteenth Century, 1973.
3172 Holyoake, G.J., Self Help a Hundred Years Ago, 2nd ed. 1890. Essays on the history of English social reform movements.

(g) The standard of living controversy

3173 [Ashton, T.S., 'The standard of life of the workers in England, 1790-1830'. in Hayek, ed. (57), listed above, 127-59.
3174 ——— Changes in standards of comfort in eighteenth-century England', Proceedings of the British Academy, XLI, 1955, 171-87.
3175 Barnsby, G., 'The Standard of living in the Black Country during the nineteenth century' Ec.H.R., 2nd Ser., XXIV, 1971, 220-33.
3176 Chaloner, W.H., The Hungry Forties, Historical Association pamphlet, 1957. 3rd rev. ed. 1963.
3177 Gilboy, Elizabeth, W., Wages in Eighteenth-Century England, Cambridge, Mass., 1934.
3178 ——— The cost of living and real wages in eighteenth-century England', Review of Economic Statistics, XVIII, 1936, 134-43.
3179 Hartwell, R.M., 'Interpretations of the Industrial Revolution in England', J.E.H., XIX, 1959, 229-49.
3180 ——— 'The standard of living controversy: a summary'. In Hartwell, ed., (2157) listed above, 167-79.
3181 ——— 'The rising standard of living in England, 1800-1850'. In Hartwell (2160) listed above, 313-45.
3182 Hilton, G.W., The British Truck System in the nineteenth century', Jnl. of Political Economy, LXV, 1957, 237-56. See also Hilton, Mr. (3143), listed above.
3183 Hobsbawm, E.J., 'The British standard of living, 1790-1850', Ec.H.R., 2nd ser. X, No. 1, Aug. 1957, 46-48. (Reprinted with additions in Hobsbawm (3046), listed above, 64-104).
3184 ——— and Hartwell, R.M., 'The standard of living during the Industrial Revolution: a discussion', Ec.H.R., 2nd ser., XVI, 1963, 120-46.
3185 Inglis, B., Poverty and the Industrial Revolution, 1971. Largely an attack on the Classical Economists.
3186 Neale, R.H., 'The standard of living, 1780-1844: a regional and class study', Ec.H.R., 2nd ser., XIX, 1966, 590-606.
3187 Pollard, S., 'Investment, consumption and the Industrial Revolution', Ec. H. R., 2nd ser., XI, 1958, 215-36.
3188 Taylor, A.J., 'Progress and poverty in Britain, 1780-1850', History, XLV, 1960, 16-31. Reprinted in Carus-Wilson, Ed., (164), listed above, III, 380-93.
3189 Tucker, R.S., 'Real wages of artisans in London, 1729-1935', Jnl. of the American Statistical Assn., XXXI, 1936, 73-84.
3190 Williams, J. E., 'The British standard of living, 1750-1850', Ec.H.R., 2nd ser., XIX 1966, 581-9.

3191 Wilsher, P., The Pound in Your Pocket, 1870-1970, 1970.
3192 Woodruff, W., 'Capitalism and the Victorians: a contribution to the discussion on the Industrial Revolution', J.E.H., XVI, 1956, 1-17.

(h) Police, popular disturbances and Luddism

3193 Beloff, M., Public Order and Popular Disturbances, 1660-1714, 1st ed., 1938, new imp., 1963.
3194 Browne, D.G. The Rise of Scotland Yard: A History of the Metropolitan Police, 1956.
3195 Church, R.A., and Chapman, S.d., 'Gravener Henson and the English working class'. In Jones and Mingay (2346), listed above, 131-61.
3196 Darvall, F.O., Popular Disturbances and Public Order in Regency England, 1934, 2nd ed., 1970, with new introduction.
3197 Divine, D., Mutiny at Invergordon, 1970. Includes new material, badly handled.
3198 Dugan, J., The Great Mutiny, Spithead and the Nore, 1797, 1966. See Gill (3200) and Manwaring and Dobrée (3204) listed below.
3199 Edwards, K., The Mutiny at Invergordon, 1937.
3200 Gill, C., The Naval Mutinies of 1797, 1913. See Dugan (3198), listed above, and Manwaring (3204), listed below.
3201 Hart, Jenifer M., The British Police, 1951. Useful for administrative history.
3202 ——— 'The reform of the borough police, 1835-1856', E.H.R., LXX, 1955, 411-27.
3203 Hobsbawm, E.J., 'The Machine breakers', (in Hobsbawm, (3046) listed above.
3204 Manwaring, G.E., and Dobrée, B., The Floating Republic: An Account of the Mutinies at Spithead and the Nore in 1797, 1935. See also Dugan (3198) and Gill (3200) listed above.
3205 Midwinter, E.C., Law and Order in Early Victorian Lancashire, 1968.
3206 Munby, L.M., ed., The Luddites and Other Essays, 1971. Contributions by Marxist historians.
3207 Peel, F., The Risings of the Luddites, Chartists and Plugdrawers, 1st ed., 1880, 4th ed., with new introduction, 1968.
3208 Read, D., Peterloo: The 'Massacre' and its Background, 2nd ed., 1973. see also Walmsley (3220), listed below.
3209 Reith, C., The Police Idea: Its History and Evolution in England in the Eighteenth Century and After, 1938.
3210 ——— British Police and the Democratic Ideal, 1943.
3211 ——— A Short History of the British Police, 1948
3212 Rose, A.G., 'The Plug Riots of 1842 in Lancashire and Cheshire', T.L.C.A.S., LXVII, 1958, 75-112.
3213 Rudé, G., The Crowd in History, 1730-1848: A Study of Popular Disturbances in France and England, N.Y., 1964.
3214 Shelton, W.J., English Hunger and Industrial Disorders, 1973 (confined to the 1760s)
3214a Stevenson, J., and Quinault, R., Popular Protest and Public Order: Six Studies in British History, 1790-1920, 1975.
3215 Thomis, M.I., The Luddites, 1970.
3216 ——— ed., Luddism in Nottinghamshire, 1972. (a collection of documents of 1811-16 with short introduction).
3217 ——— Politics and Society in Nottingham, 1785-1835, 1969. Luddism, chapter V.
3218 Thompson, E.P., 'The moral economy of the crowd in eighteenth-century England', P.P., 50, 1971, 76-136.
3219 Tobias, J.J., Crime and Industrial Society in the Nineteenth Century, 1967.
3220 Walmsley, R., Peterloo: The Case Reopened, 1969. See also Read (3208) listed above, and Mather (3230), listed below.
3221 Ward, J.T., ed., Popular Movements c. 1830-1850, 1970. Includes chapters on the factory movement, the anti-New Poor Law agitation, trade unionism, Chartism, the agitation against the Corn Laws, and the public health movement.

(i) Chartism

(1) General studies

3222 Dolléans, E., Le Chartisme, 1831-1848, 2nd rev.ed., Paris, 1949.
3223 Faulkner, H.U., Chartism and the Churches, 1st ed., 1916. Reprinted 1970.
3224 Gammage, R.G., History of the Chartist Movement, 1st ed., 1854, 2nd ed., 1895, reprinted 1969 with introduction by J.Saville, 4-66.
3225 Hadfield, Alice M., The Chartist Land Company, 1970.
3226 Hammond, J.L. and Barbara, The Age of the Chartists, 1832-1854: A Study of Discontent, 1930.
3227 Harrison, B., 'Teetotal Chartism', History, 58, 1973, 193-217.
3228 Hovell, M., The Chartist Movement, 1st ed. 1918, 3rd ed., 1966, 4th ed., 1970, with bibliographical additions (iii-ix, 318) which give details of literature up to 1970.
3229 MacAskill, Joy, 'The Chartist Land Plan', In Briggs, ed. (3238), listed below, 304-41.
3230 Mather, F.C., Public Order in the Age of the Chartists, 1959.
3231 ——— Chartism, Historical Association pamphlet, 1965, 3rd rev. ed., 1974. Sums up research since 1925.
3232 Rosenblatt, F.F., The Chartist Movement in its Social and Economic Aspects, 1st ed., 1916. Reprinted 1967.
3233 Slosson, P.W., The Decline of the Chartist Movement. 1st ed., 1916. Reprinted 1967.
3234 Smith, F.S., Radical Artisan: William James Linton, 1812-1897, 1973.
3235 Thompson, Dorothy, The Early Chartists, 1871. Covers the period 1837-41 only; documents, with commentary.
3236 Ward, J.T., Chartism, 1973.
3237 West, J., History of Chartism, 1920.
For Christian Socialism see 3825-3830 below.

88   England 1700-1970

(2) Regional studies

3238 Briggs, A., ed., Chartist Studies, 1959. Mainly essays on local aspects of the movement.
3239 Cannon, J., The Chartists in Bristol, 1964.
3240 Howell, G., ed. D.J. Rowe, A History of the London Working Men's Association from 1836 to 1850, 1972.
3241 Peacock, A.J., Bradford Chartism, 1838-1840, 1969.
3242 Rowe, D.J., ed., London Radicalism, 1830-1843: A Selection from the Papers of Francis Place, London Record Society, 1970. See also Thale (3024), listed above, and Wallas (3251), listed below.
3243 Wilson, A., The Chartist Movement in Scotland, 1970.
3244 Wright, L.C., Scottish Chartism, 1953.

(3) Biographies

3245 Cole, G.D.H., Chartist Portraits, 1st ed., 1941, 2nd ed., 1965. Useful bibliography of Chartist literature, 359-66.
3246 Conklin, R.J., Thomas Cooper the Chartist (1805-1892), Manila, 1935.
3247 Plummer, A., Bronterre: A Political Biography of Bronterre O'Brien, 1801-1864, 1971.
3248 Read, D., and Glasgow, E.L.H., Feargus O'Connor, Irishman and Chartist, 1961.
3249 Saville, J., ed., Ernest Jones, Chartist: Selections from the Writing and Speeches of Ernest Jones ... 1952.
3250 Schoyen, A.R., The Chartist Challenge: A Portrait of George Julian Harney, 1958.
3251 Wallas, G., The Life of Francis Place, 4th ed., 1951. See also Thale (3024) listed above, and Rowe (3242), listed above.
3252 Williams, D., John Frost: A Study in Chartism, 1939. Reprinted 1969.

(j) Owenism and Utopianism

3253 Armytage, W.H.G., Heavens Below: Utopian Experiments in England 1560-1960. 1961. Includes Scotland, Wales and Ireland.
3254 Butt, J. ed., Robert Owen, Prince of Cotton Spinners, 1971. Essays in honour of Owen's 200th anniversary.
3255 Cole, G.D.H., The Life of Robert Owen, 1st ed., 1925, 3rd ed., 1965, with new introduction by Margaret I. Cole.
3256 Cole, Margaret I., Robert Owen of New Lanark, 1953.
3257 Garnett, R.G. Co-operation and the Owenite Socialist Communities in Britain, 1825-45, 1972
3258 Harrison, J.F.C., Robert Owen and the Owenites in Britain and America: the Quest for the New Moral World, 1969. Detailed bibliography, 263-369.
3259 Morton, A.L., The Life and Ideas of Robert Owen, 1962. A Marxist view with extracts from Owen's writings.
3260 Owen, R., The Life of Robert Owen Written by Himself, Vol. 1, 1857, vol. 1A, 1858 (supplementary appendix). Reprinted 1967.

3261 ——— The Life of Robert Owen Written by Himself, Vol. 1, 1857. Reprinted 1971 with introduction by J. Butt.
3262 ——— A New View of Society and other Writings, ed. J. Butt, 1974.
3263 ——— A New View of Society and Report to the County of Lanark, ed. with introduction by V.A.C. Gatrell, 1969.
3264 ——— A New View of Society, ed. with introduction by J. Saville, Clifton, N.J., 1972.
3265 Podmore, F., The Life of Robert Owen, 2 vols. 1906. Reprint in 1 vol., 1923.
3266 Pollard, S. and Salt, J., eds., Robert Owen: Prophet of the Poor, 1971. Essays in honour of Owen's 200th anniversary.

INTERNAL TRANSPORT, PORTS AND COASTING TRADE

Note: for books and articles on river navigation, see 1623-1633 above.

(a) General

3266a Aldcroft, D.H., British Transport since 1914, 1975.
3267 Bagwell, P.S., The Transport Revolution from 1770, 1973.
3267a Barker, T.C., and Savage, C.I., An Economic History of Transport in Britain 3rd rev. ed. 1974.
3268 Dyos, H.J., and Aldcroft, D.H., British Transport: An Economic Survey from the Seventeenth Century to the Twentieth, 1969. Excellent bibliography, 401-38.
3269 Jackman, W.T., The Development of Transportation in Modern England, 1st ed., 1916, 2 vols., 2nd rev. ed., with new bibliographical introduction, 1962, 3rd ed., 1966.
3270 Pratt, E.A., A History of Inland Transport and Communication in England, 1912.
3271 Sherrington, C.E.R., One Hundred Years of Inland Transport in Great Britain, 1934, Reprinted 1970.
3271a Simmons, J., Transport, 1962 (short text and numerous well-chosen illustrations).

(b) Roads

3272 Ballen, Dorothy, Bibliography of Roads and Roadmaking in the United Kingdom, 1914.
3273 Albert, W.A., The Turnpike Road System in England, 1663-1840, 1971. The indispensable work on the subject.
3274 Copeland, J., Roads and Their Traffic, 1750-1850, 1968. Unsatisfactory
3275 Earle, J.B.F., A Century of Road Materials; The History of the Roadstone Division of Tarmac Ltd., 1971.
3276 Haldane, A.R.B., New Ways through the Glens, 1962. Telford's roadmaking in the Highlands.
3277 Jeffreys, R., The King's Highway: An Historical and Autobiographical Record of the Developments of the Past Sixty Years, 1949.
3278 Searle, M., Turnpikes and Toll-bars, 2 vols., 1930.

3278a Williams, L. A., Road Transport in Cumbria in the Nineteenth Century, 1974.
3279 Woodforde, J., History of the Bicycle, 1970.

(c) Coasting trade

3280 Read, A., The Coastwise Trade of the United Kingdom, Past and Present and its Possibilities, 1925.
See Willan (1551), listed above.

(d) Ports and their trade

3281 Andrews, JH., 'Two problems in the interpretation of the port books', Ec.H.R., 2nd ser., IX, 1956, 119-22.
3282 —— 'The port of Chichester and the grain trade, 1650-1750' Sussex Archaeological Collections, XCII, 1954, 93-105.
3283 —— 'The Thanet seaports 1650-1750', Archaeologia Cantiana, LXVI, 1953, 37-44.
3284 —— 'The trade of the port of Faversham, 1650-1750', Archaeologia Cantiana, LXIX, 1955, 125-31.
3285 Clark, E.A.G., The Ports of the Exe Estuary, 1660-1860: A Study in Historical Geography, 1960.
3286 Craig, R., 'Shipping and shipbuilding in the port of Chester in the eighteenth and early nineteenth centuries', T.H.S.L.C., CXVI, 1964, 39-68.
3287 —— and Jarvis, R.C., Liverpool Registry of Merchant Ships, Chet. Soc., 3rd Ser., XV, 1967.
3288 George, Barbara J., 'Pembrokeshire sea-trading before 1900', Field Studies, II, 1964, 1-39.
3289 Hyde, F.E., Liverpool and the Mersey: An Economic History of a Port, 1700-1970, 1971. See also Parkinson (1595) listed above and Harris (3605) listed below.
3290 Jarvis, R.C., Customs Letter Books of the Port of Liverpool, 1711-1813, Chet. Soc., 3rd ser., VI, 1954.
3291 Minchinton, W.E., The Trade of Bristol in the Eighteenth Century, Bristol Record Society, XX, 1957.
3292 Swann, D., 'The pace and progress of port investment in England 1660-1830', Yorks. Bull. XII, 1960, 32-44.

(e) Canals

3293 Barker, T.C., 'The Sankey Navigation', T.H.S.L.C., C., 1948, 121-55, (the first eighteenth-century canal in Great Britain, 1755-57).
3293a Broadbridge, S.R., The Birmingham Canal Navigations I (1768-1846), 1974.
3294 Hadfield, C., British Canals: An Illustrated History, 1950, 2nd ed., rev. and enlarged, 1959.
3295 —— The Canals of South Wales and the Border, 1960.
3296 —— The Canals of the West Midlands, 1st ed., 1966, 2nd rev. ed., 1969.
3297 —— and Biddle, G., The Canals of North-West England, 2 vols., 1970.
3298 Malet, H., The Canal Duke: A Biography of Francis, Third Duke of Bridgewater, 1961.
3299 De Maré, E., The Canals of England, 1950. Well illustrated.
3300 Mather, F. C., After the Canal Duke: A Study of the Industrial estates Administered by the Trustees of the Third Duke of Bridgewater in the Age of Railway Building, 1825-1872, 1970.
See also Richards, E. (4048) listed below.
3301 Patterson, A.T., 'The making of the Leicestershire canals, 1766-1814', Trans. Leicestershire Archaeological Society, XXVII, 1951, 1-35.
3302 Phillips, J., A General History of Inland Navigation, Reprint of 5th Ed., 1805, with introduction by C. Hadfield, 1970.
3303 Priestley, J., Historical Account of the Navigable Rivers, Canals, and Railways throughout Great Britain, 1831. Reprinted, with introduction by W.H. Chaloner, 1967.
3304 Rolt, L.T.C., The Inland Waterways of England, 1950.
3304a Ward, J.R., The Finance of Canal Building in Eighteenth-century England, 1974.

(f) Postal history and telecommunications

3305 Archer, M.S., The Welsh Post Towns before 1840, 1970.
3306 Baker, W.J., A History of the Marconi Company, 1970.
3307 Baldwin, F.G.C., The History of the Telephone in the United Kingdom, 1925.
3308 Briggs, A., A History of Broadcasting in the United Kingdom, 3 vols., 1961-70. I: The Birth of Broadcasting, 1961; II: The Golden Age of Wireless, 1965; III: The War of Words, 1970.
3309 Clear, C.R., John Palmer (of Bath), Mail Coach Pioneer, 1955.
3310 Coase, R.H., British Broadcasting: A Study in Monopoly, 1950.
3311 Ellis, K.L., The Post Office in the Eighteenth Century: A Study in Administrative History, 1958.
3312 Haldane, A.R.B., Three Centuries of Scottish Posts, 1971.
3313 Hemmeon, J.C., The History of the British Post Office, Cambridge, Mass., 1912.
3314 Hill, R. and Hill, G.B., The Life of Sir Rowland Hill ... and the History of Penny Postage, 2 vols., 1880.
3315 Kieve, J.L., The Electric Telegraph: A Social and Economic History, 1973, (an early and unprofitable experiment in nationalisation)
3316 Robertson, J.H., The Story of the Telephone: A History of the Telecommunications Industry of Britain, 1948.
3317 Robinson, H., The British Post Office: A History, Princeton, N.J., 1948.
3318 Staff, F., The Penny Post, 1680-1918, 1964.
3319 Vale, E., The Mail Coach Men of the Late Eighteenth Century, 1960.

(g) Motor transport

see also Dyos (3258), listed above.
3320 Andrews, P.W.S., and Brunner, Elizabeth, The Life of Lord Nuffield, 1955.

England 1700-1970

3321 Cornwell, E.L., Commercial Road Vehicles, 1960. (emphasis on technical history).
3322 Hibbs, J., A History of British Bus Services, 1970.
3323 —— ed., The Omnibus: Readings in the History of Road Passenger Transport, 1971.
3324 Lambert, Z.E., and Wyatt, R.J., Lord Austin the Man, 1968.
3325 Plowden, W., The Motor Car and Politics, 1896-1970, 1971. Contains an up-to-date bibliography, 421-4.
3326 Saul, S.B., 'The motor industry in Britain to 1914', Business History, V, 1962, 23-44.

(h) The Channel Tunnel

3327 Slater, H., Barnett, C., and Geneau, R.H., The Channel Tunnel, 1958; bibliography, 205-6.
3328 Whiteside, T., The Tunnel under the Channel, 1962.

(i) Railways

(1) Bibliographies

3329 Bryant, E.T., Railways: A Reader's Guide, 1968.
3330 Ottley, G., A Bibliography of British Railway History, 1965.
3331 Peddie, R.A., Railway Literature, 1556-1830, a Handlist, 1931.

(2) General

3332 Acworth, W., The Railways of England, 1st ed., 1889, 5th and best ed., 1900.
3333 —— The Railways of Scotland, 1890.
3334 Aldcroft, D.H., British Railways in Transition: The Economic Problems of Britain's Railways since 1914, 1968.
3335 —— 'The efficiency and enterprise of British railways, 1870-1914', Explorations in Economic History, 2nd Ser., V, No. 2, Wisconsin, 157-74.
3336 Alderman, G., The Railway Interest, 1972. (examines the growth of the railway lobby in the nineteenth century).
3337 Bagwell, P.S., The Railway Clearing House in the British Economy, 1844-1922, 1968.
3338 Baxter, B., Stone Blocks and Iron Rails, 1966. Deals with the pre-steam railway.
3339 Bell, R., History of the British Railways during the War, 1939-45, 1946.
3340 Broadbridge, S., Studies in Railway Expansion and the Capital Market in England, 1825-1873, 1970. Deals mainly with the finances on the Lancashire & Yorkshire Railway Company.
3341 Campbell, C.D., British Railways in Boom and Depression: An Essay in Trade Fluctuations and Their Effects, 1878-1930, 1932.
3342 Ellis, C., Hamilton, British Railway History: An Outline from the Accession of William IV to the Nationalisation of Railways, 2 vols., 1954-59. The two volumes divide at 1876-7.
3343 Francis, J., A History of the English Railway 2 vols., 1852. Reprinted 1968.
3344 Hawke, G.R., Railways and Economic Growth in England and Wales, 1840-1870, 1970. The first large-scale attempt to apply the methods of the 'new economic history' to a British subject.
3345 Lee, C.E., The Evolution of Railways, 2nd ed., rev. and enlarged, 1943.
3346 Lewin, H.G., Early British Railways: A Short History of Their Origin and Development, 1801-1844, 1925.
3347 —— The Railway Mania and its Aftermath, 1845-1852, 1936.
3348 Lewis, M.J.T., Early Wooden Railways, 1970.
3349 Marshall, C.F. Dendy, A History of British Railways down to the Year 1830, 1st ed., 1938, 2nd rev. ed., 1971.
3350 Mitchell, B.R., 'The coming of the railway and United Kingdom economic growth' in Reed (3354), listed below, 13-32.
3351 Parris, H., Government and the Railways in Nineteenth-Century Britain, 1965.
3352 Perkin, H.J., The Age of the Railway, 1970. Social and economic effects, c. 1780-1914.
3353 Pratt, E.A., British Railways and the Great War, 2 vols., 1921.
3354 Reed, M.C., ed., Railways in the Victorian Economy: Studies in Finance and Economic Growth, 1969.
3355 Robbins, M.R., The Railway Age, 1962, An analytical study with useful 'Notes on Sources', 199-212.
3356 Simmons, J., The Railways of Britain: An Historical Introduction, 1st ed., 1961, 2nd ed., 1969. Includes a useful chapter 'Literature and Maps'.
3357 Stephens, C. Cleveland, English Railways: Their Development and Their Relation to the State, 1915.

(3) Railway biographies

3358 Gourvish, T.R., Mark Huish and the London and North Western Railway, 1972. (exhaustive survey of a general manager).
3359 Lambert, R.S., The Railway King, 1800-71: A Study of George Hudson and the Business Morals of his Time, 1934.
3360 Rolt, L.T.C., George and Robert Stephenson: The Railway Revolution, 1960.
3361 —— Isambard Kingdom Brunel: A Biography, 1957.
3362 Webster, N.W., Joseph Locke: A Railway Revolutionary, 1971. A neglected contemporary of the Stephensons.

(4) Locomotives

3363 Ahrons, E.L., The British Steam Railway Locomotive, 1825-1925, 1927.
3364 Anon., History of the North British Locomotive Co., 1953.
3365 Clark, E.K., Kitson's of Leeds, 1938.
3366 Kidner, R.W., The Early History of the Locomotive, 1804-1876, 1956.
3367 Marshall, C.F. Dendy, A History of Railway Locomotives down to the end of the Year 1831, 1953.
3368 Warren, J.G.H., A Century of Locomotive Building by Robert Stephenson and Company 1823-1923, 1923. An account of the Stephensons' works at Newcastle upon Tyne.

(5) Individual lines and regional studies

The histories of individual lines are now so numerous, and of such varying quality, that the reader is referred to pages 236-38 of the first edition (1961) of J. Simmons, The Railways of Britain, and to the bibliographies above. A few of the most recent or significant are given below.

3369 Barker, T.C., and Robbins, R.M., A History of London Transport: Passenger Travel and the Development of the Metropolis, Vol. I, 1963, vol. II, 1974.

3370 Carlson, R.E., The Liverpool and Manchester Railway Project, 1821-1831, 1969.

3371 Nokes, G.A., (pseud. G.A. Sekon), Locomotion in Victorian London, 1938.

3372 Webster, N.W., Britain's First Trunk Line: The Grand Junction Railway, 1972.

OVERSEAS TRADE

(a) General and statistical

3373 Clark, G.N., Guide to English Commercial Statistics, 1696-1782, 1938.

3374 Davis, R., 'English foreign trade, 1700-1774', Ec.H.R., 2nd ser., XV, 1962.

3375 Schlote, W., British Overseas Trade from 1700 to the 1930s, 1952. English translation of a German book published in 1938; bibliography of books and articles since 1938, v-vi.

3376 Schumpeter, Elizabeth B., English Overseas Trade Statistics, 1697-1808, 1960. With an introduction by T.S. Ashton.

3377 Crouzet, F., L'Economie britannique et le blocus continental (1806-13), 2 vols., Paris, 1958.

3378 Ehrman, J., The British Government and Commercial Negotiations with Europe, 1783-1793, 1962.

3379 Heckscher, E.F., The Continental System: An Economic Interpretation, 1922.

3380 Henderson, W.O., 'The Anglo-French Commercial Treaty of 1786', Ec.H.R., 2nd ser., X, 1957, 104-12.

3381 Hertz (later Hurst), G.B., The Old Colonial System, 1905.

3382 Hoon, Elizabeth, E., The Organisation of the English Customs System, 1969-1786, N.Y., 1938.

3383 Olson, M., The Economics of the War-time Shortage: A History of British Food Supplies in the Napoleonic war and in World Wars I and II, Durham, N.C., 1963.

3384 Parkinson, C.N., ed., The Trade Winds: A Study of British Overseas Trade during the French Wars, 1793-1815, 1948.

3385 Schuyler, R.L., The Fall of the Old Colonial System: A Study in British Free Trade, 1770-1870, N.Y., 1945. Useful bibliography, 327-36.

3386 Sherwig, J.M., Guineas and Gunpowder: British Foreign Aid in the Wars with France, Cambridge, Mass., 1969.

3387 Williams, Judith B., British Commercial Policy and Trade Expansion, 1750-1850, 1972.

(b) Trade with specific areas mainly up to c. 1800-15

3388 Armytage, Frances, The Free Port System in the British West Indies: A Study in Commercial Policy, 1766-1822, 1953.

3389 Davis, R., Aleppo and Devonshire Square: English Traders in the Levant in the Eighteenth Century, 1967.

3390 Farnie, D.A., 'The commercial empire of the Atlantic, 1607-1783', Ec.H.R., 2nd ser., XV, No. 2, 1962, 205-18.

3391 Fisher, H.E.S., The Portugal Trade: A Study of Anglo-Portuguese Commerce, 1700-1770, 1971. Excellent bibliography, 153-62.

3392 Gill, C., Merchants and Mariners in the Eighteenth Century, 1961. Based on the papers of Thomas Hall, 1692-1748.

3393 Kent, H.S.K., War and Trade in the Northern Seas. Anglo-Scandinavian Economic Relations in the Mid-eighteenth Century, 1973.

3394 Pares, R., Merchants and Planters, 1960. The anatomy of the colonial trade.

3395 —— War and Trade in the West Indies, 1739-1763, 1936. Reprinted 1963.

3396 —— A West India Fortune, 1950 (the Pinneys of Bristol).

3397 Parkinson, C.N., Trade in the Eastern Seas, 1793-1813, 1937.

3398 Shillington, V.M. and Chapman, A.B.W., The Commercial Relations of England and Portugal, 1907.

3399 Sutherland, Lucy S., A London Merchant, 1695-1774, (William Braund), 1933. Reprinted 1962.

3400 Thomsen, Birgit N., Thomas, B. and Oldam, J.W., Dansk-Engelsk Samhandel: Et Historisk Rids, 1661-1963, Aarhus, 1966 (an historical sketch of Anglo-Danish trade: long English summary of Danish text).

3401 Walford, R., The British Factory in Lisbon, Lisbon, 1940.

3402 Wilson, C., Anglo-Dutch Commerce and Finance in the Eighteenth Century, 1941.

(c) The repeal of the Corn Laws, the free trade era and after

(1) The repeal of the Corn Laws and the coming of free trade

3403 Barnes, D.G., A History of the English Corn Laws from 1660-1846, 1930. Useful statistical tables, 297-302, and excellent bibliography, 303-31.

3404 Brown, Lucy, The Board of Trade and the Free Trade Movement, 1830-42, 1958.

3405 Chaloner, W.H., 'The agitation against the Corn Laws'. In J.T. Ward, ed., Popular Movements c. 1830-1850, 1970, 135-48. Bibliographical notes, 149-51.

3406 Fay, C.R., The Corn Laws and Social England, 1932.

3407 Grampp, W.D., The Manchester School of Economics, 1960. Good bibliography, 139-49, inferior text.

3408 Hyde, F. E., Mr Gladstone at the Board of Trade, 1934.
3409 Imlah, A. H., 'The fall of protection in Britain'. In D. E. Lee and G. E. McReynolds, eds., Essays in History and International Relations in Honor of G. H. Blakeslee, Worcester, Mass., 1949, 306-20.
3410 McCord, N., The Anti-Corn Law League, 1838-1846, 1958. Important study based on private papers of Cobden and George Wilson.
3411 Prentice, A., History of the Anti-Corn Law League, 2 vols., 1853. Reprinted, with new bibliographical introduction 1968.
3412 Prouty, R., The Transformation of the Board of Trade, 1830-1855: A Study of Administrative Reorganization in the Heyday of Laissez-faire, 1957.
3413 Read, D., Cobden and Bright: A Victorian Political Partnership, 1967.

(2) The free trade era and after, 1860-1939

3414 Abel, D., A History of British Tariffs, 1923-1942, 1945.
3415 Beveridge, W. H. et al., Tariffs: The Case Examined, 1931.
3416 Brown, B. H., The Tariff Reform Movement in Great Britain 1881-1895, N.Y., 1943.
3417 Drummond, I. A., British Economic Policy and the Empire, 1919-1939, 1972. Contains useful extracts from original documents.
3417a ——— Imperial Economic Policy, 1917-39, 1974.
3418 Dunham, A. L., The Anglo-French Treaty of Commerce of 1860 and the Progress of the Industrial Revolution in France, Ann Arbor, Mich., 1930.
3419 Fuchs, C. J., The Trade Policy of Great Britain and her Colonies since 1860, 1905. English translation of a book first published in 1893.
3420 Hutchinson, H. J., Tariff-making and Industrial Reconstruction, 1965 (an account of the work of the Import Duties Advisory Committee).
3421 Imlah, A. H., Economic Elements in the Pax Britannica: Studies in British Foreign Trade in the Nineteenth Century, Cambridge, Mass., 1958.
3422 McCord, N., Free Trade: Theory and Practice from Adam Smith to Keynes, 1970. Documents, with commentary.
3423 McGuire, E. B., The British Tariff System, 1939. Good on technical points of the working of tariffs.
3424 Richardson, J. H., British Economic Foreign Policy, 1936.
3425 Saul, S. B., Studies in British Overseas Trade, 1870-1914, 1960.
3426 Snyder, R. K., The Tariff Problem in Great Britain, 1918-1923, Stanford University Publications in History, Economics and Political Science, V, No. 2, 1944, Stanford, Calif.
3427 Turner, B., Free Trade and Protection, 1971. Documents with commentary.

(d) Trade relations affecting specific areas from c. 1800-15 onwards

3428 Buck, N. S., The Development of the Organisation of Anglo-American Trade, 1800-1850, New Haven, Conn., 1925.
3428a Davies, P. N., The Trade Makers: Elder Dempster in West Africa, 1852-1972, 1973.
3429 Ewart, E. A. (pseud. Boyd Cable), A Hundred Year History of the Peninsular and Oriental Steam Navigation Company 1837-1937, 1937.
3430 Greenberg, M., British Trade and the Opening of China, 1800-1842, 1951.
3431 Hoffman, R. J. S., Great Britain and the German Trade Rivalry, 1875-1914, Philadelphia, 1933.
3432 Hyde, F. E., Far Eastern Trade, 1860-1914, 1973.
3433 ——— and Harris, J. R., Blue Funnel: A History of Alfred Holt and Company of Liverpool, 1865-1914, 1956.
3433a ——— Shipping Enterprise and Management 1830-1939: Harrisons of Liverpool, 1967.
3434 John, A. H., A Liverpool Merchant-House, Being the History of Alfred Booth and Company, 1863-1958, 1959.
3435 Marriner, Sheila, Rathbones of Liverpool, 1845-73, 1961 (the China trade).
3436 Marriner, Sheila and Hyde, F. E., The Senior: John Samuel Swire, 1825-98: Management in Far Eastern Shipping Trade, 1967.
3437 Murray, M., Union Castle Chronicle, 1853-1953, 1953.
3438 Redford, A. et al., Manchester Merchants and Foreign Trade 1794-1858, 1934.
3439 ——— and Clapp, B. W., Manchester Merchants and Foreign Trade, vol. II: 1850-1939, 1956.

(e) The slave trade

3439a Anstey, R., The Atlantic Slave Trade and British Abolition, 1710-1810, 1975.
3440 Ashton, T. S., ed., Letters of a West African Trader, Edward Grace, 1767-70, 1950.
3441 Coupland, R. G., The British Anti-Slavery Movement, 1933, 2nd ed., with new introduction, 1964.
3442 Mackenzie-Grieve, Averil, The Last Years of the English Slave Trade. Liverpool, 1750-1807, 1941. Reprinted with corrections 1968.
3443 Mellor, G. R., British Imperial Trusteeship, 1783-1850, 1951.
3444 Merritt, J. E., 'The triangular trade', Business History, III, 1960, 1-7.
3445 Temperley, H., British Antislavery, 1833-1870, 1972.
3446 Williams, E., Capitalism and Slavery, Chapel Hill, N.C., 1944.
3447 ——— British Historians and the West Indies, 1966 (attempts to rebut Coupland (3441) and Mellor (3443), listed above).
3448 Williams, G., Liverpool Privateers and Letters of Marque with an Account of the Liverpool Slave Trade, 1897. Reprinted 1966.

(f) Imperialism

3449 Bartlett, C. J., ed., Britain Pre-eminent: Studies in British World Influence in the Nineteenth Century, 1969. Essays by various authors.
3450 Blaug, M., Economic Theory in Retrospect, 2nd rev. ed., 1968. Pages 261-71 contain the best short refutation of the theories of Marx and Lenin on imperialism.
3451 Bodelsen, C. A. G., Studies in Mid-Victorian Imperialism, Copenhagen, 1924; new impression, London, 1960.
3452 Chamberlain, M. E., The New Imperialism, 1970. A useful pamphlet on the period 1870-1914, with bibliography, 43-6.
3453 Court, W. H. B., 'The Communist doctrines of Empire'. In W. K. Hancock, Survey of British Commonwealth Affairs, II, Part I, 1940, 293-305.
3454 Fieldhouse, D. K., Economics and Empire 1830-1914, 1973.
3455 Hobson, J. A., Imperialism: A Study, 1st ed., 1902, 3rd rev. ed., 1938. Once influential, but now largely outdated; written in the shadow of the Boer War, 1899-1902.
3456 Koebner, R. and Schmidt, H. D., Imperialism: The Story and Significance of a Political Word, 1840-1960, 1964.
3457 Platt, D. C. M., Finance, Trade and Politics in British Foreign Policy, 1815-1914, 1968. The standard work; excellent bibliography, 418-33.
3458 Semmel, B., Imperialism and Social Reform: English Social-Imperial Thought 1895-1914, 1960.
3459 —— The Rise of Free Trade Imperialism: Classical Political Economy, the Empire of Free Trade and Imperialism, 1750-1850, 1970.
3460 Shaw, A. G. L., ed., Great Britain and her Colonies, 1815-1865, 1970. A collection of articles.
3461 Varga, E. and Mendelson, L., eds., New Data for V. I. Lenin's 'Imperialism: the Highest Stage of Capitalism', n.d. (1939).
3462 Winks, R. W., British Imperialism: Gold, God, Glory, N.Y., 1966. Extracts from the literature on British Imperialism.

OVERSEAS INVESTMENTS

3463 Cairncross, A. K., Home and Foreign Investment 1870-1913: Studies in Capital Accumulation, 1953.
3464 Feis, H., Europe, the World's Banker 1870-1914. New Haven, Conn., 1930. Sections on British overseas investments.
3465 Hall, A. R., ed., The Export of Capital from Britain 1870-1914, 1969. A collection of articles.
3466 Jenks, L. H., The Migration of British Capital to 1875, 1927.

OVERSEAS EMIGRATION

3467 Berthoff, R. T., British Immigrants in Industrial America, 1790-1850, Cambridge, Mass., 1953.
3468 Bloomfield, P., Edward Gibbon Wakefield, 1961.
3469 Boston, R. J., British Chartists in America, 1971.
3470 Carrothers, W. A., Emigration from the British Isles, with Special Reference to the Development of the Overseas Dominions, 1929.
3471 Coleman, T., The Atlantic Passage, 1972.
3472 Conway, A., The Welsh in America, 1961.
3473 Cowan, Helen I., British Emigration to British North America: The First Hundred Years, 2nd rev. and enlarged ed., Toronto, 1961.
3474 Dodd, A. H., The Character of Early Welsh Emigration to the United States, 2nd rev. ed., 1967.
3475 Duncan, R., 'Case studies in emigration: Cornwall, Gloucestershire and New South Wales, 1877-1886', Ec.H.R., 2nd ser., XVI, 1963, 272-89.
3476 Erickson, Charlotte, 'The encouragement of emigration by British trade unions, 1850-1900', Population Studies, III, 1949-50, 248-73.
3477 Hitchins, F. H., The Colonial Land and Emigration Commission, 1840-78, Philadelphia, 1931.
3478 Johnson, S. C., Emigration from the United Kingdom to North America, 1763-1912, 1913. Reprinted 1966.
3478a Johnston, H. J. M., British Emigration Policy, 1815-1830, 1972.
3478b Jones, M. A., 'The background to emigration from Great Britain in the nineteenth century', Perspectives in American History, Cambridge, Mass., VII, 1973, 3-92.
3479 Taylor, P. A. M., Expectations Westwards: The Mormons and the Emigration of their British Converts in the Nineteenth Century, 1965.
3480 Thistlethwaite, F., 'The Atlantic migration of the pottery industry', Ec.H.R., 2nd ser., XI, 1958, 264-78.
3481 Thomas, B., Migration and Economic Growth: A Study of Great Britain and the Atlantic Economy, 1954.
3482 —— Migration and Urban Development: A Reappraisal of British and American Long Cycles, 1972.

TOURISM

3483 Lickorish, J. and Kershaw, A. G., The Travel Trade, 1958.
3484 Pudney, J., The Thomas Cook Story, 1953.
3485 Rae, W. F., The Business of Travel, 1891 (fifty years of Thomas Cook and Son).

SHIPPING AND SHIPBUILDING

(a) General

See also Davis (1402), listed above.

3486 Jarvis, R. C., 'Eighteenth-century London shipping'. In Hollaender and Kellaway (484), listed above.
3487 Kirkaldy, A. W., British Shipping: Its History, Organisation and Importance, 1914. Excellent treatment; useful on shipping conferences, Lloyd's Register and marine insurance, bibliography, XIII-XX.
3488 Lindsay, W. S., History of Merchant Shipping, 4 vols., 1871-6.
3489 Sturmey, S. G., British Shipping and World Competition, 1962.
3490 Syrett, D., Shipping and the American War, 1775-83: A Study of British Transport Organisation, 1970.

(b) Personnel

3491 Course, A. G., The Merchant Navy: A Social History, 1963.
3492 Kemp, P., The British Sailor: A Social History of the Lower Deck, 1971.
3493 Lewis, M., A Social History of the Navy (1793-1815), 1960.
3494 Lloyd, C., The Nation and the Navy: A History of Naval Life and Policy, 2nd rev. ed., 1961.

(c) Steam

3495 Hughes, J. R. T. and Reiter, S., 'The first 1945 British steamships', Jnl. of the American Statistical Association, 53, June 1958, 360-81 (see however, T.L.S., 29 September, 13 and 27 October 1966).
3496 Kennedy, J., The History of Steam Navigation, 1903. Useful for the Liverpool lines.
3497 Moyse-Bartlett, H., From Sail to Steam, 1946.
3498 Spratt, H. P., The Birth of the Steamboat, 1958.
3499 Tyler, D. B., Steam Conquers the Atlantic, N.Y., 1939.

(d) Shipbuilding

3500 Dougan, D., The History of North East Shipbuilding, 1968.
3501 Jones, L., Shipbuilding in Britain, Mainly Between the two World Wars, 1957. Chapter I is on the nineteenth century, but contains a number of inaccuracies.
3502 Scott, J. D., Vickers: A History, 1962.

AIR TRAVEL

See also Dyos and Aldcroft (3268), listed above.

3503 Pudney, J., The Seven Skies: A Study of B.O.A.C. and its Forerunners since 1919, 1959.

ARCHITECTURE AND HOUSING

3504 Barley, M. W., The House and Home, 1963 (part of J. Simmons, ed., A Visual History of Modern Britain).
3505 Beard, G., Georgian Craftsmen and their Work, 1966.
3506 Brunskill, R. W., Illustrated Handbook of Vernacular Architecture, 1970. Excellent bibliography, 212-24.
3507 Chadwick, G. F., The Works of Sir Joseph Paxton, 1803-1865, 1961.
3508 Chapman, S. D., ed., The History of Working-Class Housing: A Symposium, 1971.
3509 Chesher, V. M. and F. J., The Cornishman's House: An Introduction to the History of Traditional Domestic Architecture in Cornwall, 1968.
3510 Cook, O. and Smith, E., English Cottages and Farmhouses, 1954.
3511 —— The English House through Seven Centuries, 1968; bibliography, 313-16.
3512 Clifton-Taylor, A., The Pattern of English Building, 1962; bibliography, 343-7.
3513 Dunbar, J. G., The Historic Architecture of Scotland, 1966.
3514 Dutton, R., The Victorian Home: Some Aspects of Nineteenth-century Taste and Manners, 1954.
3515 Eden, P. M., Small Houses in England, 1520-1820: Towards a Classification, 1969.
3516 Fletcher, V., Chimney Pots and Stacks: An Introduction to Their History, Variety and Identification, 1968.
3517 Forrester, H., The Smaller Queen Anne and Georgian House, 1700-1840, 1964.
3518 Gauldie, Enid M., Cruel Habitations: A History of Working-class Housing, 1780-1918, 1974.
3519 Gloag, J., The English Tradition in Architecture, 1963; bibliography, 241-7.
3520 —— Victorian Comfort: A Social History of Design from 1830-1900, 1961. Should be used with caution.
3521 —— Victorian Taste: Some Social Aspects of Architecture and Industrial Design, from 1820 to 1900, 1962; bibliography, 159-65.
3522 Goodhart-Rendel, H. S., English Architecture since the Regency: An Interpretation, 1953.
3523 Hadfield, M., Landscape with Trees, 1967; bibliography, 186-92.
3524 Hartley, Marie and Ingilby, Joan, Life and Tradition in the Yorkshire Dales, 1968.
3525 Henderson, A., The Family House in England, 1964.
3526 Hitchcock, H.-R., Architecture, Nineteenth and Twentieth Centuries, 1958; bibliography, 473-83.
3527 Hussey, C., English Country Houses: Early Georgian, 1715-1760, 1955.
3528 —— English Country Houses: Mid-Georgian, 1760-1800, 1956.
3529 —— English Country Houses: Late Georgian, 1800-1840, 1958.
3530 —— English Gardens and Landscapes 1700-1750, 1967.
3531 Iredale, D., This Old House, 1968.
3532 Jenkins, F., Architect and Patron, 1961.
3533 Jones, S. R., English Village Homes and Country Buildings, 1936.
3534 Kerr, Barbara, Dorset Cottages, Dorset Monographs No. 4, 1965.
3535 Lees-Milne, J., English Country Houses: Baroque, 1685-1715, 1970.

3536 Lloyd, N., A History of the English House from Primitive Times to the Victorian Period, 1931.
3537 Peate, I. C., The Welsh House: A Study in Folk Culture, 2nd rev. ed., 1944; bibliography, 215-23.
3538 Potter, M. and A., 'The changing shape of things'; Houses, Being a Record of the Changes in Construction, Style and Plan of the Smaller English Home from Medieval Times to Present Day, 1948.
3539 Richards, J. M., The Functional Tradition in Early Industrial Buildings, 1958.
3540 Summerson, J., Architecture in Britain, 1530-1830, 1953, 4th ed., 1963; bibliography, 363-70.
3541 —— Heavenly Mansions and Other Essays on Architecture, 1949.
3541a —— The London Building World of the 1860s, 1974.
3542 Tann, Jennifer, The Development of the Factory, 1970.
3543 Tarn, J. N., Working-class Housing in Nineteenth Century Britain, 1971.
3543a —— Five Per Cent Philanthropy: An Account of Housing in Urban Areas, 1840-1914, 1974.
3544 Winter, J., Industrial Architecture, 1970. A study of early factories.
3545 Woodforde, J., The Truth about Cottages, 1969.
3546 Wood-Jones, R. B., Traditional Domestic Architecture of the Banbury Region, 1963; bibliography, 298-9.

THE BUILDING INDUSTRY

3547 Bowley, Marian, The British Building Industry: Four Studies in Response to Resistance and Change, 1969. Covers the twentieth century.
3548 —— Housing and the State, 1919-1944, 1946.
3549 —— Innovations in Building Materials, 1960.
3550 Brown, Joyce M., 'W. B. Wilkinson (1819-1902) and his place in the history of reinforced concrete', Trans. Newcomen Society, XXXIX, 1966-7, 129-42.
3551 Cooney, E. W., 'The origins of the Victorian master builders', Ec.H.R., 2nd ser., VIII, 1955-6, 167-76.
3552 —— 'Long waves in building in the British economy of the nineteenth century'. In Aldcroft and Fearon (2193), listed above, 220-35.
3553 Davey, N., Building in Britain: The Growth and Organisation of Building Processes in Britain from Roman times to the Present Day, 1964.
3554 —— A History of Building Materials, 1961.
3555 Habakkuk, H. J., 'Fluctuations in house-building in Britain and the United States in the nineteenth century'. In Aldcroft and Fearon (2193), listed above, 236-67.
3556 Hobhouse, Hermione, Thomas Cubitt, Master Builder, 1971.

3557 Lewis, J. Parry, Building Cycles and Britain's Growth, 1965. Covers period from 1700 to the present.
3557a Lindsay, Jean, A History of the North Wales Slate Industry, 1974.
3558 Lloyd, N., A History of English Brickwork from Mediaeval Times to the End of the Georgian Period, 1925.
3559 Middlemas, R. K., The Master Builders: Thomas Brassey; Sir John Aird; Lord Cowdray; Sir John Norton-Griffiths, 1963.
3560 North, F. J., The Slates of Wales, 3rd rev. ed., 1946.
3561 Richardson, H. W. and Aldcroft, D. H., Building in Britain Between the Wars, 1968.
3562 Saul, S. B., 'House building in England, 1890-1914', Ec.H.R., 2nd ser., XV, 1962-3, 119-37.
3563 Skempton, A. W., 'Portland cements, 1843-1887', Trans. Newcomen Society, XXXV, 1964, 117-52.

BUILDING SOCIETIES

3564 Bacon, R. K., The Life of Sir Enoch Hill: The Romance of the Modern Building Society, 1934.
3565 Bellman, H., The Thrifty Three Millions: A Study of the Building Society Movement and the Story of the Abbey Road Society, 1935.
3566 Clearly, E. J., The Building Society Movement, 1965. The best general history.
3567 Hobson, O. R., A Hundred Years of the Halifax: The History of the Halifax Building Society, 1853-1953, 1953.
3568 Mansbridge, A., Brick upon Brick, 1934. History of the Co-operative Permanent Building Society from 1884.
3569 Price, S. J., Building Societies: Their Origins and History, 1958.
3570 —— From Queen to Queen: The Centenary History of the Temperance Permanent Building Society, 1854-1954, 1954.

URBAN HISTORY

(a) General

3570a Attention is drawn to Urban History Newsletter, No. 1, 1963, which is supplemented by the Urban History Year book No. 1, 1974.
3571 Ashworth, W., The Genesis of Modern British Town Planning: A Study in the Economic and Social History of the Nineteenth and Twentieth Centuries, 1954. Excellent bibliography.
3572 Briggs, A., Victorian Cities, 1st ed., 1963, 2nd rev. ed., 1968. Includes London, Manchester, Leeds, Birmingham and Middlesbrough.
3572a Chalklin, C. W., The Provincial Towns of Georgian England: A Study of the Building Process 1740-1820, 1974.

3573 Clapham, J. H. and Mary H., 'Life in the new towns'. In G. M. Young, ed., Early Victorian England, 1830-1865, I, 227-44.
3574 Coleman, B. I., The Idea of the City in Nineteenth Century Britain, 1973. A collection of documents with useful commentary, and good bibliography, 235-8.
3575 Dickinson, H. W., Water Supply of Greater London, 1954.
3576 Dyos, H. J. and Wolff, M., The Victorian City: Images and Reality, 2 vols., 1973.
3577 Dyos, H. J. ed., The Study of Urban History, 1968. The best introduction to the subject. See also Everitt (1414a) listed above.
3578 Fay, C. R., et al., Round about Industrial Britain 1830-1860, Toronto, 1952. Chapters on inventions, patent law, Birkenhead, Birmingham, Bradford, Dundee, the Clyde, Manchester, Merthyr Tydfil, and Sheffield.
3579 Hartley, Dorothy, Water in England, 1964.
3580 Kellett, J. R., The Impact of Railways on Victorian Cities, 1969.
3581 Laski, H. J., Jennings, W. I. and Robson, W. A., eds., A Century of Municipal Progress, 1835-1935, 1935. Published to mark the centenary of the Municipal Corporations Act, 1835.
3582 Lipman, V. D., Local Government Areas, 1834-1945, 1949.
3583 Mottram, R. H., 'Town life'. In G. M. Young, ed., Early Victorian England 1830-1865, 1934, 155-233.
3584 Pfautz, H., Charles Booth on the City, Chicago, Ill., 1967.
3585 Savage, W., The Making of our Towns, 1952.

(b) **Individual cities and towns**

Note: These entries are listed alphabetically by the name of the city or town described and not alphabetically by author.

3586 Townsend J., ed., News of a Country Town, Being Extracts from 'Jackson's Oxford Journal', relating to Abingdon, 1753-1835 A.D., 1914.
See also Marshall (2185), listed above (for Barrow-in Furness, 1757-1897).
3587 Stephens, W. B., ed., V.C.H. Warwickshire VII: The City of Birmingham, 1964.
3588 Gill, C. and Briggs, A., History of Birmingham, 2 vols., 1952, vol. I: Manor and Borough to 1865; vol. II: Borough and City 1865 to 1938.
3589 Musgrave, C., Life in Brighton, 1970.
3590 Little, B., The City and County of Bristol: A Study in Atlantic Civilisation, 1954.
3591 Minchinton, W. E., 'Bristol: metropolis of the west in the eighteenth century', T.R.H.S., 5th ser., IV, 1954, 69-89.
3592 Heape, R. G., Buxton under the Dukes of Devonshire, 1948.
3593 Dyos, H. J., Victorian Suburb: A Study of the Growth of Camberwell, 1961.
3594 Richardson, K., Twentieth-century Coventry, 1972.
3595 Chaloner, W. H., The Social and Economic Development of Crewe, 1780-1923, 1950,
new impression 1974.
3596 Hoskins, W. G., Industry, Trade and People in Exeter, 1688-1800, with Special Reference to the Serge Industry, 1935.
3596a Gillett, E., A History of Grimsby, 1973.
3597 Thompson, F. M. L., Hampstead: Building a Borough, 1650-1964, 1974.
3597a Jackson, G., Hull in the Eighteenth Century: A Study in Economic and Social History, 1971.
3598 Schofield, M. M., Outlines of an Economic History of Lancaster, 1680-1860, 2 vols., 1946-51.
3599 Greaves, R. W., The Corporation of Leicester, 1689-1836, 1st ed., 1939, 2nd ed., 1969.
3600 Patterson, A. T., Radical Leicester: A History of Leicester, 1780-1850, 1954.
3600a Hill, J. W. F., Georgian Lincoln, 1966.
3600b —— Victorian Lincoln, 1975.
3601 Chandler, G., Liverpool, 1957. A badly-arranged chronicle.
3602 White, B. D., A History of the Corporation of Liverpool, 1834-1914, 1951.
3603 Lawton, R., 'The population of Liverpool in the mid-nineteenth century', T.H.S.L.C., CVII, 1956, 89-120.
3604 Frazer, W. M., Duncan of Liverpool, Being an Account of the Work of Dr W. H. Duncan, Medical Officer of Health of Liverpool, 1847-1863, 1947.
3605 Harris, J. R. ed., Liverpool and Merseyside, 1969.
3606 Jones, J. R., The Welsh Builder on Merseyside: Annals and Lives, 1946.
See also Vigier (3630), and Simey (3760), listed below.
3607 George, M. Dorothy, London Life in the Eighteenth Century, 1st ed., 1925, 3rd corrected ed., 1951.
3608 Rudé, G., The History of London: Hanoverian London, 1714-1808, 1971.
3609 —— Paris and London in the Eighteenth Century, 1970. Concerned mainly with problems of public order and disorder.
3610 Olsen, D. J., Town Planning in London: The Eighteenth and Nineteenth Centuries, Yale, 1967.
3611 Mayhew, H., London Labour and the London Poor; 1st ed. in 3 vols., 1851, 2nd enlarged ed. in 4 vols., 1861-2, new impression, 1967.
3612 Mayhew, H., ed. S. Rubinstein, The Street Trader's Lot—London, 1851, 1947.
3613 Quennell, P., ed., Mayhew's London, Being Selections from London Labour and the London Poor, 1969.
3614 —— ed., London's Underworld: Selections from London Labour and the London Poor, 1969.
3615 Thompson, E. P. and Yeo, Eileen, The Unknown Mayhew: Selections from the Morning Chronicle, 1849-50, 1971.
3616 Thompson, E. P., 'The political education of Henry Mayhew', Victorian Studies, XI, 1967-8, 41-62.
3617 Hughes, J. R. T., 'Henry Mayhew's London', J.E.H., N.Y., XXIX, 1969, 526-36.

3618 Jackson, A. A., Semi-detached London, 1973.
3619 Jones, G. Stedman, Outcast London, 1972.
3620 Robson, W. A., The Government and Misgovernment of London, 1939. Contains much historical material mainly from 1835 to date of publication.
3621 Gomme, G. L., London in the Reign of Queen Victoria (1837-1897), 1898. Still extremely useful, as it covers many aspects of the capital's development.
3622 Dyos, H. J., 'The slums of Victorian London', Victorian Studies, XI, 1967-8, 5-40.
3623 Smith, D. H., The Industries of Greater London, Being a Survey of the Recent Industrialisation of the Northern and Western Sectors, 1933. Useful for the period c. 1900-32.
3624 Hall, P. G., The Industries of London since 1861, 1962.
3625 Winter, G., Past Positive: London's Social History Recorded in Photographs, 1971. Covers period from 1840s to 1914.
3626 Robbins, R. M., Middlesex, 1953. Covers many aspects of London's economic and social history; good bibliography, 397-417.
3627 Redford, A. and Russell, Ina S., History of Local Government in Manchester, 3 vols., 1939-40.
3627a Marcus, S., Engels, Manchester and the Working Class, 1974.
3628 Marshall, L. S., The Development of Public Opinion in Manchester, 1780-1820, Syracuse, N.Y., 1946. Neither very satisfactory nor very accurate: now largely superseded by later works.
3628a Kennedy, M., Portrait of Manchester, 1970. The best one-volume treatment.
3629 Stewart, C., The Stones of Manchester, 1956. The Victorian buildings of the city.
3630 Vigier, F., Change and Apathy: Liverpool and Manchester During the Industrial Revolution, Cambridge, Mass., 1970.
3631 Mottram, R. H., Success to the Mayor: A Narrative of the Development of Local Self Government in a Provincial Centre (Norwich) During Eight Centuries, 1937.
3632 Church, R. A., Economic and Social Change in a Midland Town: Victorian Nottingham, 1815-1900, 1966.
3633 Bateson, H., A Centenary History of Oldham, 1949. Largely a chronicle; little historical understanding.
3634 Childs, W. M., The Town of Reading During the Early Part of the Nineteenth Century, 1910.
3635 Hinton, M., A History of the Town of Reading, 1954; bibliography, 166-8.
3636 Taylor, Rebe P., Rochdale Retrospect, 1956. Useful summary: source references, 207-8.
3637 Morgan, J. B. and Peberdy, P., eds, Collected Essays on Southampton, 1968. Aspects of civic history from Anglo-Saxon times to the present.
3638 Patterson, A. T., A History of Southampton, 1700-1914, vol. I, 1966 (covers 1700-1835), vol. II, 1972 (covers the period 1836-67).

3639 Bailey, F. A., History of Southport, 1955.
3640 Barker, T. C. and Harris, J. R., A Merseyside Town in the Industrial Revolution: St Helens, 1750-1900, 1954.
3641 Grinsell, L. V. et al., Studies in the History of Swindon, 1950.
3642 Homeshaw, E. J., The Corporation of the Borough and Foreign of Walsall, 1960.
3643 Hunt, Edith M., The History of Ware, 1st ed., 1946. Reprinted 1949.
3644 Carter, G. A. et al., Warrington Hundred, 1947. A short history of the town from prehistoric times to 1947.
3645 Ede, J. F., History of Wednesbury, 1962.
3646 Wood, R., West Hartlepool: The Rise and Development of a Victorian New Town, 1967.
3647 Daysh, G. H. J., ed., A Survey of Whitby and the Surrounding Areas, 1958. Contains much historical information.
3647a Armstrong, W. A., Stability and Change in an English County Town: A Social Study of York, 1801-51, 1974.

(c) The seaside holiday

3648 Gilbert, E. W., 'The holiday industry and seaside towns in England and Wales'. In Festschrift Leopold G. Scheidl zum 60. Geburtstag, I, Vienna, 1965, 235-47.
3649 Hern, A., The Seaside Holiday: The History of the English Seaside Resort, 1967.
3650 Marsden, C., The English at the Seaside, 1947.
3651 Pimlott, J. A. R., The Englishman's Holiday, 1947.

ECONOMIC THOUGHT AND STATE POLICY

3652 Bowley, Marian, Nassau Senior and Classical Economics, 1937.
3653 Brebner, J. B., 'Laissez-faire and state intervention in nineteenth-century Britain' in Carus-Wilson ed. (164), listed above, III, 252-62.
3654 Cheyney, E. P., Modern English Reform, from Individualism to Socialism, Philadelphia, 1931.
3655 Clark, G. Kitson, 'Statesmen in disguise', Hist. Jnl., II, 1959, 19-39.
3656 Coats, A. W., ed., The Classical Economists and Economic Policy, 1971.
3657 Cromwell, Valerie, 'Interpretations of nineteenth-century administration: an analysis', Victorian Studies, IX, 1965-6, 245-58.
3658 Dicey, A. V., Lectures on the Relation between Law and Public Opinion in England During the Nineteenth Century, 1905, 2nd ed., 1914. Reprinted 1952.
3659 Halévy, E., The Growth of Philosophic Radicalism, Eng. trans., 1928, rev. ed., 1952.
3660 Harrod, R. F., The Life of John Maynard Keynes, 1951.
3661 Hart, Jenifer M., 'Nineteenth-century social reform: a Tory interpretation of history', P.P., 31, 1965, 39-61.

3662 Hutchinson, T.W., A Review of Economic Doctrines, 1870-1929, 1953.
3663 Jha, N., The Age of Marshall: Aspects of British Economic Thought, 1890-1915, 2nd ed., 1973.
3664 Lekachman, R., The Age of Keynes: A Biographical Study, 1967.
3665 Levy, S.L., Nassau W. Senior, 1790-1864, 1970.
3666 Lubenow, W.C., The Politics of Government Growth: Early Victorian Attitudes Towards State Intervention, 1853-1848, 1971.
3667 MacDonagh, O., A Pattern of Government Growth 1800-60: The Passenger Acts and their Enforcement, 1961.
3668 —— 'The nineteenth-century revolution in government: a reappraisal', Hist. Jnl. I, 1958, 52-67.
3669 McGregor, O.R., 'Social research and social policy in the nineteenth century', British Jnl. of Sociology, VIII, 1957, 146-57.
3670 Mack, Mary P., 'The Fabians and Utilitarianism', Jnl. of the History of Ideas, XVI, 1955, 76-88.
3671 Parris, H., Constitutional Bureaucracy: The Development of Central Administration since the Eighteenth Century, 1969.
3672 —— 'The nineteenth-century revolution in government: a reappraisal reappraised', Hist. Jnl. III, 1960, 17-37.
3673 Roberts, D., The Victorian Origins of the Welfare State, New Haven, Conn., 1960.
3674 Robbins, L., The Theory of Economic Policy in English Classical Political Economy, 1952.
3675 Stark, W., ed., Economic Writings of Jeremy Bentham, 1952, I, (introduction).
3676 Taylor, A.J., Laissez-faire and State Intervention in Nineteenth Century Britain, 1972.
3677 Winch, D., Economics and Policy: An Historical Study, 1970. Covers Britain 1900-60. See also Tucker (1718), listed above.

THE FACTORY SYSTEM AND LEGISLATION

3678 Babbage, C., On the Economy of Machinery and Manufactures, 4th enlarged ed., 1835. Reprinted 1963.
3679 Blaug, M., 'The classical economists and the Factory Acts — a re-examination'. In Coats (3656), listed above, 104-22.
3680 Bready, J. Wesley, Lord Shaftesbury and Social-Industrial Progress, 1926.
3681 Clarke, A., The Effects of the Factory System, 1st ed. 1899, 4th ed., 1904.
3682 Cowherd, R.G., The Humanitarians and the Ten Hour Movement in England, Boston, Mass., 1956. Should be used with caution.
3683 Djang, T.K., Factory Inspection in Great Britain, 1942.
3684 Dodd, W., The Factory System Illustrated, 1st ed. 1842, 3rd ed., with introduction, 1968.
3685 Driver, C., Tory Radical: The Life of Richard Oastler, N.Y., 1946.
3686 Fielden, J., The Curse of the Factory System, 1st ed., 1836, 2nd ed., 1969, with introduction by J.T. Ward. The introduction is the best life of Fielden.

3687 Gaskell, P., Artisans and Machinery: The Moral and Physical Condition of the Manufacturing Population Considered with Reference to Mechanical Substitutes for Human Labour, 1836. Reprinted 1968.
3688 —— The Manufacturing Population of England, 1833.
3689 Hammond, J.L., and Barbara, Lord Shaftsbury, 1st ed., 1923, 4th rev. ed., 1939. Reprinted 1969.
3690 Henriques, Ursula R.Q., The Early Factory Acts and their Enforcement, Historical Association pamphlet, 1971.
3691 Hutchins, B.L., and Harrison, A., A History of Factory Legislation, 1st ed. 1903, 2nd rev. ed., 1911, 3rd ed., 1926. Reprinted 1966. Covers the period up to 1910.
3692 Hutt, W.H., 'The factory system of the early nineteenth century'. In F. A. Hayek, ed., Capitalism and the Historians, 1954, 160-88.
3693 Kydd, S.H.G., (pseud. 'Alfred') The History of the Factory Movement, 2 vols., 1857. Reprinted N.Y., 1966.
3694 Langenfelt, G., The Historic Origin of the Eight Hours' Day, Stockholm, 1954.
3695 Lee, W.R., 'Robert Baker, the first doctor in the factory department' (Part I: 1803-1858; Part II: 1858 onwards), British Jnl. of Industrial Medicine, XXI, 1964, 85-93, 167-79.
3696 Martin, Bernice, 'Leonard Horner: a portrait of an inspector of factories', International Review of Social History, XIV, 1969, 412-43.
3697 Melada, I., The Captain of Industry in English Fiction, 1821-1871, Albuquerque, New Mexico 1970.
3698 Moseley, Maboth, Irascible Genius: A Life of Charles Babbage, Inventor, 1964.
3699 Sorenson, L.R., 'Some classical economists, laissez-faire and the Factory Acts', J.E.H., XII, 1952, 247-62.
See also Tawney (53), listed above, 283-6 (important for Sadler and the factory question).
3700 Taylor, R.W. Cooke, Introduction to a History of the Factory System, 1886.
3701 Taylor, W. Cooke, Notes of a Tour in the Manufacturing Districts of Lancashire, 1st ed., 1841, 2nd ed., 1842, 3rd ed., 1968.
3702 Thomas, M.W., The Early Factory Legislation: A Study in Legislative and Administrative Evolution, 1948. Covers the period 1802-53 in some detail.
3703 Ure, A., The Philosophy of Manufactures, 1st ed., 1835, 3rd ed. 1861. Reprint of 1st ed., 1967.
3704 Walker, K.O., 'The classical economists and the factory Acts', J.E.H. I, 1941, 168-77. Takes the question to 1833.
3705 Ward, J.T., The Factory Movement, 1830-1855, 1962.
3706 —— 'The factory movement' (with bibliographical notes). In Ward (3211), listed above, 54-77.
3707 —— 'The Factory Movement in Lancashire, 1830-1855' T.L.C.A.S., LXXV-VI, 1969, 186-210.
3708 —— 'The Factory reform movement in Scotland', Scot.H.R., XLI, 1962, 100-23.

3709 —— The Factory System, I, 1870; II, 1971. Documents and commentary.
3710 —— 'Leeds and the Factory Reform Movement', Thoresby Society Miscellany, 13, Part II, 1961, 87) 118.
3711 —— and Treble, J.J., 'Religion and education in 1843: reaction to the 'Factory Education Bill' ', Jnl. of Ecclesiastical History, XX, 1969, 79-110.
3712 Wing, C., Evils of the Factory System Demonstrated by Parliamentary Evidence, 1837 Reprinted 1967. A summary of the Parliamentary Papers and debates.
See also Chapman (2680), listed above.

POOR LAW, CHARITY AND SOCIAL PROTECTION

(a) Poor Law

3713 Ashby, A.W., One Hundred Years of Poor Law Administration in a Warwickshire Village, 1912.
3714 Beales, H.L., 'The New Poor Law', History, XV, 1930-31, 308-19.
3715 Blaug, M., 'The myth of the Old Poor Law and the making of the New', J.E.H., XXIII, 1963, 151-84.
3716 —— 'The Poor Law Report re-examined', J.E.H., XXIV, 1964, 229-45.
3717 Boyson, R., 'The New Poor Law in North East Lancashire, 1834-71', T.L.C.A.S., LXX, 1960, 35-56.
3717a Checkland, S.G. and E.O.A., eds., The Poor Law Report of 1834, 1974.
3718 Coats, A.W., 'Economic thought and poor law policy in the eighteenth century', Ec.H.R., 2nd ser., XIII, 1960, 39-51.
3719 Cormack, Una, 'The Royal Commission on the Poor Laws and the Welfare State', In A.V.S., Lockhead, A Reader in Social Administration, 1968.
3720 Cowherd, R.G., 'The humanitarian reform of the English Poor laws from 1782-1815', Proceedings of the American Philosophical Society, civ, June 1960, 328-42.
3721 Cuttle, G., The Legacy of the Rural Guardians: A Study of Conditions in Mid-Essex, 1934.
3722 Eden, F.M., The State of the Poor, abridged and ed. A.G.L. Rogers, 1928.
3723 Edsall, N.C., The Anti-Poor Law Movement, 1834-44, 1971.
3724 Fearn, H., 'The apprenticing of pauper children in the incorporated Hundreds of Suffolk', Proceedings of the Suffold Institute of Archaeology, XXVI, 1953, 85-96.
3725 —— 'The financing of the poor law incorporations for the Hundreds of Colneis and Carlford in Suffolk, 1758-1820', Proceedings of the Suffolk Institute of Archaeology, XXVII, 1956, 96-111.
3726 Gray, I., ed., Cheltenham Settlement Examinations, 1815-1826, Bristol and Gloucestershire Archaeological Society, 1969.
3727 Henriques, Ursula, 'How cruel was the Victorian poor law?', Hist. Jnl., XI, 1968, 365-71.
3728 Keith-Lucas, B., 'Poplarism', Public Law, Spring 1962, 52-80.
3729 Marshall, Dorothy, The English Poor in the Eighteenth Century: A Study in Social and Administrative History, 1926.
3730 —— 'The Old Poor Law, 1662-1795', In Carus-Wilson, ed. (164), listed above, I, 295-305 (ineffectiveness of law of settlement and removal as a brake on mobility of labour).
3731 Marshall, J.D., The Old Poor Law, 1795-1834, 1968; Select bibliography, 47-8.
3732 —— 'The Nottinghamshire reformers and their contribution to the Old Poor Law', Ec.H.R., 2nd ser., XIII, 1961, 382-96.
3733 Mitchelson, N., The Old Poor Law in East Yorkshire, 1953.
3734 Oxley, G.W., 'The relief of the permanent poor in S.W. Lancashire under the Old Poor Law'. In Harris, ed. (3605), listed above, 16-49.
3735 Postgate, R., Life of George Lansbury, 1951 (Poplarism).
3736 Poynter, J.R., Society and Pauperism: English Ideas on Poor Relief, 1795-1834, 1969.
3737 Proctor, Winifred, 'Poor law administration in Preston Union, 1838-1848', T.H.S.L.C., 117, 1965, 145-66.
3738 Roberts, D., 'How cruel was the Victorian Poor Law?' Hist. Jnl., VI, 1963, 97-107.
3739 Rose, M.E., The English Poor Law 1780-1930, 1971. Select documents with commentary.
3740 —— The Relief of Poverty, 1834-1914, 1972.
3741 —— 'The allowance system under the New Poor Law', Ec.H.R., 2nd ser., XIX, 1966, 607-20.
3742 —— 'The Anti-Poor Law agitation'. In Ward (3211), listed above, 78-94, with bibliographical note.
3743 —— 'The Anti-Poor Law Movement in the North of England', Northern History, I, 1966, 70-91.
3744 Taylor, G., The Problem of Poverty, 1660-1834, 1969. Useful short textbook.
3745 Webb, Beatrice, My Apprenticeship, 1926.
3746 Webb, S. and Beatrice, English Poor Law History: Part I: The Old Poor Law (to 1832) 1927, 2nd ed., with new introduction, 1963.
3747 —— English Poor Law History: Part II: The Last Hundred Years, 2 vols., 1929, 2nd ed., 1963.
3748 —— English Poor Law Policy, 1909. Reissued 1963.

(b) Charity and social protection

3749 Binfield, C., George Williams and the Y.M.C.A., 1973.
3750 Briggs, A., Social Thought and Social Action: A Study of the Work of Seebohm Rowntree, 1871-1954, 1961.
3751 Fried, A., and Elman, R.M., Charles Booth's London: Portrait of the Poor at the Turn of the Century, Drawn from his 'Life and Labour of the People of London', 1969.
3752 Hanes, D.G., The First British Workmen's Compensation Act, 1897, Yale, 1968.
3753 Harrison, B., 'Philanthropy and the Victorians', Victorian Studies, IX, 1965-6, 353-74.

3754 Hennock, E.P., 'Finance and politics in urban local government, 1835-1900', Hist. Jnl., VI, 1963, 226-52.
3755 Mowat, C.L., The Charity Organisation Society, 1869-1913: Its Ideas and Work, 1961.
3756 Owen, D., English Philanthropy, 1660-1960, Cambridge, Mass., 1965. Useful, although the time-span clearly hampered the author. See also Harrison (3753), listed above.
3757 Schweinitz, K. de, England's Road to Social Security, 1943.
3758 Seldon, A., ed., The Long Debate on Poverty 1972. (Essays on the history of social welfare).
3759 Simey, Margaret B., Charitable Effort in Liverpool in the Nineteenth Century, 1951.
3760 Simey, T.S., and Margaret B., Charles Booth, Social Scientist, 1960.
3761 Young, A.F., and Ashton, E.T., British Social Work in the Nineteenth Century, 1956.
3762 Woodroofe, Kathleen, From Charity to Social Work: A History of Social Work in England and the United States, 1962.

PUBLIC HEALTH AND MORALITY

3763 Acton, W., Prostitution, 2nd ed., 1870, 3rd abridged ed., 1968, with introduction by P. Fryer, 4th unabridged ed., 1972, with introduction by Anne Humpherys.
3764 Ayers, Gwendoline M., England's First State Hospitals and the Metropolitan Asylums Board, 1867-1930, 1971.
3765 Briggs, A., 'Cholera and society in the nineteenth century', P.P., 19, 1961, 76-96.
3766 Brockington, C.F., Medical Officers of Health, 1848-1855, 1957.
3767 ——— A Short History of Public Health, 1956.
3768 Brotherston, J.H.F., Observations on the Early Public Health Movement in Scotland, 1952.
3769 Chadwick, Edwin, Report on the Sanitary Conditions of the Labouring Population of Great Britain, 1842, ed. M.W.Flinn, 1965.
3770 Chesney, K., The Victorian Underworld, 1970. Chiefly about London.
3771 Eversley, D.E.C., 'The cholera in England in 1831-32' In L. Chevalier, ed., Le Choléra: la Première Epidémie du XIXe siècle, La Roche-Sur-Yon, 1958, 157-88.
3772 Finer, S.E., The Life and Times of Sir Edwin Chadwick, 1952, 2nd ed., 1970.
3773 Flinn, M.W., Public Health Reform in Britain, 1968. Excellent bibliography, 69-70.
3774 Frazer, W.M., A History of English Public Health, 1834-1939, 1950.
3775 Hodgkinson, Ruth G., The Origins of the National Health Service: The Medical Services of the New Poor Law 1834-1871, 1967.
3776 Lambert, R.J., Sir John Simon, 1816-1904, and English Social Administration, 1963.
3777 ——— 'A Victorian National Health Service: state vaccination, 1855-77', Hist. Jnl., V, 1962, 1-18.
3778 Lewis, R.A., Edwin Chadwick and the Public Health Movement, 1832-1854, 1952.
3779 Longmate, N., King Cholera: The Biography of a Disease, 1966.
3780 McLeod, R.M., 'The Alkali Acts Administration, 1863-84: the emergence of the civil scientist', Victorian Studies, IX, 1965-66, 85-112.
3781 Marcus, S., The Other Victorians, 1966.
3782 Midwinter, E.C., Social Administration in Lancashire: 1830-1860: Poor Law, Public Health and Police, 1969.
3783 ——— Victorian Social Reform, 1968.
3784 Newsholme, A. Fifty Years in Public Health: A Personal Narrative with Comments: The Years Preceding 1909, 1935.
3784a Pearsall, R., The Worm in the Bud: The World of Victorian Sexuality, 1969, (excellent references, 529-44).
3785 Simon, J., English Sanitary Institutions, 1890.

FOREIGNERS' IMPRESSIONS

There are numerous accounts of England, Wales and Scotland by foreign observers, from which the following are selected.

3786 Fussell, G.E., and Goodman, C., 'Travel and topography in eighteenth-century England: a bibliography of sources for economic history', The Library, 4th Ser., X, 1929-30, 84-103.
3787 Bell, V., To Meet Mr. Ellis: Little Gaddesden in the Eighteenth Century, 1956. Material on a Hertfordshire village, visited by the Swede Peter Kalm.
3788 Blouet, P. (pseud. Max O'Rell), John Bull and his Island, n. d. (1883)
3789 Faucher, L., Etudes sur l'Angleterre, 2 vols. Paris, 1845.
3790 Fond, B. Faujas de Saint, A Journey through England and Scotland to the Hebrides in 1784, ed. A. Geikie, 2 vols., 1907.
3791 Henderson, W.O., Industrial Britain under the Regency: The Diaries of Escher, Bodmer, May and le Gallois, 1814-18, 1968.
3792 ——— J.C.Fischer and his Diary of Industrial England, 1814-1851, 1966.
3793 Kohl, J.G., England and Wales, 1844. Reprinted 1968 (early (1840s).
3794 Von Raumer, F., England in 1835, During a Residence in London and Excursions into the Provinces, 3 vols, 1836.
3795 ——— England in 1841, 2 vols., 1842.
3796 La Rochefoucauld, F.de., A Frenchman in England, 1784, ed. and trans. J. Marchand and S.C. Roberts, 1933.
3797 Rydberg, S., Svenska Studieresor till England under Frihetstiden, Uppsala, 1951, Swedish travellers in England in the eighteenth century: summaries in English.
3798 Svedenstierna, E.T., Svedenstierna's Tour: Great Britain, 1802-3: The Travel Diary of an Industrial Spy, ed. M.W.Flinn, trans. E.M. Dellow, 1973.
3799 Taine, H., Taine's Notes on England, trans. and ed. E. Hyams, 1957. (covers 1860-70).

RELIGION, SOCIETY AND ECONOMIC LIFE

(a) General works

3800 Gay, J.D., The Geography of Religion in England, 1971. Deals mainly with the period after 1750. Useful on the Religious Census of 1851.

(b) Nonconformity and economic development

3801 Emden, P.H., Quakers in Commerce, 1939.
3802 Grubb, Isobel, Quakerism and Industry before 1800, 1930.
3803 Holt, R.V., The Unitarian Contribution to Social Progress in England, 1938, 2nd rev. ed., 1952.
3804 Isichei, Elizabeth, Victorian Quakers, 1970.
3805 Raistrick, A. Quakers in Science and Industry in the Seventeenth and Eighteenth Centuries, 1950.

(c) Religion and the working class

3806 Armstrong, A. The Church of England, the Methodists and Society 1700-1850, 1973.
3807 Clark, G. Kitson, Churchmen and the Condition of England, 1832-1885, 1973. See also Soloway (3814), listed below.
3808 Himmelfarb, Gertrude, 'Postscript on the Halévy thesis', Victorian Minds, 1968, 292-9.
3809 Hobsbawm, E.J., 'Methodism and the threat of revolution in Britain', In (3046), listed above, 23-33.
3810 Inglis, K.S., Churches and the Working Classes in Victorian England, 1963.
3811 McEntee, G.P., The Social Catholic Movement in Great Britain, N.Y., 1927.
3812 Mayor, S.H. The Churches and the Labour Movement, 1967. Deals mainly with the period 1848-1914.
3813 Smith, A., The Established Church and Popular Religion, 1750-1850, 1971. A collection of documents with commentary.
3814 Soloway, R.A., Prelates and People: Ecclesiastical Social Thought in England 1783-1852, 1969. See also Kitson Clark (3807) listed above.
3815 Taylor, E.R., Methodism and Politics 1791-1831, 1935.
3816 Thompson, D.M., Nonconformity in the Nineteenth Century, 1972. A very useful collection of documents with an introduction and bibliography.
3817 Wagner, D.O., The Church of England and Social Reform since 1854, N.Y., 1930.
3818 Ward, W.R., Religion and Society in England 1790-1850, 1972. Based largely on unpublished sources.
3819 Wearmouth, R.F., Methodism and the Common People of the Eighteenth Century, 1945.
3820 —— Methodism and the Working-class Movements of England, 1800-1850, 1937.
3821 —— Methodism and the Struggle of the Working Classes 1850-1900, 1954.
3822 —— Some Working Class Movements of the Nineteenth Century, 1948.
3823 —— The Social and Political Influence of Methodism in the Twentieth Century, 1957.
3824 Wickham, E.R., Church and People in an Industrial City, 1957. A pioneer work on the social history of religion. The city is Sheffield.

(d) Christian Socialism

3825 Christensen, T., Origins and History of Christian Socialism, Aarhus, 1962.
3826 Jones, P.D'A., The Christian Socialist Revival, 1877-1914: Religion, Class and Social Conscience in Late Victorian England, Princeton, N.J., 1968.
3827 Mack, E.C, and Armytage, W.H.G., Thomas Hughes, 1952.
3828 Masterman, N., C., John Malcolm Ludlow: The Builder of Christian Socialism, 1963.
3829 Raven, C.E., Christian Socialism, 1848-1854, 1920.
3830 Saville, J. 'The Christian Socialists of 1848' In Saville (2996) listed above, 135-59.

THE WOMAN QUESTION

3831 Banks, J.A. and Olive, Feminism and Family Planning in Victorian England, 1964.
3832 Bott, A. and Clephane, Irene, Our Mothers ... Late Victorian Women, 1870-1900, 1932.
3833 Crow, D., The Victorian Woman, 1971.
3834 Dunbar, Janet, The Early Victorian Woman: Some Aspects of Her Life, 1837-1857, 1953.
3835 Fulford, R., Votes for Women: The Story of a Struggle, 1957, 2nd ed., 1958. Good bibliographical index, 273-83.
3836 Hecht, J.J., The Domestic Servant Class in Eighteenth-Century England, 1956.
3837 Hewitt, Margaret, Wives and Mothers in Victorian Industry, 1958.
3837a Holcombe, Lee, Victorian Ladies at Work: Middle-class Working Women in England and Wales, 1850-1914, 1974.
3838 McGregor, O.R., Divorce in England: A Centenary Study, 1957.
3839 —— 'The social position of women in England, 1850-1914: a bibliography', British Jnl. of Sociology, VI, 1955, 48-60.
3840 Marshall, Dorothy, The English Domestic Servant in History, Historical Association 1949.
3841 Mitchell, D., The Fighting Pankhursts: A Study of Tenacity, 1967. Select bibliography, 341-4.
3842 Mitchell, G., ed., The Hard Way Up: The Autobiography of Hannah Mitchell, Suffragette and Rebel, 1968.
3843 Neff, Wanda F., Victorian Working Women: An Historical and Literary Study of Women in British Industries and Professions, 1832-1850, 1929, 2nd ed., 1966.
3844 O'Neill, W., The Woman Movement in Britain and America, 1969.
3845 Pinchbeck, Ivy, Women Workers and the Industrial Revolution, 1750-1850, 1930.
3846 Rover, Constance, Women's Suffrage and Party Politics in Great Britain, 1866-1914, 1967.
3847 —— Love, Morals and The Feminists, 1970.

England 1700-1970

EDUCATION

(a) Schools

3848 Maclure, J.S., Educational Documents: England and Wales, 1816-1967, 2nd rev. ed., 1968.
3849 Journal of Educational Administration and History, I, 1968-9 to date.
3850 Adamson, J.W., English Education, 1789-1902, 1930.
3851 Armytage, W.H.G., Four Hundred Years of English Education, 1964.
3852 Arnold, M., Reports on Elementary Schools, 1852-1882, new ed., 1910, with introduction by F.S. Marvin.
3853 Barnard, H.C., History of English Education from 1760, 1961.
3854 Bardshaw, D.C.A., ed., Studies in the Government and Control of Education since 1860, 1970.
3855 Bayne-Powell, Rosamond, The English Child in the Eighteenth Century, 1939.
3856 Curtis, S.J., The History of Education in Great Britain, 6th ed., 1965. Bibliography, 711-28.
3857 Hurt, J., Education in Evolution: Church, State, Society and Popular Education, 1800-1870, 1971.
3858 Johnson, Marion, Derbyshire Village Schools in the Nineteenth Century, 1970.
3859 Jones, M.G., The Charity School Movement: A Study of Eighteenth-century Puritanism in Action, 1938.
3860 Lawson, J. and Silver, H., A Social History of Education in England, 1973. A general survey extending from the Middle Ages to the present day. The main emphasis is on the post-1760 period.
3861 Kay-Shuttleworth, J.P., Public Education as Affected by the Minutes of the Committee of Privy Council from 1846 to 1852 with suggestions as to further Policy, 1853 (vol. I).
3862 —— Four Periods of Public Education as Reviewed in 1832-1839-1849-1862, 1862 (vol. II).
3863 Lowndes, G.A., The Silent Social Revolution: An Account of the Expansion of Public Education in England and Wales 1895-1935, 1950.
3864 McLachlan, H., English Education under the Test Acts, 1931. Covers Dissenting academies, 1663-1820.
3865 Maclure, J.S., One Hundred Years of London Education, 1870-1970, 1970.
3866 Murphy, J., Church, State and Schools in Britain, 1800-1870, 1971.
3867 —— The Education Act, 1870: Text and Commentary, 1972.
3868 —— The Religious Problem in English Education: The Crucial Experiment, 1959, (the non-denominational Liverpool Corporation schools).
3869 Peterson, A.D.C., A Hundred Years of Education, rev. ed., 1971.
3870 Pinchbeck, Ivy and Hewitt, Margaret, Children in English Society, Vol. 2: From the Eighteenth Century to the Children Act, 1948. 1973. See also vol. I (1845), listed above.
3871 Rich, E.E., The Education Act, 1870, 1970.
3872 Robson, D., Some Aspects of Education in Cheshire in the Eighteenth Century, 1966.
3873 Selleck, R.J.W., English Primary Education and the Progressives, 1914-1939, 1972.
3874 Simon, B., Studies in the History of Education: The Two Nations and the Educational Structure 1780-1870, 1960.
3875 —— Studies in the History of Education: Education and the Labour Movement, 1870-1920, 1965.
3875a —— Studies in the History of Education: The Politics of Educational Reform 1920-1940, 1974
3876 Smith, J.W. Ashley, The Birth of Modern Education: The Contribution of the Dissenting Academies, 1660-1800, 1954.
3877 Sturt, Mary, The Education of the People, 1967. The growth of English elementary education in the nineteenth century.
3878 Sutherland, Gillian, Policy-making in Elementary Education, 1870-1895, 1974.
3879 Tompson, R.S., Classics or Charity?: The Dilemma of the Eighteenth-century Grammar School, 1971. A re-assessment of the condition and functions of the grammar schools. Useful bibliography, 144-64.
3880 Wardle, D., English Popular Education, 1780-1970, 1970.

(b) The public schools

3881 Bamford, T.W., The Rise of the Public Schools, 1967.
3882 Mack, E.C., Public Schools and British Opinion, 1780-1860, 1938.
3883 —— Public Schools and British Opinion since 1860, N.Y., 1941. Covers the period up to 1914.

(c) Adult education, including public libraries

3884 Harrison, J.F.C., Learning and Living, 1790-1860, 1961.
3885 Kelly, T., Early Public Libraries: A History of Public Libraries in Great Britain before 1850, 1966.
3886 —— George Birkbeck: Pioneer of Adult Education, 1957.
3887 Munford, W.A., William Ewart, M.P., 1798-1869: Portrait of a Radical, 1960. Prominent in the free public library movement.
3888 Stocks, Mary D., The Workers' Educational Association: The First Fifty Years, 1953.
3889 Tylecote, Mabel, The Mechanics Institutes of Lancashire and Yorkshire before 1851, 1956.

(d) The universities

3890 Sanderson, M., The Universities and British Industry, 1850-1970, 1972. Excellent select bibliography, 398-419.
3891 Ward, W.R., Georgian Oxford, 1958 (Excellent bibliography).
3892 —— Victorian Oxford, 1965.

WALES 1700-1966

Items on Wales before 1700 are in the appropriate English sections of the bibliography.

3893 Bowen, I., The Great Enclosures of Common Lands in Wales, 1914.
3894 Davies, A.E., 'Some aspects of the operation of the Old Poor Law in Cardiganshire, 1750-1834', Jnl. of the Cardiganshire Antiquarian Society, VI, 1968, 1-44.
3895 Dodd, A.H., The Industrial Revolution in North Wales, 1933, 3rd ed., with corrections and additions, 1971.
3896 Gray-Jones, A., A History of Ebbw Vale, 1970.
3897 Howell, D.W., 'The economy of the landed estates of Pembrokeshire, c. 1680-1830, Welsh Hist. Rev., III, 1967, 265-86.
3898 John, A.H., The Industrial Development of South Wales, 1750-1850, 1950.
See also Davies (147) listed above
3899 Jones, D.J.V., Before Rebecca: Popular Protests in Wales, 1793-1835, 1973.
3900 Jones, E.D., ed., Victorian and Edwardian Wales from Old Photographs, 1972.
3901 Lewis, E.D., The Rhondda Valleys: A Study in Industrial Development, 1800 to the Present Day, 1959.
3902 Minchinton, W.E., ed., Industrial South Wales, 1750-1914: Essays in Welsh Economic History, 1969.
3903 Roberts, R.O., ed., Farming in Caernarvonshire around 1800. 1973. (documents on the Vaenol estate).
3904 Thomas, B., ed., The Welsh Economy: Studies in Expansion, 1962.
3905 Thomas, D., Agriculture in Wales During the Napoleonic Wars, 1963.
3906 Williams, D., A History of Modern Wales, 1950.
3907 ──── The Rebecca Riots: A Study in Agrarian Discontent, 1955.

SCOTLAND 1066-1700

GENERAL WORKS

(a) Bibliographies

3908 Hancock, P.D., Bibliography of Works Relating to Scotland, 2 vols., 1959-60.
3909 Keith, Theodora., Bibliography of Scottish Economic History, 1914. Now obviously very inadequate and out of date.
3910 Mackie, J.D., Scottish History, 1956.
3911 Marwick, W.H., 'A bibliography of Scottish business history', In P.L.Payne, ed., Studies in Scottish Business History, 1967, 77-99.
3912 —— 'A bibliography of Scottish economic history', Ec.H.R., III, 1931-2, 117-37.
3913 —— 'A bibliography of Scottish economic history, 1931-51', Ec.H.R., 2nd ser., IV, 1951-2, 376-82.
3914 —— 'A bibliography of Scottish economic history, 1951-62', Ec.H.R., 2nd ser., XVI, 1963-4, 147-54.
3915 —— 'A bibliography of Scottish economic history, 1963-70', Ec.H.R., 2nd ser., XXIV, 1971, 469-79.
3916 Scott, W.R., Scottish Economic Literature to 1800, 1911.

(b) Sources

3917 Anderson, A.O., ed., The Early Sources of Scottish History, A.D. 500-1286, 2 vols., 1922.
3918 Brown, P.H., ed., Scotland Before 1700 from Contemporary Documents, 1893.
3919 Dickinson, W.Croft, A Source Book of Scottish History to 1707, 3 vols., 1952-4. Vol. I: From the Earliest times to 1424: Vol. II: 1424-1567 and Vol. III. 1567-1707.
3920 Donaldson, G., ed., Scottish Historical Documents, 1970. A useful source book covering the medieval and early modern periods. See also Browning, ed., (970), listed above, which contains a substantial section, 591-698 on Scotland.

(c) Surveys

(1) Medieval

3921 Barbé, L.A., Sidelights on the History, Industries and Social Life of Scotland, 1919.
3922 Barrow, G.W.S., The Kingdom of the Scots. Government, Church and Society from the Eleventh to the Fourteenth Century, 1973.
3922a —— 'The beginnings of feudalism in Scotland', B.I.H.R., XXIX, 1956, 1-31. An important article.
3923 Brown, P.H., Early Travellers in Scotland, 1891. The accounts range in date from 1295 to 1689
3924 Campbell, J., 'England, Scotland and the 100 Years War in the fourteenth century'. In J.R. Hale, ed., Europe in the Late Middle Ages, 1965, 184-216.
3925 Coutts, J., The Anglo-Norman Peaceful Invasion of Scotland, 1057-1200, 1923.

3926 Dickinson, W. Croft, Scotland from the Earliest Times to 1603, 1961. A useful textbook; bibliography.
3927 Grant, I.F., Social and Economic Development of Scotland before 1603, 1930, 2nd ed., Westport, Conn., 1971.
3928 Mackenzie, W.C., The Highlands and Isles of Scotland: An Historical Survey, 1937, 2nd ed., 1949.
3929 Mackie, J.D., History of Scotland, 1964.
3929a Nicholson, R., The Edinburgh History of Scotland. II. The Later Middle Ages, 1974.
3930 Rait, R.S., An Outline of the Relations between England and Scotland, 500-1707, 1901.
3931 Ritchie, R.L.G., The Normans in Scotland, 1954.
See also Barrow (178), listed above, a general survey which devotes more space than usual to Scottish history, and Mitchison (3940), listed below.

(2) Early modern

3932 Carstairs, A.M., 'Some economic aspects of the union of the Parliaments', Scottish Jnl. of Political Economy, II, 1955, 64-72.
3933 Donaldson, G., Scotland, James V to James VII, 1965. Mainly of value on political and ecclesiastical aspects.
3934 —— Shetland Life under Earl Patrick, 1958.
3935 Insh, G.P., Scotland and the Modern World, 1932.
3936 Keith, Theodora., 'The influence of the Convention of the Royal Boroughs of Scotland on the economic development of Scotland before 1707', Scot. H.R., X, 1914, 250-71.
3937 Lythe, S.G.E., The Economy of Scotland in its European Setting, 1550-1625, 1960.
3938 —— 'The Union of the Crowns in 1603 and the debate on economic integration', Scottish Jnl. of Political Economy, V, 1958, 219-28.
3939 Mathew, D., Scotland under Charles I, 1955.
3939a Meikle, H.W., Some Aspects of Seventeenth Century Scotland, 1947.
3940 Mitchison, Rosalind, A History of Scotland, 1970. A general survey of Scottish history, particularly weighted, however, towards the seventeenth century—'the key period for the understanding of modern Scotland' (ix). A useful critical bibliography is appended, 430-42.
3941 Nobbs, D., England and Scotland, 1560-1707, 1952.
3942 Notestein, W., The Scot in History, New Haven, Conn., 1946.
3943 Paul, J.B., 'Social life in Scotland in the sixteenth century', Scot. H.R., XVII, 1919-20, 296-309.
3944 Pryde, G.S., Scotland from 1603 to the Present Day, 1962. A useful textbook.
3945 Smout, T.C., A History of the Scottish People, 1560-1830, 1969. Strong on econo-

Towns 105

mic and social aspects. Useful aids to further reading are appended to each chapter.

3946 Warrack, J., Domestic Life in Scotland, 1488-1688, 1920. Deals mainly with furniture and household effects.

3946a Willson, D. H., 'King James I and Anglo-Scottish unity'. In Aiken and Henning (1907), 41-56.
See also Dickinson (3926), Grant (3927), and Mackie (3929), listed above, and Ferguson (4071-4072), listed below.

POPULATION

(a) Medieval

3947 Barrow, G. W. S., 'Rural settlement in central and eastern Scotland: the medieval evidence', Scottish Studies, VI, 1962, 123-44.

3948 Cooper, Lord, 'The numbers and distribution of the population in medieval Scotland', Scot. H. R., n. s., I, 1947, 2-9. Rather unsatisfactory.

(b) Early modern

3949 Walton, K., 'The distribution of population in Aberdeenshire, 1696', Scottish Geographical Magazine, LXVI, 1950, 17-25.

AGRICULTURE AND RURAL SOCIETY

(a) Medieval

3950 Anderson, M. L., A History of Scottish Forestry. Vol. I: From the Ice Age to the French Revolution, ed. C. J. Taylor, 1967.

3951 Franklin, T. B., A History of Scottish Farming, 1952.

3952 Marwick, H., Medieval Lairds, 1936, 2nd ed., 1939.

3953 Murray, A., 'The crown lands in Galloway, 1455-1543', Trans. Dumfriesshire and Galloway Natural History and Antiquarian Society, XXXVII, 1960, 9-25.

3954 Symon, J. A., Scottish Farming Past and Present, 1959.

(b) Early modern

3955 Fenton, A., ed., 'Skene of Hallyard's Ms. of Husbandrie', Ag. H. R., XI, 1963, 65-81. A seventeenth-century account.

3956 Donaldson, G., 'Sources for Scottish agrarian history before the eighteenth century', Ag. H. R., VIII, 1959, 82-90.

3957 Fenton, A., 'The rural economy of East Lothian in the seventeenth and eighteenth centuries', Trans. East Lothian Antiquarian and Field Naturalists' Society, IX, 1963, 1-23.

3958 —— 'Farm servant life in the seventeenth to nineteenth centuries', Scottish Agriculture, XLIV, 1965, 281-5.

3959 Mackerral, A., Kintyre in the Seventeenth Century, 1948.

3960 Murray, J. E. L., 'The agriculture of Crail, 1550-1600', Scottish Studies, VIII, 1964, 85-95.

3961 Smout, T. C., 'Problems of timber supply in later seventeenth-century Scotland', Scottish Forestry, XIV, 1960, 3-13.

3962 —— 'Scottish landowners and economic growth 1650-1850', Scottish Jnl. of Political Economy, XI, 1964, 218-34. See also Smout (4048a), listed below.

3963 —— 'Goat keeping in the old highland economy: 4', Scottish Studies, IX, 1965, 186-9. Assesses the significance of earlier contributions on this subject.

3964 —— and Fenton, A., 'Scottish agriculture before the improvers—an exploration', Ag. H. R., XIII, 1965, 73-93.

INDUSTRY

(a) Medieval

3965 Cochran-Patrick, R. W., ed., Early Records Relating to Mining in Scotland, 1878.

3966 Adams, I. H., 'The salt industry of the Forth Basin', Scottish Geographical Magazine, LXXXI, 1965, 153-62.
See also Arnot (3099), listed above.

(b) Early modern

3967 Knoop, D. and Jones, G. P., The Scottish Mason and Mason Word, 1939.

3968 Lumsden, H., ed., The Records of the Trades House of Glasgow, 1605-1678, 1910.

3969 —— History of the Skinners, Furriers and Glovers of Glasgow: A Study of a Scottish Craft Guild in its Various Relations, 1937.

3970 —— and Aitken, P. H., History of the Hammermen of Glasgow, 1912.

3971 Marwick, J. D., Edinburgh Gilds and Crafts, Scottish Burgh Record Society, 1909.

3972 Scott, W. R., ed., Records of a Scottish Cloth Manufactury at New Mills, Haddingtonshire, 1681-1703, Scottish History Society, 1905.

3973 Smout, T. C., 'The early Scottish sugar houses, 1660-1720', Ec. H. R., 2nd ser., XIV, 1961, 240-53.

3974 —— 'Lead-mining in Scotland, 1650-1850'. In P. L. Payne, ed., Studies in Scottish Business History, 1967, 103-35.
See also Nef (1354), listed above, and Scott (1507), vol. III of which deals with Scottish joint stock companies.

TOWNS

(a) Medieval

3975 Dickinson, W. Croft., ed., Early Records of Aberdeen, 1317, 1398-1407, Scottish Historical Society, 1957.

3976 Ballard, A., 'The theory of the Scottish burgh', Scot. H. R., XIII, 1916, 16-29.

3977 Lythe, S. G. E., 'The origin and development of Dundee', Scottish Geographical Magazine, LIV, 1939, 344-57.

3978 Mackenzie, W. M., The Scottish Burghs, 1949. Covers both the medieval and early modern periods.

(b) Early modern

3979 Roberts, F. and MacPhail, I. M. M., eds., Dumbarton Common Goods Accounts 1614-1660, 1972.

3979a Shearer, A., ed., Extracts from the Burgh Records of Dunfermline in the Sixteenth and Seventeenth Centuries, 1951.

3979b Taylor, Louise B., ed., Aberdeen Council Letters 1552-1681, 6 vols., 1942-61.

3979c —— ed., Aberdeen Shore Works Accounts 1596-1670, 1972. Lists ships and their cargoes entering and leaving the harbour.

3980 Lythe, S. G. E., Life and Labour in Dundee from the Reformation to the Civil War, Abertay Historical Society publications, No. 5, 1958.

3981 Murray, D., Early Burgh Organisation in Scotland, as Illustrated in the History of Glasgow and of Some Neighbouring Burghs, 2 vols., 1924.

3982 Pagan, Theodora (née Keith), The Convention of the Royal Burghs of Scotland, 1926. Deals with the burghs' relations with the state and with each other.

3983 Smout, T. C., 'Development and enterprise of Glasgow, 1556-1707', Scottish Jnl. of Political Economy, VII, 1960, 194-212.

COMMERCE

(a) Medieval

3984 Dilley, J. W., 'German merchants in Scotland, 1297-1327', Scot. H. R., XXVII, 1948, 142-55.

3985 Reid, W. S., 'Trade, traders and Scottish independence', Speculum, XXIX, 1954, 210-22.

3986 Rooseboom, M. P., The Scottish Staple in the Netherlands, 1292-1676, The Hague, 1916.

(b) Early modern

3987 Davidson, A. and Gray, A., The Scottish Staple at Veere, 1909.

3988 Dow, J., 'Scottish trade with Sweden, 1512-80', Scot. H. R., XLVIII, 1969, 64-79.

3989 —— 'Scottish trade with Sweden 1580-1622', Scot. H. R., XLVIII, 1969, 124-50.

3989a —— 'A comparative note on the Sound Toll registers, Stockholm customs accounts, and Dundee shipping lists 1589, 1613-1622', Scand. Ec. H. R., XII, 1964, 79-85.

3990 Elder, J. R., Royal Fishery Companies of the Seventeenth Century, 1912.

3991 Hart, F. R., The Disaster of Darien: The Story of the Scots Settlement, 1699-1701, 1930.

3992 Insh, G. P., Scottish Colonial Schemes, 1620-86, 1922.

3993 —— The Company of Scotland trading to Africa and the Indies, 1932.

3994 —— The Darien Scheme, Historical Association pamphlet, 1947.

3995 —— ed., Darien Shipping Papers: Papers Relating to the Ships and Voyages of the Company of Scotland Trading to Africa and the Indies, 1696-1707, Scottish Historical Society, 3rd ser., VI, 1934.

3996 Keith, Theodora, Commercial Relations of England and Scotland 1603-1707, 1910.

3996a Lythe, S. G. E., 'Scottish trade with the Baltic 1550-1650'. In J. K. Eastham, ed., Economic Essays in Commemoration of the Dundee School of Economics, 1955, 63-84.

3997 Prebble, J., The Darien Disaster, 1968.

3998 Smout, T. C., Scottish Trade on the Eve of the Union, 1660-1707, 1963.

3999 —— 'The overseas trade of Ayrshire, 1660-1707', Ayrshire Archaeological Collections, 2nd ser., VI, 1961, 56-80.

4000 —— 'Scottish commercial factors in the Baltic at the end of the seventeenth century', Scot. H. R., XXXIX, 1960, 122-8.

4001 —— 'The foreign trade of Dumfries and Kirkcudbright, 1672-1696', Trans. Dumfriesshire and Galloway Natural History and Antiquarian Society, XXXVII, for 1958-9, 1960, 36-47.

4002 —— 'The Glasgow merchant community in the seventeenth century', Scot. H. R., XLVII, 1968, 53-71.

PRICES, PUBLIC FINANCE AND BANKING

(a) Medieval

4003 Cochran-Patrick, R. W., Records of Coinage, 1357 to the Union, 2 vols., 1876.

4004 Stewart, I. H., The Scottish Coinage, 1955.

(b) Early modern

4005 Mitchison, Rosalind, 'The movement of Scottish corn prices in the seventeenth and eighteenth centuries', Ec. H. R., 2nd ser., XVIII, 1965, 278-91.

4006 Murray, A., 'The procedure of the Scottish Exchequer in the early sixteenth century', Scot. H. R., XL, 1961, 89-117.

4007 —— 'The pre-Union records of the Scottish Exchequer', Jnl. of the Society of Archivists, II, 1961, 89-100.

4008 —— 'The Scottish treasury, 1667-1708', Scot. H. R., XLV, 1966, 89-104.
See also Yamey, Edey and Thomson (1719), listed above.

COMMUNICATIONS

4009 Hardie, R. P., The Roads of Medieval Lauderdale, 1942.

4010 Taylor, W., 'The King's mails, 1603-25', Scot. H. R., XLII, 1963, 143-7.
See also Haldane (2380), listed above, for an introductory chapter on 'The early drovers' (i.e., before 1700).

POOR RELIEF

4011 Cormack, A., Poor Relief in Scotland: An Outline of the Growth and Administration of

the Poor Laws in Scotland from the Middle Ages to the Present Day, 1923.
4012 McPherson, J. M., The Kirk's Care of the Poor, 1941.
4013 Nicholls, G., A History of the Scotch Poor Law, 1856. Reprinted 1968.

EDUCATION

4014 Boyd, W., Education in Ayrshire through Seven Centuries, 1961.
4015 Cant, R. G., 'The Scottish universities in the seventeenth century', Aberdeen University Review, XLIII, 1970, 323-33.
4015a —— The College of St Salvator, 1950.
4016 Durkan, J., 'Education in the century of the Reformation'. In McRoberts (4017), listed below, 145-68.
4016a Henderson, G. D., The Founding of Marischal College, Aberdeen, 1947.
4016b Mackie, J. D., The University of Glasgow 1451-1951. A Short History, 1954.
4017 Scotland, J., The History of Scottish Education, 1973.
4017a Simpson, I. J., Education in Aberdeenshire before 1872, 1947.
4017b Withrington, D. J., ed., 'List of schoolmasters teaching Latin, 1690', Miscellany of the Scottish History Society, X, 1965, 121-42.

RELIGION

(a) Medieval

4018 Coulton, G. G., Scottish Abbeys and Social Life, 1933.
4019 Cowan, I. B., The Parishes of Medieval Scotland, Scottish Record Society, XCIII, 1967.
4019a Easson, D. E., Medieval Religious Houses: Scotland, 1957.
4020 Levy, A., 'The origins of Scottish Jewry', Trans. Jewish Historical Society, XIX, 1960, for 1955-9, 129-62.
4020a Morgan, M., 'The organisation of the Scottish church in the twelfth century', T. R. H. S., 4th ser., 29, 1947, 135-49.

(b) Early modern

4021 Burrell, S. A., 'The apocalyptic vision of the early Covenanters', Scot. H. R., XLIII, 1964, 1-24.
4022 Cowan, I. B., 'The Covenanters: a revision article', Scot. H. R., XLVII, 1968, 35-52.
4023 Donaldson, G., The Scottish Reformation, 1960.
4023a Foster, W. R., Bishop and Presbytery: The Church of Scotland 1661-1688, 1958.
4024 Henderson, G. D., Religious Life in Seventeenth-century Scotland, 1937.
4025 —— The Scottish Ruling Elder, 1935.
4026 Lee, M., jnr., 'Revision article: the Scottish Reformation after 400 years', Scot. H. R., XLIV, 1965, 135-47.
4027 McRoberts, D., ed., Essays on the Scottish Reformation, 1513-1625, 1962.
4027a Stevenson, D., The Scottish Revolution 1637-1644. The Triumph of the Covenanters, 1973.
4028 Trevor-Roper, H. R., 'Scotland and the Puritan Revolution'. In H. E. Bell and R. L. Ollard, eds., Historical Essays, 1600-1750, Presented to David Ogg, 1963, 78-130.
4029 Wedgewood, C. Veronica, 'The Covenanters in the first Civil War', Scot. H. R., XXXIX, 1960, 1-15.

SCOTLAND SINCE 1700

GENERAL WORKS

4030 Campbell, R. H. and Dow, J. B. A., Source Book of Scottish Economic and Social History, 1968.
4031 Grant, I. F., The Economic History of Scotland, 1934. List of books for further reading, 283-5.
4032 Mackinnon, J., The Social and Industrial History of Scotland, 2 vols., 1920-1. See Marwick (4042) and Smout (3945).

POPULATION AND EMIGRATION

4032a Donaldson, G., The Scots Overseas, 1966 (excellent bibliography).
4032b Kyd, K. D., Scottish Population Statistics, Scottish History Society, 1952.

TRADE AND BUSINESS HISTORY

4033 Pryde, G. S., The Treaty of Union of Scotland and England of 1707, 1950. See also Payne (87), listed above (contains copious bibliography of Scottish economic and business history, 79-99), and Smout (3998), listed above.

INDUSTRIAL GROWTH

4034 Bremner, D., The Industries of Scotland: Their Rise, Progress and Present Condition, 1869, 2nd ed., with new introduction, 1969.
4035 Butt, J., The Industrial Archaeology of Scotland, 1968.
4036 Cairncross, A. K., ed., The Scottish Economy, 1954.
4037 Campbell, R. H., Scotland from 1707: The Rise of an Industrial Society, 1964.
4038 Gulvin, C., The Tweedmakers: A History of the Scottish Fancy Woollen Industry, 1600-1914, 1973.
4039 Hamilton, H., An Economic History of Scotland in the Eighteenth Century, 1963.
4040 ――― The Industrial Revolution in Scotland, 1932, 2nd ed., 1966.
4041 Marwick, W. H., Economic Developments in Victorian Scotland, 1936.
4042 ――― Scotland in Modern Times: An Outline of Economic and Social Development since the Union of 1707, 1964.
4042a Thomson, A. G., The Paper Industry in Scotland, 1590-1861, 1974.
See also Coleman (1393) and Shorter (2816a), listed above.

AGRICULTURE

4043 Donaldson, J. E., Caithness in the Eighteenth Century, 1938.
4044 Gray, M., The Highland Economy, 1750-1850, 1957.
4045 Handley, J. E., Scottish Farming in the Eighteenth Century, 1953.
4046 Jones, D. T., Duncan, J. F., Conacher, H. M., and Scott, W. R., Rural Scotland During the War, 1926.
4047 Mitchison, Rosalind, Agricultural Sir John, 1962. Definitive biography of Sir John Sinclair.
4048 Richards, E., The Leviathan of Wealth: The Sutherland Fortune in the Industrial Revolution, 1973.
4048a Smout, T. C., 'The landowner and the planned villages in Scotland, 1730-1830'. In G. Phillipson and Rosalind Mitchison, eds., Scotland in the Age of Improvement, 1970. See also Smout (3962), listed above.
4049 Youngson, A. J., After the Forty-Five: The Economic Impact on the Scottish Highlands, 1973 (covers period up to 1840s). See also Haldane (2380), listed above.

LABOUR

4050 Buckley, K. D., Trade Unionism in Aberdeen, 1878-1900, 1955.
4051 Gillespie, Sarah C., A Hundred Years of Progress: The Record of the Scottish Typographical Association, 1853-1952, 1953.
4052 Handley, J. E., The Irish in Scotland, 1798-1845, 2nd rev. ed., 1945.
4053 ――― The Irish in Modern Scotland, 1947.
4054 ――― The Navvy in Scotland, 1970.
4055 Macdonald, D. F., Scotland's Shifting Population, 1770-1850, 1937.
4056 McDougall, I., ed., The Minutes of Edinburgh Trades Council, 1859-1873, Scottish History Society, 1968.
4057 Marwick, W. H., A Short History of Labour in Scotland, 1967.
4058 Trickett, Ann, The Scottish Carter: The History of the Scottish Horse and Motormen's Association, 1898-1960, 1967.

SOCIAL LIFE AND INTELLECTUAL DEVELOPMENT

4059 Cowan, R. M. W., The Newspaper in Scotland, 1815-60, 1946.
4060 Davie, G. E., The Democratic Intellect: Scotland and her Universities in the Nineteenth Century, 1961.
4061 Ferguson, T., Dawn of Scottish Social Welfare: A Survey from Medieval Times to 1863, 1948.

4062 —— Scottish Social Welfare, 1864-1914, 1958.
4063 Graham, H. G., The Social Life of Scotland in the Eighteenth Century, 1st ed., 1899, 2nd rev. ed., 1900, 4th ed., 1937. Reprinted 1950, 1964.
4064 Minto, C. S., Victorian and Edwardian Scotland from Old Photographs, 1970.
4065 Plant, Marjorie, The Domestic Life of Scotland in the Eighteenth Century, 1952.
4066 Mechie, S., The Church and Scottish Social Development, 1780-1870, 1960.
4067 Meikle, H. W., Scotland and the French Revolution, 1st ed., 1912. Reprinted 1969.
4068 Saunders, L. J., Scottish Democracy, 1815-40: The Social and Intellectual Background, 1950.

IRELAND 1066-1700

GENERAL WORKS

(a) Bibliographies

4069 Asplin, P. W. A., Medieval Ireland, c. 1170-1495. A Bibliography of Secondary Works, 1970.
4070 Eager, A. R., ed., A Guide to Irish Bibliographical Material, 1964.
4071 Edwards, R. D. and Quinn, D. B., 'Thirty years' work in Irish history: sixteenth-century Ireland', Irish Historical Studies, XVI, 1969, 15-32. One of a series of very useful bibliographical articles.
4072 Johnston, Edith M., ed., Irish History: Select Bibliography, Historical Association, 1969.
4073 Kavanagh, M., ed., A Bibliography of the County Galway, 1965.
4074 Mulvey, H. F., 'Modern Irish history since 1940: a bibliographical survey, 1600-1922', The Historian, XXVIII, 1965, 516-59.
4075 Otway-Ruthven, J., 'Thirty years' work in Irish history: medieval Ireland, 1169-1485', Irish Historical Studies, XV, 1967, 359-65.
4076 Povey, K., 'The sources for a bibliography of Irish history, 1500-1700', Irish Historical Studies, 1, 1939, 393-403.
4077 Prendeville, P. L., 'Bibliography of Irish history', Ec. H. R., III, 1931-2, 274-92, and ibid., IV, 1932, 81-90.
4078 Simms, J. G., 'Thirty years' work in Irish history: seventeenth-century Ireland, 1603-1702', Irish Historical Studies, XV, 1967, 366-75.

(b) Sources

4079 Curtis, E. and MacDowell, R. B., eds., Irish Historical Documents, 1172-1922, 1943. Overwhelmingly constitutional.
4080 Maxwell, Constantia, Irish History from Contemporary Sources, 1509-1610, 1932. A useful collection, with sections on social and economic conditions and on Tudor efforts at colonisation.
See also Browning (970), listed above. Part VIII, 701-83, deals with Ireland.

(c) Surveys

(1) Medieval

4081 Beckett, J. C., A Short History of Ireland, 1952, 3rd ed., 1966.
4082 Chart, D. A., An Economic History of Ireland, 1920. An elementary textbook.
4083 Curtis, E., A History of Ireland, 1936, 6th ed., 1950.
4084 —— A History of Medieval Ireland from 1086 to 1513, 1923, enlarged ed., 1938. Bibliography.
4084a Edwards, Ruth D., An Atlas of Irish History, 1973.
4085 Lydon, J. F., The Lordship of Ireland in the Middle Ages, 1972.
4086 —— Ireland in the Later Middle Ages, 1973.
4087 Nicholls, K., Gaelic and Gaelicised Ireland in the Middle Ages, 1972.
4088 O'Brien, Maire and C. C., A Concise History of Ireland, 1972.
4089 O'Domhnall, S., 'Magna Carta Hiberniae', Irish Historical Studies, III, 1942, 31-8.
4090 O'Sullivan, M. J. D., Old Galway: The History of a Norman Colony in Ireland, 1942.
4091 Orpen, G. H., Ireland under the Normans, 1169-1333, 4 vols., 1911-20.
4092 Otway-Ruthven, J., A History of Medieval Ireland, 1968. Mainly political. Good bibliography.
4093 —— 'The character of Norman settlement in Ireland', Irish Historical Studies, XV, 1965, 75-84.
4094 Richardson, H. G. and Sayles, G. O., The Administration of Ireland, 1172-1377, 1963.

(2) Early modern

4095 Bagwell, R., Ireland under the Tudors, 3 vols., 1885-90. Reprinted 1963.
4096 —— Ireland under the Stuarts and During the Interregnum, 3 vols., 1909-16. Reprinted 1963.
4097 Beckett, J. C., The Making of Modern Ireland, 1603-1923, 1969. Mainly political but some coverage of economic and social aspects is attempted. Bibliography.
4098 Butler, W. F. T., Gleanings from Irish History, 1925. Has chapters on the Irish lordships, on the Tudor policy of surrender and re-grant and on the Cromwellian confiscations in Ireland.
4099 Cullen, L. M., Life in Ireland, 1968. A useful social history, although the weight is on post-1700 developments.
4100 Dunlop, R., 'Ireland, to the settlement of Ulster: from the beginning of the sixteenth century to 1611', Cambridge Modern History, III, 1904, 579-616.
4101 —— 'Ireland from the Plantation of Ulster to the Cromwellian Settlement, 1611-59', Cambridge Modern History, IV, 1906, 513-38.
4102 —— 'Ireland from the Restoration to the Act of Resumption, 1660-1700', Cambridge Modern History, V, 1908, 301-23.
4103 —— Ireland under the Commonwealth, 1913.
4104 Hinton, E. M., Ireland through Tudor Eyes, Philadelphia, 1935.
4104a MacCurtain, Margaret, Tudor and Stuart Ireland, 1972.
4105 Maclysaght, E., Irish Life in the Seventeenth Century, 1939, 2nd ed. enlarged and revised 1950. A very useful survey. Has chapters on rural and urban life, communications, recreations. Documentary appendices and bibliography.
4106 O'Brien, G., The Economic History of Ireland in the Seventeenth Century, 1919. Vintage polemics, urgently in need of replacement.

4107 Quinn, D. B., The Elizabethans and the Irish, Ithaca, N. Y., 1966.
4108 —— 'Ireland and sixteenth-century European expansion'. In T. D. Williams, ed., Historical Studies, 1958, 20-32.
4109 Rowse, A. L., The Expansion of Elizabethan England, 1955. Has two chapters on Ireland.
4110 Simms, J. G., Jacobite Ireland, 1685-91, 1969.
4111 White, D. G., 'The reign of Edward VI in Ireland: some political, social and economic aspects', Irish Historical Studies, XIV, 1964-5, 197-211.
4112 Woodward, G. W. O., Reformation and Resurgence, 1485-1603, 1963. Has a section on Ireland.
See also Black (993) and Salaman (2438), listed above.

POPULATION

(a) Medieval

4113 Gwynn, A., 'The Black Death in Ireland', Studies, XXIV, 1935, 25-42.
4114 Russell, J. C., 'Late thirteenth-century Ireland as a region', Demography, III, 1966, 500-12.

(b) Early modern

4115 Pender S., ed., A Census of Ireland, c. 1659, 1939.
4116 Butlin, R. A., 'The population of Dublin in the late seventeenth century', Irish Geography, V, 1965, 51-66.
4117 Lee, Grace L., The Huguenot Settlements in Ireland, 1936.
4118 MacLysaght, E., 'Seventeenth-century hearth money rolls with full transcript relating to County Sligo', Analecta Hibernica, XXIV, 1967, 1-89.
4119 Paterson, T. G. F., 'County Armagh householders, 1664-5', Seanchas Ardmhacha, III, 1958, 96-142.

AGRICULTURE AND RURAL SOCIETY

4120 Aalen, F. H. A., 'Enclosures in eastern Ireland: report of a symposium', Irish Geography, V, 1965, 29-39.
4121 Fitzpatrick, H. M., ed., The Forest of Ireland: An Account of the Forests of Ireland from Early Times until the Present Day, 1966.
4122 McCracken, Eileen, 'The woodlands of Ireland c. 1600', Irish Historical Studies, XI, 1959, 271-96. See also McCracken (4184), listed below.
4123 O'Donovan, J., The Economic History of Livestock in Ireland, 1940.
4124 Otway-Ruthven, J., 'The organisation of Anglo Irish agriculture in the Middle Ages', Jnl. Royal Society of Antiquaries of Ireland, LXXXI, 1951, 1-13.

INDUSTRY

4125 Boyle, E., 'Irish embroidery and lace-making, 1600-1800', Ulster Folk Life, XXI, 1966, 52-65.
4126 Breathnach, B., 'The Huguenots and the silk weaving industry in Ireland, Eire-Ireland, II, 1967, 11-18.
4127 Kearney, H. F., 'Richard Boyle, ironmaster', Jnl. Royal Society of Antiquaries of Ireland, LXXXIII, 1953, 156-62.
4128 Longfield, Ada K., 'History of tapestry making in Ireland and in the seventeenth and eighteenth centuries', Jnl. Royal Society of Antiquaries of Ireland, LXVIII, 1983, 91-105.
4129 McCracken, Eileen, 'Charcoal-burning ironworks in seventeenth- and eighteenth-century Ireland', Ulster Jnl. of Archaeology, XX, 1957, 123-38.
4130 O'Sullivan, D., 'The exploitation of the mines of Ireland in the sixteenth century', Studies, XXIV, 1935, 442-52.
See also Gill (2741), listed above, 1-30, on the linen industry in Stuart Ireland.

ANGLO-IRISH RELATIONS IN THE SIXTEENTH AND SEVENTEENTH CENTURIES

4131 Hogan, J., ed., Letters and Papers relating to the Irish Rebellion Between 1642-6, Irish Manuscripts Commission, 1936.
4132 Moody, T. W., ed., 'Ulster Plantation Papers, 1608-13', Anatecta Hibernica, VIII, 179-297.
4132a Barnard, T. C., Cromwellian Ireland: English Government and Reform in Ireland, 1649-60, 1975.
4133 Bottigheimer, K. S., English Money and Irish Land: The 'Adventurers' in the Cromwellian Settlement of Ireland, 1971.
4234 Butler, W. F. T., Confiscation in Irish History, 1917.
4135 Clarke, A., The Old English in Ireland, 1625-42, 1966.
4136 Dunlop, R., 'Sixteenth-century schemes for the plantation of Ulster', Scot. H. R., XXII, 1924-1925, 51-60, 115-26, 199-212.
4137 Kearney, H. F., Strafford in Ireland, 1633-41: A Study in Absolutism, 1959.
4138 —— 'The Court of Wards and Liveries in Ireland, 1622-24', Proceedings of the Royal Irish Academy, C, 1956, 29-68.
4139 Mayes, C. R., 'The early Stuarts and the Irish peerage', E. H. R., LXXIII, 1958, 227-51.
4140 Moody, T. W., The Londonderry Plantation, 1939. The main work on the subject.
4141 —— 'The treatment of the native population under the scheme for the plantation in Ulster', Irish Historical Studies, I, 1938, 59-63.
4142 Morton, R. G., 'The enterprise of Ulster', History Today, 17, 1967, 114-21. Deals with Elizabethan efforts at plantation.
4143 Prendergast, J. P., The Cromwellian Settlement of Ireland, 1865, 3rd ed., 1922.

Ireland 1066-1700

4144 Quinn, D. B., The Elizabethans and the Irish, Ithaca, N. Y., 1966.
4145 —— 'The Munster Plantation: problems and opportunities', Jnl. Cork Historical and Archaeological Society, LXXI, 1966, 19-40.
4146 Ranger, T. O., 'Strafford in Ireland: a revaluation', P. P., 19, 1961, 26-45. Reprinted in Aston (990), listed above, 271-94.
4147 Simms, J. G., The Williamite Confiscation in Ireland, 1609-1703, 1956.
4148 —— 'The Civil Survey, 1654-56', Irish Historical Studies, IX, 1954-5, 253-63.
4149 Treadwell, V., 'The Irish Court of Wards under James I', Irish Historical Studies, XII, 1960, 1-27.

PRICES AND PUBLIC FINANCE

(a) Medieval

4150 Dolley, R. H. M., Medieval Anglo-Irish Coins, 1972.
4150a Lydon, J. F., 'Edward II and the revenues of Ireland in 1311-12', Irish Historical Studies, XIV, 1964, 39-57.
4151 —— 'Survey of the memoranda rolls of the Irish Exchequer, 1294-1509', Analecta Hibernica, XXII, 1966, 49-134.
4152 Nolan, D., A Monetary History of Ireland, 2 vols., 1926. Vol. 2 covers the period from the Anglo-Norman invasion to the death of Elizabeth.
4153 O'Sullivan, M. D., Italian Merchant Bankers in Ireland in the Thirteenth Century: A Study in the Social and Economic History of Medieval Ireland, 1962.
4154 O'Sullivan, W., The Earliest Anglo-Irish Coinage, 1950. Reprinted 1964.
4155 Richardson, H. G. and Sayles, G. O., 'Irish revenue, 1278-1384', Proceedings of the Royal Irish Academy, LXII, 1961-3, 87-100.

(b) Early modern

4156 Quinn, D. B., 'Guide to English financial records for Irish history, 1461-1558, with illustrative extracts, 1461-1509', Analecta Hibernica, X, 1941, 1-69.

COMMERCE

Early modern

4157 Kearney, H. F., ed., 'The Irish wine trade, 1614-15' (document), Irish Historical Studies, IX, 1955, 400-42.
4158 O'Brien, G., 'The Irish staple organisation in the reign of James I', Ec. J. Economic History Supplement, I, 1920, 42-56.
See also Cullen (1574), and Longfield (1587), listed above.

TOWNS

4159 Pender, S., ed., Council Books of the Corporation of Waterford, Irish Manuscripts Commission, 1964.

4160 Camblin, G., The Town in Ulster: An Account of the Origin and Building of the Towns of the Province and the Development of their Rural Setting, 1951. Illustrated.
4161 O'Sullivan, W., The Economic History of Cork City from the Earliest Times to the Act of Union, 1937. One of the best of Irish urban studies. Documentary and statistical appendices. Good bibliography.
4162 Simms, J. G., 'Dublin in 1685', Irish Historical Studies, XIV, 1965, 212-26.

RELIGION

4163 White, N. B., ed., Extents of Irish Monastic Possessions, 1540-41, Irish Manuscripts Commission, 1943.
4164 Beckett, J. C., Protestant Dissent in Ireland, 1687-1780, 1948.
4165 Coonan, T. L., The Irish Catholic Confederacy and the Puritan Revolution, 1954. Bibliography. Needs to be used with great care.
4166 Douglas, J. M., 'Early Quakerism in Ireland', Jnl. of the Friends' Historical Society, XLVIII, 1956, 3-32.
4167 Edwards, R. D., Church and State in Tudor Ireland: A History of the Penal Laws against Irish Catholics, 1534-1603, 1935. Bibliography. A scholarly work.

MISCELLANEOUS

(a) Medieval

4168 Hand, G. J., 'The status of the native Irish in the Lordship of Ireland, 1272-1331', The Irish Jurist, n. s., I, 1966, 93-115.
4169 Lydon, J. F., 'The problem of the frontier in medieval Ireland', Topic, XIII, 1967, 5-22.
4170 Otway-Ruthven, J., 'Knight service in Ireland', Jnl. of the Royal Society of Antiquaries of Ireland, LXXXIX, 1959, 1-15.
4171 —— 'The medieval county of Kildare', Irish Historical Studies, XI, 1959, 181-99.
4172 Richardson, H. G. and Sayles, G. O., The Irish Parliament in the later Middle Ages, Philadelphia, 1952. Reprinted 1964.

(b) Early modern

4173 Gleeson, D. F., The Last Lords of Ormond: A History of the 'Countrie of the three O' Kennedys' During the Seventeenth Century, 1938.
4174 Goodbody, O. C., 'Anthony Sharp, wool merchant, 1643-1707, and the Quaker community in Dublin', Jnl. of the Friends' Historical Society, XLVIII, 1956, 38-50.
4175 Knox, S. J., Ireland's Debt to the Huguenots, 1959.
4176 Nicholls, G., A History of the Irish Poor Law in Connection with the State of the Country and Condition of the People, 1856. Reprinted 1968.
4177 Ranger, T. O., 'Richard Boyle and the making of an Irish fortune, 1588-1614', Irish Historical Studies, X, 1956-57, 257-97.

IRELAND SINCE 1700

GENERAL

4177a Adams, W. F., Ireland and Irish Emigration to the New World from 1815 to The Famine, New Haven, Conn., 1932.
4178 Coyne, W. P., ed., Ireland, Industrial and Agricultural, 1902.
4179 Cullen, L. M., Economic History of Ireland since 1660, 1972.
4180 —— (ed.) The Formation of the Irish Economy, 1969.
4181 —— 'Problems in the interpretation and revision of eighteenth-century Irish economic history', T.R.H.S., 5th ser., 17, 1967, 1-22.
4182 —— 'The value of contemporary printed sources for Irish economic history in the eighteenth century', Irish Historical Studies, XIV, 1964, 142-55.
4183 Freeman, T. W., Pre-Famine Ireland, 1957.
4183a Lee, J. P., The Modernisation of Irish Society, 1848-1918, 1973.
4183b Lyons, F. S. L., Ireland since the Famine, 1971.
4184 McCracken, Eileen, The Irish Woods since Tudor Times: Their Distribution and Exploitation, 1971.
4184a Meenan, J., The Irish Economy since 1922, 1970.
4185 Moody, T. W. and Beckett, J. C., eds., Ulster since 1800: A Political and Economic Survey, 1954.
4186 —— and Beckett, J. C., Ulster since 1800, Second Series: A Social Survey, 1957. Bibliography, 236-40.
4186a —— and Martin, F. X. (eds.), The Course of Irish History, 1967.
4187 O'Brien, G., Economic History of Ireland in the Eighteenth Century, 1918.
4188 —— Economic History of Ireland from the Union to the Famine, 1921. Vintage polemic.
4188a O'Tuathaigh, G., Ireland before the Famine, 1798-1848, 1972.
4189 Public Record Office of Northern Ireland (H. M. Stationery Office, Belfast), Irish Economic Documents, 1967.
4190 Wilson, T., ed., Ulster under Home Rule: A Study of the Political and Economic Problems of Northern Ireland, 1955.

SOCIAL

4191 Boyd, A., The Rise of the Irish Trade Unions, 1729-1970, 1972. (Should be used with caution).
4192 Burns, R. E., 'The Catholic Relief Act in Ireland, 1778', Church History, XXXII, 1963, 181-206.
4193 Ellis, P. B., A History of the Irish Working Class, 1972.
4194 Inglis, B., The Freedom of the Press in Ireland, 1784-1841, 1954.
4195 McDowell, R. B., ed., Social Life in Ireland, 1800-45, 1952.
4196 Maxwell, Constantia, Country and Town in Ireland under the Georges, 1940.
4197 —— The Stranger in Ireland from the Reign of Elizabeth to the Great Famine, 1954.
4198 Munter, R., The History of the Irish Newspaper, 1685-1760, 1967.
4199 Quane, M., 'The Diocesan Schools, 1570-1870', Jnl. Cork Historical and Archaeological Society, LXVI, 1961, 26-50.
4200 Wall, Maureen, 'The rise of a Catholic middle class in eighteenth-century Ireland', Irish Historical Studies, XI, 1958, 91-115.

TRADE

See Cullen (1574), listed above.

4201 Murray, Alice E., A History of the Commercial and Financial Relations Between England and Ireland from the Period of the Restoration, 1907.
4202 Wall, Maureen, 'The Catholic merchants, manufacturers and traders of Dublin, 1778-1782'. Reportorium Novum: Dublin Diocesan Historical Record, II, 1959-60, 298-323.

TRANSPORT AND INDUSTRY

4203 Barker, T. C., 'The beginnings of the canal age in the British Isles' (the Newry Canal). In Pressnell, ed. (2170), 1-22.
4203a Casserley, H. C., Outline of Irish Railway History, 1974.
4204 Coe, W. E., The Engineering Industry of the North of Ireland, 1969.
4205 Conroy, J. C., A History of Railways in Ireland, 1928 (needs revision).
4206 Delany, V. T. H. and D. R., The Canals of the South of Ireland, 1966.
4207 Green, E. R. R., The Industrial Archaeology of County Down, 1963.
4208 —— The Lagan Valley, 1800-50: A Local History of the Industrial Revolution, 1949.
4209 Gribbon, H. D., The History of Water Power in Ulster, 1969.
4210 Irvine, H. S., 'Some aspects of passenger traffic between Britain and Ireland, 1820-1850', Jnl. of Transport History, IV, 1960, 224-41.
4211 Kane, R., Industrial Resources of Ireland, 2nd ed., 1845.
4212 Lee, J. P., 'The constructional costs of early Irish railways, 1830-52', Business History, IX, 1967, 95-109.
4213 —— 'The provision of capital for early Irish railways', Irish Historical Studies, XVI, 1968, 33-63
4214 Lynch, P. and Vaizey, J., Guinness's Brewery in the Irish Economy, 1759-1876, 1960.

114 *Ireland Since 1700*

4215 McCutcheon, W. A., The Canals of the North of Ireland, 1968.
4216 Murray, K. A., The Great Northern Railway (Ireland), 1944.
4217 Nowlan, K. B., Travel and Transport in Ireland, 1973.
4218 Bianconi, M. A. and Watson, S. J., Bianconi, King of the Irish Roads, 1962.
4219 Petree, J. F., 'Charles Wye Williams (1780-1866) a pioneer in steam navigation and fuel efficiency', Trans. Newcomen Society, XXXIX, 1966-7, 35-46. Steam navigation in Irish waters.
4220 Swift, J., History of the Dublin Bakers, 1949. On the Irish linen trade and industry see Horner (2741) and Gill (2742), listed above.

FINANCE, BANKING AND ACCOUNTANCY

4220a Barrow, G. L., The Emergence of the Irish Banking System, 1820-45, 1974.
4221 Dillon, M., The History and Development of Banking in Ireland, 1889.
4222 Fetter, F. W., ed., The Irish Pound, 1797-1826: A Reprint of the Committee of 1804 of the British House of Commons on the Condition of the Irish Currency, 1955.
4223 Hall, F. G., History of the Bank of Ireland, 1783-1946, 1949.
4224 O'Kelly, E., The Old Private Banks and Bankers of Munster, 1959.
4225 ——— 'The old Limerick private bankers', Jnl. Old Limerick Society, I, No. 1, December 1946, 5-27.
4226 Tenison, C. M., 'The Dublin bankers', Jnl. of the Cork Historical and Archaeological Society, 1st ser., II, 1893, 246-8; III, 1894, 16-18, 36-8, 54-6, 102-6, 120-3, 143-6, 168-71, 193-7, 221-2, 241-3, 256-60 and I, 2nd series, 1895 passim.
4227 ——— 'The private bankers of Cork and the South of Ireland', Jnl. of the Cork Historical and Archaeological Society, 1st ser., I, 1892, 221-4, 242-7; II, 1893, 8-9, 26-30, 46-8, 69-72, 94-7, 113-15, 134-7, 159-62, 184-6, 205-8; III, 1894, 56.
4228 Robinson, H. W., A History of Accountants in Ireland, 1964.

LAND AND AGRICULTURE

4228a Solow, Barbara L., The Land Question and the Irish Economy, 1870-1903, 1971.

POPULATION

4229 Black, R. D. C., Economic Thought and the Irish Question, 1817-1870, 1960.
4230 Connell, K. H., The Population of Ireland, 1750-1845, 1950.
4230a ——— Irish Peasant Society, 1968.
4231 Drake, M., 'The Irish demographic crisis of 1740-41', Historical Studies, VI, ed. T. W. Moody, 1968, 101-24.
4232 ——— 'Marriage and population growth in Ireland, 1750-1845', Ec. H. R., 2nd ser., XVI, 1963, 301-13.
4233 Edwards, R. D. and Williams, T. D., eds., The Great Famine: Studies in Irish History, 1845-1852, 1956.
4234 Woodham-Smith, Cecil, The Great Hunger: Ireland, 1845-9, 1962.

URBAN STUDIES

4235 Beckett, J. C., and Glasscock, R. E., Belfast, the Origin and Growth of an Industrial City, 1967.
4236 Chart, D. A., A History of Dublin, 1932.
4237 Craig, M., Dublin, 1660-1860, 1952.
4238 Harvey, J., Dublin: A Study in Environment, 1949.
4239 Maxwell, Constantia, Dublin under the Georges, 1714-1830, 1936, 2nd rev. ed., 1956. See also O'Sullivan (4161), listed above.

INDEX OF AUTHORS AND EDITORS

NUMBERS REFER TO ENTRIES IN THE BIBLIOGRAPHY

Aalen, F. H. A., 4120
Abel, D., 3414
Abel-Smith, B., 2285
Abrams, P., 2268
Abramsky, C., 3111
Acton, W., 3763
Acworth, A. W., 2849, 3342-3
Adams, I. H., 3966
Adams, J. W. R., 750
Adams, L. P., 2327
Adams, W. F., 4177a
Adamson, J. W., 2075-7, 3850
Adburgham, Alison, 2476, 2787
Addis, J. P., 2627
Addison, W., 917
Adler, M., 518
Agricola, G., 1356
Ahrons, E. L., 3363
Aiken, W. A., 1907
Aitken, H. G. J., 1
Albert, W. A., 3273
Albion, R. G., 1398
Aldcroft, D. H., 2192-4, 2411, 2504, 2930, 3266a, 3268, 3334-5, 3351
Alderman, G., 3336
Alexander, D., 2458
Alford, B. W. E., 1305, 2420, 2785
Allan, D. G. C., 1284, 1908
Allen, E., 2665, 3076
Allen, G. C., 2195, 2627a
Allen, J. E., 2840
Allison, K. J., 712-4, 1073, 1162, 1251, 1332-3
Allman, A. H., 2897a
Allmand, C. T., 844, 923
Altick, R. D., 2788
Altschul, M., 166, 241
Ambrose, P., 2393a
Ames, E., 824
Amherst, Alicia, 1163
Anderson, A. O., 3917
Anderson, B. L., 2952a
Anderson, D., 2576
Anderson, M., 2673
Anderson, M. L., 3950
Andréades, A. M., 1700
Andreano, R., 2
Andrews, C. B., 1358
Andrews, C. M., 1555-6
Andrews, J. H., 3281-4
Andrews, K. R., 1572
Andrews, P. W. S., 2628, 3320
Anstey, R., 2439a
Appleby, A. B., 1111
Archer, M. S., 3305
Armitage, Susan M. H., 2196
Armstrong, A., 3806
Armstrong, W. A., 3647a
Armytage, Frances, 3388

Armytage, W. H. G., 2551, 2933, 3253, 3827, 3851
Arnold, M., 3852
Arnot, R. P., 3096-3100
Ashby, A. W., 3713
Ashby, Mabel K., 2394
Ashley, M., 988-9, 1724, 1766
Ashley, W. J., 3, 4, 302
Ashmore, O., 1884, 2177
Ashton, E. T., 3761
Ashton, R., 1573, 1680-3, 1909-10, 2003
Ashton, T. S., 6, 7, 116, 2114, 2139-40, 2410, 2577, 2620-30, 2682, 2850, 2898, 3173-4, 3440
Ashworth, W., 9, 2197, 3571
Aspin, W., 2178, 2674
Aspinall, A., 2790, 3000
Asplin, P. W. A., 4069
Aston, Margaret, 933-4
Aston, T. H., 351, 990
Aström, S. E., 1516-18
Atkinson, F., 751, 2578, 2710
Atkinson, T., 1417
Atton, H., 1725
Ault, W. O., 627-9, 662, 691
Axtell, J. L., 2078
Aydelotte, F., 1819
Ayers, Gwendoline M., 3764
Ayerst, D., 2791
Aylmer, G. E., 1684-5, 1726-6a, 1911

Babbage, C., 3678
Bacon, R. K., 3564
Baernreither, J. M., 3168
Bagley, A. J., 1820
Bagley, J. J., 170, 1820
Bagwell, P. S., 3031a, 3090, 3267, 3337
Bagwell, R., 4095-6
Bailey, F. A., 3639
Bailey, W. Milne, 3001
Baily, L., 2219, 2220
Bailyn, B., 1557
Bain, G. S., 3117
Baines, E., 2675
Baker, A. R. H., 383, 630-1, 692, 708, 1235-6
Baker, J. N. L., 503
Baker, N., 2835
Baker, R. L., 770, 882
Baker, T., 174
Baker, W. J., 3306
Baldwin, F. E., 1727
Baldwin, F. G. C., 3307
Baldwin, J. F., 881
Ballam, H., 1060
Ballard, A. 249, 469-70, 3976
Ballard, M., 10

Ballen, Dorothy, 3272
Ballin, H. H., 2547
Balogh, T., 2851
Bamford, F., 1898
Bamford, S., 3015
Bamford, T. W., 3861
Bankes, Joyce, 1155
Banks, A. G., 2579
Banks, C. E., 1106
Banks, J. A., 2296, 3026, 3831
Banks, Olive, 3831
Barbé, L. A., 3921
Barbour, H., 2004
Barbour, V., 1399
Bardshaw, D. C. A., 3854
Barker, T. C., 738b, 1305, 2423, 2444, 2511, 2749, 2880, 3293, 3359, 3630, 4193
Barley, M. W., 913, 1885-6, 3504
Barlow, F., 175-6
Barnard, H. C., 3853
Barnard, T. C., 4132a
Barnes, D. G., 3403
Barnes, T. G., 1758
Barnett, C., 3327
Barnett, D. C., 2381
Barnie, J., 844a
Barnsby, G., 3175
Barraclough, G., 177
Barron, Caroline M., 575
Barou, N., 2465, 3032
Barrow, G. L., 4220a
Barrow, G. W. S., 178, 3922-2a 3947
Barry, E. E., 2198
Bartlett, C. J., 3449
Bartlett, J. N., 895
Barton, D. B., 2522
Barton, R. M., 2768
Baskerville, G., 1269
Basmann, R. L., 11
Bassett, D. K., 1527
Bateman, J., 2370
Bateson, H., 3643
Bateson, Mary, 471-2
Batho, G. R., 1211, 1217, 1767, 1880
Baxter, B., 3338
Baxter, R., 1899
Baxter, S. B., 1686
Bayne-Powell, Rosamond, 3855
Beales, A. C. F., 2079
Beales, H. L., 2115, 2141, 2199, 2221, 2978, 3714
Bean, J. M. W., 567, 600, 668
Beard, G., 3505
Beardwood, Alice, 924-6
Beazley, F., 3033
Bebb, E. D., 2005
Beckerman, W., 2200

Beckett, J.C., 4081, 4097, 4164, 4185-6, 4235
Beckinsale, R.P., 2711-2
Beer, E.S. de, 2106
Beer, M., 568, 2328, 2979
Beier, A.L., 1821
Bell, R., 3339
Bell, S.P., 2940a
Bell, V., 3787
Bell, W.G., 1112
Bellamy, Joyce, 2512, 2969a
Bellman, H., 3565
Bellot, H.H., 132
Beloff, M., 3193
Benians, E.A., 1565
Bennett, A., 3138a
Bennett, H.S., 352, 569, 2080
Bennett, M.K., 303
Bennett, R., 2515
Berens, C.H., 1989
Beresford, M.W., 12, 13, 304 476, 601-2, 632, 693-5, 712- 13, 715-16, 1237, 1728, 2941
Berry, E.K., 743
Berthoff, R.T., 3467
Bessemer, H., 2631
Best, G.F.A., 2142
Bevan-Evans, M., 2618
Beveridge, W.H., 305, 438-9, 1652, 2222, 3415
Bianconi, M.A., 4218
Biddle, G., 3297
Bidwell, W.H., 2899
Billson, C.J., 477
Bindoff, S.T., 991-2, 1285, 1306, 1474, 1701a, 1729
Binfield, C., 3749
Binney, J.E.D., 2836
Birch, A., 2622, 2623
Birch, L., 3034
Birnbaum, N., 2053
Birrell, J.R., 720
Bischoff, J., 2713
Bishop, T.A.M., 250, 353, 384
Bisschop, W.R., 1702
Black, J.B., 993
Black, R.D.C., 2116, 4229
Blackman, Janet, 2425
Blackwood, B.G., 1973, 2006
Bladen, V.W., 2769
Blagden, C., 1307
Blair, E., 2223
Blake, J.B., 771-2
Blanchard, I., 1080
Bland, A.E., 141
Blaug, M., 3450, 3679, 3715-16
Blaxland, G., 3148
Blitz, R.C., 1605
Bloch, M., 14, 179
Bloomfield, P., 3468
Blouet, P, 3788
Blythe, R., 2224
Bogdanov, V., 2225
Bolitho, H., 2740
Bonar, J., 1081
Bond, R.P., 2811
Bonser, K.J., 2388
Bonser, W., 167

Booker, F., 2179
Bossy, J., 2007
Boston, R.J., 3469
Bott, A., 2226, 3832
Bottigheimer, K.S., 4133
Bouch, C.M.L., 1046, 2008
Boucher, C.E., 603
Boucher, C.T.G., 2552-3
Bowden, P.J., 1198, 1653
Bowden, W., 2942
Bowditch, J., 2125
Bowen, I., 3893
Bowker, B., 2676
Bowley, A.L., 2269
Bowley, Marian, 3547-9, 3652
Boxer, C.R., 1544-5
Boyd, A., 4191
Boyle, A., 2852
Boyle, E., 4125
Boynton, L., 1730
Boyson, R., 2677, 3717
Boyd, W., 4014
Brace, H.W., 2786
Bracegirdle, B., 2554
Bradac, J., 570
Brailsford, H.N., 1990
Branch-Johnson, W., 2395
Brand, C.F., 3035
Branson, Noreen, 2227
Braudel, F.P., 1654
Brauer, G.C., 2081
Bray, J.F., 2980-1
Breach, R.W., 2126
Bready, J. Wesley, 3680
Brears, C., 1047
Breathnach, B., 4126
Breen, T.H., 2054
Brebner, J.B., 3653
Bremner, D., 4034
Brenner, Y.S., 1655-7
Breslow, M.A., 2009
Brett-James, N.G., 1418
Brewer, J.G., 1232
Bridbury, A.R., 15, 571, 602a 773, 1163a
Bridenbaugh, C., 1107, 1475
Bridenbaugh, Roberta, 1475
Bridgwater, D., 2649
Briggs, A., 2228, 2988-9, 3238, 3308, 3572, 3588, 3750, 3765
British Association, 2201-2
Britnell, R.H., 633
Broadbridge, S.R., 3293a, 3340
Broadley, H., 2429
Broadway, F., 2203
Brockington, C.F., 3766-7
Brodrick, G.C., 2381
Brooke, C.N.L., 180, 946
Brooke, G.C., 409
Brooks, F.W., 251
Brotherston, J.H.F., 3768
Brown, A.F.J., 2127
Brown, A.H., 3416
Brown, E.H. Phelps, 1658-61, 3036, 3142
Brown, J.H., 2082
Brown, Joyce M., 3550
Brown, K.D., 2229, 2989a

Brown, Lucy, 3404
Brown, P.A., 141
Brown, P.H., 3918, 3923
Brown, R., 2924
Brown, R., 3129a
Brown, R.A., 181-2, 425
Brown, R.G., 2312
Browne, D.G., 3194
Browne, Margaret H., 3142
Browning, A., 970
Bruce, M., 2230
Brunner, Elizabeth, 2628, 3320
Brunskill, R.W., 3506
Brunton, D., 1913
Brutzkus, J., 504
Bryant, E.T., 3329
Bryant, W.N., 832
Buchanan, R.A., 2180
Buck, N.S., 3428
Buckatzch, E.J., 143, 1100-1, 1851
Buckley, H., 1703
Buckley, K.D., 4050
Buer, M.C., 2287
Bulletin of the Society for the Study of Labour History, 2968
Bulley, J.A., 2580
Bullock, A., 3149
Bulow, G. von, 1061-2
Bundock, C.J., 3111
Burke, P., 994
Burn, D.L., 2634-5
Burnett, J., 825, 2426, 3015a
Burnley, J., 2912a
Burns, Eveline M., 2231
Burns, R.E., 4192
Burrell, S.A., 2055, 4021
Burstall, A.F., 1292
Burt, R., 2181, 2614
Burton, Kathleen M., 971
Burwash, Dorothy, 1400
Business History, 2513
Butler, R.F., 2636
Butler, R.M., 696
Butler, W.F.T., 4098, 4134
Butlin, R.A., 306, 393, 1238-9 4116
Butt, J., 2143, 2581-2, 3254, 3261.2, 4035
Byrne, Muriel St.C., 995
Bythell, D., 2678

Caird, J., 2339, 2382
Cairncross, A.K., 2327, 3463, 4036
Calder, A., 2270
Calthrop, D.C., 525
Calvert, A.F., 1385
Cam, Helen M., 510-11, 572
Camblin, G., 4160
Cameron, K., 390
Campbell, C.D., 3331
Campbell, E.M., 254
Campbell, J., 3924
Campbell, Mildred, 1108, 1768

Campbell, R. H., 2637, 2957, 4030, 4037
Camrose, Lord, 2792
Cannan, E., 1822, 2853
Cannery, Margaret, 2117
Cannon, J., 3239
Cant, R. G., 4015-5a
Cantor, L. M., 721
Cantor, N. F., 16
Cardwell, D. S. L., 2523
Carlson, R. E., 3370
Carney, J. J., 2232
Carr, A. M., 2466
Carr, C. T., 1504
Carr, J. C., 2638
Carrothers, W. A., 3470
Carr-Saunders, A. M., 2233-4, 2466, 2934
Carstairs, A. M., 3932
Carswell, J., 2825
Carter, Allice C., 1445, 2822
Carter, G. A., 3644
Carter, G. R., 2505
Carter, H. B., 2330
Carter, T., 3016
Carus-Wilson, Eleanora M., 164, 394, 397-8, 478-9, 505, 726, 774-9, 817-19, 896
Cash, M., 1881
Caspari, F., 2083
Casserley, H. C., 4203a
Catling, H., 2679
Cave, C. H., 2900
Cell, G. T., 1558
Chadwick, E., 3769
Chadwick, G. F., 3507
Chalklin, C. W., 559, 995a, 1048, 1126, 1623, 3572a
Challinor, R., 3101-2
Challis, C. E., 1662-3
Chaloner, W. H., 393, 1231, 1386, 2445, 2639, 2735, 3027, 3176, 3405, 3595
Chamberlain, M. E., 3452
Chambers, J. D., 17, 117, 996, 2144-5, 2182, 2313, 2331
Chancellor, Valerie, E., 3017
Chandler, A. D., 18
Chandler, D., 2543
Chandler, G., 2901, 3601
Chapman, A. B. W., 3398
Chapman, S. D., 133a, 2145, 2680-80a, 2786a, 3195, 3508
Chapman, S. J., 2681-3
Chapman, V., 697
Chappell, E. L., 2640
Charlton, K., 2084
Chart, D. A., 4082, 4236
Chaudhuri, K. N., 1528-30
Checkland, E. O. A., 3707a
Checkland, S. G., 2146, 3717a
Cheke, V., 1406
Chesher, F. J., 3509
Chesher, V. M., 3509
Chesney, K., 3770
Chevalier, C. T., 183
Cheyney, E. P., 859, 3654
Chibnall, A. C., 332, 883

Chibnall, Marjorie, 372
Child, J., 3115
Childs, W. M., 3634
Chilton, D., 1184
Chitty, C. W., 1446-7
Chivers, K., 2427
Chrimes, S. B., 512
Christensen, T., 3825
Christy, M., 2902
Church, R. A., 3195, 3632
Cipolla, C. M., 1499
Clair, C., 2793
Clapham, J. H., 19, 144, 2147, 2714, 2736, 2817, 2154, 3573
Clapham, Mary H., 3573
Clapp, B. W., 2684, 3439
Clarendon, Earl of, 1900
Clark, Alice, 1852
Clark, A., 860
Clark, E. A. G., 3285
Clark, E. K., 3365
Clark, G. Kitson, 2148, 3655, 3807
Clark, G. N., 21, 997-9, 2118, 2493, 3373
Clark, P., 1412
Clarke, A., 3681, 4135
Clarke, I. F., 2143
Clarke, J. F., 3076
Clarkson, L. A., 1000, 1389-91
Clay, C., 1222, 1785
Clay, H., 2855
Clay, Rotha M., 1806
Clear, C. R., 3309
Cleary, E. J., 3566
Clegg, H. A., 3002, 3150
Clements, P., 2565
Clephane, Irene, 2245, 3832
Cliffe, J. T., 1786
Clifton-Taylor, A., 3512
Clough, R. T., 2619
Clow, A., 2751
Clow, Nan L., 2751
Clyde, W. M., 2107
Coate, M., 1001
Coates, B. E., 534
Coates, Mary, 1974
Coates, K., 3303
Coates, W. H., 1915
Coats, A. W., 22, 1606, 3656, 3718
Cobb, H. S., 762
Cobbett, W., 2399
Cochran-Patrick, R. W., 3965, 4003
Coe, W. E., 4204
Cohen, J. M., 2752
Cohen, P., 2236
Cole, G. D. H., 2115, 2237, 2390, 2467, 2974, 2987, 3004, 3037, 3245, 3255
Cole, Margaret, 2247, 3256
Cole, W. A., 23, 1991, 2011, 2119
Coleman, B. I., 3574
Coleman, D. C., 1002, 1222a, 1301, 1308, 1323, 1334, 1448, 1607, 1853, 2715, 2737
Coleman, Olive, 763, 779, 884

Coleman, T., 3091, 3471
Collet, C. D., 2794
Collier, Frances, 2685
Collins, E. J. T., 2332
Collins, H., 3077, 3161
Collins, K., 2373
Collinson, P., 2012-14
Colvin, H. M., 402-3, 526, 1731
Conacher, H. M., 4046
Conant, J. B., 2085
Conklin, R. J., 3246
Connell, K. H., 2288, 4230
Connell-Smith, G., 1476
Connelly, T. J., 3084
Conrad, A. H., 24-5, 79
Conroy, J. C., 4205
Consitt, F., 1309
Conway, A., 3472
Cook, O., 3510-1
Cooke, C. A., 2958
Coonan, R., 4165
Cooney, E. W., 3551-2
Cooper, J. P., 983, 1003, 1732, 1787
Cooper, Lord, 3948
Coote, C., 2658
Copeland, J., 3274
Copeman, W. S. C., 1113
Coppetiers, E., 2856
Corbett, J., 3138b
Corley, T. E. B., 2428
Cormack, A., 4011
Cormack, Una, 3719
Cornwall, J., 1074, 1082, 1102, 1132-3, 1252, 1413, 1788
Cornwell, E. L., 3320
Cossons, A., 1634
Cossons, N., 2180
Costello, W. T., 2086
Coulton, G. G., 184-6, 4018
Coupland, R. G., 3441
Course, A. G., 3491
Court, W. H. B., 26-7, 1293, 2128, 2149, 3453
Coutts, J., 3925
Covina, M., 2477
Cowan, Helen, I., 34 3
Cowan, I. B., 4019, 4022
Cowan, R. M. W., 4059
Cowgill, Ursula M., 1134
Cowherd, R. G., 3682, 3720
Cowley, F. G., 541
Coyne, W. P., 4178
Cracknell, B. E., 643
Craig, J., 410
Craig, M., 4237
Craig, R., 3286-7
Cramp, A. B., 2857
Cranfield, G. A., 2795
Crathorne, Nancy, 2753
Crawford, W., 2429
Cregeen, E., 2389
Creighton, C., 604
Cressy, D., 2087
Crick, W. F., 2903
Croft, Pauline, 1573a
Crofts, J. E. W., 1635
Cromarty, D., 698

Cromwell, Valerie, 3657
Cronne, H. A., 187, 309, 897
Crook, W. H., 3151-2
Cross, F. W., 1441
Cross, M. Claire, 1212, 2015
Crossley, D. W., 158, 1359, 1395
Cronse, N. M.. 1109
Crouzet, F., 2953, 3377
Crow, D., 3833
Crowther, G., 2414
Crump, C. G., 827
Crump, W. B., 2716-7
Cule, J. E., 2524
Cullen, L. M., 1574, 4099, 4179-82
Cunningham, Audrey, 28
Cunningham, W., 145, 1449
Cunnington, C. W., 1887
Cunnington, Phillis, 527, 1887
Curtis, E., 4079, 4083-4
Curtis, M. H., 2088-9
Curtis, S. J., 3856
Curtis-Bennett, N., 2430
Curtler, W. H., 1240
Cuthbert, N. H., 3133
Cutlack, S. A., 1808
Cutting, C. L., 1407
Cuttle, G., 3721

Dacey, H. M., 2858
Dale, M. K., 660, 861
Dalton, R., 2818
Dane, E. S., 2640a
Daniels, G. W., 127, 2686
Darby, H. C., 146, 242, 252-7. 709, 1253
Darlington, R. R., 188
Darvall, F. O., 3196
Darwin, B., 2487
Davenport, F. G., 354, 862
Davey, N., 3553-4
David, P., 29
Davidson, A., 3987
Davie, G. E., 4060
Davies, A. E., 3894
Davies, A. S., 2904
Davies, C. S. L., 1286-7, 1733-4, 1823
Davies, C. Stella, 1419-2406
Davies, D. J., 147
Davies, G., 964, 1004, 1916
Davies, J. C., 426, 506, 1992
Davies, K. G., 1324, 1506, 1533, 1769
Davies, Margaret G., 1854
Davies, P. N., 3428a
Davis, Dorothy, 2459
Davis, L. E., 30-2
Davis, R., 33, 1325, 1402, 1477-9, 1521, 1575, 1735, 3374, 3389
Davis, W. J., 2819, 3038
Davison, R. C., 2238-9
Dawson, T. R., 2783
Day, C., 2990
Day, Joan, 2614a
Day, L. J. C., 542
Dayson, G. H. C., 3647

Deane, Phyllis, 2119, 2121, 2150
Deardorff, N. R., 1519
Debus, A. G., 1113a
Deerr, N., 2431
Delany, D. R., 4206
Delany, V. T. H., 4206
Dell, E. M., 1902
Denham, R. D., 1855
Denholm-Young, N., 189, 300, 573, 669
Denman, D. R., 133, 365
Denney, A. H., 666
Department of Labour and Productivity, 2970
Desai, M., 34
Dewar, H. S. L., 752-3
Dewar, Mary, 972
Dicey, A. V., 3658
Dickens, A. G., 1420, 2016
Dickinson, H. W., 2525-30, 3575,
Dickinson, J. C., 190, 543
Dickinson, W. Croft, 3919, 3926, 3975
Dickson, P. G. M., 2823, 2927
Dietz, F., 1687-8
Dilks, T. B., 893
Dilley, J. W., 3984
Dillon, M., 4221
Divine, D., 3197
Djang, T. K., 3683
Dobb, M., 35, 148
Dobrée, B., 3204
Dobson, R. B., 867, 898, 946a
Dodd, A. H., 149, 1005-6, 1049 1414, 1421, 1537, 2905, 3474, 3895
Dobbd, W., 3684
Dodwell, Barbara, 258, 440-1, 687
Dolléans, E., 3222
Dolley, R. H. M., 411-12, 4150
Donald, M. B., 1360-61
Donaldson, G., 3920, 3933-4, 3956, 4023, 4032a
Donaldson, J. E., 4043
Donkin, R. A., 544-9
Donnelly, J. S., 947
Dony, J. G., 2745
Dore, R. N., 1985
Dougan, D., 2556, 3500
Douglas, D. C., 171, 191-2
Douglas, J. M., 4166
Douring, F., 36
Dow, J., 3988-9a, 4030
Dow, J. C. R., 2204
Dowell, S., 427, 2827
Down, C. G., 2583
Dowse, R. E., 3162
Drake, M., 35a, 2289, 4231-2
Drescher, L., 2343
Drew, B., 2928
Drew, J. S., 355
Driver, C., 3685
Drummond, I. A., 3417-7a
Drummond, J. C., 874
Du Bois, A. B., 2959
Du Boulay, F. R., 560, 574-5, 670-2

Duby, G., 307-8
Duckham, B. F., 2584-8
Duckham, H., 2585
Duffy, J., 3198
Dukes, G., 2108
Dulley, A. J. F., 780, 899
Dunbabin, J. P. D., 2391a, 3066
Dunbar, Janet, 3834
Dunbar, J. G., 3513
Duncan, J. F., 4046
Duncan, R., 3475
Dunham, A. L., 3418
Dunham, W. H., jnr., 973
Dunlop, O. J., 1855
Dunlop, R., 4100-3, 4136
Dunsheath, P., 2548
Durkan, J., 4016
Dutton, R., 3514
Dyer, A. D., 1422
Dyer, C., 634, 717
Dymond, D. P., 1135
Dyos, H. J., 3538, 3576-7, 3593, 3622

Eager, A. R., 4070
Earle, J. B. F., 3275
Earle, P., 1006a
Early, R. E., 2726
Easson, D. E., 4019a
Ede, J. F., 3645
Edelen, G., 974
Eden, F. M., 1824, 3722
Eden, P. M., 3515
Edey, H. C., 1719
Edie, C. A., 1423
Edler, F., 1576
Edsall, N. C., 3723
Edwards, A. C., 1050
Edwards, G., 3067
Edwards, J. G., 404
Edwards, K., 3199
Edwards, M. M., 2687
Edwards, R. D., 4071, 4167, 4233
Edwards, Ruth D., 4084a
Ehrenberg, R., 1704
Ehrman, J., 3378
Ekwall, E., 391, 597, 605
Elliott, Blanche, B., 2487a
Elliott, G., 1241, 1335
Ellis, C. Hamilton, 3342
Ellis, C. M., 2516
Ellis, H., 247-9
Ellis, K. L., 3311
Ellis, M. J., 1207
Ellis, P. B., 4193
Ellison, Mary, 2688
Ellison, T., 2689
Elman, P., 519-20
Elman, R. M., 3751
Elsas, Madeleine, 2641
Elton, G. R., 37, 134, 1007-8, 1689, 1721, 1736-40, 1825, 1917
Elton, J., 2515
Emden, A. B., 954
Emden, P. H., 3801

Emmison, F. G., 699, 1636-8, 1809-10, 1888
Engberg, J., 1918
Engels, F., 2991
English, W., 2690
Erickson, Charlotte, 2943, 3476
Ernle, Lord, 310
Erskine, A. M., 598
Evans, G. H., 2960
Evans, J. D., 2642
Evelyn, J., 975
Everard, S., 2544
Everitt, A. M., 1009, 1199, 1200, 1414a, 1770, 1856, 1919-20, 1976-7, 2017
Eversley, D. E. C., 1083, 1136, 2290, 2460, 3771
Ewald, W. B., 2796
Ewart, E. A., 3429
Eyre, A., 1156

Fagan, H., 869
Faith, R. J., 688
Falkus, M., 2545
Fanfani, A., 2056
Faraday, M. A., 1075
Farley, A., 246
Farman, C., 3152a
Farmer, D. L., 413-14
Farnell, J. E., 1547
Farnie, D. A., 2690a, 3390
Farnsworth, A., 2829
Farrar, W. J., 1978
Farriers, K. G., 2517
Faucher, L., 3789
Faulkner, H. U., 3223
Faulkner, P. A., 528
Fay, C. R., 2151-2, 3406, 3578
Fearn, H., 3724-5
Fearon, P., 2203, 2421
Feavearyear, A. E., 415
Federn, K., 38
Feis, H., 3464
Fell, A., 1362
Fenton, A., 3955, 3957-8
Fereday, R. P., 2643
Ferguson, T., 4061-2
Fessler, A., 1826
Fetter, F. W., 2817a, 2859, 4222
Ffrench, Yvonne, 2797
Field, E., 2488
Fielden, J., 3686
Fieldhouse, D. K., 3454
Filby, F. A., 2432
Filson, A. W., 2974
Finberg, H. P. R., 39-41, 333, 480, 700, 900, 948, 1051 1055
Finch, Mary, E., 1789
Finer, Ann, 2770
Finer, S. E., 3772
Finn, R. W., 256, 260-269
Firth, C., 1921
Fish, S., 1811
Fischoff, E., 2057
Fisher, F. J., 1010-11, 1201, 1310, 1424-5, 1480-1, 1664

Fisher, F. M., 42
Fisher, H. E. S., 3391
Fisher, P., 644
Fisher, W. B., 644
Fishlow, A., 43
Fitton, R. S., 2671
Fitgerald, P., 2506
Fitzgibbon, C., 2271
Fitzpatrick, H. M., 4121
Flanagan, D., 2468
Flemming, Jessie, H., 561
Flenley, R., 781
Fletcher, T. W., 2334, 2397-8
Fletcher, V., 3516
Flinn, M. W., 142, 150, 1363-5, 2153, 2291, 2633, 3644-5, 2860, 3773
Florence, P. S., 2466
Floud, R., 43a, 165a
Fogel, R. W., 43-5
Fond, B. Faujas de Saint, 3790
Ford, T. D.,
Fordham, H. G., 1639
Formoy, R. R., 2961
Forrester, H., 3517
Forster, G. C. F., 1426, 1759
Foster, B., 764
Foster, C. W., 270
Foster, J., 2991a
Foster, W., 1522
Foster, W. R., 4023a
Fowler, G. H., 271
Fowler, J., 901
Fowler, K., 845
Fox, A., 3002, 3134
Fox, H. G., 1741
Fox, L., 481
France, R. S., 1357
Francis, J., 3343
François, M. E., 1427
Frank, J., 2109
Franklin, T. B., 3951
Fraser, C. M., 606, 782
Fraser, D., 2240
Fraser, H. M., 272
Fraser, P. 2110
Fraser, W. H., 3040
Fraser-Stephen, Elspet, 2589
Frazer, W. M., 3604, 3774
Freeman, T. W., 4183
Freese, S., 754
French, A., 1922
French, J. O., 3085
French, P., 2267
French, R. V., 2449
Frewer, L. B., 135
Fried, A., 3741
Friis, Astrid, 1482
Frow, E., 2999, 3005, 3041
Frow, Ruth, 2999, 3005
Fry, A. Ruth, 1812
Fryde, E. B., 783-5, 833-4, 885
Fuchs, C. J., 3419
Fulford, R., 3835
Fuller, Margaret D., 3169
Furber, E. C., 136
Furniss, D. A., 949
Furniss, E. S., 1857

Furnivall, F. J., 976
Fussell, G. E., 311, 576, 635 1059, 1157, 1164-70, 1185-6, 1254, 1858, 2325, 2335-8, 3068, 3786
Fyrth, H. J., 3077

Gainer, B., 2320
Gairdner, J., 562
Galambos, L., 18
Galbraith, V. H., 273
Gale, W. K. V., 2531, 2646-8
Galloway, R. L., 1351-2
Galpin, W. E., 2339
Galton, F. W., 3135
Gammage, R. G., 3224
Ganshof, F., 193
Garbati, J., 3042
Gardiner, Dorothy, 1901
Gardiner, S. R., 1012, 1923-4
Garnett, F. W., 2399
Garnett, R. G., 2929, 3257
Gartner, L. P., 2321
Gash, N., 2382
Gaskell, P., 3687-8
Gatrell, V. A. C., 3263
Gauldie, Enid M., 3518
Gaut, R. C., 2400
Gay, E. F., 1242, 1288
Gay, J. D., 3800
Gayer, A. D., 2412
Geneau, R. H., 3317
Gentles, I., 1218
George, Barbara J., 3288
George, C. H., 2058-9
George, C. O., 2843-4
George, Katherine, 2059
George, M. Dorothy, 3006-7, 3607
Gerrard, J. A., 2322
Ghorbal, Gertrude, 2717
Gibb, A., 2557
Gilbert, B. B., 2241-2
Gilbert, E. W., 3648
Gilboy, Elizabeth W., 2461, 3177-8
Gilchrist, J., 935
Giles, Phyllis M., 2746
Gill, C., 902, 1428, 2741, 3200, 3392, 3588
Gillespie, Frances E., 3043
Gillespie, J. E., 1559
Gillespie, Sarah C., 4051
Gillet, E., 3586a
Gillett, W., 2893
Girling, F. A., 786
Girouard, M., 1450
Giuseppi, J., 2861
Giuseppi, M. S., 737
Giusseppi, J. A., 1466
Glasgow, E. L. H., 3248
Glasgow, G., 3153
Glass, D. V., 1076, 1083, 1137, 1859, 2292-3
Glasscock, R. E., 645, 4235
Gleason, J. H., 1760
Gleeson, D. F., 4173

Gloag, J., 2649, 3519-11
Glynn, S., 46
Goetschin, P., 2862
Golding, D., 2243
Gomme, A. A., 2494
Gomme, G. L., 3621
Gonner, E. C. K., 2364
Goodbody, O. C., 4174
Goodhart, C. A. E., 2863
Goodhart-Rendel, H. S., 3522
Goodman, C., 3786
Goodrich, C., 47
Gordon, M. D., 1993
Gosden, P. H. J. H., 3170-1
Gottschalk, L., 48
Gough, J. W., 1326-8, 1366
Gould, J. D., 718, 1138, 1483
    1577-9, 1665-8, 2340
Gourvish, T. R., 3358
Graham, H. G., 4063
Graham, J. Q., jnr., 103
Graham, W., 2864
Grampp, W. D., 1608, 3407
Grant, A. T. K., 2865
Grant, I. F., 3927, 4031
Gras, E. C., 335
Gras, N. S. B., 49, 50, 335, 1202
Grassby, R., 1538-9, 1705
Graves, E. B., 167a
Graves, R., 2244
Gravil R., 1580
Gray, A., 2982, 3987
Gray, B. K., 1827
Gray, E. M., 2693
Gray, H. L., 442, 636, 734,
    1243
Gray, I., 3726
Gray, M., 2446, 4044
Gray-Jones, A., 3896
Grayzel, S., 521
Greaves, R. L., 2089a, 3599
Green, E. R. R., 4207-8
Green, F., 2906
Green, F. E., 3069
Green, J. R., 151
Green, Mrs. J. R., 903
Green, R. W., 2060
Green, V. H. H., 2090
Greenaway, G. W., 171
Greenberg, M., 3430
Gregg, Pauline, 1994, 2245
Gregory, D., 2817a
Gregory, R., 3103
Gregory, T. E., 1860, 2866
Grether, E. T., 2478
Gribbon, H. D., 4209
Griffith, G. T., 2294
Griffin, A. R., 2590, 3104-5
Griffiths, S., 2650
Grigg, D. B., 2401
Grindon, L. H., 2907
Grinsell, L. V., 3641
Grose, C. L., 965
Gross, C., 168, 467, 729
Groves, R., 3070
Grubb, Isobel, 3802
Gulvin, C., 4038
Gunderson, G., 51

Gwynn, A., 4113
Gwynn, R. D., 1451

Habakkuk, H. J., 52, 1084, 1213,
    1223-4, 1861, 1925-8, 2295-
    6, 2341, 2495, 3555
Haber, L. F., 2754-5
Hadfield, Alice M., 3225
Hadfield, C., 3294-7
Hadfield, M., 3523
Haigh, C., 1270
Hair, P. E. H., 1085, 2591
Hair, T. H., 2592
Halcrow, E. M., 648
Haldane, A. R. B., 2390, 3276
    3312
Hale, B., 2018
Halévy, E., 2154, 2983, 3659
Hall, A. R., 3465
Hall, D. J., 936
Hall, F. G., 4223
Hall, H., 169
Hall, N. F., 2891
Hall, P. G., 3624
Hallam, H. E., 282-4, 334, 646-
    7, 744, 1187
Haller, W., 2019-20
Hambling, W., 3139
Hamer, S. H., 2818
Hamilton, E. J., 1669
Hamilton, H., 1367, 4039-30
Hammersley, G., 1188, 1367a,
    1929
Hammond, Barbara, 2155, 2383,
    2992-3, 3226, 3689
Hammond, J. L., 2155, 2383
    2992-3, 3226, 3689
Hancock, P. D., 3908
Hancock, W. K., 54
Hand, G. J., 4168
Handley, J. E., 4045, 4052-4
Handover, P. M., 2798
Hanes, D. G., 3752
Hanley, H. A., 599
Hannington, W., 2256-9
Hanson, L., 2799
Hanson, L. W., 2120
Hardacre, P. H., 1930
Hardie, D. W. F., 2756-8
Hardie, R. P., 4009
Harding, A., 152
Hare, A. E. C., 2593
Hargreaves, E. L., 2824
Harland, J., 1882
Harper, L. A., 1484
Harris, A., 701
Harris, A., 2651
Harris, Helen, 2183
Harris, J. R., 2532, 2615, 2781,
    3433, 3433a, 3605, 3640
Harris, José, 2250
Harris, L. E., 1255
Harris, R. W., 2251
Harris, S. A., 2546
Harris, T. R., 2558
Harrison, A., 3691
Harrison, B., 2450-2, 3227

Harrison, G., 2479
Harrison, J., 1143
Harrison, J. F. C., 2129, 2156,
    3258, 3884
Harrison, M., 3044
Harrison, R., 3045
Harriss, G. L., 1690-1, 1742
Harrod, R. F., 3660
Hart, A. T., 2021-2
Hart, C. E., 1862
Hart, F. R., 3991
Hart, Jenifer M., 3201-2, 3661
Harte, N. B., 55, 2672
Hartley, Dorothy, 1158
Hartley, Marie, 2718, 3524
Hartwell, R. M., 1013, 2127,
    2157-60, 2944, 3179-81,
    3184
Harvey, Barbara, 607, 673, 868
Harvey, J., 4238
Harvey, J., 746
Harvey, J. B., 285
Harvey, N., 2326
Harvey, P. D. A., 336, 415a
Harvey, S., 274
Harvie, C., 2130
Hasbach, W., 1863
Hassall, W. O., 529
Hatcher, J., 649-50, 663, 738a-
    8b
Havinden, M. A., 995a, 1189a,
    1256-6a, 1883, 2402
Haward, W. I., 847
Hawke, G. R., 3344
Hawtrey, R. G., 2867
Hay, D., 848
Hayek, F. A., 57
Hayward, J. F., 1452
Hawke, G. R., 56
Heal, F., 1214
Healey, H. A. H., 3112
Heape, R. G., 3592
Heater, D., 58
Heaton, H., 20, 1336, 1609
Hecht, J. J., 3836
Heckscher, E. F., 59, 1610-11,
    3379
Hedges, R. Y., 3008
Heginbotham, S., 3086
Heinemann, Margot, 2227
Helleiner, K. E., 608
Hembry, Pauline M., 2023
Hemmeon, J. C., 3313
Henderson, A., 3525
Henderson, G. D., 4006a,
    4024-25
Henderson, W. O., 2692, 3380,
    3791-2
Henning, B. D., 1907
Hennings, Margaret A., 172
Hennock, E. P., 3734
Henriques, Ursula R. Q., 3690,
    3727
Herbert, G., 3018
Herlitz, L., 826, 1612
Hern, A., 3649
Hertz, G. B., 2738, 3381
Hewitt, H. J., 651, 849

Hewitt, Margaret, 1845, 3837, 3870
Hey, D., 1051a, 1367b, 2651a
Hexter, J. H., 60-1, 1771-2, 1790, 2091
Hibbert, A., 482
Hibbert, F. A., 730, 1265
Hibbs, J., 3322-3
Hicks, J., 62
Hicks, Ursula K., 2837-8
Higgins, J. P. R., 2954
Higgs, H., 312
Hill, B. D., 550
Hill, C., 1014-15a, 1208, 1829-30, 1864, 1902, 1932-7, 2024-9, 2061
Hill, G. B., 3314
Hill, J. W. F., 483, 1429, 3600a-00b
Hill, Mary C., 914
Hill, R., 3314
Hillier, J., 2518
Hills, R. L., 2533
Hilton, G. W., 3143, 3182
Hilton, R. H., 337-9, 356-8, 373, 381, 443-6, 637, 667, 674, 702, 863, 869, 904
Hilton, W. S., 3087
Himes, N. E., 2307
Himmelfarb, Gertrude, 3808
Hines, A. G., 3144
Hinton, E. M., 4104
Hinton, J., 3045a
Hinton, M., 3635
Hinton R. W. K., 1520, 1569, 1613
Hirst, F. W., 2839-40
Hitchcock, H.-R., 3526
Hitchins, F. H., 3487
Hoare, H. P. R., 2908
Hobhouse, Hermione, 3556
Hobsbawm, E. J., 64-5, 1938, 2161, 2384, 2945, 2975, 3028-29, 3046-7, 3183-4, 3203, 3809
Hobson, J. A., 3455
Hobson, O. R., 3567
Hockey, S. T., 950
Hodge, A., 2244
Hodgett, C. A. J., 577, 638, 1271
Hodgkinson, Ruth G., 3775
Hodgskin, T., 2984
Hoffman, P. C., 3118
Hoffman, R. J. S., 3431
Hoffmann, W. G., 2162
Hogan, J., 4131
Hogg, O. F. G., 1408
Holcombe, Lee, 3837a
Holden, J. M., 1706, 2820
Hole, Christina, 1865, 1889
Holiday, P. G., 1939
Hollaender, A. E. J., 484
Holland, H. H., 1725
Holland, J., 2594
Hollings, M., 194
Hollingsworth, T. H., 1086-7
Hollis, Patricia, 2162a, 2800, 2994
Hollister, C. W., 195-203

Holloway, J., 3019
Holloway, S. J. F., 63
Holmes, C., 1979a
Holmes, D. T., jnr., 530
Holmes, G., 578
Holmes, G. A., 675, 787, 927
Holmes, M., 1430, 1453
Holt, J. C., 204-7
Holt, R. V., 3803
Holyoake, G. J., 2469, 3172
Homans, G. C., 313-15, 336, 385
Homer, S., 416
Homeshaw, E. J., 3642
Hoon, Elizabeth E., 3382
Hope-Jones, A., 2830
Hopkins, Sheila V., 1658-61
Hopkinson, G. G., 1353, 1368
Hopkinson, J., 3020
Hopwood, E., 3128
Horn, Pamela L. R., 3071
Horne, H. O., 2894
Horner, J., 2742
Horniker, A. L., 1523
Horrocks, S., 2514
Horsefield, J. K., 1670, 1707, 2868
Hosford, W. A., 1233
Hoskins, W. G., 66, 153, 243, 275, 286, 316, 340, 485, 639, 703, 719, 1052-5, 1139, 1171-2, 1190, 1257, 1415, 1431, 1540, 1791, 1866, 1890, 2403, 3596
Hovell, M., 3228
Howe, E., 2946, 3113-5
Howell, D. W., 3897
Howell, G., 3009, 3240
Howell, R., 1131
Howell, R. junr., 1980
Howell, W. S., 2092
Howells, B., 652
Hower, R. M., 2771
Howson, W. G., 1140
Hoyt, R. S., 276, 367, 513
Hudson, K., 2947
Hudson, W. S., 2062
Hughes, A., 827
Hughes, Dorothy, 563
Hughes, E., 1743-4, 2595-6
Hughes, F., 3119
Hughes, H. S., 69
Hughes, J., 2909
Hughes, J. R. T., 67-8, 2413, 3495, 3617
Hughes, M., 3154
Hughes, P. L., 1722
Hulme, E. W., 2652-4
Humphreys, B. V., 3120
Hunnisett, R. F., 886
Hunt, B. C., 2962
Hunt, C. J., 2621
Hunt, Edith M., 3643
Hunt, E. H., 70, 3145
Hunter, D. M., 2719
Hurst, G. B. see Hertz
Hurst, J. G., 712-13, 716
Hurstfield, J., 992, 1016, 1692-3, 1745-6

Hurt, J., 3857
Husain, B. M. C., 722
Hussey, C., 3527-30
Hutchinson, H. J., 3420
Hutchinson, Lucy, 1903
Hutchins, B. L., 3691
Hutchinson, T. W., 3662
Hutt, A., 2252
Hutt, W. H., 3692
Hyams, P. R., 368
Hyamson, A. M., 1467
Hyde, F. E., 2910, 3289, 3408, 3432-3, 3433a, 3436
Hyde, H. M., 2433
Hynes, S., 2253

Imlah, A. H., 3409, 3421
Imray, Jean, 731
Insh, G. P., 3935, 3992-5
Ingilby, Joan, 2718, 3524
Inglis, B., 3185, 4194
Inglis, K. S., 3810
Innis, H. A., 1581
Iredale, D., 3531
Iredale, D. A., 2759-60
Irvine, H. S., 4210
Isaac, A. W., 2911
Isichei, Elizabeth, 3804
Ives, E. W., 1774, 1940

Jack, I. R., 564, 676
Jack, S., 1272
Jackman, W. T., 3269
Jackson, A. A., 3618
Jackson, G., 3597a
Jackson, J. A., 2332a
Jacob, E. F., 579
James, F. G., 1141
James, J., 1337
James, L., 2801
James, Margaret, 1831, 1904
James, Margaret K., 788, 820
James, M. E., 1055a, 1289-9a
Jarvis, R. C., 1571, 3287, 3290, 3486
Jeffreys, J. B.. 2480, 2963, 2976, 3078
Jeffreys, R., 3277
Jenkin, A. K. Hamilton, 1867
Jenkins, F., 3532
Jenkins, J. G., 1338
Jenkins, J. T., 1582
Jenkins, R., 1294, 1369-71, 2529
Jenkins, R. T., 137
Jenks, L. H., 3466
Jennings, B., 1380, 2622
Jennings, W. I., 3581
Jevons, H. S., 2597
Jevons, W. S., 2598
Jewitt, Ll., 2772
Jewkes, J., 2693
Jha, N., 3663
John, A. H., 8, 2342-5, 3434, 3898
John, E., 71, 208

Johnson, A. H., 1244
Johnson, B. L. C., 1372-5, 2656
Johnson, C., 423-4, 827
Johnson, H. T., 405
Johnson, Marion, 3858
Johnson, P. B., 2272
Johnson, S. C., 3478
Johnston, E. M., 4072
Johnston, H. J. M., 3478a
Jones, A. G. E., 2912
Jones, D. C., 2233
Jones, D. J. V., 3899
Jones, D. T., 4016
Jones, D. W., 1583
Jones, E. D., 3900
Jones, E. L., 1173, 1295, 2344-7
Jones, G. H., 1832
Jones, G. P., 406, 448-9, 864, 1046, 1833, 1871-3, 2205
Jones, G. R. J., 244, 447
Jones, G. Stedman, 72, 3619
Jones, G. T., 2694
Jones, H. G., 2122
Jones, J. R., 1584, 3606
Jones, L., 3501
Jones, M. A., 3478b
Jones, M. G., 3859
Jones, P. d'A., 3826
Jones, P. E., 1142
Jones, R. J., 209
Jones, S. R., 3533
Jones, T. I. G., 1585
Jones, W. J., 1585
Jones, W. R. D., 1017
Jope, E. M., 875
Jordan, W. K., 1018-19, 1834-9
Joseph, J. K. St., 304
Journal of Educational Administration and History, 3849
Judge, A., 3123
Judges, A. V., 1142, 1614, 1840
Jusserand, J. J., 581

Kaeuper, R. W., 428
Kahl, W. F., 1304
Kahn, A. E., 2206
Kane, R., 4211
Katanka, M., 2999, 3005, 3041
Kavanagh, M., 4063
Kay-Shuttleworth, J. P., 2859, 3853
Kearney, H. F., 2062, 2093, 4117, 4127-8, 4147
Keeler, Mary F., 1941
Keen, M., 851
Keil, I., 677
Keith, Theodora, 3909, 3936, 3982, 3996
Keith-Lucas, B., 3728
Kelf-Cohen, R., 2207
Kellaway, W., 138, 486
Kellenbenz, H., 1296
Kellett, J. R., 1312, 3570
Kelly, T., 3885-6
Kelsall, R. K., 1868-70
Kemp, D., 2683
Kemp, P., 3492

Kennedy, J., 3496
Kennedy, M., 3628a
Kennedy, W., 2828
Kent, H. S. K., 3393
Kenyon, G. H., 1396
Kenyon, J. P., 1723
Kepler, J. S., 1485
Kerling, Nellie J. M., 789, 928
Kerr, Barbara M., 2323, 2385, 3534
Kerridge, E., 1088, 1155, 1174-6, 1191, 1206, 1230, 1258-60, 1290, 1432
Kershaw, A. G., 3483
Kershaw, I., 317, 678
Kesteven, G., 870
Ketton-Cremer, R. W., 1981
Kew, J., 1273
Kidd, A. T., 3079
Kiddier, W., 3136
Kidner, R. W., 3366
Kiernan, V. G., 1841
Kieve, J. L., 3315
Kimball, Janet, 2985
Kindleberger, C. P., 2208
King, E., 369
King, G., 1077
King, P., 154
King, W. T. C., 2869
Kingsford, C. L., 582, 790
Kingsford, P. W., 3092
Kirby, C., 2434-5
Kirk, E. F., 1442
Kirk, R. E. G., 1442
Kirkaldy, A. W., 2841, 3487
Kirkham, Nellie, 2623
Kitch, M. J., 2064
Klingender, F. D., 2163
Klugmann, J., 3163
Knappen, M. M., 2030
Kneisel, E., 1203
Knight, C., 2802
Knoop, D., 406, 448-9, 864, 1871-3
Knorr, K. E., 1560
Knott, D., 2117
Knowles, D., 551-2, 951, 1274
Knowles, K. G. J. C., 3048
Knox, S. J., 4175
Koebner, R., 3456
Koenigsberger, H., 1586
Khol, J. G., 3793
Kosminsky, E. A., 318, 382, 450, 640
Koss, S. E., 2761
Kramer, Stella, 1313-14
Krause, J. T., 296, 2298-2301
Krishna, B., 1531
Kuznets, S., 73
Kyd, K. D., 4032b
Kydd, S. H. G., 3693

Labarge, Margaret W., 531
Lacey, A. D., 2543
La Mar, V., 1641
Lambert, R. J., 3776-7
Lambert, R. S., 2221, 2481, 3359

Lambert, Z. E., 3324
Lamond, Elizabeth, 298, 977
Lamont, W. M., 1995, 2031
Lancaster, J. C., 139
Lander, J. R., 583, 850
Landes, D. S., 2164
Lane, F. C., 1403
Lane, N., 1708-9
Lang, R. G., 1540a
Langenfelt, G., 3694
Langford, A. W., 609
Lapsley, G. T., 738, 887
Larkin, J. F., 1722
Laski, H. J., 3581
Laslett, P., 155, 1089, 1142 1792
Latham, L. C., 359
Large, D., 3139a
Laver, H., 1387
Lavington, E., 2870
Lavrovsky, V. M., 1793
Laws, P., 2190
Lawson, J., 2094, 3860
Lawton, R., 2315, 2324, 3603
Layton, W. T., 2414
Leach, A. F., 955
Leach, A. L., 1982
Leadam, I. S., 1234
Leader, R. E., 2913
Leconfield, Lord, 1209-10
Lee, C. E., 3345
Lee, C. H., 2208a, 2695
Lee, Grace L., 4117
Lee, J. P., 4183a, 4212-3
Lee, L. G., 1875
Lee, M., jnr., 4026
Lee, W. R., 3695
Lees-Milne, J., 3535
Le Fanu, W. R., 1454
Leff, G., 937, 956
Leifchild, J. R., 2599, 2616
Leighton-Boyce, J. A. S. L., 2914
Lekachman, R., 3664
Lennard, R. V., 74, 274, 319, 341, 374, 451-5. 704, 1020, 1177, 1983
Leonard, Elizabeth M., 1245, 1842
Le Patourel, J., 473
Lerry, G. C., 2600
Letts, M., 1063
Letwin, W., 1021
Leventhal, F. M., 3049
Levett, A. E., 360, 610-11, 888
Levine, M., 966
Lewis, E. D., 3901
Lewis, J. Parry, 3557
Lewis, R. A., 3778
Levy, A., 4020
Levy, H., 1114-15
Levy, H., 2375, 2508
Levy, S. L., 3665
Lewin, H. G., 3346-7
Lewis, E. A., 727, 791, 1570, 1644
Lewis, G. R., 1376
Lewis, M., 3493

Index of Authors and Editors 123

Lewis, M. J. T., 3348
Lewis, R., 2935
Lewis, R., 1060
Lewis, R. A., 3093
Lewis, W. J., 1377, 1388
Leys, Mary D. R., 2032
Li, Ming-Hsun, 1671
Lickorish, J., 3483
Lindley, E. S., 952
Lindsay, Jean, 3557a
Lindsay, W. S., 3488
Lingelbach, W. E., 1508, 1511
Link, R. G., 2415
Lipman, V. D., 522, 3582
Lipsey, R. G., 3146
Lipson, E., 156, 1339, 2720
Lister, J., 765
Little, B., 3590
Littleton, A. C., 2924
Llafur, 2969
Lloyd, A., 2033
Lloyd, A. L., 2601
Lloyd, C., 3494
Lloyd, E., 664
Lloyd, G. I. H., 1409
Lloyd, H. A., 1794
Lloyd, J. E., 210
Lloyd, N., 3536, 3558
Lloyd, T. H., 417, 456
Lobel, Mary D., 486
Local Population Studies, 2284
Lodge, Eleanor, 1159
London Trades Council, 3050
Longfield, Ada K., 1587, 4128
Longley, T., 270
Longmage, N., 2273, 2453, 3779
Loomie, A. J., 1588
Lopez, R. S., 211, 507, 535
Lord, J., 2534
Lounsbury, R. G., 1589
Lovell, J., 3051, 3130
Lovett, W., 3021
Lowe, N., 1340
Lowndes, G. A., 3863
Loyn, H. R., 212-13
Lubenow, W. C., 3666
Lucas, A. F., 2509
Lucas, C., 527
Lucas, C. P., 1561
Lucas, H. S., 612
Luethy, M., 2065
Lumsden, H., 3968-70
Lydon, J. F., 4085-5a, 4150a-41, 4169
Lyle, H. M., 871
Lyman, R., 3138
Lynch, P., 4214
Lynd, Helen M., 2264
Lyons, F. S. L., 4183b
Lythe, S. G. E., 75, 653, 3937-8, 3977, 3980, 3996a

MacAskill, Joy, 3229
McBriar, A. M., 3164
MacCaffrey, W. T.. 1433
McCloskey, D. N., 2209, 2376, 2656a

Maccoby, S., 3052
McCord, N., 3076, 3410, 3422
McCracken, Eileen, 4122, 4129, 4184
Mack, E. C., 3827, 3882-3
Mack, Mary P., 3670
Macrosty, H. W., 2510
McCulloch, J. R., 1472, 1650
MacCurtain, Margaret, 4086 4104a
McCusker, J. J. jnr., 793
McCutcheon, W. A., 4215
MacDonagh, O., 3667-8
McDonald, D., 301
MacDonald, D. F., 3053, 4055
McDougall, I., 4056
MacDowell, R. B., 4079, 4195
McElwee, W., 2255
McEntee, G. P., 3811
Macfarlane, A., 1120
MacFarlane, L. J., 3165
MacFarlane, K. B., 584, 835, 852-3, 938
McGrath, P. V., 1509, 1591 2034
McGregor, O. R., 3669, 3838-9
McGuire, E. B., 3423
Macinnes, C. M., 1590
MacIntyre, Sylvia, 468
Mackay, T., 1844, 2948
McKecknie, W. S., 216
Mackenzie, C., 2773
McKenzie, J. C., 2423
Mackenzie, W. C., 3928
Mackenzie, W. M., 3978
Mackenzie-Grieve, Averil, 3442
McKendrick, N., 2949
McKeown, T., 2312-13
Mackerral, A., 3959
Mackie, J. D., 1022, 3910, 3929, 4016b
McKibbin, R., 3053a
McKillop, N., 3094
Mackinnon, J., 4032
McKisack, May, 585
McLachlan, H., 3854
McLachlan, Jean O., 1486
McLeod, R. M., 3780
Maclure, J. S., 3848, 3865
MacLysaght, E., 4105, 4118
McMahon, C., 957
McNeil, I., 2559
McPherson, J. M., 4012
McRoberts, D., 4027
Mace, F. A., 792
Machin, F., 3106
Madden, J. E., 553
Madge, S. J., 1942
Madocks, R. T., 2210
Maehl, W. H., 2971
Maitland, F. W., 214
Malet, H., 3298
Mallet, B., 2842-4
Mallet, M. E., 794
Maloney, F. X., 1592
Mann, Julia de L., 1341, 1350, 2721-13

Manning, B., 1943-4, 1996
Mansbridge, A., 3568
Mantoux, P., 2165
Manwaring, G. E., 3204
Marcus, S., 3627a, 3781
Marczewski, J., 76
Mare, E. de, 3299
Marlow, Joyce, 3072
Marriner, Sheila, 3435-6
Marsden, C., 3650
Marsh, D. C., 2256
Marshall, C. F. Dendy, 3349, 3367
Marshall, Dorothy, 1843, 2166, 3729-20, 3840
Marshall, J. D., 2185, 2462, 3731-2
Marshall, L. S., 3628
Marshall, Lydia M., 1144-5
Marshall, T. H., 1315, 2304-5, 2348
Martin, Bernice, 3696
Martin, F. X., 4186a
Martin, G., 2130
Martin, G. H., 468, 474, 487-8, 795, 1416
Martin, K., 3155
Martin, R., 3054
Marwick, A., 77, 2257, 2274-5
Marwick, H., 3952
Marwick, J. D., 3971
Marwick, W. H., 3911-5, 4041-2 4057
Mason, A., 3156
Mason, M. G., 2517
Masterman, N. C., 3828
Mather, F. C., 3230-1, 3300
Mathew, D., 554, 1023-4, 3939
Mathias, P., 78, 2167, 2454, 2482, 2497, 2821
Matthew, D. J. A., 215
Matthews, P. W., 2915
Matthews, R. C. O., 2416
Maude, A., 2935
Maxwell, Constantia, 4080, 4196-7, 4239
Maxwell, I. S., 255
May, Teresa, 375
Mayes, C. R., 4139
Mayes, L. R., 1694
Mayhew, H., 3611-2
Mayor, S. H., 3812
Mead, W. E., 876
Mechie, S., 4066
Meekings, C. A. F., 1127-8
Meenan, J., 4184a
Meikle, H. W., 3939a, 4067
Melada, I., 3697
Melling, Elizabeth, 1813, 2404
Mellor, G. R., 3443
Mellows, W. T., 1266
Mendelson, L., 3461
Mendenhall, T. C., 1342
Mercer, E., 1891
Mercer, T. W., 2470
Merritt, J. E., 3444
Meteyard, Eliza, 2774
Meyer, J. R., 24, 79

Middlemas, R. K., 3559
Midwinter, E. C., 3205, 3782-3
Miles, Patricia H., 2554
Miller, E., 217-18, 227, 376, 399, 489, 514-15
Miller, L. R., 1593
Mills, G. H. Saxon, 2489
Mills, W. H., 2803
Milne, A. T., 132, 140
Milne, M., 2804
Milward, A. S., 2276
Minchinton, W. E., 165, 1487, 1615, 1874, 2657, 3291, 3591, 3902
Mingay, G. E., 17a, 2331, 2346, 2349-50, 2367, 2373-4
Mining Association of Great Britain, 2602
Miskimin, H. A., 828, 1025
Mitchell, B. R., 2121-2, 3350
Mitchell, D., 3831
Mitchell, F. L., 2479
Mitchell, G., 3842
Mitchell, S. K., 429-30, 836
Mitchelson, N., 3733
Mitchison, Rosalind, 3940, 4005, 4047
Minto, C. S., 4064
Moens, W. J. C., 1443-4
Moffitt, L. W., 2168
Moggridge, D. E., 2871-2
Moir, Esther A. L., 1026, 1343, 1761, 2724
Mollat, M., 796
Monroe, A. E., 1672
Montgomery, J., 2258-9
Moody, T. W., 4132, 4140-1, 4185
Moore, J. S., 278, 342
Moran, J., 3116
Morant, Valerie, 1455
Morazé, C., 80
More, T., 978
Morgan, E. S., 1121
Morgan, E. V., 2409, 2873-5
Morgan, J. B., 3637
Morgan, M., 4020a
Morison, S. E., 1106
Morrah, D., 2930
Morrell, W. P., 1554
Morrill, J. S., 1983a
Morris, C., 979
Morris, Helen, 2436
Morris, J. H., 2603
Morris, Margaret, 3157
Morris, M., 2977
Morris, W. A., 516
Morrison, E. J. D., 1146
Mortimer, J. E., 3080-1
Morton, A. L., 2035, 3259
Morton, R. G., 4142
Morton, W. A., 2845
Moseley, Maboth, 3698
Moser, C. A., 2234
Mosley, L., 2277
Mott, R. A., 739, 2604
Mottram, R. H., 2658, 3583, 3631
Mousley, J. E., 1795

Mowat, C. L., 2260, 2972-3, 3755
Moyse-Bartlett, H., 3497
Muggeridge, M., 2261
Muir, A., 2696
Mullett, C. F., 613, 1116-17
Mulligan, Lotte, 1795a
Mulvey, H. F., 4074
Munby, L., 1078
Munby, L. M., 3206
Munford, W. A., 3887
Munro, J. H. A., 796a
Munter, R., 4198
Murphy, B., 157
Murphy, G. G. S., 81
Murphy, J., 3866-8
Murray, Alice E., 4201
Murray, A., 3953, 4006-8
Murray, D., 3981
Murray, J. E. L., 3960
Murray, J. J., 1456
Murray, K. A., 4216
Murray, Kathleen M. E., 408 490
Murray, M., 3437
Musgrave, C., 3589
Musgrave, P. W., 2659
Musson, A. E., 393, 2471, 2498-9, 2535, 2538, 2762, 3010, 3055-5a, 3116a
Myers, A. R., 565, 586
Myers, R., 2094a

Namier, L. B., 2660
Nash, V., 3132
National Association for the Promotion of Social Science, 3056
Neale, R. S., 2995, 3186
Nef, J. U., 740, 854, 1027, 1297, 1302-3, 1354, 1673, 1747
Neff, Wanda F., 3843
Neilson, Nellie, 320
Nelson, N., 840
Nettels, C. P., 1594
Nevin, E., 2846
Nevinson, J. C., 532
Newman, J. R., 3088
Newsholme, A., 3784
Newton, A. P., 1110, 1562, 1565
Newton, K. C., 654
Nicholls, G., 1844, 4013, 4176
Nicholls, K., 4087
Nicholson, R., 3929a
Nieuwerts, J. H., 2620
Nixon, F., 2186
Nobbs, D., 3941
Nohl, J., 614
Nokes, G. A., 3371
Nolan, D., 4152
Noonan, J. T., 841
Norman, F. A., 1875
Norris, J. H., 2519
North, D. C., 82-4
North, F. J., 3560
Notestein, W., 3942
Nowell-Smith, S., 2262
Nowlan, K. B., 4217

O'Brien, C. C., 4088
O'Brien, G., 4106, 4158, 4187-8
O'Brien, Maire, 4088
O'Dea, W. T., 2542
Oddy, D. J., 2424
O'Domhnall, S., 4089
O'Donovan, J., 4123
Ogg, D., 1028-9
O'Kelly, E., 4224-5
Oldam, J. W., 3400
Oliver, J. G., 918
Olsen, D. J., 3610
Olson, M., 3383
Oman, C., 418
O'Neal, R., 2624
O'Neill, W., 3844
Orme, N., 958
Orpen, G. H., 4091
Orton, W. A., 3057
Orwin, C. S., 705
Orwin, Christobel S., 705, 2351
Osborn, F. M.. 2661
Osborne, J. W., 2391
O'Sullivan, D., 4130
O'Sullivan, M. D., 1453
O'Sullivan, M. J. D., 4090
O'Sullivan, W., 4154, 4164
Oschinsky, Dorothea, 299, 377
Osterman, N., 1468
Ottley, G., 3330
O'Tuathaigh, G., 4188a
Otway-Ruthven, J., 4075, 4092-3, 4124, 4170-71
Outhwaite, R. B., 1225-6, 1674, 1710-11
Owen, D., 3756
Owen, Dorothy M., 745, 939
Owen, H., 2777
Owen, J., 3082
Owen, L., 1090
Owen, R., 3260-4
Oxley, G. W., 3734
Oxley, J. E., 1275

Padley, R., 2763
Pagan, T., see Keith, Theodora
Page, F. M., 348, 679
Painter, S., 219, 297
Palais, H., 797
Palliser, D. M., 1146a
Palmer, A., 2437
Palmer, R. E., 1065
Palmer, W. M., 475
Pankhurst, R. K. P., 2986
Pantin, W. A., 877-8
Parain, C., 321
Pares, R., 3394-6
Pargellis, S., 973
Parker, L. A., 1147, 1246
Parker, R. A. C., 2352
Parker, W. N., 85
Parkes, Joan, 1642
Parkinson, C. N., 1595, 3384, 3397
Parris, H., 3351, 3371-2
Parry, A. W., 959
Parry, J. H., 1500

Index of Authors and Editors

Parry, O., 1148
Parry, R. H., 1945
Parsons, R. H., 2549
Paterson, T. G. F., 4119
Patten, J., 1091
Patterson, A. T., 3301, 3600, 3638
Paul, J. B., 3943
Pawson, H. C., 2353
Payne, P. L., 86-7, 2782, 2949a
Peacock, A. J., 2386, 3241
Pearce, B., 1748
Pearl, M., 2392
Pearl, Valerie, 1946-9, 1984
Pearsall, R., 3784
Pease, E. R., 3166
Peate, I. C., 3537
Peberdy, P., 3637
Peddie, R. A., 3331
Pedlar, Ann, 3131
Peel, Dorothy C., 2263, 2278
Peel, F., 3207
Peers, R., 2466
Pelham, R. A., 615, 755, 889, 919-21, 1103, 1378-9, 2520
Pelling, H. M., 2279, 3011, 3030, 3033, 3058-60, 3167
Pender, S., 4115, 4159
Pennington, D. H., 1913, 1985
Pepys, S., 980
Perkin, H. J., 88-9, 2169, 3121, 3352
Perkins, H. E., 2483
Perkins, M., 2916
Perry, P. J., 2354, 2354a
Petegorsky, D. W., 1997
Peterson, A. D. C., 3869
Pettit, P. A. J., 1192
Petty, W., 1079
Petree, J. F., 4219
Pfautz, H., 3584
Philips, A. W., 3147
Phillips, G. A., 2210
Phillips, J., 3302
Phillips, M., 2917
Pickard, R., 1149
Pierce, T. J., 457, 586a, 655, 665, 1215
Pigott, S. C., 2697
Pigou, A. C., 2211
Pike, E. R., 2130a-34
Pilgrim, J. E., 1344
Pimlott, J. A. R., 3651
Pinchbeck, Ivy, 1845, 3865, 3870
Pinker, R., 2285
Pitkin, D. S., 689
Plant, Marjorie, 2805, 4065
Platt, C., 953
Platt, D. C. M., 3457
Playne, Caroline E., 2280
Plowden, W., 3325
Plucknett, T. F. T., 680
Plumb, J. H., 90
Plummer, A., 2212, 2725-26, 3247
Pocock, E. A., 386
Podmore, F., 3265
Poirier, P. P., 3061

Pole, W., 2560
Political and Economic Planning, 2698, 2806
Pollard, S., 91, 158, 2213, 2472, 2662, 2876, 2950, 2954-5, 3012, 3140, 3187, 3266
Ponko, V., jnr., 1204
Ponting, K. G., 2672, 2727-9
Pool, A. G., 2205
Poole, A. L., 220-2, 322
Poole, R. L., 431
Population Studies, 2283
Porter, J., 2918
Postan, M. M., 92-4, 223-7, 279, 323-6, 378-9, 458-60, 508, 587, 616, 798-801, 804, 821, 855-6, 946
Postgate, M. R., 706
Postgate, R., 2987, 3735
Postgate, R. W., 3089
Potter, A., 3538
Potter, M., 3538
Pound, J. F., 1434, 1846-7
Pound, R., 2484
Pounds, N. J. G., 802
Povey, K., 4076
Powell, C. L., 1122
Powell, E. T., 1712
Power, Eileen, 95, 736, 803-4, 982, 2123
Powicke, F. M., 96-7, 228
Powicke, M., 229
Poynter, F. N. L., 2306
Poynter, J. R., 3736
Prall, S. E., 1905, 1998
Pratt, D., 756
Pratt, E. A., 3270, 3353
Pratt, J. D., 2758
Prebble, J., 3997
Prendergast, J. P., 4143
Prenderville, P. L., 4077
Prentice, A., 3411
Pressnell, L. S., 2170, 2877, 2895
Prest, J., 2699
Prest, W. R., 2095-5a
Preston, R. A., 1534
Prestwich, J. O., 432
Prestwich, Menna, 1750
Prestwich, M., 433, 890
Pribicevic, B., 3062
Price, J. M., 1488, 1675
Price, L. L., 98
Price, R., 3031
Price, R. G. G., 2807
Price, S. J., 3560-70
Price, W. H., 1751
Prichard, M. E. Lloyd, 2730
Priestley, J., 3303
Priestley, M., 1489
Proctor, Winifred, 3737
Prouty, R., 3412
Pryde, G. S., 3944, 4033
Public Record Office of Northern Ireland 4189
Pudney, J., 3484, 3503
Pugh, A., 3083
Pugh, R. B., 842, 1219

Purvis, J. S., 1267
Putnam, Bertha, 891

Quane, M., 4199
Quennell, P., 3613-14
Quinault, R., 3214a
Quinn, D. B., 766, 1563-4, 4071, 4107-8, 4144-5, 4156

Rabb, T. K., 1490, 1596
Radford, F. H., 3122
Rae, W. F., 3485
Raftis, J. A., 588, 617, 681, 690
Raistrick, A., 1380, 2625-26, 2664-5, 3805
Rait, R. S., 3930
Ralph, E., 1150
Ramsay, G. D., 1316, 1345-7, 1491, 1541, 1552
Ramsey, P., 1030, 1492, 1542, 1676
Ramsland, C., 2125
Ranger, T. O., 4146, 4177
Ransome, D. R., 1457, 1876
Rashdall, H., 960
Raumer, F. von, 3794-5
Raven, C. E., 3829
Raybould, T. J., 2666
Raymond, J., 2264
Razzell, P. E., 2307-8
Read, A., 3280
Read, C., 967, 1752
Read, D., 2135, 2265, 2808, 3208, 3248, 3413
Reader, W. J., 2575, 2764, 2936
Record, R. G., 2303
Reddaway, T. F., 829, 1317, 1435
Redfern, P., 2472-3
Redford, A., 491, 2318, 3438
Redlich, F., 99, 100
Redwood, B. C., 349
Reed, M. C., 3354
Rees, G., 2421, 2485
Rees, J. F., 2878
Rees, W., 137, 587, 1381
Reid, K. C., 757
Reid, W. S., 3985
Reiter, S., 3495
Reith, C., 3209-11
Reitzel, W., 2399
Renshaw, P., 3157a
Reynolds, G. W., 3123
Reynolds, P., 1597
Reynolds, Susan, 492
Rich, E. E., 226-7, 1031, 1104, 1505, 1535, 3871
Richards, E., 4048
Richards, J. M., 3539
Richards, R. D., 1695-6, 1713-14, 2879
Richards, T., 1151
Richards, T., 2036-9
Richardson, H., 536, 805
Richardson, H. G., 461, 517, 523, 4094, 4155, 4172

Richardson, H.W., 2194, 2422, 3561
Richardson, J.H., 3424
Richardson, K., 3594
Richardson, R.C., 1151a, 1949a, 2040
Richardson, W.C., 1227, 1697
Riches, Naomi, 2405
Riemersma, J.C., 1753
Rimmer, W.G., 1436, 2743
Ritchie, Nora, 865
Ritchie, R.L.G., 3931
Rive, A., 1553, 1892
Robbins, L., 3674
Robbins, R.M., 3355, 3369, 3626
Robbins, W.G., 1536
Roberts, B.C., 3051, 3063
Roberts, B.K., 287
Roberts, D., 3673, 3738
Roberts, F., 3679
Roberts, R.O., 2617, 3903
Roberts, R.S., 1118
Robertson, D.W., 905
Robertson, H.M., 1329, 2066
Robertson, J.H., 3316
Robertson, N., 3013
Robinson, C.B., 1160
Robinson, E.H., 2463, 2499, 2535, 2538
Robinson, H., 3317
Robinson, H.W., 4228
Robinson, P., 2667
Robinson, W.C., 590
Robo, E., 618
Robson, D., 3872
Robson, J.A., 961
Robson, R., 2700
Robson, R., 2937
Robson, W.A., 3581, 3620
Rochefoucauld, F. de, 3796
Roden, D., 370, 707-8
Rodgers, B., 1848
Rodgers, H.B., 1193, 1645
Roe, J.W., 2561
Roehl, R., 230
Roepke, H., 2668
Rogers, J.E.T., 101, 419-20
Rogers, P.G., 2387
Roll, E., 2536
Rolt, L.T.C., 2562-6, 2774a, 3304, 3360-1
Rooseboom, M.P., 3986
Roots, I., 1796, 1950, 1985
Roover, R. de, 830, 1715
Rörig, F., 906
Rose, A.G., 3212
Rose, J.H., 1565
Rose, M.E., 3739-43
Rose-Troup, Frances, 1566
Rosenblatt, F.F., 3232
Rosenthal, J.H., 591
Rosenthal, J.T., 682
Roseveare, H., 434
Ross, C., 683
Ross, D., 1775
Rostenberg, L., 2110a
Rostow, W.W., 102, 159, 2412, 2417

Roth, C., 574
Roth, H.L., 2919
Rousseaux, P., 2418
Rover, Constance, 3846-7
Rowe, D.J., 3076, 3242
Rowe, J., 2187
Rowlands, Marie B., 1410
Rowney, D.K., 103
Rowse, A.L., 1032, 1567, 4109
Rubens, A., 1469
Rubin, S., 618a
Rubini, D., 1716
Rudé, G., 2384, 3213, 3608-9
Ruddock, A.A., 806-8, 929, 1598
Rudishill, G., jnr., 435
Rudkin, E.H., 745
Russell, C., 1033, 1951
Russell, E.J., 2355-6
Russell, J.C., 288-94, 619-20, 4114
Russell, R.C., 3073
Ruston, A.G., 656
Rydberg, S., 3797
Ryder, Judith, 2266
Rye, W.B., 1066, 1458

Sabine, B.E.V., 2831, 2847
Sachse, W.L., 968
Salaman, R.N., 2438
Salt, J., 3266
Salter, E.G., 1067
Salter, F.R., 1814
Salter, H.E., 493
Saltmarsh, J., 592, 621, 709
Salusbury, G.T., 907
Salzman, L.F., 395, 509, 661, 728, 747, 1034
Sambrook, J., 2393
Sampson, H., 2490
Sams, K.I., 3013
Samuel, A.M., 2447
Samuel, E.R., 1470
Samuelsson, K., 2067
Sandberg, L.G., 2701-1a
Sanderson, M., 3890
Saul, S.B., 2214, 2501, 2567-8, 3326, 3425, 3562
Saunders, I.J., 231, 908, 4068
Saunders, P.T., 2920
Savage, G., 2770
Savage, W., 3585
Saville, J., 2215, 2319, 2988-9, 2969a, 2996, 3249, 3264, 3830
Savine, A., 1276
Sawyer, O.H.M., 133
Sawyer, P.H., 232, 280, 392
Sayers, R.S., 2848, 2850, 2880-2, 2921
Sayles, G.O., 233, 517, 4094, 4155, 4172
Scammell, G.V., 1404-5, 1501
Scammell, Jean, 621a
Scarfe, N., 922
Scharf, A., 2130
Schidrowitz, P., 2783
Schlatter, R.B., 2041

Schlote, W., 3375
Schmidt, H.D., 3456
Schofield, M.M., 3598
Schofield, R.B., 2579
Schofield, R.E., 2502
Schofield, R.S., 104, 593, 2096
Schoyen, A.R., 3250
Schreiner, J., 831
Schubert, H.R., 400
Schumpeter, Elizabeth B., 1677, 3376
Schuyler, R.L., 3385
Schwartz, Anna J., 2412
Schweinitz, K. de, 3757
Scotland, J., 4017
Scott, J.D., 2569, 3502
Scott, Richenda, 343
Scott, W.D. Robson, 1068
Scott, W.R., 5, 1507, 3916, 3972, 4046
Scouloudi, Irene, 1459
Scoville, W.C., 1460
Scrivenor, H., 2663
Searle, E., 683a
Searle, M., 3278
Seaver, P.S., 2042
Sée, H., 105
Seebohm, M.E., 327
Seldon, A., 3758
Seligman, E.R.A., 106
Sella, D., 1298
Selleck, R.J.W., 3873
Sellers, Maud, 767, 1515
Selley, E., 3074
Semler, E.G., 2570
Semmel, B., 3458-9
Shaaber, M.A., 2111
Shafter, R.J., 107
Shannon, H.A., 2964-6
Shapiro, S., 2702
Sharp, I.G., 3064
Shaw, A.G.L., 3460
Shaw, R. Cunliffe, 723
Shaw, W.A., 421, 1651
Shearer, A., 3979a
Shears, P.J., 1461
Shehab, F.A., 2832
Shelby, L.R., 462
Shelton, W.J., 3214
Sheppard, D.K., 2883
Sheppard, F.H.W., 1462
Sherborne, J.W., 809, 857
Sherrington, C.E.R., 3271
Sherwig, J.M., 3386
Shillington, V.M., 3398
Shorter, A.H., 1394, 2816a
Shrewsbury, J.F.D., 622
Siddle, D.J., 344
Siebert, F.S., 2809
Sigsworth, E.M., 2309-10, 2455, 2731
Silberling, N.J., 2884
Silver, A., 2703
Silver, H., 2266, 3860
Simey, Margaret B., 3759-60
Simey, T.S., 3760
Simmons, J., 494, 2571, 3095, 3271a, 3356

Simms, J. G., 4078, 4110, 4147-8, 4162
Simon, A. L., 810
Simon, B., 2097, 3874-5a
Simon, Daphne, 2997
Simon, Joan, 962, 2098-101
Simon, J., 3785
Simon, J., 3158
Simpson, A., 1261, 1646, 1797
Simpson, I. J., 4017a
Simpson, J. B., 741
Singer, C. J., 1411
Singleton, F., 2188
Sissons, M., 2267
Sitwell, O., 3159
Skeat, W. W., 1161
Skeel, Caroline A. J., 1205, 1348
Skempton, A. W., 1624, 3563
Skidelsky, R. W., 2225
Skipp, V. H. T., 1189
Slack, P., 1412
Slade, C. F., 331
Slater, G., 2368
Slater, H., 3327
Slicher van Bath, B. H., 160, 328
Slosson, P. W., 3233
Smart, W., 2171
Smelser, N. J., 2704
Smiles, Aileen, 2951
Smiles, S., 2572
Smith, A., 3813
Smith, A., 657
Smith, A. G. R., 1016, 1035, 1754
Smith, B. S., 909
Smith, C. Manby, 3022
Smith, C. T., 1152
Smith, D. H., 3623
Smith, D. M., 2189
Smith, E., 1069
Smith, E., 3510-11
Smith, F. B., 3234
Smith, H. L., 3132
Smith, J. T., 1893
Smith, J. W. Ashley, 3876
Smith, P., 1894
Smith, R. A., 1550
Smith, R. A. L., 684
Smith, R. B., 658, 1178
Smith, R. E. F., 866
Smith, R. S., 1382, 1397
Smith, T. J., 2922
Smout, T. C., 3945, 3961-4, 3973-4, 3983, 3998-4002, 4048a
Snell, L. S., 1277
Sneyd, C. A., 1070
Snyder, R. K., 3426
Social Science Research Council, 2113
Sogner, S., 2316
Solow, Barbara L., 4228a
Soloway, R. A., 3814
Solt, L. F., 2043
Sombart, W., 108, 2068
Somerville, A., 3023
Sorenson, L. R., 3699
Southern, R. W., 234, 940
Spain, Nancy, 2439

Speck, W. A., 1776
Spangler, J. J., 1092
Sperling, J. G., 2826
Spiegel, H. W., 109
Spooner, F., 1654
Spoor, A., 3124
Sprandel, R., 742
Spratt, H. P., 3498
Spring, D., 2375
Springall, L. Marion, 2388
Spufford, Margaret, 659, 1153, 1178a, 2102
Spufford, P., 422, 1105
Stacey, J., 941
Stacey, N. A H., 2926
Staff, F., 3318
Stamp, L. D., 703
Stark, W., 3675
Steel, A., 837, 858, 892
Steffan, T. G., 2044
Steinbicker, C. R., 1849
Stenton, Doris M., 161, 235-6, 537
Stenton, F. M., 173, 237-8, 361, 463, 495, 538
Stephens, C. Cleveland, 3357
Stephens, W. B., 110, 1437, 1493, 1599-1601, 1625, 3587
Stephenson, C., 496
Stern, F., 111
Stern, W., 2448
Stevens, H., 1526
Stevenson, D., 4027a
Stevenson, J., 3214a
Stewart, C., 3629
Stewart, I. H., 4004
Stewart, Margaret, 3137
Stitt, F. B., 371
Stocks, Mary D., 3888
Stone, L., 115, 1330, 1355, 1698, 1717, 1755, 1777-81, 1798-9, 1952, 2103-4
Stone, T. G., 981
Stoye, J. W., 1036
Straker, E., 1383
Strayer, J. R., 435
Sturmey, S. G., 3489
Sturt, G., 2573
Sturt, Mary, 3877
Stuyvenberg, J. H. van, 2440
Styles, P., 1154, 1782, 1850
Summerson, J., 3540-1a
Supple, B. E., 112, 1037, 1495, 1678, 1783, 2069, 2931
Sussmann, H. L., 2172
Sutherland, Gillian, 3878
Sutherland, Lucy S., 3399
Svedenstierna, E. T., 3798
Swale, W. E., 2550
Swales, T. H., 1278
Swann, D., 3292
Swanson, J., 113
Sweezy, P. M., 2605
Swift, A. G., 3125
Swift, J., 4220
Switzer, J. F. Q., 133
Sykes, J., 2577, 2896
Sylvester, D. W., 2074

Sylvester, Dorothy, 345, 362, 710
Symon, J. A., 3954
Symons, J., 3160
Syrett, D., 3490
Syson, L., 2521

Taine, H., 3799
Tait, J., 281, 497-8
Talbot, C. H., 623
Tames, R. L., 2136
Tann, Jennifer, 1349, 3542
Tanner, J. R., 1815
Taplin, W., 2638
Tarn, J. N., 3543-3a
Tate, G. K., 3140a
Tate, Mavis, 831a
Tate, W. E., 1247, 1762, 2369
Taube, E., 1463
Tawney, R. H., 52, 114, 141, 982, 1038, 1179, 1602, 1699, 1800-1, 1877-8, 2070
Taylor, A. J., 407
Taylor, A. J., 2606-10, 3107, 3188, 3676
Taylor, Audrey M., 2923
Taylor, C. C., 724-5
Taylor, E. G. R., 641
Taylor, E. R., 3815
Taylor, G., 3744
Taylor, H., 1496, 1679
Taylor, Louise B., 3979b-9c
Taylor, P. A. M., 1953, 2137, 3479
Taylor, Rebe P., 3636
Taylor, R. W. Cooke, 3700
Taylor, W. Cooke, 3701
Taylor, W., 4010
Temin, P., 118-19
Temperley, H., 3445
Tenison, C. M., 4226-27
Terrett, I. B., 253
Tewson, W. F., 2705
Textile History, 2671
Thale, Mary, 3024
Thirsk, Joan, 387-8, 983, 1093, 1124-5, 1180-2, 1194-7, 1248-9, 1262-2a, 1299, 1300, 1349a, 1438, 1954-5
Thistlethwaite, F., 3480
Thomas, B., 3400, 3481-2, 3904
Thomas, C., 346
Thomas, D., 3905
Thomas, J., 2775-6
Thomas, Joan, 2733
Thomas, K., 120-1, 1895, 1999, 2000
Thomas, M. W., 3702
Thomas, P. J., 1532
Thomas, S. E., 2795, 2897
Thomas, W. A., 2875, 2956
Thomis, M. I., 2997a, 3215-17
Thompson, A., 2173
Thompson, A. F., 3002
Thompson, A. H., 879, 942-4
Thompson, D. M., 3816
Thompson, Dorothy, 3235

Thompson, E. P., 2952, 2898 3218, 3615-16
Thompson, F. M. L., 122, 1216, 2357, 2376, 2938, 3497
Thompson, R., 1038a
Thomsen, Birgit N., 3400
Thomson, A. G., 4042a
Thomson, C., 3025
Thomson, Gladys Scott, 1643, 1896
Thomson, H. W., 1719
Thompson, J. W., 963
Thornley, Isobel, 566
Thornton, H., 2886
Thrupp, Sylvia, 624-5, 732-3, 822, 930-1, 1319
Tierney, B., 1807
Tippett, L. H. C., 2706
Tipping, D. G., 2217
Titley, A., 2530
Titow, J. Z., 295, 329-30, 389, 460, 464
Tobias, J. J., 3219
Tomkieff, O. G., 239
Todd, A. C., 2190, 2574
Tompson, R. S., 3879
Tooke, T., 2887
Topham, T., 3003
Tout, T. F., 910
Townsend, J., 3586
Toynbee, A., 2174
Trades Union Congress, 3065, 3075
Tranter, N. L., 2321-1a
Treadwell, V., 4149
Treble, J. H., 3711
Trevelyan, G. M., 162, 1956
Trevor-Roper, H. R., 123, 1784, 1802, 1957-8, 2045, 2071, 4028
Trickett, Ann, 4058
Trimble, W. R., 2046
Trinder, B., 2191
Troeltsch, E., 2072
Tropp, A., 3126
Trotter, Eleanor, 1763
Trow-Smith, R., 642, 2358
Truptil, R. J., 2888
Tucker, G. S. L., 1094, 1718
Tucker, R. S., 3189
Tuke, A. W., 2915
Tuma, E. H., 124
Tunzelmann, G. N. von, 125, 2539
Tupling, G. H., 539, 1057, 1647, 1986
Turner, B., 3427
Turner, E. S., 2491
Turner, H. A., 3129
Twining, S., 2441
Tyacke, N., 2047
Tylecote, Mabel, 3889
Tyler, D. B., 3499
Tyrer, F., 2406

Ugawa, K., 363
Ullman, W., 594

Underdown, D., 1959-60, 1987, 2048
Unwin, G., 126, 838, 1320-1, 1512, 2707
Unwin, Jane C., 2442
Upton, A. P., 1803
Urban History Newsletter, 3570a
Urban History Yearbook, 3570a
Ure, A., 693
Urry, W., 499
Usher, A. P., 843
Usher, G., 811
Utley, F., 2708
Utterstrom, G., 1095

Vaizey, J., 2456, 4214
Vale, E., 3319
Van der Wee, H., 813
Vann, R. T., 2049-50
Varga, E., 3461
Varley, F. J., 2112
Veale, Elspeth M., 748, 812
Veall, D., 2001
Verlinden, O., 540
Vigier, F., 3630
Vincent, W. A. L., 2104a-4b
Viner, J., 1616
Vinogradoff, P., 240, 364, 465
Vollans, E. L., 347
Vries, L. de, 2492

Wade, J., 2939
Wadsworth, A. P., 1350, 2691
Wadsworth, J. E., 2903
Wagner, D. O., 3817
Waight, L., 2892
Wailes, R., 758-60
Waite, H. H., 3114
Waites, B., 401, 555-7
Walcott, R., 969
Walford, R., 3401
Walker, F., 1058
Walker, K. O., 3704
Walker, S. F., 2611
Walker, V. W., 911
Wall, Maureen, 4200, 4202
Wallace, A. R., 2359
Wallas, G., 3251
Walmsley, R., 3220
Walton, K., 3949
Walzer, M., 1961
Warburg, J., 2138
Warburton, W. H., 3141
Ward, J. C., 380
Ward, J. R., 3304a
Ward, J. T., 2387, 2417, 3221 3236, 3705-11
Ward, W. R., 2833-4, 3818, 3891-2
Ward-Perkins, C. N., 2419
Warden, A. J., 2744
Wardle, D., 3880
Warner, F., 2739
Warner, G. F., 768, 823

Warrack, J., 3946
Warren, J. G. H., 3368
Warren, K., 2669
Warren, W. L., 872
Warrington, A. J., 2583
Waters, D. W., 1497
Watkins, G., 2540-1
Watkins-Pritchard, W., 1129
Watson, S. J., 4218
Watts, D. G., 595
Wearmouth, R. F., 3819-23
Weatherill, Lorna, 2778
Webb, Beatrice, 128, 1764, 3014, 3745-8
Webb, Catherine, 2475
Webb, J., 1543, 1816
Webb, R. K., 2810
Webb, S., 128, 1764, 3014, 3108, 3746-8
Webber, R., 1183, 2443
Weber, M., 2073
Webster, N. W., 3362, 3372
Wedgwood, C. Veronica, 1962-4, 4029
Weed, K. K., 2811
Weinbaum, M., 894
Weinstock, Maureen, 1130, 1904, 2740
Welbourne, E., 2962, 3109
Wells, F. A., 2709, 2748
Wernham, R. B., 1039
Werveke, H. van, 500
West, J., 3237
Westerfield, R. B., 1648
Whale, P. B., 2889
Wheeler, J., 1510
Whetham, Edith H., 2351, 2360
Whitaker, W. B., 2051
Whitaker, W. B., 3127
White, A. W. A., 2612
White, B. D., 3602
White, Cynthia L., 2812
White, D. G., 4111
White, G. H., 436
White, L., jnr., 396
Whiter, L., 2779
White, N. B., 4163
Whitfield, R., 3139a
Whitney, Dorothy Williams, 2052
Whiteside, T., 3328
Whitwell, R. J., 437
Wicker, E. R., 2361
Wickham, E. R., 3824
Wickwar, W. H., 2813
Wiener, J. H., 2814-15
Wightman, W. E., 245
Wilbraham, Anne, 874
Wiles, R. M., 2816
Wilkins, H. J., 1817
Wilkinson, B., 596, 873
Willan, T. S., 1473, 1498, 1513-14, 1524, 1551, 1626-32, 1897, 2464
Willard, J. F., 839, 915-16
Willcock, H. D., 2486
Willcox, W. B., 1765
Williams, C., 1071
Williams, C. H., 984, 992

Williams, D., 3252, 3906-7
Williams, D. H., 558
Williams, E., 3436-7
Williams, E. N., 985, 1818
Williams, G., 945, 1279-80
Williams, G., 3448
Williams, G. A., 501
Williams, J. E., 3110, 3190
Williams, Judith B., 2124, 3387
Williams, L., 1464
Williams, L. A., 3278a
Williams, L. J., 1384, 2216, 2603, 2760
Williams, M., 1263
Williams, M. E., 1150
Williams, N., 814, 1291, 1603, 1649
Williams, N. J., 1331
Williams, P., 1040, 1756
Williams, T. D., 4233
Williams, W. O., 1041-2, 1804
Williamson, J., 113
Williamson, J. A., 1043, 1502-3
Willson, D. H., 3946a
Wilsher, P., 3191
Wilshore, J. E. O., 1119
Wilson, A., 3243
Wilson, A. E., 349
Wilson, B. R., 129
Wilson, C., 130, 932, 1031, 1044-5, 1548-9, 1617-22, 1757, 1965, 2575, 2765-6, 3402
Wilson, C. Anne, 879a
Wilson, F. M., 1072
Wilson, G. B., 2457
Wilson, J. Dover, 986
Wilson, K. P., 769, 815

Wilson, P., 2934
Wilson, P. N., 761
Wilson, R. G., 2377, 2732
Wilson, T., 4190
Wilson, T., 987
Winch, D., 3677
Winks, R. W., 3462
Wing, C., 3712
Winter, G., 2408, 3625
Winter, J., 3544
Winterbottom, A., 3008
Withers, H., 2932
Withrington, D. J., 4017b
Witney, D., 656
Woledge, G., 912
Wolf, L., 1471
Wolff, M., 3516
Wolff, P., 816
Wolffe, B. P., 685-6, 1220-1
Wood, A. C., 1525, 1633, 1805, 1988
Wood, E., 2840
Wood, E. B., 1250
Wood, M., 880
Wood, M. E., 533
Wood, O., 2613
Wood, R., 3646
Wood, S. M., 559
Woodcroft, B., 2503
Woodforde, J., 3279, 3545
Woodham-Smith, Cecil, 4234
Woodhead, J. R., 1439
Woodhouse, A. J. P., 1906
Wood-Jones, R. B., 3546
Woodroofe, Kathleen, 3762
Woodruff, W., 2784, 3192
Woodward, D. M., 1392, 1604, 1879, 2362

Woodward, G. W. O., 1228, 1281, 4112
Woodward, J. H., 2312
Woodward, L., 2282
Woolrych, A., 1966-7
Worswick, G. D. N., 2217
Wray, Margaret, 2734
Wright, A. E. G., 2638
Wright, Jane, A., 749
Wright, L. C., 3244
Wrigley, E. A., 1096-9, 1440
Wyatt, R. J., 1465
Wyatt, T., 1465

Yamey, B. S., 1719-20, 2925
Yelling, J., 1264
Yeo, Eileen, 3675
Youd, G., 711
Youings, Joyce, 1268, 1282-3, 1322
Young, A. F., 3761
Young, C. R., 502
Young, G. M., 2175-6
Youngson, A. J., 131, 2218, 4039
Yudkin, J., 2423-24, 2444
Yule, G., 1968-9, 2002

Zagorin, P., 1970-2
Ziegler, P., 626
Zins, H., 1520a
Zupco, R. E., 163

ADDENDA

Explorations in Economic History, Kent State University, Ohio, has published two issues of interest:

(a) Vol. 10, No. 4 (summer 1973), 321-459, on problems on the 'new economic history' arising from various topics in British economic and social history 1700-1850.

(b) Vol. 11, No. 4 (summer 1974), 317-444, on problems on the 'new economic history' arising from various topics in British economic history 1870-1914.

Kellaway, W., Bibliography of Historical Works Issued in the U.K., 1961-5, 1967.

Kellaway, W., Bibliography of Historical Works Issued in the U.K., 1966-70, 1972.

Rowlands, Marie B., Masters and Men in the West Midland Metalware Trades Before the Industrial Revolution, 1975.

Salaman, R. A., Dictionary of Tools Used in the Woodworking and Allied Trades, c. 1700-1970, 1975.

Chandaman, G. D., The English Public Revenue 1660-1688, 1975.

Wrigley, E. A., ed., Nineteenth-century Society: Essays in the Use of Quantitative Methods for the Study of Social Data, 1972. Chiefly concerned with the problems arising from census data.

Hudson, Patricia, ed., The West Riding Wool Textile Industry: A Catalogue of Business Records from the Sixteenth to the Twentieth Century, 1975.

Vicinus, Martha, The Industrial Muse: A Study of Nineteenth-century British Working-class Literature, 1974.

Roseveare, H., The Treasury, 1660-1870: The Foundations of Control, 1973.

Campbell, R. H. and R. G. Wilson, Entrepreneurship in Britain, 1750-1939, 1975. A collection of documents.

Jones, E. L., Agriculture and the Industrial Revolution, 1973.

Kirby, R. G. and A. E. Musson, The Voice of the People: John Doherty, 1798-1854, Trade Unionist, Radical and Factory Reformer, 1975.

Hanson, Harry, The Canal Boatmen, 1760-1914, 1975.

Hyde, F. E., Cunard and the North Atlantic, 1840-1973, 1975.

Vicinus, Martha, ed., Suffer and Be Still: Women in the Victorian Age, Bloomington, Ind., 1972.

Checkland, S. G., Scottish Banking: A History 1695-1973, 1975.

Devine, T., The Tobacco Lords, 1975.